EXCAVATIONS AT TLACHTGA, HILL OF WARD, CO. MEATH, IRELAND

EXCAVATIONS AT TLACHTGA, HILL OF WARD, CO. MEATH, IRELAND

by

STEPHEN DAVIS AND CAITRÍONA MOORE

OXBOW | books
Oxford & Philadelphia

Published in the United Kingdom in 2024 by
OXBOW BOOKS
The Old Music Hall, 106–108 Cowley Road, Oxford, OX4 1JE

and in the United States by
OXBOW BOOKS
1950 Lawrence Road, Havertown, PA 19083

Paperback Edition: ISBN 979-8-88857-044-9
Digital Edition: ISBN 979-8-88857-045-6 (epub)

A CIP record for this book is available from the British Library

Library of Congress Control Number: 2024931277

Printed in Malta by Melita Press

Typeset in India by Lapiz Digital Services, Chennai.

For a complete list of Oxbow titles, please contact:

UNITED KINGDOM
Oxbow Books
Telephone (0)1226 734350
Email: oxbow@oxbowbooks.com
www.oxbowbooks.com

UNITED STATES OF AMERICA
Oxbow Books
Telephone (610) 853-9131, Fax (610) 853-9146
Email: queries@casemateacademic.com
www.casemateacademic.com/oxbow

Oxbow Books is part of the Casemate Group

Front cover: The Hill of Ward – UCD Excavation – 2015 (Photograph courtesy of Noel Meehan, Copterview)
Back cover: The Hill of Ward (Photograph courtesy of Noel Meehan, Copterview)

Contents

Acknowledgements

There are many people who made this project possible, quite apart from the specialists who have given their expertise in the volume below. Initially the project received significant encouragement from Jean O'Dowd and especially from John Gilroy who helped secure support from the Office of Public Works in the first season. We are also indebted to Mark and Elaine Clarke, the owners of the field where Tlachtga stands, for allowing us to excavate and providing us with facilities for three years of fieldwork. Special thanks are due to Joe Conlon – the keeper of the hill, who helped out in a host of ways over the excavation campaign, and to Francis Mac Donncha, a hardy man with a shovel and the last man on site in the last season of excavation. Many thanks also to the communities of Athboy and Ráth Chairn who welcomed us and kept the excavation teams supplied with home baked treats. The late Ultan Ó Conmhidhe is also fondly remembered and thanked for contribution to local history studies.

John and David Gilroy were instrumental in the success of the project, in particular by introducing us to Jackie Maguire at Meath County Council. Funding for the project was a collaborative effort, with invaluable contributions both towards Research Excavation and post-excavation grants schemes through the Royal Irish Academy, and also through the good auspices of Meath County Council, without whom the project simply would not have been able to run. The content of this publication is solely the responsibility of the authors and does not necessarily represent the official views of the Royal Irish Academy. In the second year of excavation we were also thankful to receive funding for a dedicated outreach position through the Heritage Council, a role that was filled admirably by Katherine McCormack.

A great many UCD students experienced their first, or at least second archaeological excavation at the Hill of Ward, in addition to some more esoteric participants who arrived from the US, Canada, Spain and Finland. Many of those have gone on to have successful careers in commercial archaeology. We are incredibly grateful to everyone who gave their time and labour to the project, usually in exchange for tea, cake and cheese sandwiches over three seasons of inclement Irish summer weather. It would have been impossible without you all and you have our thanks. Thanks are also due to our supervisors through the three seasons of excavation: Siobhan Ruddy, Niamh Kelly, Clíodhna Ní Líonain, Mick Corcoran, Stephen McLeod, Maeve McCormick and Clare Ryan (in approximate trench order). Thanks are also due to Neil Jackman for briefly stepping in as trench supervisor in 2014, and for help with publicity in that first year. Special thanks should go to Mick Drumm who was not only trench supervisor in 2015 but also directed the final year of excavations before departing to non-archaeological pastures new.

Similarly, the geophysical survey required the help of a large number of people. From the very first surveys, thanks go to Dr Karen Dempsey, and subsequent surveys where Dr Chris Carey wishes to thank Hannah Ventre, Leila Abdullah and Kristine Buckley for all their help in the field. Chris also wishes to thank Dr Nick Crabb for commenting on his original text, and Kimberley Colman for proof reading. Special mention also should go to Dr Lizzie Richley for her GPR survey, which hopefully will be published at a later date.

Beyond excavation, a number of students were instrumental in the post excavation phase, in particular Katherine McCormack, Rebecca Swayne, Karen O'Toole, Catríona Baldwin, Christine Brown and Jeanne Connolly with additional support from Patrizia la Piscopia in the 2016 season. Special thanks too should go to Noel Carroll for his excellence and dedication in sieving. In preparing this document for print we are also grateful to Maggie Kobik for revisiting the drawings and to Conor McDermott for help with images. Thank you also to Noel Meehan of Copterview for providing aerial images of the site.

Beyond the project we would like to extend our thanks to long-suffering family members who have tolerated the write-up phase and, occasionally, have helped out in one capacity or another.

1

Introduction: The Hill of Ward, Co. Meath

The Hill of Ward, Co, Meath, Ireland is a low hill (119 m OD) located just east of the town of Athboy (*Baile Átha Buí*, 'the town of the yellow ford') – an outcrop of calp limestone, the bedrock typical of much of County Meath and North Co. Dublin. Like many elevations in low-lying Meath, it has been a focus of intensive human activity for millennia. Its location is striking – like its more famous neighbour, the Hill of Tara, it possesses panoramic views – on an average day extending to Tara and neighbouring Skryne, to Faughan Hill in the middle distance to the northeast, to the Loughcrew cairns in the west and north to the Hill of Lloyd, topped by its ornamental lighthouse the Spire of Lloyd (Fig. 1.1). On a clear day the views are spectacular and include the Dublin and Wicklow Mountains, with their cairns and tombs, the red and white stripes of the Poolbeg chimneys and, most striking of all, the bulk of Slieve Gullion (Fig. 1.2), site of the highest surviving passage tomb in Ireland, over 60 km to the north. As a location, therefore, the Hill of Ward possesses views to a remarkable collection of Bronze Age and Neolithic sites and landscapes both within Meath and far beyond.

The Hill of Ward today is topped by the remains of an enormous quadrivallate earthwork known as Tlachtga (ME030-001). The site has been greatly disturbed in recent centuries: the culprits for this have been suggested to include some of the 'usual suspects' in monument defacement during this time, in particular Oliver Cromwell and, earlier still, Owen Roe O'Neill both of whom local legend has it encamped upon the hill. Whoever the culprits, there are several clear episodes of damage evident: the southeastern portion of the monument has been ploughed almost flat, the western portion is occupied by an enormous depression, most likely a quarry, and the central platform is cut by a shallow, sinuate ditch, splitting it into north and south sections. The best-preserved part of the site is to the north where the banks remain undamaged

and give the visitor some feel for what the site may have been like when intact – a hugely impressive monument, with high stone and earthen ramparts surrounding a substantial, flat-topped central mound.

Tlachtga is one of a very small number of quadrivallate enclosures within Ireland: it was long suggested that there were only three enclosures of this type: Tlachtga, Rathra near Rathcroghan, Co. Roscommon (Fenwick 2021) and the Rath of the Synods on the Hill of Tara (Grogan 2008). Newman (1997, 178–180) considered that these formed a coherent group of monuments, most likely of late Iron Age date, and presumably of very high status.

Tlachtga is recorded as a 'Ringfort-rath' within the Sites and Monuments Record (SMR). Ringforts are considered to be the dominant settlement type of the Irish early medieval period (*c.* AD 400–1100, with most enclosures occupied between the 6th and 9th centuries AD (O'Sullivan and Nicholl 2011, 65), where they functioned as enclosed and defended farmsteads (see Stout 1997; Curran 2019b; O'Sullivan *et al.* 2021a). They are the dominant archaeological monument within the Irish landscape, with approaching 50,000 currently recorded using a broad definition (Stout and Stout 2010, Fig. 42) and undoubtedly many more to be found with increasing availability of remote sensing data (see Curran 2019a; 2019b). While the majority of ringforts – up to 80% (Stout 1997, 17) – are small (*c.* 28–35 m diameter – Stout 1997, 15) and univallate, a proportion are more elaborate in design with two, or even three vallations. The number and scale of these vallations has been linked to status: early medieval Ireland was a strongly hierarchical society (*e.g.* Aitchison 1994; Powell 1995; Boyle 2004; O'Sullivan and Nicholl 2011, 61–62; Kelly 2000, 445–448) and that stratification has long been regarded as codified into the structure of settlement enclosures (Curran 2019b, 53; O'Sullivan *et al.* 2021a, 53; 82–84). O'Sullivan *et al.* (2021a, 84) note that while there is an implicit relationship

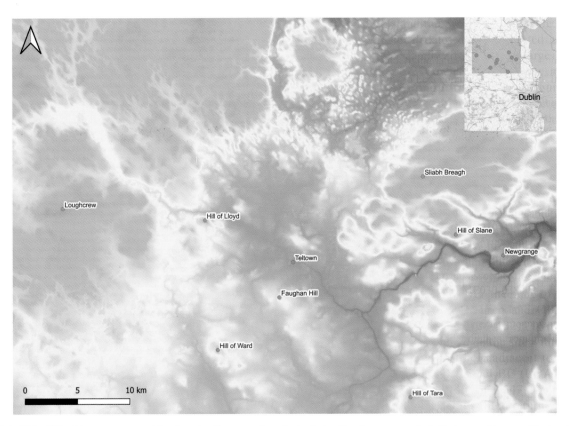

Fig. 1.1. Hill of Ward location map with other significant archaeological sites/landscapes marked. Ordnance Survey of Ireland 30 m Digital Terrain Model basemap.

Fig. 1.2. Slieve Gullion, Co. Down, over 60 km from the Hill of Ward and site of the highest surviving passage tomb in Ireland.

between social status and the level of vallation in these sites, there is no explicit discussion of this in the early Irish law tracts. The height and scale of rampart construction is, however, more strongly linked textually to status (*ibid.* 82–83), and is more important in this regard than the actual area enclosed.

Relatively few trivallate enclosures have been excavated. Classic sites at Garranes, Co. Cork (Ó Ríordáin 1941; O'Brien and Hogan 2021) and Ballycatteen, Co. Cork (Ó Ríordáin and Hartnett 1943) revealed the presence of high-quality non-ferrous metalworking and glassworking, as well as of trade with the continent in the form of amber, non-native glass objects and pottery, including a significant imported element with links to the Mediterranean and to Atlantic France (see Comber 2001; O'Brien and Hogan 2021).

These sites have been supplemented more recently by community-led excavations at Rathnadrinna, Co. Tipperary (O'Brien 2012) and by development-led excavations at Knockhouse Lower, Co. Waterford (Walsh 2020a; 2020b) and Lissaniska, Co. Kerry (Lyne 2021; 2022). These excavations increasingly support the view that conflating sites based solely on morphology is sometimes problematic, and that trivallate sites may have had a range of functions, and indeed of inhabitants (see Fitzpatrick 2009). While some sites do seem to include significant high-status and/or exotic material this does not appear to be universally the case – for example at Knockhouse Lower, Walsh (2020a) is of the opinion that the site was occupied over a number of generations by a sort of social climbing *nouveau riche* – 'who thought it necessary to emphasise their social standing in the community through the construction and modification of this impressive multivallate ringfort' (p. 137).

The chronology of ringforts has also been extensively discussed (Stout 1997, 22–31; Kerr *et al.* 2013; McLaughlin *et al.* 2018; O'Sullivan *et al.* 2021a, 64–70; Hannah 2023), with consensus being that multivallate enclosures begin slightly earlier than other forms – perhaps before AD 500 (O'Sullivan *et al.* 2021a, 66). Recent radiocarbon dating from Garranes is in agreement with this, with most dates spanning the period from the early 5th century AD to the early 7th century (O'Brien and Hogan 2021, 93–94); however, at Knockhouse Lower most of the dates are significantly later, almost all between the mid-7th century to the mid- to late 8th century AD. At Lissaniska too, the dates range from the mid-8th century to the mid-12th century AD, although there are two earlier dates from the mid-5th century to mid-8th century AD (Lyne 2022, 64–65). The abandonment of early medieval settlement enclosures in Ireland – both in terms of when and why – is still open for discussion. O'Sullivan *et al.* (2021a, 78) suggest two major declines – the first at *c.* AD 800, the second at *c.* AD 1000, but the reasons for this are obscure and not synchronous in any sort of island-wide

fashion. Perhaps of relevance here are suggestions of changes in social organisation based upon socioeconomic changes (Kerr 2007, 114–115), and the potential re-organisation of the landscape around central lordly 'fortress' sites (O'Sullivan *et al.* 2021a, 78).

If one considers overall size, number and scale of ringfort enclosing elements as indicators of status then Tlachtga at 148 m diameter and with four vallations is almost unmatched within the monument class. The presence of more than three vallations is also vanishingly rare and suggests something beyond a normal high-status settlement. As Macalister (1949, 264) noted, Tlachtga is an 'altogether exceptional' monument and provided us with the opportunity to examine one of the most spectacular multivallate enclosures in Ireland over three seasons of excavation.

1.1. Project rationale

This work initially began as a small-scale remote sensing study: following on from previous work using lidar data for archaeological prospection in the Brú na Bóinne World Heritage Site. Tlachtga and its environs offered an intriguing and little-studied target for further investigation. From the ground the site is difficult to get a sense of, but archival aerial imagery better demonstrated its remarkable nature; however, prior to the examination of the lidar data and subsequent geophysical survey, the monument stood somewhat alone. Non-invasive methods showed this not to be the case – in addition to some significant and impressive monuments within the hinterland of Tlachtga, the monument itself provided some unexpected twists that warranted further investigation, and required excavation to address (see Davis 2011; 2013; Davis *et al.* 2017).

Initial questions revolved around site chronology and function. At least three clear construction phases were evident from the earliest stages of geophysical survey: the present enclosure of Tlachtga, a larger and earlier triple-ditched enclosure partially overbuilt by the present monument, a smaller plectrum-shaped enclosure partially overlapping Tlachtga to the south (the 'Southern Enclosure') and a series of ditches and linear anomalies to the east (Carey and Curran, this volume). The discovery of these monuments raised a number of questions:

1. Was the monument of Tlachtga centred on an earlier feature, for example a mound barrow or megalithic tomb? Given its intervisibility with the passage tomb cemetery of Loughcrew, the Hill of Tara and especially with Slieve Gullion, it would present an ideal location for such a monument.
2. Given significant high-status material recovered from a number of other large multivallate sites is there any evidence to demonstrate that Tlachtga was a regional centre of trade/exchange?

3. What were the dates of activity within the three clearly defined phases of activity on site? Is Tlachtga itself an early medieval site, a late Iron Age site or something else?
4. When was the Southern Enclosure constructed? How does this relate chronologically to Tlachtga?
5. What was the character of the larger, earlier monument?
6. What is the latest evidence of activity on the hill? Is there any archaeological evidence of reported encampments from Owen Roe O'Neill or Cromwellian forces?
7. Is there any archaeological evidence in favour of Geoffrey Keating's reported ritual burning events (the 'Fire of Tlachtga')?

Given that the original focus of many of the research questions was chronological, initial trenches targeted isolated sections of each feature. This approach in 2014 led to good dates for the Southern Enclosure, the outermost vallation of Tlachtga, the inner ditch of the earlier multivallate monument and to an extent a timber stockade constructed on the hilltop. In 2015 it was decided to build upon this approach, and also to focus on the junction between the Southern Enclosure and Tlachtga, the relationship between which had remained unclear from previous dates. The final season of excavation sought to better understand the central platform of the site, in particular the question of whether this represented an earlier monument or was part of the original construction. It also sought to characterise the eastern complex of features, and to understand whether these were contemporary with or distinct from the main phases of activity seen elsewhere.

1.2. The Ordnance Survey at Tlachtga

The earthworks at the Hill of Ward were first identified as being the site of Tlachtga by the Ordnance Survey of Ireland in the 1830s. John O'Donovan, the well-known placename researcher, began his tour of Meath in Kells during July 1836 and wrote to Lieutenant Thomas Larcom regarding his attempt to identify the 'situation of Tlachtga' on 3 August (O'Donovan 1836 – OS Letter 14E 2/25ii, p. 317). In this letter he notes that he had encountered traditions about its being located near Athboy, Co. Meath and not, as some of his informants suggested, in Co. Dublin. By 8 August he had travelled about 16 miles in search of information about Tlachtga in the Athboy. He visited the Hill of Ward in the company of an old soldier who was also keen to discover the location and, despite finding the site under cultivation for oats, was soon convinced that this was the place he had been looking for.

By the 1830s O'Donovan already noted that the original 'palace' had been 'variously dissected and modelled into a modern entrenchment' which he attributes to the encampment of Owen Roe O'Neill at the site in 1641. He notes (and indeed underscores) the presence of four concentric embankments (suggesting even the possibility of a fifth), and the central mound, although the diameter he noted of 136 yards is considerably smaller than the actual diameter of the site. Continuing his enquiries, O'Donovan spoke to a local antiquarian who noted that the site was known as a 'place of meeting established for bards by *Túathal Techtmar* (ibid., 318). It is questionable whether this association with *Túathal* relates to local folklore or, given the apparently educated nature of the informant, might relate to a written source (e.g. a familiarity with Keating's '*Foras Feasa ar Érinn*').

1.3. The historical and literary associations of Tlachtga (Edel Bhreathnach)

The significant archaeology that survives at Tlachtga forms one element in an impressive landscape of large-scale monuments located in the medieval kingdom of Brega. At the height of its extent, this kingdom stretched from around Ardee south to the river Liffey, and westwards from the Irish Sea coast to the borderlands of modern counties Meath and Westmeath. These monuments included the Neolithic Boyne Valley tombs, the ceremonial landscapes of Tara (Temair) and Teltown (Tailtiu) and the many hilltop earthworks on the low hills that gave Brega its name. Close to Tlachtga are Faughan Hill (Ocha) and the Hill of Lloyd (Mullach Aite). During the early medieval period, this landscape inspired poets and historians to compose metrical and prose literary cycles of topographical lore, accorded the title *dindsenchas* 'the lore or history of places' (*cf.* Hicks and Ward Elder 2003; Theuerkauf 2022). Prominent natural features and man-made monuments became the focus of the compositions of accomplished poets and traditional historians. These places triggered memories of stories, likely to be a combination of popular stories and more literary mythology, while very occasionally recording actual historical events. The specific place names were often explained by normally traditional – and unscientific – etymologies, and as in the cases of Tlachtga, Tailtiu and Temair, the names were said to have been personal names of women who died and were buried at these sites in extraordinary circumstances. Whether this memorialisation of women and significant places originated from the belief in the feminine fecundity of the land or from an echo of the link between the death of a woman, sometimes at the time of her giving birth – as in the case of Tlachtga – and the foundation of a religious centre or an assembly site is difficult to prove. Was this the imposition of literary knowledge on a landscape or was it a learned transformation of popular traditions? This note on Tlachtga is a brief contribution to this debate.

The etymology of the word *tlachtga* is uncertain. *Tlacht* means 'a garment, covering, protection'[1] and hence the place name could possibly mean 'a covered/protected place'. More significantly, another noun *tlacht* is cited in Dinneen's Irish English Dictionary as meaning 'a market, fair, meeting' and also 'earth, ground'. An associated verb *tlachtuighim* can mean 'I bury, inter' (Dineen 1927, 204; for more detail see Müller-Lisowski 1923, 145–163; 1938, 46–70). Tlachtga's function as an assembly place would fit well with the use of other prehistoric sites, including Tailtiu (Teltown, Co. Meath) and Óenach Carmain (perhaps Silliothill, Co. Kildare (Ó Murchadha 2002) or possibly a peripatetic event held at prehistoric sites in Leinster). The 11th-century poem on the royal women of Ireland, the *Banshenchas*, actually describes Tlachtga as *tulach na trét* 'the hill of the flocks/hosts' (Dobbs 1930) and one version of the *dindshenchas* calls it *Tlachtga na treb* 'Tlachtga of the tribes' (Gwynn 1926–28, 77, section 11). This, of course, may simply be a poetic phrase used to complete a rhyme, but is nonetheless worth noting. Most of these sites consisted of prehistoric burial monuments and attracted ambitious kings and their traditional historians (*senchaide*) to hold ceremonies affirming their authority and to celebrate their power publicly in poetry and prose (Bhreathnach 2011; 2022a; Gleeson 2015). The notion that the hill was an assembly site or a place for mustering troops is borne out somewhat by the few historical references to Tlachtga. In 908, for example, the northern kings of Cenél nEogain, Domnall and Niall son of Áed came on an expedition southward and are said to have burned Tlachtga (Annals of Ulster 908.1; Annals of the Four Masters 903.8). This was probably a show of force against Flann mac Maíl Sechnaill, king of Tara, who was dominant in the midlands during this period. What is meant by burning Tlachtga is unclear, unless the hill was defended by some form of wooden structure. According to the Annals of the Four Masters, a late source, more than a hundred years later, in 1022, Máel Sechnaill mac Domnaill, king of Tara, defeated the Vikings of Dublin at Áth Buide-Tlachtga (Athboy-Tlachtga). It was his last battle as he died a month later. Máel Sechnaill was instrumental in the revival of *óenach Tailten* ('the assembly of Tailtiu') during his reign and from surviving literature composed by his household poet, Cúan úa Lothcháin, it appears that he was keenly aware of the symbolism associated with such monuments and landscapes (Downey 2013; Bhreathnach 2022a). According to the Annals of the Four Masters, the most spectacular of these assemblies was convened in 1167 by Ruaidrí Ua Conchobair, high-king of Ireland, at which all the prominent nobles and clergy gathered to agree on military, political and ecclesiastical matters and, in effect, to recognise Ruaidrí as their overlord. This was one of a series of such assemblies that were convened by kings of Ireland during the 12th century, often at sites of historical or mythological significance (Flanagan 2010, 113). The events at Tlachtga recorded in the annals were probably the most noteworthy but it is likely that many others were held there. As a place where people gathered

it is not surprising that finds such as the small coin hoard of 10th-century English coins was discovered during the excavations. As noted by Andrew Woods (this volume), this could be a deposit that reflects the exchange economy of Dublin's hinterland with the regional kings of Clann Cholmáin or could be associated with the ecclesiastical economy. The nearest large monastery at Kells and its wealth were a focus of constant raids by Irish kings and especially the Vikings of Dublin during the 10th and 11th centuries. The possibility raised by Wood that this was a Viking deposit at a prehistoric site, a pattern noted from other discoveries, presumably with some votive intention, is plausible. I have argued recently that this might explain the Viking hoards discovered at Dunmore Cave, Co. Kilkenny (Bhreathnach 2022b). However, the more likely explanation is that the hoard was deposited in the eastern complex, the site of contemporary metalworking, simply as bullion. In sum, while not as prominent an assembly site as Tailtiu, nevertheless Tlachtga was recognised as one of a number of prehistoric sites in the region that attracted gatherings, for peaceful purposes and otherwise. It was sufficiently important during the 5th/6th centuries, and again during the 8th to 10th century and later, to warrant building on and extending a Bronze Age/Iron Age hillfort and enclosure.

None of the prosaic meanings of the place name Tlachtga inspired early medieval traditional etymologists who spun a tale around the death of a woman Tlachtga daughter of the famous magical wizard Mog Ruith ('Slave of the Wheel'). This tale is part of a greater cycle that centres around Mog Ruith who appears in genealogical and toponymic texts as a wise druid, poet and advisor to the king of Munster. This early tradition, reflected in an Old Irish poem (Carey 2005), also mentions his alliance with the great sorcerer and heretic of the east, Simon Magus (Eastman 2016; 2022), against the Apostle Peter (Carey 2005, 117–118):

> When he was a sage of those arts, the noble grandson of Fer Glan, he went to Simon in the east to learn druidry.

> He waged that struggle along with Simon – enduring the report – against Peter, for the sake of a blessing on [his] wisdom and weapons.

Mog Ruith's association with Simon Magus expands further in a later tale in which he is implicated in the beheading of John the Baptist as a pupil of Simon (Müller-Lisowski 1923), which Aideen O'Leary in a recent study of Mog Ruith's extensive biography describes as 'a remarkable interaction in the Celtic world between pre-Christian magical vestiges and medieval Christian realities' (O'Leary 2017). Mog Ruith and his magical arts are at the heart of the early Irish saga *Forbuis Droma Damhghaire* 'The siege of Knocklong' in which he comes to the aid of the men of Munster in their battle with Cormac mac Airt, king of Tara (Ó Duinn 1992). In return he was given the fertile territory of Mag Féne and his descendants, Fir Maige Féne (from which the place name Fermoy, Co. Cork originates), were designated to be the preeminent warriors of Munster. The tale of his daughter Tlachtga is one strand of the Mog Ruith cycle and while she does not appear in the Old Irish poem mentioned above, she forms part of the summary of Mog Ruith's life in the early genealogies (O'Brien 1962, 279–280[2]):

> Mog Ruith son of Fergus from whom are descended the Fir Maigi Féine. It is he who went to learn druidry from Simon the druid and it is they who together made the *roth rámach* that comes across Europe before the Day of Judgement in the year before Simon's battle with Peter and Paul. And this is why Europe was blamed because there was a pupil of every nation with Simon in the conflict against Peter.
>
> Cacht ('a slave') daughter of Cathmind, king of the Britons, was Mog Ruith's mother. Roth son of Riguill, fostered him. Hence he was named Mog Ruith ('?slave of Roth/the wheel').
>
> Mog Ruith's two sons were Buan and Fer Corb. Der Draigen ('daughter of the blackthorn') was the mother of Mog Ruith's two sons and Coirpre Lifechair's mother were two sisters of the Corcu Bárddéine from Dún Cermna (?Old Head of Kinsale).
>
> However, Dron daughter of Láirín was Mog Ruith's lawful wife, and others say that Tlachtga was Mog Ruith's daughter, who the three sons of Simon impregnated before she came west and she bore three sons for them. It is she who brought with her Coirthe Chnámchaille ('the pillarstone of Cnámchaill'), namely, a fragment of the wheel, and it is she who broke it. Blind everyone who will see it, deaf everyone who will hear it, dead everyone against whom it will strike.

The metrical and prose texts relating the story of Tlachtga add some extra details to the above genealogical extract. She went with Mog Ruith to learn magic from Simon where she was ravished by the latter's sons (Gwynn 1906, 186–191; Müller-Lisowski 1923, 158–161). Their names, Nero, Carpent and Uetir, are clearly Latin, Carpent, presumably used with *carpentum* 'a cart' or *artifex carpentarius* 'a maker of wooden carts' and wooden wheels in mind. Her sons' names are laden with doom: *Muach* ('gloom, dejection'), *Cumma* ('grief, sorrow') and *Doirb* ('hard to please, discontented'). The *dindshenchas* poem associates them with the men of Torach, Tory Island, thus fitting them into the mythical Balor of the

One Eye and the Fomóiri who were said to have lived there. The poet also places Tlachtga and her sons in the realms of gloomy and apocalyptic prophecies that had a long tradition in Hiberno-Latin and vernacular literature, and gained particular traction during the 11th and 12th centuries (Gwynn 1906, 188–189; see also discussion in Carey 2020, 156–171):

> The names of her sons – no meagre utterance – were Muach and Cumma and darling Doirb: 'tis for the men of Torach, that claimed them for its own, to hear their names – and mark ye them!
>
> As long as the names of her sons shall be held in honour throughout Banba – this is a true saying to spread abroad – there comes no ruin to her men.

In one tradition, the *roth rámach* 'rowing or paddle wheel' was constructed by Mog Ruith and Simon Magus, and part of it brought to Ireland by Tlachtga. In another version, Tlachtga herself is the artificer of the wheel (for a detailed summary see Chadbourne 1994; see also Macalister 1919, 350–351; Shingurova 2018). This wheel is regarded as one of the most bizarre and devastating objects of doom portending the end of the world for the Irish. It was foretold that the wheel would come from the east and smash against the pillarstone of Cnámchaill, causing untold destruction (Carey 2020, 158–159; see also O'Curry 1878, 385). In another version Simon Magus's adherents would be crushed by the wheel on the feast of St John the Baptist in divine retribution (Chadbourne 1994, 109). The feast of St John the Baptist was often cited as Doomsday for the very reason that Mog Ruith was implicated in the saint's beheading. Clearly, magic wheels and wheels of doom are a universal phenomenon, and there have been many theories associating this particular object and Mog Ruith with sun or fire worship and the image of a boat with oars or a chariot wheel representing the power of the sun god (*cf.* Müller-Lisowski 1938). In his study of this apocalyptic phenomenon, John Carey, however, admits that its true origins remain obscure. One possible explanation for the *roth rámach* is that the object in question is a wooden horizontal millwheel with its paddles and that the remnant (*fuidel*) was the shaft of the wheel.[3] Although he did not make this deduction in his study of the horizontal mill in Ireland, A.T. Lucas's comments were perceptive (Lucas 1953, 31):

> In an age and place where the mill was the only automatic machine in existence its symbolic appeal to the imagination must have been irresistible and it is not surprising to find it the subject of that numerical exaggeration characteristic of the heightened language of many passages of Old Irish literature.

The *roth rámach* may be a perfect example of Lucas's theory!

In recent years Tlachtga has become increasingly associated with the festival of Samhain, which fell at the same time as Halloween, based on late medieval and early modern literary reference to a druidic fire cult having existed on the hill. This tradition first appears in an Irish text on the chief places of Meath which relates that the young men of Munster used to guard Tlachtga with its fires and that no fire would be kindled in Ireland unless it was permitted by them (McCaughey 1960, 172). The 17th-century historian Geoffrey Keating includes a more expansive version in his history of Ireland, *Foras Feasa ar Éirinn* (Keating 1776, 146). The mythical king *Túathal Techtmar* created the central province of Mide and Tlachtga was that part of Mide representing Munster. Keating continues:

> It is then that it was ordained that the Fire of Tlachtga be kindled as it was a custom among them that the druids of Ireland used to meet and assemble on the eve of Samain to make offerings to all the gods. It is in that fire that they used to burn their offerings, and under the pain of a tax the fires of Ireland had to be extinguished that night, and none of the men of Ireland would dare kindle a fire unless it was kindled from that fire; and for every fire that was kindled from it the king of Munster was due a tribute or three pennies as a tax for it because the soil on which Tlachtga is situated was the part of Munster that came to Mide.

This section of Keating's history is part of a greater narrative in which the historian contends that Ireland was governed in an agreed and ordered manner since ancient times, thus countering Elizabethan descriptions of a wild and barbarous ungovernable people (for the context of Keating's *Foras feasa*, see Cunningham 2000). The island was ruled by the king of Tara, druids were in charge of religion and great assemblies were held at key times of the year (Samain, Beltaine and Lugnasad). The most important assembly, *Feis Temro* 'the feast of Tara' was held every third year at Samain, preceded by the lighting of the fire at Tlachtga. As demonstrated many decades ago by D.A. Binchy (1958, 113–138) in discussing *Feis Temro* and *Óenach Tailten* (the Fair of Tailtiu), very little of Keating's narrative is reliable history, although there are instances, as Rose-anne Schot (2006) has argued in relation to Uisneach, in which archaeological evidence can shed light on activities at these sites. While not associated with major Samain celebrations, it is interesting to note that the middle enclosure at Tlachtga was filled in by a large mound during the late 10th or early 11th century, and that there is some evidence of contemporary and later burning and feasting occurring on this mound. This might

be explained by the holding of occasional celebrations on the site, as reflected in the few annalistic records mentioned earlier.

One connection between Tlachtga and Munster, which is mentioned in very complex early genealogies, are the Fir Tlachtga 'The descendants of Tlachtga' who are named as one of the four Araid, a group of people who were settled around the eastern shore of Lough Derg and Limerick/Tipperary border. While their ancestry appears to be a genealogical fiction, that they were descended from Fer Tlachtga son of the Ulster hero Fergus mac Róich, suggests another strand in the Tlachtga story (O'Brien 1962, 320–321). William Mahon (1988) has demonstrated, based on ogham inscriptions from the Gap of Dunloe, Co. Kerry, that the information contained in these complicated genealogical tracts possibly reflects the movement and settlement of people around Ireland, perhaps during the 6th century, and how their genealogies were fitted into a structure dominated by dynasties who came to the fore at that time. If this analysis is correct, then there might just be a connection between these texts and the reconstruction of Tlachtga during the same period. What that connection might be depends on finding comparable archaeological activity in the territories of the Araid, and even of the Ulaid in the northeast from which Fer Tlachtga reputedly came, as well as further distillation of the genealogical tracts. Keating's claim of a link between the fire of Tlachtga and the feast of Tara may be fabricated but it is clear that the kings of Tara, or at least their historians, regarded Tlachtga as forming part of the inner ceremonial landscape of their kingship. In the gift of the king of Tara were such items as fish from the Boyne and the water of the well of Tlachtga, presumably a source imbued with some healing properties (Dillon 1951, 8).

The historical and mythological associations with Tlachtga fall in line with the profile of many similar prehistoric and medieval assembly sites. The early medieval Irish literary class wove marvellous fictional tales to explain place names such as Tlachtga and the monuments that were visible to them. They composed histories about them to enhance their aristocratic patrons' claims to long, distinguished ancestries and to contemporary ambitions. And yet unknown to them, archaeology would actually prove the genuine importance of Tlachtga and a long history dating back to the early Bronze Age. If there is one feature of the excavation at Tlachtga that speaks to the rituals that were actually held there, it is the possible foundational burial of an infant and the cattle bones placed around the rock cut ditch during the 5th century, at the very period that Christianity, a new religion, was being introduced especially into the kingdom of Brega due to its extensive trading networks with the world as far as north Africa and the eastern Mediterranean.

1.4. The archaeological landscape of the Hill of Ward

1.4.1. The Mesolithic

While no Mesolithic sites are recorded within the vicinity of the Hill of Ward, a number of late Mesolithic radiocarbon dates were obtained on the M3 Navan–Kells road construction project, which runs in a northwest–southeast direction approximately 8.5 km to the east of Tlachtga (Walsh 2021, 48). Only one site – Cakestown Glebe 2 – is regarded by Walsh (*ibid.*) as a bona fide Mesolithic site, comprising a pair of late Mesolithic hearths from which a butt-trimmed flake was recovered. Previous work on the Dunshaughlin–Navan section of the M3 at Clowanstown, Co. Meath identified a series of four remarkably preserved late Mesolithic fish traps at the edge of a small terrestrialised lake (FitzGerald 2007). These very partial snapshots demonstrate the potential of this landscape for Mesolithic occupation sites; however, they also demonstrate the difficulty in locating such sites, especially through non-invasive methods. The numerous eskers within the area may well have offered significant dry islands overlooking more low-lying boggy ground and it is likely that Bohermeen Bog (Jamestown Bog) comprised lake or fen in earlier prehistory (see Maguire, this volume).

1.4.2. Neolithic and Bronze Age

From the summit of the Hill of Ward a number of significant middle Neolithic sites are visible, in particular the passage tomb cemetery at Loughcrew, and other passage tomb locations including the Hill of Tara and Slieve Gullion. The nearby Faughan Hill, to the north of the Hill of Ward has been shown to encompass a large middle Neolithic (*c.* 3635–3380 cal BC) palisaded enclosure, *c.* 250 m in diameter (Dowling and Schot 2023, 33). Meanwhile, the potentially destroyed passage tomb at Drewstown Great (ME023-013; *cf.* Herity 1974) is the closest megalithic monument, *c.* 6.5 km northwest of Tlachtga.

The absence of more local recorded Neolithic archaeology, especially settlement archaeology is likely to be a function of preservation and visibility. This is again suggested by the M3 Navan–Kells project, which identified a wide range of sites spanning the entire Neolithic period (Walsh 2021). In particular, at least eight rectilinear early Neolithic houses were identified within an area just south of Kells at Kilmainham/Cookstown. These ranged from classic 'trench built' examples to more unusual post-built structures. At Kilmainham 1C these were accompanied by a range of other prehistoric timber constructions that demonstrated continued re-use of the location from the early Neolithic through to at least the early medieval period (*ibid.*, 15). While the Blackwater Valley seems to have been a focus for early

Neolithic activity, many of the excavated features would have been difficult or impossible to identify other than through open area excavation.

In the middle Neolithic, settlement activity across Ireland appears to decline, or at least becomes more cryptic. This has been previously highlighted elsewhere within the Irish archaeological record, with discussions of an early Neolithic agricultural 'boom' followed by a middle Neolithic 'bust' (Whitehouse *et al.* 2014; Colledge *et al.* 2019). While changes in settlement and in agricultural practice do occur (*e.g.* McClatchie *et al.* 2016), there is still significant discussion about what these lines of evidence actually mean in terms of the lived experience of Neolithic people. In particular, there is a tension between apparent agricultural decline and the increase in the construction of funerary monuments seen at this time.

Middle to late Neolithic remains were comparatively sparse along the M3 Navan–Kells project, but included a Grooved Ware circle ('4-post structure' – see Carlin and Cooney 2017) at Kilmainham 3 ('Structure 2'; Walsh 2021, 85) as well as other structural and artefactual remains at Phoenixtown 5 (*ibid.*, 80) and pottery sherds at Kilmainham 1C (*ibid.*, 81). A late Neolithic charcoal deposit and a pit of similar date (*c.* 2800–2500 cal BC) were also identified through excavation at Faughan Hill (Dowling and Schot 2023, 31–32). Within the immediate area of the Hill of Ward a typical Boyne-style embanked enclosure (henge) was identified through early lidar surveys (now recorded as ME030-035 Large enclosure; Davis 2011).

While the middle and late Neolithic represent a comparative lull in the monumental record around the Hill of Ward, the same cannot be said for the Bronze Age. Returning to the M3 Navan–Kells project, the Bronze Age represents the most frequently encountered time period, with 26 sites overall and a further 11 sites attributed to the Chalcolithic period. The nature of Chalcolithic activity in the area remains largely unclear: although Beaker pottery was recovered from a number of sites on the scheme, it was only at Kilmainham 1C that more extensive activity was hinted at, with significant deposition of Beaker sherds within an earlier Grooved Ware structure (Walsh 2021, 81). At the Hill of Ward itself, a barbed and tanged projectile point attributable to this period was recovered from the top of the central mound in a secondary context, as well as a bifacially worked plano-convex knife. This provides little information beyond the suggestion that people with Beaker affinities were present in the local area.

Bronze Age activity within the hinterland of the Hill of Ward is much more extensive. This includes a number of burnt mounds/fulachta fiadh (eight within the immediate area, with 20 excavated on the M3 Navan–Kells road project) and settlement sites from the early and middle

Bronze Age (Walsh 2021, 109–139). A number of ring-ditches of probable Bronze Age date have been identified through aerial survey including clusters at Faughan Hill (ME024-022004; ME024-022005; ME024-022006) and at Moymet (ME030-054001; ME030-054002; ME030-054003; ME030-05400 and ME030-05405), with a further cluster identified through geophysical survey north of Tlachtga and other probable examples to the east (see Carey and Curran, this volume). Given the levelled nature of monuments within this class it is likely that they are significantly under-represented in the known archaeological record. Significant potential for crop-mark archaeology exists in the area, especially in tilled fields south and east of the Hill of Ward, with some previously unknown sites identified in the unusually dry summer of 2018 (*e.g.* Enclosure ME030-051). A number of burial monuments and cremations were noted by Walsh (2021, 135–139), including one early Bronze Age ringditch (Kilmainham 3), middle Bronze Age unenclosed cremation pits (*e.g.* Kilmainham 1C; Cakestown Glebe 2). While human remains were not recovered from the former site, in the latter two examples these appear to represent complete (as opposed to token) cremation burials.

As highlighted by the first two seasons of excavation, the Hill of Ward was clearly a location of significance in the later Bronze Age. The same is likely to have been the case for the nearby Hill of Lloyd and Faughan Hill (see Dowling 2015) where recently published dates place the construction of a large Class 2 hillfort at *c.* 1200 BC (Dowling and Schot 2023, 15). A number of later Bronze Age structures were recorded on the M3 Navan–Kells road, including at Cakestown Glebe 2, Townparks 3 and Nugentstown 1 (*ibid.*, 124). These sites are all roughly contemporary with the start of the earliest phase at the Hill of Ward, *c.* 1200–1000 BC. Only a single later Bronze Age funerary structure was excavated on the road development – a small barrow monument at Grange 3. As at Kilmainham 3, no human bone was recovered with the site interpreted as a cenotaph rather than a grave marker. Cremated human bone of late Bronze Age date (1192–938 cal BC) was also recovered within two burnt spreads excavated by Moraghan at Curleyland/Mill Land (Morahan 2014) most likely representing ploughed out cremation burials. Dowling and Schot (2023, 36–38) highlight the stray find of a Ballintober-type bronze rapier (NMI 1970:215) from the nearby Bohermeen/Jamestown Bog (see Maguire, this volume), most likely contemporary with the early phases of hillfort construction at both Faughan Hill and the Hill of Ward (*cf.* Matthews 2011).

A hoard of late Bronze Age gold items was discovered by Martin and Michael Coffey during ploughing in 1953 at Drissoge, 2 km east of the Hill of Ward. These were published by George Eogan (1957) and comprised a 'sunflower' pin and three penannular bracelets (Fig. 1.3).

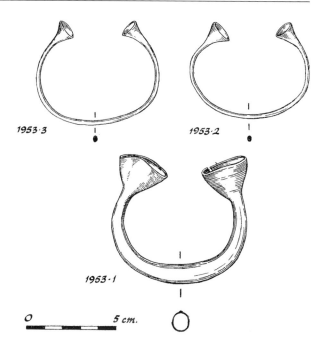

Fig. 1.3. Group of penannular gold bracelets from Drissoge, Co. Meath. Published by George Eogan (1957).

This group of objects likely dates to the early to middle 1st millennium BC and are therefore contemporary with late Bronze Age activity at the Hill of Ward.

1.4.3. Iron Age to early medieval

Early Iron Age activity, contemporary with the end of the Hillfort Phase at the Hill of Ward, was limited to isolated pits (*e.g.* at Kilmainham 1C and Cookstown Great 1), a burnt mound (Cookstown Great 3) and a cereal drying kiln at Kilmainham 2 (Walsh 2021). Drying kilns remained the most frequently recorded Iron Age feature within the N52 Navan–Kells project (22 were excavated) and have also been noted in profusion elsewhere in Meath (*e.g.* on the M3 motorway – O'Connell 2009; 2013, 115–121). Of the 22 kilns excavated, 15 returned dates that were transitional or early medieval dates between early 5th and mid-6th centuries AD. However, one example at Kilmainham 2 (Kiln C33) returned a middle Iron Age date of 510–387 cal BC (UBA-12065). Four other kilns have date ranges that are either all, or in part within the late Iron Age. Three of these are located at Kilmainham 1C (C81; C689 and C13), with the fourth at Kilmainham 1B. A group of late Iron Age metalworking features was identified at Grange 3 (Walsh 2021, 149), dating to between 390 cal BC and cal AD 30.

As regards burial monuments, a small barrow was excavated at Cakestown Glebe 2. This was similar in dimensions to the Bronze Age barrow/ringditch excavated at Grange 3. While a small amount of burnt animal bone was recovered, the site produced no human remains.

Two disparate Iron Age radiocarbon dates were obtained, one of 380–110 cal BC (SUERC-29337), the other AD 28–128 (UBA-12069), suggesting a main period of use in the late Iron Age. Two further inhumations dated to the early medieval period (cal AD 434–598; UBA-12933) were located adjacent to a middle Iron Age rectangular enclosure. This unusual structure was compared with Iron Age shrine structures such as that excavated by O'Connell at Lismullen, Co. Meath (2013, 57–60), Collierstown, Co. Meath (O'Hara 2009) and a number of British examples (Walsh 2021, 160).

Most likely belonging to the same transitional period, Wood-Martin (1886) recorded a ladle 'of extremely thin bronze' found by turf cutters at Bohermeen/Jamestown Bog, perhaps within the context of a destroyed crannog (*ibid.*, 82), the location of which remains unknown. This object is suggested as of Roman manufacture by Ó Ríordáin (1945) rather than being an insular object of Roman design, and is one of only seven such items he catalogues. A wooden vessel of bog butter (M1951:22)

was recovered from Tullaghstown, Co. Meath (within Jamestown Bog). This was retrieved from a depth of 6 ft (1.83 m), and the vessel is described as being held together with strips of willow, implying this was stave-built (Karen O'Toole pers. comm.). Again, the majority of such vessels belong to the late Iron Age to early medieval transition (Cronin *et al.* 2007).

Several townland names in the vicinity of the Hill of Ward suggest possible early medieval activity – *e.g.* Fordrath, Rathmore, Raith Cairn; however, the 'rath' townland name cannot be regarded as a sure indicator of early medieval activity (see Fitzpatrick 2009, 273). At least 17 recorded ringforts are present within the local area (all classified as 'ringfort – rath'), with these including both Tlachtga (ME030-001) and the Southern Enclosure (ME030-001002; Fig. 1.4). A single souterrain has been recorded in the immediate area, located at Fraine, *c.* 4 km southwest of the Hill of Ward (Rynne and Prenderdast 1962). At Trim to the southeast there are several religious foundations and ecclesiastical

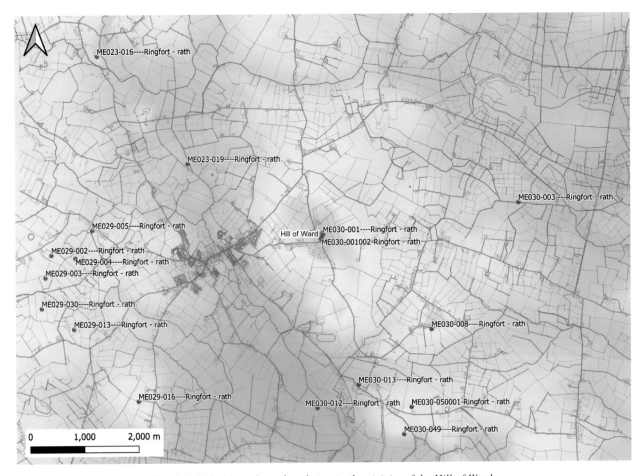

Fig. 1.4. Probable early medieval sites in the vicinity of the Hill of Ward.

Fig. 1.5. St Laurence's Stone, now in St Lawrence's churchyard, Rathmore. Photograph courtesy John Gilroy.

enclosures (*e.g.* at Kiltoome – ME036-011004); however, none have yet been identified in the immediate area of the Hill of Ward.

Just north of the summit of the hill a 'holy/saint's stone' is recorded (ME024-014), marked on the 6" map as 'St. Laurence's Stone'. This large holed stone is reputed to have originally stood at Rathmore Castle (ME024-018001) but now resides in the modern churchyard of St Lawrence, Rathmore – ironically a different St Laurence for whom the stone is named (Fig. 1.5). This may represent an inauguration stone (*e.g.* Lynn 2007).

There has also been some discussion as to whether the Hill of Ward represents an ancient *oenach* or assembly site (*e.g.* Chadbourne 1994; MacLeod 2003). According to Myles Dillon, a 'horse fair' used to be held approximately half a mile east of the hill at a field known as 'the Crothy' (Ettlinger 1952). This may correspond with the substantial archaeological remains noted in the geomagnetic survey (Carey and Curran, this volume) and is likely derived from the irish *crotach* ('small eminence, humps, hummocks' – T. O'Hagan, pers. comm.). In part, this highlights difficulties in defining assembly sites highlighted by Gleeson (2015), but it seems likely that given broad associations of the site with Samhain, the suggestion of an adjacent horse fair and the later Synod of Athboy or 1167 (Dumville 1997) that Tlachtga was a site of seasonal gatherings through the early medieval period and beyond.

1.4.4. Later medieval

Immediately after the arrival of the Anglo-Normans in Ireland in AD 1169 Tlachtga was the scene of a dramatic incident between Hugh de Lacy and Tighernán Ua Ruairc, King of Breifne over the grant of the lordship of Mide by Henry II. The two delegations met at Tlachtga, named by Giraldus Cambrensis as 'O'Roric's [*sic*] Hill', each with a small number of armed followers (Forester 2001, 41). Here, Cambrensis suggests that ua Ruairc – 'the one-eyed villain, meditating treachery' attempted to slay de Lacy. Despite de Lacy reportedly being felled twice, ua Ruairc was slain and subsequently beheaded, and his head sent to Dublin. In Geraldus, these events are attributed to having taken place on the Hill of Tara, but the Annals of the Four Masters place them at Tlachtga and describe ua Ruairc as having been 'treacherously slain' by de Lacy.

The granting of Mide to de Lacy meant that Athboy became the centre of an important manor and was granted to William de Muset by Hugh de Lacy in the early 1170s (Orpen 1911–20, ii, 86). The manor changed hands several times over the next two centuries. There are suggestions of motte-type fortification within the area of Athboy from the very early 13th century (Pipe Roll of 14 John – Davies and Quinn 1941, 38–39), at which point the castle of Athboy was described as being in the process of fortification. Moore (2022) believes that this original castle may have been located at Tlachtga, with the adaptation of pre-existing native fortifications as motte castles being a not infrequent occurrence (*e.g.* at Dundrum Castle – Waterman 1951; see discussion in O'Sullivan *et al.* 2021a, 79).

After the 12th century little factual information is recorded about Tlachtga until the 17th century. In 1643 the town of Athboy was captured by Owen Roe O'Neill. It is recorded to have been recaptured by the Parliamentarians under General Michael Jones in October 1647. This recapture is described in detail within Jones' diary, where he described the taking of the town as 'little less than miraculous' (Jones and Young 1897, 157) having cost the Leinster Army only four men and taken only two hours. Cromwell's forces arrived in Ireland in August 1649 and proceeded to take both Drogheda and Trim. While there is no clear evidence of his presence in Athboy (*e.g.* no mention in Murphy 1893), there is certainly local folklore relating Cromwell to the Hill of Ward, for example as murder of the Plunkets [*sic*] of Rathmore and their children (*e.g.* Schools' Collection, Rathcarran roll number 4370), varying in number from 7 to 12. As always, it is difficult to unpick the reality of Cromwell's activities in Ireland from what he is alleged to have been responsible for.

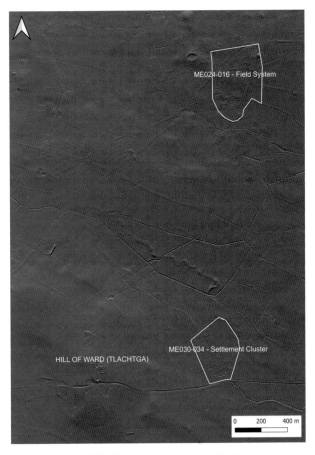

Fig. 1.6. Hill of Ward showing location of adjacent deserted settlements. Multidirection hillshade baselayer.

A number of substantial medieval sites are present in the immediate area of the Hill of Ward. These include the churches at Wardstown southeast of Tlachtga (ME030-002), its associated graveyard (ME030-002001) and font (ME030-002002), and two deserted medieval settlements (Fig. 1.6). These comprise the impressively well-defined settlement associated with Rathmore Church *c.* 2 km to the north (ME024-017001; Rheinisch 2013; see also Leask 1933) and the deserted medieval settlement of Wardstown (ME030-034 – Settlement cluster) 700 m to the east. Rathmore was traditionally associated with the Plunkett family (see above) and the site is known for the ruins of a 15th-century church with a corbelled bell tower, an effigial tomb (ME024-017005) believed to represent Sir Thomas Plunket (d. 1471) and his wife, Mary Cruise, a 'labyrinth stone' (Leask 1933, 166) and an octagonal stone font (*ibid.*, 160–161) that was stolen and then returned in recent years (Condit 2013). Rheinisch (2013) suggests this continued as a functioning manor up until the 17th century. While Rathmore was noted as a manorial village by Graham (1975) in his review of Anglo-Norman settlement in Meath, Wardstown has no reference in historical documents.

Notes

1   The author wishes to thank Dr Kevin Murray, UCC Scoil Léann na Gaeilge for providing me with the unpublished entry on Tlachga in the Historical Dictionary of Ireland.
2   Author's own translation.
3   The author owes this suggestion to Dr Raghnall Ó Floinn.

2

Previous archaeological research in the Hill of Ward environs

2.1. Remote sensing

In 2010 a small area of lidar data (2.5 km × 2.5 km) was purchased from the Ordnance Survey Ireland to assess the structural of the monument itself and to elaborate upon its wider landscape setting. This revealed a range of new features of archaeological interest (Davis 2011; 2013), some of which have already been noted. In particular, these included.

- a pair of parallel, curving outer embankments to the north (ME030-038 – Linear Earthwork);
- a Boyne-style henge monument to the east (ME030-035 – Large Enclosure);
- a well-preserved deserted medieval settlement at Wardstown to the east (ME030-034 – Settlement Cluster).

A much larger area of lidar data, obtained from the Office of Public Works was subsequently obtained, stretching eastwards beyond Jamestown Bog and better contextualising the site. While much of Meath has been subject to intensive agriculture since at least the Anglo-Norman settlement of Ireland, a range of earthworks and possible lynchet structures are present within this dataset. These could in some cases be described as 'linear earthworks' but are more likely to be the remains of early field systems, pre-dating the 1830s 6-inch series mapping.

Focusing on Tlachtga, where the banks had been demolished it remains possible to trace the outermost embankment to the southeast using local relief modelling (Fig. 2.1). To the east elements of a field system were clearly visible. One northeast–southwest field boundary appears to mark the section of the site that was subsequently removed to the east. The depression dividing the central mound was clearly defined, as was the disrupted area west of the central platform. West of the road there is an apparent cairn or rock outcrop while to the south of

the site a clear interruption in the outer two bank circuits was noted which was interpreted as an enclosure, partially intersecting the monument of Tlachtga. A similar pattern of smaller enclosures partially incorporated by later, larger enclosures is present at sites on the Hill of Tara (see Newman 1997) and also at Freestone Hill, Co. Kilkenny (Raftery 1969; S. Dowling pers. comm.; see also Ó Floinn 2000) and the Hill of Slane, Co. Meath (Brady et al. 2011; Seaver and Brady 2011).

Geomagnetic survey in 2013 was immediately striking (see Carey and Curran, this volume). The first day of survey, northwest of the main monument, revealed three parallel, closely spaced curving ditches. These were clearly not concentric with Tlachtga and ran beneath the upstanding monument. Tlachtga itself is extremely complex geomagnetically because in some places both banks and ditches show as positive magnetic anomalies (Carey and Curran, this volume). This means that while in the outer circuits it is relatively straightforward to follow the course of the ditches, approaching the centre of the monument the overall form becomes difficult to interpret magnetically. With the outermost ditch revealed the overall diameter of the Tlachtga is c. 148 m. The breaks in the outer bank circuit evident in the lidar data to the south of Tlachtga coincide with the northern section of a plectrum-shaped ditched enclosure, c. 40 m in diameter – this is subsequently referred to as the 'Southern Enclosure'.

The three ditches observed in the first day of survey emerge from beneath Tlachtga to the southeast. They form part of a large, trivallate enclosure (the 'Hillfort Phase') of approximately 153 m internal diameter, clearly pre-dating Tlachtga itself (see Carey and Curran below). The ditches of this enclosure are closely but variably spaced: to the northwest they are c. 7.5 m apart, while the spacing narrows to 4.5 m in the southeast. The overall diameter of the site from outer ditch to outer ditch is c. 195 m. Barry

Raftery (1972) linked the development of closely spaced multivallation with inland promontory forts (his Class III hillforts) while Dowling (2011) suggests parallels with linear earthworks (*e.g.* Riverstown, Co. Meath). The development of closely spaced multivallation in Ireland has seen significant discussion, especially by Dowling (*ibid.*, 217). In particular, while noting the lack of dating he suggests that multivallate monuments in the Bronze Age are typically defined by widely spaced ramparts, and that at this time the use of closely spaced vallation was restricted to funerary and ritual monuments.

To the east of Tlachtga one of the linear anomalies noted in the lidar was revealed to have a strong magnetic signature, and to incorporate at least two curving anomalies representing enclosures or partial enclosures. The nature of these features was difficult to interpret from geophysical data alone. The linear anomaly links to a series of other linear features that are tentatively interpreted as a network of boundaries or droveways. These connect to a series of enclosures, most likely of medieval/early medieval date (with some prehistoric elements) evident in the field east of the monument (see Carey and Curran, this volume). Some quarrying is evident here also. To the southeast a double-ditched linear anomaly aligns with the central platform of Tlachtga. This pre-dates any historic mapping and probably represents a formal access to the site, possibly to the earlier phase of monument. To the north of the site, while no geomagnetic trace of the curvilinear banks is present a group of probable ring ditches was identified. These most likely represent Bronze Age funerary structures and are again discussed in more detail elsewhere in this volume.

2.2. Geophysical survey at the Hill of Ward: placing Tlachtga in space and time (Chris Carey and Susan Curran)

2.2.1. Introduction
After the lidar DTM modelling at the Hill of Ward (see Fig. 2.1), a series of geophysical surveys were undertaken to investigate the monument of Tlachtga and its immediate surroundings. The initial lidar survey defined extensive earthworks on the hilltop, with a spread of other monuments in the surrounding fields. Given that the bedrock geology of the site is Lower Carboniferous limestone and shale of the Lucan formation (Geological Survey Ireland; data available from http://www.gsi.ie) and there was little in the way of surficial geologies recorded in the immediate surroundings, a shallow gradiometer survey was initially trialled in 2012 to investigate the presence of sub-surface (<1 m) archaeological features. Initial results demonstrated a high potential for the gradiometer survey to detect archaeological monuments and features across this landscape and was extended using volunteers, staff and students from University College Dublin

and the University of Brighton, during the summers of 2013–2015.

The gradiometer surveys at the Hill of Ward attempted to not only find archaeology, but also to develop a wider narrative of the monument at the Hill of Ward and its immediate sitescape over time. To achieve this, the gradiometer data was interpreted within a structured framework, allowing for major phases of activity to be identified.

2.2.2. Methods: gradiometer field collection and data processing
The survey used a handheld Bartington Grad-601 gradiometer. This fluxgate gradiometer instrument comprises two gradiometer sensor tubes spaced at a fixed horizontal distance of 1 m, with each tube containing two magnetometers with a vertical separation of 1 m between sensors. A maximum depth of penetration into the sediment profile is *c.* <1 m. The gradiometer was balanced on site by scanning for a location of low, uniform, magnetic response over an area of 1 m². The gradiometer was then calibrated to the earth's magnetic field and the sensor tubes calibrated to each other. A maximum tolerance of 0.5 nT (nanoTesla) between sensor tubes was used in the calibration, although a lower level of sensor tolerance was routinely achieved. The survey area was divided into 30 m × 30 m survey grids, set out using a Trimble RTK GPS system, accurate to approximately 0.02 m. The traverse interval for data collection was 1 m, with a sample interval of 0.25 m, using a 'zig-zag' survey method. All data were logged automatically and collected by slowly traversing survey chains for high resolution data.

All the collected gradiometer data were downloaded into the Grad 601 software. The data were then imported into 'Terrasurveyer' (DW Consulting) software for processing. A combination of data clipping, destriping and despiking, were used to remove noise and account for directional variation of the sensors, before export of raw and processed data (ascii files) into ArcGIS 10.8.1 for georeferencing, visualisation and interpretation. A composite of multiple different gradiometer survey plots were then mosaiced into a final gradiometer GeoTIFF image. This image was displayed at 2.5 standard deviations and interpreted.

2.2.3. Methods: gradiometer data interpretation
The most subjective aspect of any geoprospection survey is interpretation. Although it is based on the observation of scientific data, the interpretation of geophysical data is 'not an exact science as there is interplay between theory and experience. While a broad knowledge of geophysical techniques and the principles of archaeological geophysics are a necessary requirement, other factors are also important. In particular, an appreciation of the nature of the archaeological features being investigated is fundamental, as is an understanding of the local conditions at the site – including the geology, pedology and topography' (Gaffney and Gater

2003, 109). Given the size of the dataset and the large number of magnetic anomalies identified, a hierarchical approach to interpretation was undertaken. This initially focused on the geophysical properties of the anomalies, but attempts to go further than a descriptive account of possible archaeological features, providing a detailed analysis of their potential chronology and site-wide development. The identified anomalies that had a high probability of an archaeological origin were digitised as shapefile polygons within a GIS framework, using structured attributes to define their likely form, function and phase.

In recent years an increasing number of interpretations of geophysical data sets have sought to perform autoclassification of anomalies for the identification of archaeological features (*e.g.* Pregesbauer *et al.* 2014), arguing for a considerable time saving on anomaly digitisation. This is largely driven by the increasing spatial extent of near surface geophysical surveys now achievable through cart-mounted arrays, as well as advancements in automated analysis (Küçükdemirci and Sarris 2020). For the Hill of Ward survey a combination of manual digitisation and image classification was utilised, as this facilitates familiarity and scrutinisation of the data, allowing the forms and relationships of the geophysical anomalies to be identified. This engagement with the gradiometer data permitted the development of interpretative chronological narratives of the local sitescape. Of course, an interpretation of geophysical data is just that, an interpretation, but the acquisition of geophysical data is a repeatable non-intrusive process that can provide a model for subsequent testing, investigation and refinement. The hierarchical attribute structure for the hand-digitised magnetic anomalies at the Hill of Ward were defined as:

- **Level 1:** Geophysical interpretation – Each anomaly was described as either positive, negative or metal interference (*e.g.* fences, gates, etc), or mixed magnetic signal (*e.g.* modern rubbish dumping).
- **Level 2:** Assessment of confidence – Each anomaly was assigned a confidence in the archaeological interpretation on a sliding scale: Definite archaeology (>90% confidence); Probable archaeology (75% confidence); Possible archaeology (50% confidence); and Unknown (<50% confidence).
- **Level 3:** Feature level interpretation – Interpretation of the cause of the anomaly, such as pit/activity area, ditch, bank, *in-situ* heating, occupation/pyrotechnological debris, building/activity area, etc. In addition, many of the ditches had areas with very magnetic fills, producing negative 'halos' surrounding the positive ditch, which were described as 'high magnetic response'.
- **Level 4:** Monument level interpretation – Many of the anomalies were constituents of larger structures, such as multiple ditches forming an enclosure. Therefore, the Level 4 interpretation identified the form of larger monuments, such as Enclosures, Ring Ditches, land plot, etc.

Beyond these four levels of interpretation, two further attributes were also assigned to each digitised anomaly; Grouping and Phasing.

- Grouping – An individual Group number was assigned to each monument, *e.g.* Enclosure Group 22, the Avenue Group 21, Land Divisions Group 12, etc. In some cases a further sub Group was defined using a decimal, to indicate association with the wider Group number, *e.g.* Group 8.1 Enclosure and associated building Group 8.2, within the enclosure.
- Phasing – based on the physical morphology of the Level 4 monument groups, an interpretation of their suspected date of construction/use was made within broad archaeological periods being: Phase 1 Prehistoric EBA–MIA (Early Bronze Age to Middle Iron Age); Phase 2 Early Medieval, Phase 3 Anglo-Norman, and Phase 4 Later Medieval to Post-Medieval.

Beyond the selection of anomalies for hand digitising, there are a large number of other magnetic anomalies in the gradiometer dataset that are potentially of archaeological origin. In general, it is extremely challenging to interpret features such as small isolated and discrete pits, stakeholes etc. in magnetic data, even though these have a magnetic signature. Therefore, the mosaiced gradiometer data were converted into integer data using the Spatial Analyst Math function, and vectorised using the Raster Conversion to Polygon Tool in ArcGIS. These anomalies were then colour coded by their polarity and are shown in some figures (Positive-other and Negative-other) in addition to the interpreted polygons. This process of data interpretation provided an overview of the salient monuments within the data set, allowing a narrative to be developed of the sitescape over time, maximising archaeological understanding without producing an overwhelming number of anomalies, descriptions and variables.

2.2.4. Geomagnetic survey: results

The geophysical results reveal a complex archaeological palimpsest at the Hill of Ward, which has been interpreted into chronological and monumental groupings. It is worth restating that this was (and still is) an interpretative model, and aspects of this model were subsequently tested by excavation, alongside providing an opportunity for further research beyond the lifetime of this project. The gradiometer survey provided a dramatic view of this sitescape, revealing a wealth of previously unknown archaeological monuments and features. Many of these archaeological sites are not visible within the lidar DTM; instead these sites are detected in the shallow subsurface (<1 m) (Fig. 2.1; Fig. 2.2).

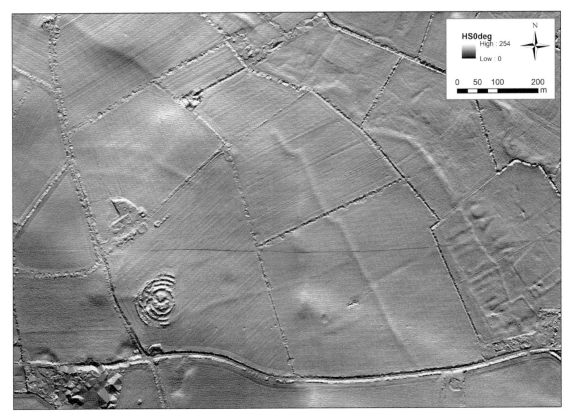

Fig. 2.1. Lidar hillshade, Hill of Ward survey area.

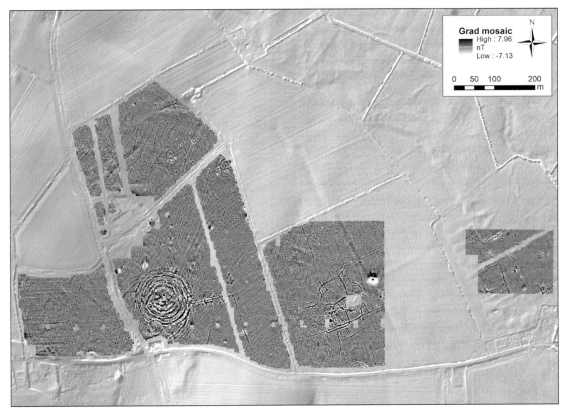

Fig. 2.2. Total area of geomagnetic survey, Hill of Ward environs.

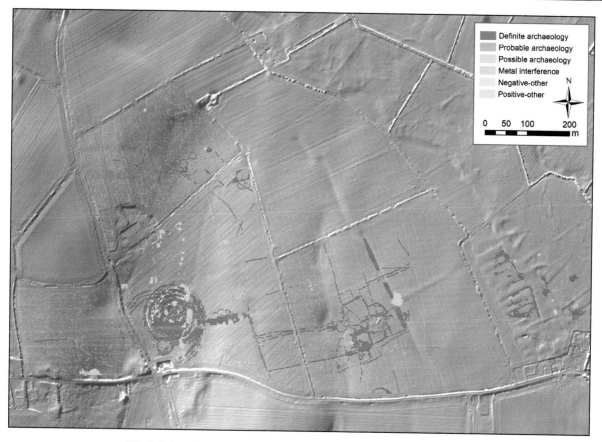

Fig. 2.3. Level 2 interpretation of geomagnetic survey data, Hill of Ward.

The processing of the Hill of Ward datasets demonstrated that many areas of this sitescape were magnetically noisy, including the main Tlachtga enclosure. This magnetic noise indicates substantial human activity and the associated use of fire, *e.g.* cooking, and potentially pyrotechnologies (*e.g.* iron working, pottery production, etc). Furthermore, many areas recorded extensive plough lines, for example, directly north of Tlachtga, plough lines can be seen trending northeast–southwest. This ploughing has undoubtedly had an impact on the preservation of many of the archaeological features and explains their lack of topographic expression.

The interpretation of the dataset comprised the hand digitisation of 2,549 polygon anomalies that were first categorised by their magnetic polarity and were then interpreted as to their likely archaeological potential (Fig. 2.3), with definite archaeology (2,049 anomalies), probable archaeology (386 anomalies) and possible archaeology (62 anomalies), defining an archaeologically rich record. In addition to these hand-digitised anomalies, a large number of other anomalies were identified through the vectorisation of the gradiometer raster and were classified by their magnetic polarity (*i.e.* negative-other or positive-other) and at least some of these anomalies are of potential archaeological origin. When

working and interpreting large geophysical data sets, the hand digitisation and interpretation of the data provides a first hand, detailed examination of the anomalies and their relationships, allowing possible relationships between intersecting features to be interpreted (*i.e.* what cuts what). However, we must be mindful that a relationship between intersecting magnetic anomalies is not based on stratigraphy, but based on the magnitude of their magnetic field, and these relationships are interpreted and not absolute, with the only way to definitively answer such questions being through excavation. The gradiometer data are presented below, primarily structured through the interpreted Phasing and Grouping framework. All diameters and lengths/widths of monuments are from the inside edge of the internal ditch/structure, unless otherwise stated.

2.2.4.1. Phase 1: prehistoric Early Bronze Age to Iron Age

Across the sitescape at the Hill of Ward numerous archaeological features and monuments were identified that have been interpreted as prehistoric and were constructed prior to the main phase of the present enclosure of Tlachtga (Table 2.1). These features have been placed into 14 groups (Fig. 2.4; Table 2.1).

Table 2.1. Summary of interpreted prehistoric monuments, presented in the order discussed in the text.

Group no.	Monument type	Interpretation
3	Enclosure/ring ditch	Either a small enclosure or substantial ring ditch, underlying later archaeology monuments.
4	Enclosure	Although only part of the monument is visible, seems to be a conjoined 'segmented' Iron Age enclosure similar to Group 23 enclosure.
6	Ring ditch/roundhouse	Small internal diameter (*c.* 4.6 m), with a central anomaly. It is most likely a funerary monument, however, it is difficult to distinguish between roundhouses and ring ditches from gradiometer data in isolation.
11	Enclosure/ring ditch	Either a large enclosure or ring ditch, possible entrance to the west. Classified as ME030-038001 – Ring ditch.
12	Land divisions – field system	These land divisions have been constructed on a NNE–SSW axis, which differs to the predominant orientation associated with the avenue (Group 21) and associated land divisions (Group 9) at the Hill of Ward. This and Group 13 are classified as ME030-038002 – Field System.
13	Land divisions – field system	These land divisions have been constructed on a NE–SW axis, which is different to the predominant orientation associated with the avenue (Group 21) and associated land divisions (Group 9) at the Hill of Ward. This and Group 12 are classified as ME030-038002 – Field System.
14	Ring ditch/roundhouse	Small internal diameter, with a central anomaly. It is most likely a funerary monument; however, it is difficult to distinguish between roundhouses and ring ditches from gradiometer data in isolation. Opening to the northwest.
15	Enclosure	Annex of Group 11 or possibly another small enclosure.
16	Enclosure/ring ditch	Either a large enclosure or ring ditch.
17	Enclosure/ring ditch	Either a small enclosure or ring ditch, underlying later archaeological monuments.
18	Tlachtga earlier enclosure	Enclosure defined by three relatively closely spaced ditches. Analogous examples at Hill of Lloyd and Faughan Hill; likely to be Bronze Age.
22	Earlier enclosure partially underlying Tlachtga avenue	Although only part of the monument is visible, seems to be a conjoined 'segmented' enclosure, most likely dating to the Iron Age.
23	Enclosure	Probable Iron Age conjoined (segmented enclosure).
29	Possible ring ditch	Possible ring ditch, however, confidence in this interpretation is only possible.

To the north of Tlachtga a number of interpreted monuments have been identified and grouped (Fig. 2.5; Table 2.1). Group 12 is a set of land divisions on an NNE–SSW axis, which is different to the predominant axis of the interpreted later land divisions of the Phase 2 (Early Medieval) sitescape. The Group 12 field system is localised to the north of the survey area and limited in its extent, although it is unclear whether this is due to fragmentary preservation or that it was a spatially localised system. The Group 12 land divisions contain one remaining fully enclosed field, which measures *c.* 40 m × 47 m, at the centre of the arrangement.

At their eastern end the Group 12 land divisions appear to have a direct relationship with those of Group 13. The Group 13 land divisions initially begin on a northwest–southeast axis, although this becomes more southerly towards its eastern extent. Again, the Group 13 land divisions are limited in extent probably as a result of fragmentary preservation, with

some possible further fragments further to the south (Fig. 2.6). The Group 12 land divisions seemingly respect the Group 11 enclosure/ring ditch, only visible to the north and south of this feature. There also appears to be a direct relationship with the Group 23 enclosure, with the enclosure possibly built over the top of this pre-existing land division, although the relationship is not possible to definitively interpret from the gradiometer data.

There has been relatively little work dating prehistoric field systems in Ireland beyond the well-known Neolithic Céide Fields, Co. Mayo (Caulfield *et al.* 1997; Verrill and Tipping 2010; see also Whitefield 2017). Land divisions on the Antrim plateau have been dated to the late Bronze Age (Gardiner *et al.* 2019). Similarly, research in the Burren, Co. Clare, has revealed some evidence for Bronze Age field systems in the form of 'mound walls'. For example, excavations at Roughan Hill demonstrated that most of the mound walls at

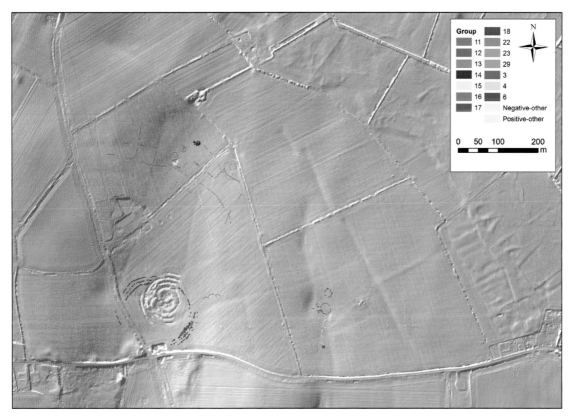

Fig. 2.4. Prehistoric features – archaeological groupings.

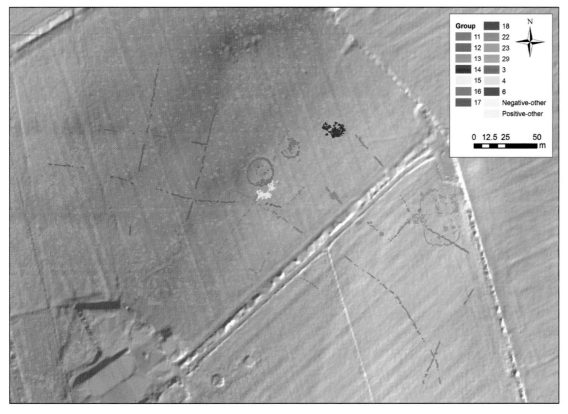

Fig. 2.5. Prehistoric features to the north of the Hill of Ward.

this site date to the Beaker period and early Bronze Age (Jones *et al.* 2011, 35). Similarities between the Roughan Hill examples and enclosure walls at Coolnatullagh suggest that they may be contemporary, while an example on the nearby Carran Plateau has been dated to the late Bronze Age (*ibid.*, 36). Roughan Hill is particularly important as it includes a range of habitation and burial monuments, including a dense concentration of wedge tombs, cairns and other unclassified megaliths (Jones *et al.* 2015, 15–20). The land divisions at the Hill of Ward have a coaxial form, albeit to a limited spatial extent, and are reminiscent of the middle Bronze Age (*c.* 1600–1000 BC) domestic landscapes in Britain (Brück 2019, 163–223).

Set within the Group 13 land divisions is the Group 11 enclosure/ring ditch. The Group 11 enclosure/ring ditch is ovoid, with an internal diameter of *c.* 20 m. There are two possible entrances/gaps identified, one to the southeast and one to the west; in both cases the circuit of the enclosure/ring ditch appears to be incomplete. The interior has some significant anomalies that might relate to pits, occupation activity or possible buildings/structures or burials. Of the two possible entrances to the Group 11 enclosure/ring ditch, the southeast one might enter into a further enclosure or structure, Group 15. The Group 15 enclosure is much smaller than the adjacent Group 11 enclosure, being only 11 m on its longest axis. It is possible that the Group 15 enclosure is an annex or further extension of the Group 11 enclosure/ring ditch.

Group 16 also represents a further enclosure/ring ditch, which is potentially cut by a land division from the Group 13 field system. This enclosure/ring ditch is relatively small and circular with an external diameter of *c.* 15 m and an internal diameter of *c.* 13 m, except for its western side where it meets the land division and is possibly truncated. The interior of Group 16 again has internal magnetic anomalies that potentially represent pits or burials.

To the northwest of the Group 16 enclosure/ring ditch is Group 14, which is interpreted as a probable ring ditch/roundhouse. This monument has an internal diameter of *c.* 6 m, with a definable ditch that is possibly incomplete/has an entrance to the north. The interior of the monument contains a central positive anomaly, with an associated negative anomaly that may represent a cremation burial or a possible hearth.

The two ring ditches excavated at Kilbrew, County Meath (Hawkes 2021) provide a good analogy for Groups 16 and 14 at the Hill of Ward. At Kilbrew, the two ring ditches with external diameters of 13 m (western) and 9.4 m (eastern) provide size ranges very similar to the Groups 16 and 14. Both of the Kilbrew ring ditches have possible entrances visible in the gradiometer data to the north of the ring ditches, very similar to Group 14. The eastern of the Kilbrew ring ditches had a central positive

anomaly in the geophysical data and this related to a cremation associated with a Collared Urn dated to 1732–1530 cal BC (UBA-40789). As such, the geophysical form of the Groups 16 and 14 are most likely to be ring ditches associated with cremation burial.

Group 23 is a further enclosure to the east and is again defined by ditches. It measures *c.* 42 m on its longest axis and *c.* 30 m wide, with straight sides and curved ends to the north and south. The enclosure either cuts or is cut by a land division from Group 13, although it is not possible to directly define the relationship from the gradiometer data. The form of this enclosure is similar to that of enclosure Group 4 and likely represents a divided or conjoined enclosure. Such enclosures come in a variety of morphologies which may be an indication as to their function, and potentially their origins (Curran 2019a, 18–19). Some are composed of two distinct circular enclosures, each with its own complete bank (*e.g.* Aghamore, Co. Leitrim SMR: LE035-002; LE035-003), others consist of two adjoining enclosures with a shared bank (*e.g.* Tech Cormaic and An Forrad at the Hill of Tara, Co. Meath), while a third possible variation comprises a sub-circular enclosure with an adjoining annexe which is more sub-rectangular than sub-circular in shape (*e.g.* Lusk, Co. Dublin; Giacometti 2011, 160).

Many of these enclosures have been identified as early medieval ringforts with an associated annexe; however, conjoined monuments also feature at 'Royal Sites', thought to have been reserved for special purposes such as kingship and inauguration. In these cases, the monuments are often interpreted to date to the late Iron Age and early medieval periods (*e.g.* Hogan 1932, 196; Bhreathnach 1995, 112; Newman 1997, 135; Byrne 2004, 27; Schot 2006). The field division that divides the enclosure makes it difficult to determine its original morphology, particularly the central section, which effectively holds the key to identifying it with any certainty. It is possible that it corresponds to a domestic enclosure with associated annexe, which could potentially point to an early medieval date. However, given that some similar sites are associated with an Iron Age date, this enclosure is tentatively placed within the prehistoric phasing of the site.

The central area of Tlachtga revealed one of the more startling outcomes from the gradiometer survey (Fig. 2.6; Table 2.1). Here, a sequence of three earlier ditches were clearly definable radiating out from the later upstanding earthworks of the monument, defined as Group 18. These ditches belong to an earlier monument that was subsequently overbuilt/remodelled. The Group 18 ditches have no topographic expression and only survive in a fragmentary form. The southern end of the Group 18 enclosure ditches is obscured by the water treatment works. To the north, the ditches are mostly overbuilt by the later monument of Tlachtga.

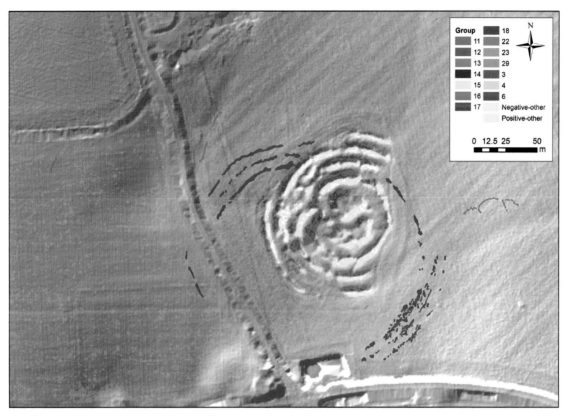

Fig. 2.6. Hill of Ward central area, prehistoric features (interpreted geomagnetic survey).

The Group 18 earlier phase of enclosure has three concentric ditches, with the distance across the ditches from the outside to the interior of the monument being *c*. 20 m. The enclosure has an internal diameter of *c*. 150 m across the innermost ditches and *c*. 190 m across the outer ditches. Whilst early multivallate enclosures are well-represented in the Irish archaeological record (*e.g.* Type 2 hillforts, Raftery 1972) the vallations are generally widely spaced. Sites with closely spaced multivallation include the Rath of the Synods on the Hill of Tara, which produced dates between the 2nd and 4th centuries AD including the addition of a fourth bank and ditch between the inner ditch and middle bank (Grogan 2008, 97; Bayliss and Grogan 2013). However, while these sites do have closely spaced multiple vallation they lack the large open central area of the Hill of Ward enclosure and are closer to the multivallate ringfort tradition than to hillforts. Recent surveys at the Hill of Lloyd and at Faughan Hill (Dowling 2015) have revealed similar large, closely spaced multivallate enclosures, with recently published dates from Faughan Hill closely matching the construction dates from the Hill of Ward (Dowling and Schot 2023; see below).

Within the main field is a further monument that is seemingly overlain by the later avenue (see below Phase 2 Early Medieval), to the east of Tlachtga. This enclosure is Group 22 and it possibly contains internal sub-divisions or is a conjoined enclosure similar to Enclosure Groups 23

and 4. This monument is defined by ditches and appears to have a 'segmented' plan and measures *c*. 40 m east to west. It is unclear whether further evidence for this enclosure still exists underneath the later avenue.

To the east of the survey area are a further set of monuments that have also been interpreted as prehistoric; these are partially overlain by substantive later archaeological monuments (Fig. 2.7; Table 2.1). Group 6 is interpreted as a ring ditch/house, defined by a ditch, with an internal diameter of *c*. 3.7 m. The interior of this monument has a clearly definable central positive anomaly, associated with negative halo anomalies, and it could represent a central burial or a hearth. This likely dates to the early–middle Bronze Age. The interpreted Group 6 ring ditch/house is immediately south of another enclosure, Group 4. This enclosure has straight sides and curved ends to the northeast/southwest and is *c*. 60 m across on its long axis and *c*. 30 m wide. The Group 4 enclosure potentially has an internal sub-division at its northern end. The monument of Group 4 is bisected by a land division of Group 9, which has been interpreted as early medieval. Therefore, the Group 4 enclosure is tentatively assigned a prehistoric date; however, it is possible that Group 4 represents a rath at the (northern section) with a field annex and as such fits more comfortably with an early medieval date. The morphology has strong parallels with the excavated site of Dowdstown 2, Co. Meath situated *c*. 20 km to the

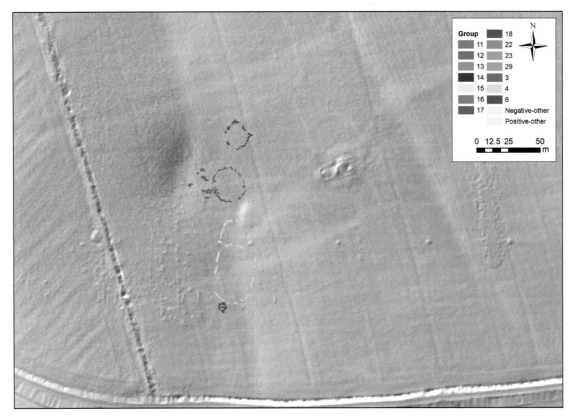

Fig. 2.7. Hill of Ward eastern area, prehistoric features (interpreted geomagnetic plot).

east, which was a multi-phase early medieval enclosure with multiple additions and re-configurations between the 6th and 9th centuries AD (*e.g.* Cagney and O'Hara 2009, 125; O'Sullivan *et al.* 2014, 190).

Immediately to the north of the Group 4 enclosure/ring ditch, are two further circular enclosures/ring ditches, Groups 3 and 17. The Group 3 enclosure/ring ditch is defined by ditches and has an internal diameter of *c.* 25 m, with a possible entrance to the southeast. The enclosure/ring ditch Group 17 to the north is partially obscured by later archaeological features and has an internal diameter of *c.* 15 m.

Lastly, further to the north is Group 29, which is interpreted as a possible ring ditch; however, the confidence of interpretation of this archaeological group is much lower than the preceding archaeological monuments, and is only defined as possible archaeology. The plough lines in this area seemingly deviate around a small upstanding topographic area, with a possible barrow/ring ditch on top, associated with some potential pit type features. For Group 29, the definition of the barrow ditch is slight, with an internal diameter of *c.* 11 m.

2.2.4.2. Phase 2 Early Medieval and Phase 2.1 Early Medieval

The interpretation of the early medieval phases of the Hill of Ward revealed the development of the main monument of Tlachtga, set within a sitescape of extensive land

divisions and enclosures (Fig. 2.8; Table 2.2). Tlachtga was extremely challenging to digitise and interpret, and is summarised as Group 19 (Fig. 2.8). Across the wider survey area, cut features revealed a reliable positive magnetic polarity when they had been plough-levelled/infilled, often with a negative 'halo' to the feature, allowing confidence in their interpretation as ditch-cut features.

However, across Group 19, the east side of the monument had been largely destroyed with a large amount of metallic interference present. Therefore, only cut features are present on the east side of the monument and again these were reliably interpretable as positive magnetic anomalies, often with large negative magnetic 'halos'. On this east side of the monument, four ditches can be identified. Contrastingly, the west side of the monument is clearly visible as an upstanding earthwork with up to four banks and ditches visible in parts of the circuit. Over the upstanding part of the monument, including the central area and the extant banks and ditches, the magnetic polarity of anomalies often do not directly relate to ditches (positive) and banks (negative). In fact, it is clearly visible that both positive and negative anomalies occur across both the extant banks and ditches (Fig. 2.9). Within the central part of the Hill of Ward complex, there were also some very high magnetic responses, some of which are caused by modern metal interference, but others of which are due to heating/use of fire, which again altered the form of the magnetic anomalies of the banks and ditches over the extant earthworks.

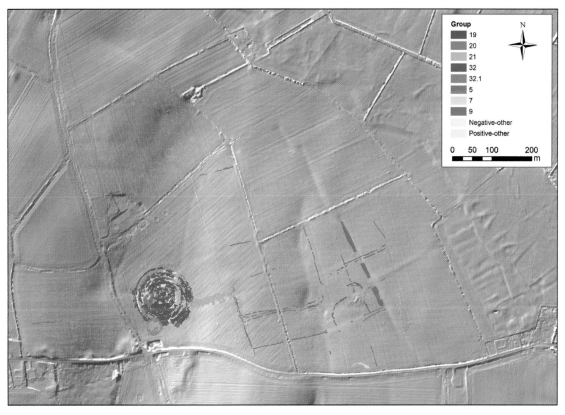

Fig. 2.8. Hill of Ward probable early medieval features (interpreted geomagnetic data).

Table 2.2. Summary of interpreted early medieval monuments presented in the order discussed in the text.

Group no.	Monument type	Interpretation
5	Enclosure, possibly D-shaped	Large enclosure to the east, possibly directly constructed on a Group 9 land division. The large size of the enclosure and its rounded ditches to the north indicate an early medieval date.
7	Enclosure lying partially under road	Probable ringfort/rath.
9	Land divisions	Land divisions on an ENE–WSW orientation, seemingly connected the end of the avenue and on the same alignment as the avenue. These are classified as ME030-040 – Field System.
19	Main Tlachtga enclosure	Extant multiple banks and ditches on the west side of the monument. Destroyed to the east, with ditches still visible. All of these features of banks and ditches overly the earlier prehistoric phase of the monument.
20	Southern enclosure at Tlachtga	A subsequent remodelling of the outer bank and ditch to accommodate a southern enclosure was interpreted from the gradiometer data, although it was interpreted as likely to form part of the main phase of early medieval monument construction.
21	Avenue extending out from the east side of the Tlachtga	Part of the construction of the main phase of the Hill of Ward quadrivallate enclosure.
32	Southern part of the central area of Tlachtga	This area is magnetically very noisy, and could well be associated with craft/production activities in the monument, such as metal production.
32.1	Probable rectangular building	Probable building in the southern part of the central area of Tlachtga.

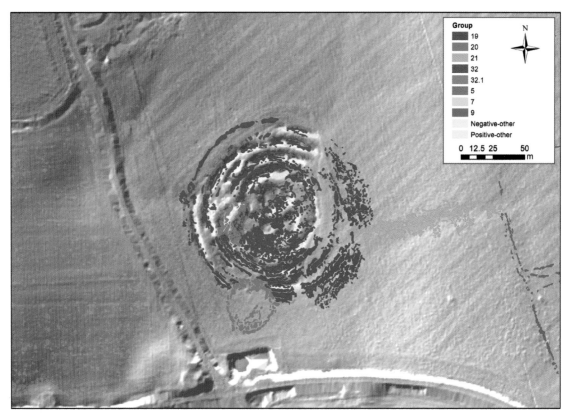

Fig. 2.9. Hill of Ward central area early medieval features (interpreted geomagnetic data).

Group 19 clearly delineates the large multivallate circular enclosure of Tlachtga. The western side of the monument was difficult to interpret from the gradiometer data, although the concentric enclosure elements are clearly visible. It is quite probable that heated materials, such as Ceramic Burnt Material (CBM), possibly slag, and hearth/furnace fills/lining have been dumped in the ditches and onto the banks, which has caused the strong magnetic signatures of both. The distance from the outer ditch, across the banks and ditches to the interior of the monument is *c*. 40 m, with an internal central area of the monument with a diameter of *c*. 65 m.

There were two areas of the monument where it is interpreted the continuous nature of the banks and ditches were interrupted, these being the southern interior and southern edge of the monument. These two areas were tentatively interpreted from the geophysical survey data as a later phase of remodelling (Phase 2.1 below). The excavated evidence at Trenches 3 and 5 provides significant further detail on this area.

Extending out from the Group 19 Tlachtga monument is the eastern avenue, defined as Group 21, which creates a formalised entrance into the monument, orientated ENE–WSW. The anomalies forming the Group 21 avenue are again noisy and prominently defined by a series of positive and negative linear anomalies, probably indicating a raised causeway, with the lidar data showing a small ridge that the avenue overlies. Both the eastern and western ends

of the Group 21 avenue have anomalies that potentially indicate buildings or more elaborate structures, which are most noticeable on the eastern side of the avenue. The avenue is *c*. 100 m long and its eastern end is downslope of the Hill of Ward, rising dramatically as it enters the main monument of Tlachtga.

The ENE-WSW axis of the Group 21 avenue is repeated across a further set of land divisions, defined as Group 9. These land divisions have been tentatively interpreted as early medieval, owing to their shared alignment with the avenue (Fig. 2.10). The Group 9 land divisions are on a different orientation to the interpreted earlier prehistoric land divisions (Groups 12 and 13), and are also more extensively represented in the data than the earlier land divisions. Some areas of these land divisions have stretches of ditch that are magnetically noisy, especially when they are close to later monuments. This has generally been interpreted as the later dumping of waste/rubbish into the ditches associated with later use of this sitescape.

The Group 9 land divisions occur to the east of the Hill of Ward, and it is noticeable that they are seemingly absent to the north where there is a concentration of earlier prehistoric activity. Therefore, it is possible that some of these prehistoric monuments were still visible when the Group 9 divisions were constructed, and this area was avoided. The Group 9 divisions seemingly intersect with the Group 21 avenue and then follow this alignment to a possible further enclosure Group 5. The Group 5 enclosure

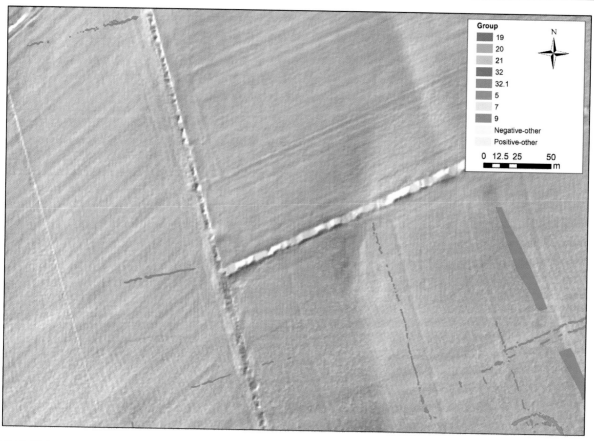

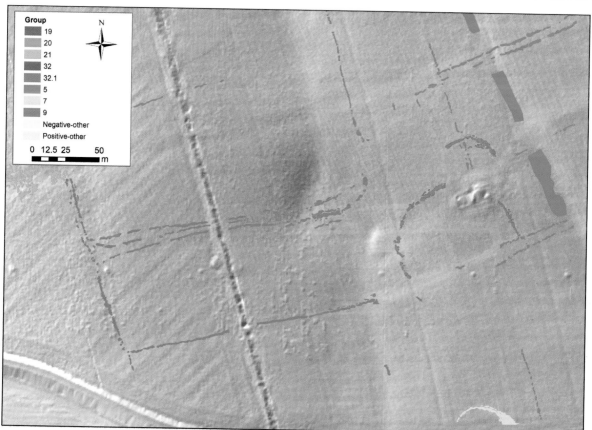

Fig. 2.10. Land divisions/field boundaries to the east of the main monument of Tlachtga (interpreted geomagnetic data).

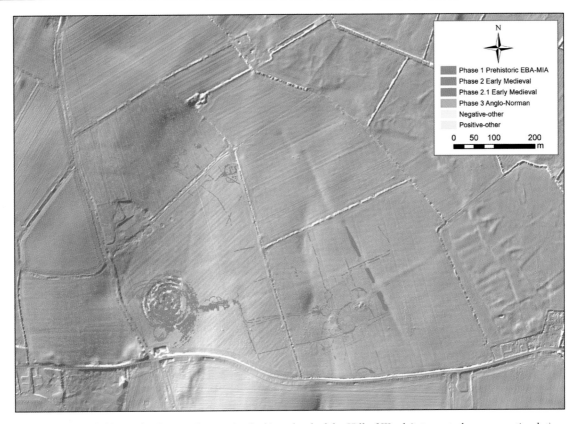

Fig. 2.11. Probable Anglo-Norman features in the hinterland of the Hill of Ward (interpreted geomagnetic plot).

is partially visible under a concentration of denser later archaeological remains (Phase 3, see below).

The Group 5 enclosure is *c.* 85 m wide between the two outer ditches, and with the length currently undefined. It has rounded corners on its north side, and its southern extent is possibly defined by the field division, forming a D-shaped enclosure, or it is possibly truncated. The dating of the Group 5 enclosure is difficult, although double ditched enclosures have been dated to the early medieval period, such as Balriggan, Co. Louth (Delaney and Roycroft 2003), and Raystown, Co. Meath (Seaver 2016; Nevin 2021). The outer ditch of the Group 5 enclosure might not fully enclose the site (for example it is not apparent on the western edge) and this is similar to the Balriggan enclosure.

Another enclosure is visible to the south of Group 5 and is defined as Group 7. Only a small portion of the monument falls within the area of the gradiometer survey and the enclosure is bisected by the road, making further interpretation difficult. It is estimated the Group 7 enclosure is *c.* 40 m in diameter, with the ditch having a relatively high magnetic response, indicating potential evidence of occupation/pyrotechnological waste in the ditch fill. The enclosure Group 7 has been interpreted as most likely early medieval in date.

It is also likely that a series of features are visible at Tlachtga that relate to the early medieval period but are created after the initial construction phase of the main Tlachtga monument (Fig. 2.9; Table 2.2). These are the Southern Enclosure, Group 20, and the southern part of the central main enclosure, Group 32. Both of these anomaly groups suggest that the main enclosure was remodelled to accommodate later development and activity at the site. The Southern Enclosure Group 20 appears to bisect the outer bank and ditch of the original monument and was subsequently considered to be later than the main Tlachtga monument phase (Phase 2) based solely on the gradiometer data. The Group 20 'plectrum shaped enclosure' (Kinsella 2010) is *c.* 34 m across on its longer axis. The interior of the main Tlachtga monument demonstrated high magnetic responses in the southern part of the enclosure, with the circuit of the bank and ditches appearing to 'dog leg' (kink) slightly to the south. Again, this change in form of the continuous circuit of the banks and ditches was interpreted as a later remodelling and defined as Group 32. The western extent of Group 32 has a somewhat rectangular appearance, potentially indicating the presence of a large building/structure, defined as Group 32.1.

2.2.4.3. Phase 3 Anglo-Norman

The field to the east of the Hill of Ward contains a further series of monuments that have a distinct rectilinear form, and are interpreted as belonging to the Anglo-Norman period. Group 8.1 defines a large multi-ditched rectilinear enclosure seemingly at the centre of this group of

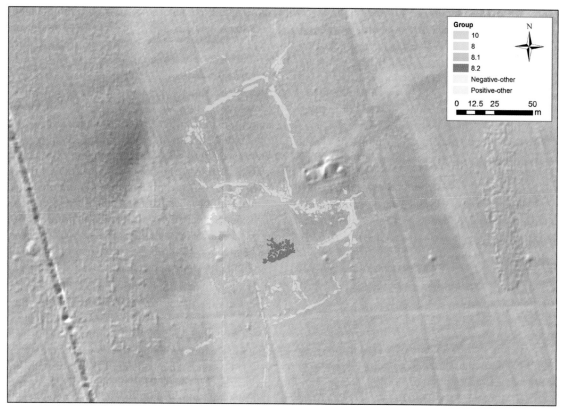

Fig. 2.12. Probable Anglo-Norman moated site, east of the Hill of Ward (interpreted geomagnetic plot).

monuments (a moated site) that is interpreted as the focus of the wider Anglo-Norman phase of the site (Fig. 2.11 and 2.12; Table 2.3). The ditches, especially to the south of the enclosure are very magnetic and indicate some form of intense occupation/heating within the enclosure. The enclosure has straight sides and tightly rounded corners, being *c.* 57 m long and *c.* 32 m wide, between the inside of the internal ditches. In the southern end of enclosure Group 8.1 is a tightly constrained group of higher magnetic anomalies that indicate some form of heating possibly within a larger structure/building, defined as Group 8.2.

Around enclosure Group 8.1 is the wider Anglo-Norman site, defined as the Group 8 enclosure. This Group 8 enclosure expands away from the main ditched enclosure to the north, south and east, producing a series of further annexes or compartments to the wider Anglo-Norman site. It is interesting that the enclosure Group 8 orientation is the same as the preceding Group 9 early medieval field system/land divisions and in places, the Anglo-Norman enclosure Group 8 incorporates some of these earlier elements of land division.

Group 10 is tentatively dated to the Anglo-Norman period and potentially comprises a dump of material associated with ferrous/heating materials. Both the northern and southern ditches of the Anglo-Norman enclosure Group 8.1 are very magnetic and this potentially relates to activities occurring within Group 10. However, the

Table 2.3. Summary of interpreted Anglo-Norman monuments presented in the order discussed in the text.

Group number	Monument type	Interpretation
8	Wider Anglo-Norman enclosure	Multiple annexes of the Anglo-Norman enclosure, on the same orientation as Enclosure Group 8.1 and early medieval field system Group 9.
8.1	Double ditched rectangular enclosure with rounded corners	This is a probable moated site, dated to the Anglo-Norman period (O'Sullivan and Downey 2006). The orientation of this enclosure follows the preceding Group 9 early medieval land divisions.
8.2	Probable building	A probable building in the southern end of the double ditched enclosure Group 8.1.
10	Spread/dump of very magnetic material	Spread/dump of very magnetic material, possibly relating to some form of pyrotechnology/ metal production, adjacent to the Group 8.1 enclosure.

magnetic signal of Group 10 is very mixed and non-definitive, with later disturbance potentially being the cause of this anomaly group.

2.2.4.4. Phase 4 Later Medieval to Post-Medieval

Following the Anglo-Norman phase, a series of monuments and features across the sitescape can be identified as late medieval to post-medieval (Fig. 2.13; Table 2.4). The main concentration of this activity is a Deserted Medieval Village (DMV) that is located to the east of the Anglo-Norman enclosure Group 8 (Fig. 2.14; Table 2.4) that was only partially surveyed (ME030-034 – Settlement Cluster). Within this area, a series of buildings (probable houses) and land plots can be identified, which are identified as Group 37, with the decimal number defining individual buildings and land plots.

- Group 37.1 is a building and land plot in the northwest of the DMV. The house is *c.* 16 m long × *c.* 7 m wide, with possible walls and a floor/interior definable. The building is adjacent to an interpreted land plot, which is *c.* 16 m × 16 m.
- Group 37.2 is a further building and land plot directly to the southeast of Group 37.1. The interpreted building is *c.* 15 m × 5 m, with the land plot *c.* 35 m across, although this may contain a further land plot sub-division.
- Group 37.3 is a further land plot, although the building is not clearly defined. The land plot is *c.* 51 m by 17 m. A building is potentially present in the northwest corner, although there are several areas of magnetic enhancement along the main ditch running southeast–northwest that are also potential buildings.

- Group 37.4 is a further land plot, with a building in the southwest corner, measuring *c.* 16 m × 7 m. The attached land plot is *c.* 40 m × 16 m. It is possible that there is another building along the main ditch, running southeast–northwest, where there is a further area of magnetic enhancement.
- Group 37.5 is the final land plot in the sequence and is only partially defined by the extent of the gradiometer survey. The building is in the southwest corner with the land plot measuring *c.* 20 m across.
- Group 37.6 is interpreted as a further building, but it does not have a definable land plot attached to it. However, the interior of the house is reasonably clear, and the building is *c.* 15 m × 6 m.
- Group 37.7 is a further building immediately to the northwest of Group 37.6 and is also without a definable land plot. The building measures *c.* 15 m × 5 m.
- Group 37.8 is in the east of the surveyed area and is interpreted as another building without a definable land plot. The building measures *c.* 15 m × 8 m. The magnetic form of this building is quite mixed, and the building shape is less well defined than the previous Groups.
- Group 37.9 is a concentration of magnetic anomalies in the south of the survey area and is interpreted as a building, although the form of the building is difficult to discern. The building dimensions are *c.* 15 m × 8 m. The lidar data indicates this is associated with a land plot and this is partially defined in the gradiometer data.

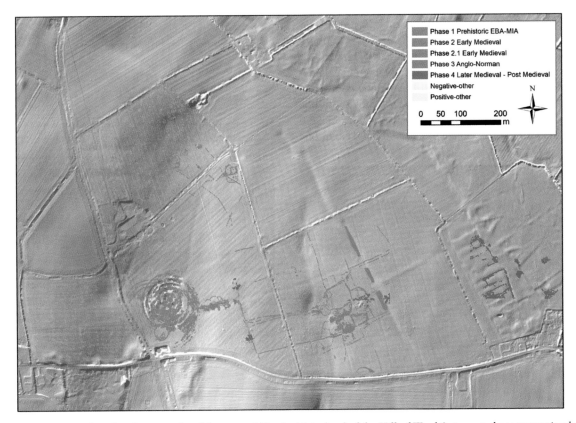

Fig. 2.13. Later medieval and post-medieval features within the hinterland of the Hill of Ward (interpreted geomagnetic plot).

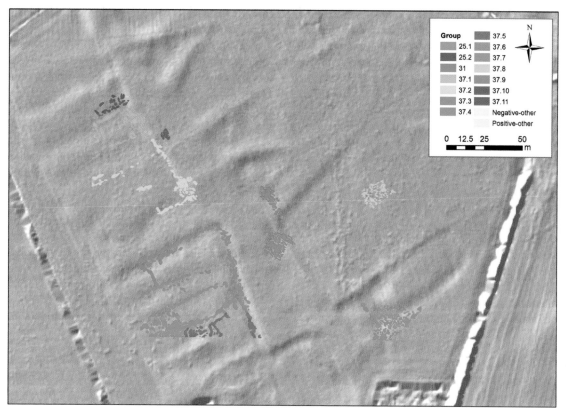

Fig. 2.14. Wardstown Settlement Cluster (ME030-034) (interpreted geomagnetic plot).

Table 2.4. Summary of interpreted late medieval–post-medieval monuments presented in the order discussed in the text.

Group number	Monument type	Interpretation
25.1	Cluster of small pits or shallow scoops	This group of anomalies is tentatively interpreted as relating to limestone quarrying, presumably dating to the post-medieval period
25.2	Evidence of *in-situ* heating, associated with some high magnetic anomalies	This group of anomalies is tentatively associated with the processing of limestone and is again placed into the post-medieval period.
37.1	DMV House and land plot	Clearly definable DMV house with land plot.
37.10	DMV Possible building	A seemingly isolated building without associated land plot.
37.11	DMV Possible building	A seemingly isolated building without associated land plot.
37.2	DMV House and land plot	Clearly definable DMV house with associated land plot.
37.3	DMV House and land plot	Clearly definable DMV house with associated land plot.
37.4	DMV House and land plot	Clearly definable DMV house with associated land plot.
37.5	DMV House and land plot	Clearly definable DMV house with associated land plot.
37.6	DMV Building	A seemingly isolated building without associated land plot.
37.7	DMV Building	A seemingly isolated building without associated land plot.
37.8	DMV Building	A seemingly isolated building without associated land plot.
37.9	DMV Building	Clearly definable DMV house with an associated land plot (interpreted primarily from the lidar data).

- Group 37.10 is interpreted as a possible building, again without a definable associated land plot. However, the definition of this group as a building is tentative and the magnetic form of the building is limited, measuring *c.* 6 m × 3m.
- Group 37.11 is interpreted as a possible building, on the northern edge of the survey area. The interpretation

of this group of anomalies is again tentative, with the building measuring *c.* 16 m × 5 m.

Group 31 is located in the same field as the Anglo-Norman enclosure Group 8, with Group 31 focused around the extant remains of a building that is visible in the lidar data. Group 31 generally demonstrates high magnetic responses and given its location next to the remains of an extant building, it has been tentatively assigned to the post-medieval period. Further to the east, between Tlachtga and the Anglo-Norman enclosures, are two more anomaly groups that are tentatively interpreted as being linked. The first of these is Group 25.1, which comprises a series of relatively weak positive anomalies. Given their size and distribution, they are interpreted as possible small-scale limestone quarrying. It is possible that Group 25.2 is linked to this process, with heating of the limestone to produce 'quicklime'. Group 25.2 indicates *in-situ* heating, with the adjacent ditch fill of the Group 9 land division displaying an enhanced magnetic fill, indicating the dumping of burnt materials. The interpretation of both the quarrying and lime production, and their date as post-medieval, is of course interpreted, and these warrant further investigation.

2.2.4.5. Unphased archaeological anomalies

In addition to the geophysical anomalies presented within the Phases and Groups of monuments, a further series of anomalies were considered to be of definite or probable archaeological potential. These anomalies are spatially scattered across the sitescape and generally comprise land divisions and ditches of undefinable date.

2.3. Tlachtga in space and time

Whilst the gradiometer survey at the Hill of Ward has only mapped a small part of this remarkable archaeological landscape, from the data produced it is possible to place Tlachtga into a spatial and chronological context. The geophysical survey reveals an area that contains both funerary and domestic architectures that are likely associated with the early–middle Bronze Age (ring ditches, possible houses, and land divisions), and segmented enclosures that are of possible Iron Age origin. It is clear that from the Bronze Age the Hill of Ward was a known locale, with a signature of activity from at least the early Bronze Age, and it is probable that a funerary landscape was one that over time, become more associated with the land divisions of a domestic landscape. It is within this landscape that an earlier phase of the Tlachtga monument was constructed, as a concentric triple-ditched enclosure. This is unusual in form for a Class 2 hillfort in Ireland (it is currently classified as a 'ceremonial enclosure') but it has been categorised as such by O'Brien and O'Driscoll (2017, Fig. 1.2). This enclosure was likely a central place to the prehistoric community, within a relatively dense collection of later prehistoric monuments. Whether the Group 18 ditches are the earliest phase of activity on the Hill of Ward monument is unknown, and it is possible that there are older elements at the centre of the monument, buried beneath later activity, or perhaps obliterated by it.

It is also probable that a number of the enclosures within this landscape are constructed and used during the late Iron Age, especially the conjoined enclosures Groups 4, 22 and 23. At this time the trivallate monument (Group 18) is overbuilt by a quadrivallate enclosure (Group 19). Subsequent excavations have shown a considerable time differential between the infilling of the trivallate enclosure and the construction of the quadrivallate (see below). It is in the early medieval period that the landscape is also seemingly reorganised, with new land divisions (Group 9) extending eastwards from Tlachtga on the same orientation as an avenue (Group 21). The avenue formalises the entrance into the monument hinting at a substantial entrance on the eastern side.

Further probable early medieval settlement has been identified in the form of a curvilinear ditched enclosure (Group 7). Further investigations in the field to the south would be required to determine the nature of this feature with more certainty. However, its proximity to other potentially early medieval features, such as the Group 5 enclosure that is *c.* 90 m to the north, may be significant and indicate expansion of early medieval settlement and activity located within and around the Group 9 land.

Tlachtga itself is magnetically noisy and defines a monument of considerable activity, almost certainly including extensive use of fire, probably associated with some form of metal production and/or other pyrotechnologies. Such magnetic data is suggestive of a central place, where activities for relatively localised production such as iron smithing, potentially precious metalworking, cooking and feasting took place. It appears that the southern part of the main monument has a subsequent phase of remodelling to form the southern plectrum-shaped enclosure (Group 20), although the evidence for this is discussed in the subsequent chapters. The Group 9 land divisions of the early medieval period potentially link to another enclosure further east (Group 5), indicating a denser pattern of early medieval settlement. However, this said, the Group 5 enclosure is only tentatively assigned to the early medieval period and is largely covered by later monuments.

Curiously, the focus of the landscape changes in the Anglo-Norman period and a series of interpreted Anglo-Norman enclosures (Groups 8 and 8.1) are visible to the east of the hill, with Group 8.1 interpreted as a moated site. A medieval 'horse fair' is recorded as occurring just to the east of Hill of Ward (Ettinger 1952), and the signatures of the enclosure Groups 8.0 and 8.1 are very magnetic, indicating a range of activities/fires/occupations and again some probable metalworking.

Despite the refocusing on the Anglo-Norman moated site to the east from the site of Tlachtga, there are elements of continuity. The orientation of the earlier Avenue (Group 21) and early medieval land divisions (Group 9) are incorporated into the Anglo-Norman enclosure. However, other earlier prehistoric enclosures in this eastern area are seemingly long forgotten and are built over by the Anglo-Norman enclosures.

In the later medieval to post-medieval period, a village (Groups 37.1–37.11) is evident in both the lidar and gradiometer data. This DMV likely developed outside the Anglo-Norman enclosure (Group 8), perhaps associated with renewed fortification of Tlachtga itself. Again, this DMV is magnetically noisy and indicates much activity within buildings and land plots of this settlement.

Overall, the spatial organisation of this landscape indicates some degree of continuity from the Bronze Age through to the post-medieval period. However, whilst this is a landscape with abundant evidence of human activity over millennia, this should not be confused with indicating the same activities occurred for millennia. Initially funerary and ritualistic landscapes of the early–middle Bronze Age seemingly gave way to domestic and communal monuments of the later Bronze Age/Iron Age. The Hill of Ward develops as an important central place, but over time this diminishes and the focus of this landscape seems to shift progressively eastwards. These changes in manner and intensity of use are likely not to have all been gradual, and include two very substantial phases of monumental construction, cut deep into the limestone bedrock through significant human effort.

2.4. Previous excavations

Despite local suggestions that R.A.S. Macalister may have dug at the site, no record for excavation at Tlachtga itself exists. Several attempts at planning the site have been published, most notably in Herity (1993), but it is large, complex and much damaged, hence difficult to plan accurately from the ground.

Prior to the 2014 season several excavations had taken place in the vicinity of the site, though none were either substantial or very close to Tlachtga itself. In 2007 test-excavations in advance of the construction of a farm building were undertaken at Wardstown to the north of the hill but yielded no material of archaeological significance (Duffy 2007). A more substantial programme of excavations in the adjacent townland of Rathcarran (Ráith Cairn) in advance of a water pipeline (Shine 2008a; 2008b) yielded a small amount of medieval pottery and lithics (see also Shine and Travers 2011). A hoard of high-quality late Bronze Age gold items from Drissoge, 2 km to the east of the Hill and comprising a sunflower pin and three penannular bracelets was published by Eogan (1957); these objects remain on display at the National Museum of Ireland. As such this project represented the first major archaeological works to take place at the Hill of Ward.

Excavations at Tlachtga: aims and objectives

Given the exceptional results from the geomagnetic survey it was clear that there were at least three overlapping phases of construction at the Hill of Ward. The initial objectives of the excavation project were:

1. To obtain good material for radiocarbon dating from each of these phases of activity and so understand the archaeological activity on the hilltop;
2. To characterise the monumental remains in terms of their material culture and ecofactual remains;
3. To understand the changing function of Tlachtga in its various forms through time, in particular with reference to other similar sites within its landscape.

The project undertook three seasons of excavation at the Hill of Ward under Ministerial Consent C568, licence E4474, with each season lasting for a month and largely reliant on student volunteers and more senior supervisory staff (Fig. 3.1).

In 2014 the project opened three trenches and three test pits:

- Trench 1 focused on the outer embankment of Tlachtga to the northeast of the site, aiming to obtain secure dating evidence and assess the composition of the outermost bank;
- Trench 2 focused on the innermost ditch of the earlier site, to the northeast of the monument;
- Trench 3 focused on the Southern Enclosure, specifically at a point away from overlap with Tlachtga;
- Test Pit 1 examined a small area of the interior of the Southern Enclosure;
- Test Pit 2 focused on an area within the central platform of Tlachtga, in the northern part of the central mound;
- Test Pit 3 was located north of Trench 1 and aimed to characterise the depth of soil slightly away from the hilltop.

In 2015 two further trenches were excavated

- Trench 4 extended across all three ditches of the trivallate enclosure to the southeast of the monument;
- Trench 5 explored the intersection of Tlachtga and the Southern Enclosure to the southeast of the site.

Finally, in 2016 three further trenches were opened:

- Trench 6 explored the northern section of the central mound, excavating this down to construction levels;
- Trench 7 focused on the innermost ditch of Tlachtga to the southeast where the bank has been levelled;
- Trench 8 examined the eastern complex, c. 30 m east of the outer ditch of the site of Tlachtga.

In all seasons all excavation was by hand, with no use of heavy machinery. In 2016 machinery was allowed for backfilling; however, in 2014 and 2015 all backfilling was also undertaken by hand owing to the perceived sensitive nature of the earthwork monument.

3.1. Excavations: the Hillfort Phase

3.1.1. Trench 2

In 2014 a small trench (10.00 × 3.00 m) was opened to the northwest of Tlachtga (Fig. 3.3). This was positioned to investigate the innermost ditch of the earlier trivallate enclosure of which there are no visible surface remains. It became clear that much of the hilltop preserved only a shallow layer of topsoil. At this location the limestone bedrock was exposed at a depth of only 0.15 m (Fig. 3.4). Within the topsoil were a number of pieces of animal bone, a flint flake (2014: SF036) and a small selection of post-medieval objects including fragments of glazed pottery and a corroded coin/token.

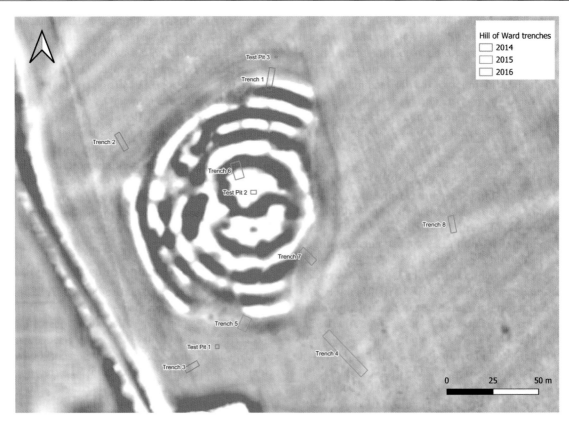

Fig. 3.1. Location of Trenches 1–8 on lidar local relief model.

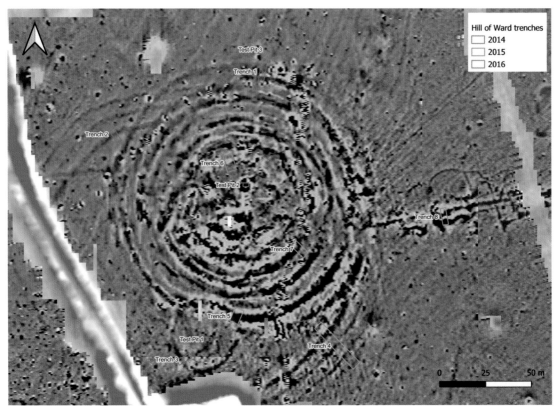

Fig. 3.2. Location of Trenches 1–8 on geomagnetic survey (ramp ±4 nT).

Fig. 3.3. Hill of Ward 2014, looking southeast over Trench 3, with Trench 1 to the left, Trench 3 to the right.

Fig. 3.4. Looking southeast over Trench 2 pre-excavation, with the ditch C076 clearly cut through the natural limestone bedrock.

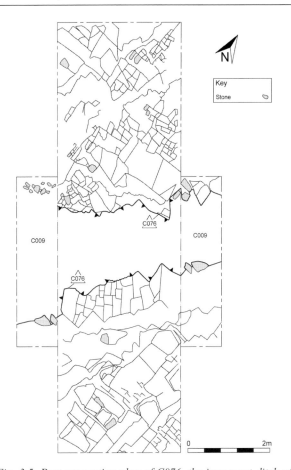

Fig. 3.5. Post-excavation plan of C076, the innermost ditch of the trivallate hillfort in Trench 2.

Excavation revealed a broad, flat-bottomed rock-cut ditch (C076), the sides of which were formed by jagged planes of broken limestone bedrock to the southwest, while the northeast edge was almost vertical (Fig. 3.5; Fig. 3.6). The ditch had a maximum width of 3.4 m at the surface, narrowing to 0.85 m at the base, and a maximum depth of 1.13 m. The base of the ditch comprised a flat, sloping bedrock plane, presumably formed by repeated breaking and lifting of limestone bedrock. Although the base included significant areas of flat bedrock, it was also clear that bedrock was not removed to the same depth or plane of fracture throughout the entire circuit. It is possible that where bedrock was not removed to significant depth that these areas served as causeways or points of access to the interior of the monument.

The sequence of fills appeared remarkably simple (Fig. 3.7). Above the bedrock was a thin deposit of reddish/yellow clay (C064), perhaps the result of bedrock erosion. A similar deposit was seen immediately above the bedrock elsewhere on the site. Above this was C046, a clayey silt with few stones, varying in depth from 0.06–0.55 m. This was overlain by C009, a silty clay containing

significant quantities of angular fractured bedrock, mostly in the sub-0.30 m range. This fill incorporated a significant quantity of highly fragmented animal bone and a small quantity of charcoal. This main fill seemingly represented a single deposit with no sign of gradual infilling. A piece of cattle bone from C009 was radiocarbon dated to 516–364 cal BC (2300±30 BP; Beta-386851). A bone awl (2014: SF058), one of a number of similar bone tools recovered from this phase of the site, was the only artefact found within this deposit.

This phase of the monument was returned to in 2015 with the opening of Trench 4 (Fig. 3.8; Fig. 3.9). Rather than focusing solely on the inner ditch of the large trivallate monument, this trench aimed to span all three ditches of this phase, measuring 30.00 × 5.00 m.

Removal of topsoil revealed a selection of largely post-medieval finds (*e.g.* a clay pipe bowl; a piece of agricultural iron debris) and pieces of unworked chert. Black chert forms part of the local limestone geology at Tlachtga and while occasional worked objects of this material were found, a significant quantity of unworked nodules was present. The topsoil at this location was slightly deeper than at Trench 2, with a maximum depth of 0.34 m.

Fig. 3.6. Trench 2 C076 post-excavation, looking northwest.

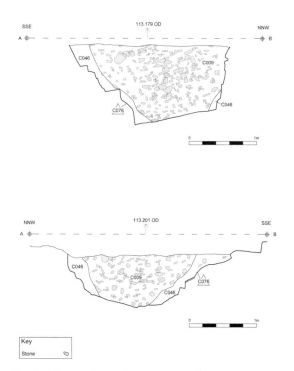

Fig. 3.7. East and west facing sections through ditch C076.

3.1.2. Trench 4 – southern extent

At the southern end of the Trench 4 adjacent to the limit of excavation was an oval pit (C481), its long axis orientated northwest–southeast (Fig. 3.10). The presence of this feature had been suggested by a discrete positive magnetic anomaly in the geophysical survey. C481 measured 1.30 × 0.87 m and was 0.25 m deep. It had vertical sides with a flat base, around both of which was a deposit of very compact orange clay (C472), which appeared to be thermally altered. Over this lay a thin (0.05 m) deposit of charcoal rich, dark brown silt with (C478). This deposit contained a concentration of charred cereal remains, predominantly hulled barley (see Stone and Gilligan, this volume). A barley grain from C478 was radiocarbon dated to 146 cal BC–cal AD 68 (2030±30 BP; Beta-436097). The uppermost fill of C481 comprised a largely sterile compact brown clay with some small stones. Although no flue was encountered, this feature was probably a truncated cereal drying kiln.

Only 2.00 m northwest of this pit was the outermost ditch of the trivallate enclosure (C404) (Fig. 3.11; Fig. 3.12). As seen at Trench 2 this was cut into the underlying limestone bedrock, which was again very close

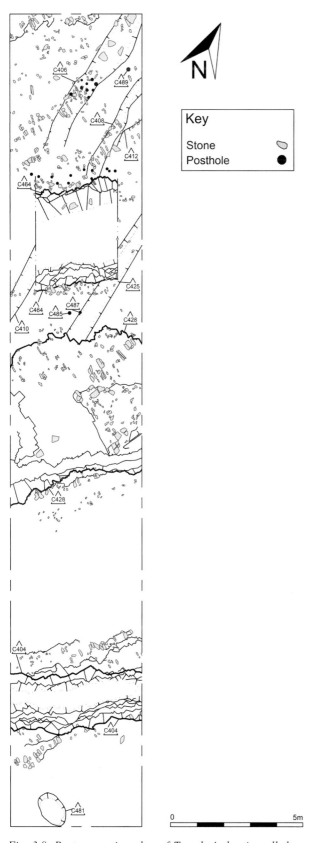

Key

Stone

Posthole

0   5m

Fig. 3.8. Post-excavation plan of Trench 4 showing all three ditches of the trivallate hillfort.

to the surface; however, it was significantly shallower, measuring only 0.90 m deep. Rather than the flat bottom seen at Trench 2, the outermost ditch had a V-shaped profile, measuring 2.40 m at the surface and narrowing to 0.60 m at the base, which once again comprised flat but slightly sloping bedrock. The primary fill of the ditch (C429) was 0.40 m deep and comprised pieces of shattered angular bedrock in a matrix of sandy clay. This was deeper on the southeastern side, suggesting that this was the direction from which the deposit had entered the ditch. C429 produced few finds, but these included a large bone blade (2015: SF058). A human mandible recovered from this deposit was subsequently radiocarbon dated to 912–807 cal BC (2710±30 BP; Beta-420642). An attempt to extract DNA from this was, unfortunately, unsuccessful (Cassidy, this volume).

Overlying C429 was a deposit of dark brown clayey silt with fewer angular stones (C414). This was deepest (0.25 m) at the northern extent, becoming shallower (0.10 m) at the southern end and produced very few finds, including a single piece of flint debitage (2015: SF047). The uppermost fill of this ditch was C403, a shallow (0.07 m) deposit of light brown silty clay containing occasional stones.

Located just south of C404, at the eastern edge of the trench and extending beyond the limit of excavation was C415, a metalled surface covering an area of at least 1.40 × 1.00 m, with a depth of 0.02–0.10 m (Fig. 3.13). Comprising an assortment of small cobbles and pebbles, mostly of limestone, similar metalled surfaces were encountered further north within the trench (C424 and C428), and was probably placed to stabilise areas of soft ground.

The southern end of Trench 4 was criss-crossed by six north–south orientated plough furrows (C416; C418; C420; C422; C430; C439), which measured an average of 0.20 m wide by 0.08 m deep.

3.1.3. Trench 4 – centre

Approximately central within Trench 4 was C428, the middle ditch of the trivallate enclosure. It was located 7.01 m north of the outer ditch and was a maximum of 1.13 m deep. This ditch was less regular than the outer ditch, and had an uneven V-shaped profile (Fig. 3.14; Fig. 3.15). While the southeastern edge was cut into the bedrock at *c.* 45 degrees, the opposite side comprised limestone bedrock gradually sloping at 15–20 degrees, this made its overall width difficult to judge but it was estimated to be 3.20 m at the top narrowing to *c.* 0.15 m at the base. The primary fill of the ditch (C427) was a dark brown silty clay with frequent inclusions of shattered bedrock, along with occasional flecks of charcoal and pieces of animal bone. This context varied from 0.10–0.70 m in depth, mirroring the variable nature of the ditch itself. A fragment of animal bone from the base of C427 has been radiocarbon dated to 1014–836 cal BC (2790±30

Fig. 3.9. Trench 4 under excavation (Photograph courtesy of Noel Meehan, Copterview).

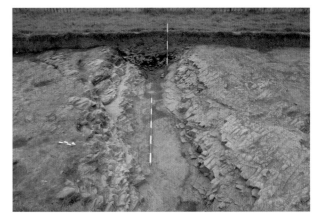

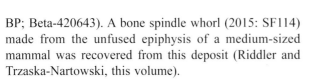

Fig. 3.10. Possible cereal drying kiln C481 mid-excavation showing fills C472 and C478.

Fig. 3.11. The shallow outermost ditch C404 post-excavation.

BP; Beta-420643). A bone spindle whorl (2015: SF114) made from the unfused epiphysis of a medium-sized mammal was recovered from this deposit (Riddler and Trzaska-Nartowski, this volume).

C428 was subject to two phases of re-cutting (Fig. 3.16), both of which followed its orientation and truncated C427.

The likely earliest of these recuts was C475, which occurred along the inner edge of C428. C475 was a linear cut (1.70–2.00 m wide and 0.10–0.50 m deep), with steep sides and a flat base, visible in both sections through C428. It was filled with C402, a deposit of yellow/brown silty clay with a maximum depth of 0.40 m containing both

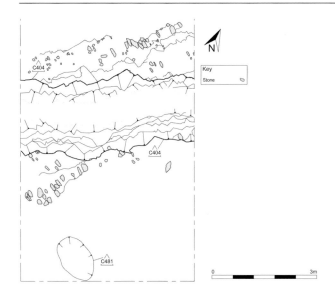

Fig. 3.12. Post-excavation plan of C404, the southernmost ditch of the trivallate hillfort.

Fig. 3.13. Trench 4, Metalled surface C415.

Fig. 3.14. Post-excavation plan of the Trench 4 middle ditch C428.

animal bone and charcoal. A cattle tooth from this deposit was radiocarbon dated to 992–828 cal BC (UBA-32856; 2764±30 BP), suggesting this recutting may have been undertaken to counteract the natural infilling of the ditch.

The second re-cut through C427 was C477, which was carried out on the opposing outer edge. C477 measured 0.25–0.80 m wide. It had concave sides and an irregular sloped base, with a maximum depth of 0.47 m. It was filled with C476, a deposit of compact silty clay with small stones, charcoal and some animal bone. Sealing all of the fills and recuts of the middle ditch was C461, a deposit of soft dark brown silt, again with flecks of charcoal and pieces of animal bone. Measuring 3.96 m wide and up to 0.20 m deep this was only evident in the northeast facing section of the ditch, presumably owing to the irregular profile of the ditch itself.

Located on the upper northeastern edge of the middle ditch was C438, another small area of metalling, similar to C415 south of the outer ditch, and comprising small pieces of angular limestone within a silty-clay matrix. This was truncated by a plough furrow (C425) but, along with C415, may represent the remnants of a much larger metalled area.

3.1.4. Trench 4 – northern extent

The inner ditch of the trivallate enclosure (C464), lay 4.03 m north of the middle ditch and was analogous with the ditch section excavated at Trench 2 (2014). Once again it comprised a very substantial rock-cut ditch with a roughly U-shaped profile, measuring 1.44–2.16 m wide at the base increasing to 3.40 m at the top, with a maximum depth of 1.26 m (Fig. 3.17; Fig. 3.18). The sides were almost vertical but again were stepped owing to the fracture patterns within the bedrock. The base comprised a flat but sloping sheet of limestone bedrock (Fig. 3.19). For reasons of health and safety two 1.0 m wide baulks were left *in situ* at each edge of the excavation trench resulting in c. 60% of the deposits being excavated. However, unlike the simple sequence of deposits seen at Trench 2 the fills at this location showed significant complexity.

The primary fill of this ditch was C492, a shallow deposit (0.07–0.11 m) of orange/brown stony clay only visible in the eastern section face of the trench and extending for a maximum of 0.60 m. Adjacent to the inner ditch edge was C516, a deposit of compact silty clay with quantities of fractured limestone and animal bone. This had a maximum depth of 0.52–0.56 m, and was overlain by C518, a localised slump of grey silty clay 0.16–0.42 m deep. A very shallow deposit of similar material (C479) covered the flat base of the ditch, from which some animal bone was recovered. A piece of cattle bone from this deposit, which lay directly on the bedrock, was radiocarbon dated to 1122–926 cal BC (2860±30 BP; Beta-420644).

Fig. 3.15. The unevenly cut middle ditch C428 during planning.

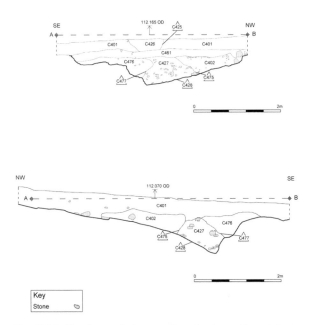

Fig. 3.16. Northeast facing section (top), southwest facing section (bottom) through middle ditch C428 showing recuts C475 and C477.

Covering these three fills was C473, a deep deposit (0.58–0.64 m) of silty clay with very frequent inclusions of shattered bedrock. An isolated human molar (B3/SK003 – see Ash, this volume), a piece of worked flint (2015: SF083) and two bone awls (2015: SF084; 2015: SF085) were recovered from this fill. Within C473 was a localised deposit (1.00–1.20 m × 0.80–1.00 m × 0.10–0.15 m depth) of compact silty clay containing charcoal and small stones (C474).

The inner ditch C464 was subject to a significant episode of re-cutting (C491), which occurred along its inner edge and truncated contexts C473 and C516. C491 was a linear cut that followed the line of the earlier ditch and had an approximately U-shaped profile with concave sides and a slightly rounded base. It had a minimum length of 3.00 m, width 0.40–1.01 m and depth of 0.42–0.50 m. This recut had two fills, the lowest of which was C517 a deposit of silty clay with frequent angular stones and charcoal flecks, measuring 0.32–0.38 m deep. Over this lay C471 a thin layer (0.04–0.24 m) of soft silty clay with fewer stones and charcoal flecks.

Sealing the re-cut and C473 was C470, a soft silty clay with frequent pieces of shattered limestone, charcoal

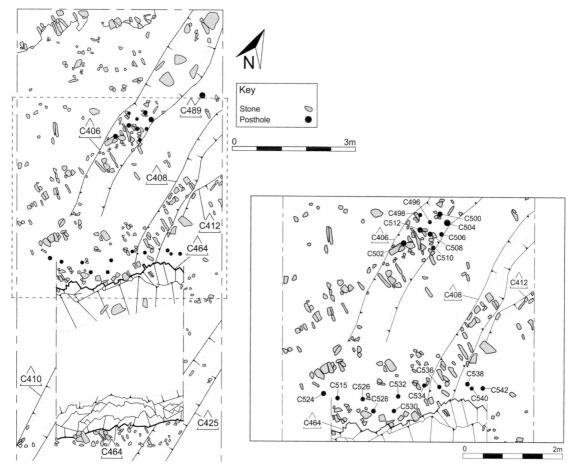

Fig. 3.17. Post-excavation plan of inner ditch C464 with insert showing the line of stakeholes along the northern edge and the cluster of stakeholes just further north.

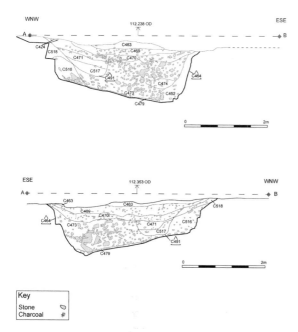

Fig. 3.18. Southwest facing (top) and northeast facing (bottom) sections through the inner ditch C464.

and animal bone. This was the earliest of three similar fills that likely post-date the use of the ditch. C470 was truncated by a small sub-circular pit (C467), which measured 0.56 × 0.46 m and was just 0.03–0.06 m deep. C467 had concave sides and a flat base and was filled with C468, a deposit of dark grey clayey silt with frequent charcoal, occasional small stones and fragments of burnt bone (Fig. 3.20). To the eastern side of the pit pieces of heat-affected bedrock were evident.

The pit was overlain by C469 (depth 0.16–0.26 m), which was very similar to C470. Finds from this context included a fragment of a lignite bracelet (2015: SF074; see Stevens, this volume). The upper fill of the ditch was C463 (depth 0.06–0.18 m), a mid-brown/grey silty clay with occasional small stones, flecks of charcoal and a moderate amount of animal bone.

Aligned along the top of the inner edge of the innermost enclosure ditch was a line of small post and stakeholes with an average diameter of 0.10 m and depth of 0.05–0.10 m (Fig. 3.21). These were arranged in a staggered pattern of regularly spaced pairs set 0.22 m apart. The distance between the pairs varied from 0.42–0.50 m.

Fig. 3.19. Inner ditch of Hillfort Phase (C464) post-excavation.

Fig. 3.20. Shallow pit C467 mid-excavation showing charcoal-rich fill C468.

Fig. 3.21. Rock-cut stakeholes along inner edge of ditch C464.

On the opposite side of the ditch, at the top of the outer edge were two postholes (C485 and C487), 0.15 m apart, the fills of which (C486 and C488 respectively) comprised grey/brown silty clay with no inclusions or artefactual remains. Partially overlying the upper ditch fill was C424, an irregularly shaped but well defined, metalled surface 3.05 m long and 1.65 m wide. Above this was a small localised deposit (C462) of dark brown/

grey silty sand with small stones and charcoal flecks, from which an unfinished bone spindle whorl was recovered (2015: SF127).

Located 1.4 m east of these features was an isolated posthole (C489) the fill of which included charcoal and burnt bone. Additional isolated features in the northern extent of Trench 4 included two possible pits (C412 and C434). C412 in the northwest corner of the trench extended beyond the limit of excavation, but the exposed portion was roughly wedge-shaped with straight sides and a flat base. It was filled with a sterile grey silt (C413). The second possible pit (C434) was located *c.* 2.5 m north of the inner edge of the inner ditch, adjacent to the eastern limit of excavation. This was a very ephemeral feature sub-circular in shape with sloped sides and an uneven base owing to the underlying bedrock. Just 0.06 m deep, C434 was filled with a deposit of dark brown silty sand (C435) with inclusions of stone, charcoal, burnt and unburnt bone, most likely representing domestic refuse.

The northern end of Trench 4 was criss-crossed by four plough furrows (C406; C408; C410; C425) oriented north–south or northeast–southwest. These ranged from 0.25–0.85 m wide and were up to 0.17 m deep. In the base of furrow C406 were nine small postholes, clustered in a restricted area of *c.* 1.00 × 0.60 m. Cut into the underlying bedrock, these postholes had a uniform fill of sterile grey silty clay.

3.2. The Southern Enclosure and environs

Trench 3 in the 2014 season aimed to explore the 'Southern Enclosure' – the 40.00 m diameter plectrum-shaped enclosure that is conjoined with Tlachtga. While this monument is not visible as upstanding archaeological remains, its circuit can be traced where the monuments intersect as the outer banks of Tlachtga are absent at this point. Trench 3 was a small cutting, measuring 8.00 × 3.00 m, positioned to target the enclosure ditch to the southeast at a point well away from its intersection with Tlachtga (Fig. 3.22). The primary aim during 2014 was to obtain dateable material without encountering significant stratigraphic complexity.

Topsoil and sod reached a depth of 0.50 m, deeper than that seen at Trench 2, and produced several finds, including two pieces of worked chert; a flake (2014: SF047) and a broken projectile point (2014: SF012). Beneath topsoil at the southwest end of the trench was a shallow linear feature (C011), probably a plough furrow. This was oriented northwest–southeast, and close to its southeast end was an isolated posthole (C061). This extended beyond the limit of excavation and was semi-circular measuring 0.26 × 0.12 m, with a maximum depth of 0.09 m. It had steep sides, a flat base and had a single sterile fill (C015) of brown/grey silty clay.

On the northwest side of C011 were a posthole (C010) and a possible posthole (C049). C010 was sub-circular and

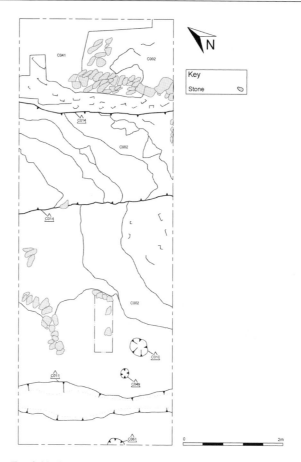

Fig. 3.22. Post-excavation plan of Trench 3 (Southern Enclosure).

measured 0.40 × 0.30 m and was 0.13 m in depth. This had steep sides and contained a single, stony fill (C005) of silty clay with frequent charcoal inclusions. C005 also contained fragments of bone, some of which were burnt. Hazel charcoal from C005 was radiocarbon dated to 1259–1015 cal BC (2937±38 BP; UBA-27559). C049 may also have been a posthole but was less well-defined. Measuring 0.24 × 0.18 m and only 0.05 m in depth it contained a single fill (C047) of compact silty clay with occasional charcoal flecks.

To the northeast end of Trench 3 was the ditch of the Southern Enclosure (C014) (Fig. 3.23). This measured 3.05 m wide and 0.80 m deep and was excavated in half-section, with the northwest half excavated first followed by the remaining southeast portion. The upper edge of C014 was steep and the sides were nearly vertical but asymmetrical, with the outer (northwest) side shorter than the opposite inner (southeast) side. The break of slope at the base of the ditch was sharp and the base sloped downwards northwest–southeast, but was stepped owing to the fractured nature of the bedrock (Fig. 3.24).

The base of the ditch was partially covered with a layer of compact yellow/grey clayey silt with occasional flecks of charcoal (C060). This was only apparent in the southeast facing section of the ditch where it was thickest, measuring 0.10 m in depth. The primary fill of

Fig. 3.23. Looking southwest at Trench 3 post-excavation. In the foreground is the Southern Enclosure ditch C014. To the rear are postholes C010 and C049 along with furrow C011.

the ditch (C018) (Fig. 3.25) measured 0.46 m in depth and comprised a moderately compact silty clay with frequent angular stones (0.10–0.20 m). This context also contained abundant and well-preserved animal bone. Several large pieces of cattle bone were apparently placed at regular intervals at the base of C018, directly on bedrock. Finds from C018 included a chert flake (2014: SF038) and a broken hammer stone. A fragmentary bone awl (2014: SF069) with evidence of fire blackening was found during examination of the animal bone assemblage.

Above C018 was C006, a moderately compact mid-brown silty clay, 0.38 m deep and containing occasional angular stones similar to those in C018. C006 contained less animal bone than C018 and much of the bone recovered was very fragmented. Finds from C006 comprised a chert flake (2014: SF014), a hammerstone fragment, a possible bone awl (2014: SF065) and a fragment of bone with a worked and rounded terminal, possibly part of a larger awl (2014: SF070). Within C006 was a small and isolated lens of charcoal (C036) measuring 0.40 × 0.30 m, with a maximum depth of 0.03 m.

Along both sides of the ditch were a number of small deposits, evident only in section, which appeared to be the result of silting episodes, and which contained small quantities of cultural material. On the outer edge of the northwest facing section was C019, a compact silty clay

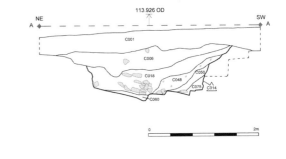

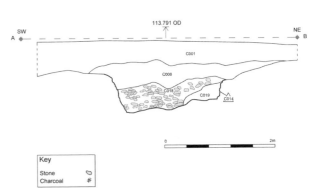

Fig. 3.24. Southeast facing (top) and northwest facing (bottom) sections through the ditch C014.

Fig. 3.25 Southeast facing section through ditch C014.

Fig. 3.26. The infant burial in Trench 3. The lower part of the remains was enclosed in a setting of small stones.

0.25 m deep. In the southeast facing section were three deposits. C075 was also 0.25 m deep and was a compact silty clay with a small amount of charcoal. This was 0.15 m deep and more friable than C050 which lay above. C050 comprised an orange sandy silt with inclusions of burnt clay, grit, small pebbles, charcoal flecks and a few fragments of animal bone.

Overlying C050 in the southeast facing section was C048 a moderately compact charcoal-rich silty clay. Measuring 0.25 m deep this appears to have been a localised fill and contained two partial cattle femurs, one of which lay directly on the bedrock and has been radiocarbon dated to cal AD 412–542 (1570±30 BP; Beta-386850) (visible in Fig. 3.25).

In the northeast corner of the exposed section of ditch an infant burial was revealed (Fig. 3.26; see Ash, this volume). This lay in C063, a deposit of mid-grey silty clay with frequent charcoal inclusions that underlay C018 (see above). The burial was oriented along the width of the ditch (northeast–southwest) with the head and torso resting directly on the bedrock and the pelvis and legs on C063. It seems likely that C063 was intentionally used to cover the burial before the larger stones were put in place. Examination suggests that they are those of a child of 3–5 months old, showing no signs of trauma. The remains have been directly radiocarbon dated to cal AD 420–556 (1530±30 BP; Beta-388456).

C063 was up to 0.15 m deep and contained abundant animal bone, most of which was highly fragmentary. Above this was a concentration of medium to large flat stones, probably acting as capstones, while adjacent to the lower part of the skeleton were a number of upright, smaller stones, creating a formal setting.

Overlying the bedrock along each edge of the ditch were C007 and C008, deposits of compact clay that appeared to be natural deposits related to the degradation of the underlying limestone. The inclusion of occasional flecks of charcoal suggests that these deposits were somewhat mixed with cultural material.

3.2.1. Test Pit 1

Test Pit 1 was located 11.25 m to the northeast of Trench 3 and was positioned to examine a linear geophysical anomaly, identified as a potentially earlier enclosure which had been overbuilt by the Southern Enclosure. It measured 3.00 × 2.00 m and was oriented east–west. Following the removal of the sod and *c.* 0.30 m of topsoil, the area was cleaned back to reveal bedrock, part of which was overlain by a deposit of compact clay (C035). This appeared to be a natural deposit, similar to C008 in Trench 3. Cut into the bedrock and C035 was a shallow north–south oriented linear feature (C033), 0.40 m wide × 0.23 m deep. U-shaped in section with vertical sides and a very flat base of uneven bedrock, most likely a plough furrow. The only inclusions in the clay-rich fill (C034) were a partial cattle tooth and stones of varying size, which appeared to be pieces of degraded bedrock. No trace of any earlier enclosure feature was encountered.

3.3. Tlachtga, outer ditches

3.3.1. Trench 1

Trench 1 was positioned to examine the outermost bank-ditch pair of Tlachtga. It was located to the north of the upstanding monument where the bank had been largely levelled and measured 12.20 × 3.00 m, oriented NNE–SSW. Trench 1 also covered part of an outer ditch with no surface remains but which was identified as a weak positive magnetic anomaly in geophysical survey.

The removal of sod and topsoil (C001) to a depth of 0.60 m produced a small quantity of unidentifiable animal bone and a number of finds including two 'minié ball' lead bullets, a type of ammunition first developed in the early 19th century (Kerr 1990, 11), and an Edward VII threepenny piece, dated to 1908. Beneath topsoil was C021, a shallow layer of compact clay-rich silt with occasional small stones, which likely equates to C030 in the inner ditch (see below). Below C021 lay the upper layer of the bank (C022) and upper fill of the outer ditch (C023). Following exposure and planning of the uppermost features, the trench was half-sectioned lengthwise and the western half was excavated. Owing to time constraints, the remaining *in-situ* deposits were half-sectioned crosswise and only the southern half was excavated (Fig. 3.27).

Close to the southern end of Trench 1 was the remains of the upstanding bank (Fig. 3.28). This had a maximum height of 1.08 m and was composed of two deposits, the lowest of which (C040) overlay a thin layer (0.09 m) of clayey silt (C042) that lay directly on bedrock. The lowest deposit of the bank was C040, which comprised a 0.50 m deep layer of very sandy silt with frequent small angular stones. Quite sterile, this appeared to be redeposited subsoil, most likely upcast during the initial excavation of the outer ditch. Finds within C040 were few but included an edge-retouched chert blade (2014: SF052). The southern extent of C040 stopped at the edge of the inner ditch (C025) suggesting that these contexts are contemporary. Overlying C040 was C022, a shallow (0.15 m) deposit of grey/brown silt with a large number of small to medium angular stones. The larger stones were concentrated at the highest point of the bank with smaller stones continuing down the southern slope but not to the north.

Within the upper surface of the bank was a piece of sandstone (2014: SF005) decorated with four parallel pecked lines; this may be a fragment of a larger panel of

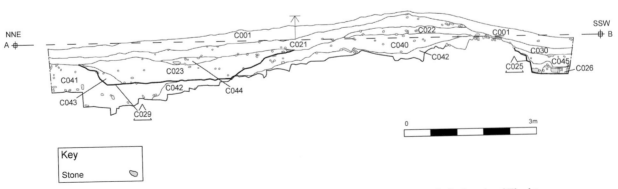

Fig. 3.27. Half-section drawing through Trench 1 showing the outermost bank-ditch pair of Tlachtga.

megalithic art or a stone vessel (Fig. 3.29; see O'Sullivan, this volume).

The inner ditch (C025) was located at the southern end of Trench 1 and excavated for a length of 1.00 m. It was 0.74 m deep and cut into the bedrock with vertical sides and a sharp break of slope at the base (Fig. 3.30), which consisted of naturally stepped and sloping layers of bedrock. The primary fill of the ditch (C026) was 0.18 m deep and comprised soft silt with frequent angular stones. A red fox tooth from the base of this cut has been radiocarbon dated to cal AD 412–542 (1550±30 BP; Beta-386849).

Fig. 3.28. Tlachtga, outer bank, pre-excavation looking north.

Overlying C026 was C045, which measured 0.30 m deep and was very similar to both C026 and C030, but with smaller and less frequent stones. The final, uppermost fill of the inner ditch was C030, a deposit of compact clayey silt with moderate amounts of grit but few larger stones. This contained significant quantities of fragmentary animal bone, most of which was unidentifiable to species. C030 was possibly a continuation of C021, above the bank. If this was the case then C030/C021 represent an earlier topsoil horizon that had slumped either side of the bank. A small piece of prehistoric pottery (2014: SF063) found in this context was identified belonging to a middle Neolithic broad-rimmed globular bowl (Helen Roche, pers. comm.), possibly contemporary with the fragmentary pecked stone object found within the bank.

The outer ditch (C029) was very wide and shallow measuring 2.90 m wide at the base expanding to 5.90 m at the top, with a maximum depth of 0.56 m. Its northern half was cut into subsoil (C041) – which in this location was moderately deep over the bedrock. The southern half of the ditch appears to have been re-cut as it truncated C040, the basal layer of the bank. C029 had very shallow gradually sloping sides and a flat base. Along its northern edge was C043 a shallow deposit of compact clayey silt, containing grit and some charcoal. This had a slightly convex profile and appears to have been redeposited subsoil mixed with cultural material, which had subsequently slumped into the ditch. The primary fill of C029 was C023, a sandy silt containing small pebbles and occasional sub-angular stones. Measuring 0.55 m deep this contained a small quantity of fragmentary and in some cases burned animal bone. Finds from C023 included a substantial quartz flake (2014: SF031), a small flake of struck flint (2014: SF034) and a fragment of a convex flint scraper (2014: SF035). Four small lenses of charcoal (C024, C027, C028 and C039) were encountered within C023. C039 occurred towards the base of the deposit while C028 and C027 were clustered towards the middle. These were small and shallow,

Fig. 3.29. Pecked stone object 2014: SF005 from the top of the outer Tlachtga bank (Illustration: Conor McHale).

Fig. 3.30. The vertical-sided rock-cut inner ditch (C025) of the outermost bank-ditch circuit of Tlachtga.

measuring a maximum of 0.46 × 0.40 m and 0.02–0.06 m deep. C024 occurred near the top of the ditch and was a little larger measuring 0.90 × 0.53 m, with a depth of 0.05 m. This produced a small fragment of a flint flake (2014: SF023). These small, isolated charcoal deposits are likely the result of short-lived events such as cooking hearths, within the lifetime of the ditch.

In the centre of the ditch, overlying C023 was C044, a deposit of compact silty clay with occasional grit and charcoal. This measured 1.40 m × 0.60 m and was likely the result of a short phase of natural siltation.

Apart from the upper bank deposits and the charcoal lenses in the outer ditch, the deposits in Trench 1 were all very similar and difficult to distinguish from one another. As a result the half-section through the trench, specifically the outer ditch, was overcut in order to identify in section the edges and base of the ditch. The difficulty encountered in recognising the cut of the outer ditch necessitated the excavation of a small test pit (Test Pit 3) to the north.

3.3.2. Test Pit 3

Test Pit 3 was located 5.50 m north of Trench 1. It was excavated to better understand the apparent deep subsoil deposits in this location and to ascertain whether the depth to bedrock observed in Trench 1 was anomalous or part of a broader trend that could be observed elsewhere away from the summit of the hill. It measured 0.77 × 0.75 m and at its base, 0.69 m below the sod was bedrock. This was overlain by C054, subsoil identical to C041 in Trench 1 (see above), which measured 0.50 m deep. Over this lay 0.30 m of topsoil. The excavation of Test Pit 3 established that in contrast to the stratigraphy encountered elsewhere at the Hill of Ward (*e.g.* at Trenches 2 and 3), a significant depth of compact subsoil overlay bedrock in this part of the field. This combined with the necessary overcutting of the deposits in the northern end of Trench 1 aided the understanding of the natural and archaeological stratigraphy at the site.

3.3.3. Trench 5

Trench 5 measured 7.80 × 5.00 m and was oriented NNE–SSW and was placed to investigate the junction of the Southern Enclosure and the second from the outermost bank and ditch of the upstanding monument of Tlachtga. Beneath the topsoil covering most of the trench was C443, an interface layer very similar to topsoil. The features exposed in the upper levels of Trench 5 were quite ephemeral and so were investigated in two large box sections at each side of the trench, leaving a central baulk. The sections were numbered Sondage 1 and Sondage 2 and lay respectively to the east and west sides of the trench (Fig. 3.31; Fig. 3.32). The northern half of Trench 5 was covered with collapsed bank material from the largely levelled bank of Tlachtga (C444) at this location. This comprised a substantial deposit of angular stone and soil,

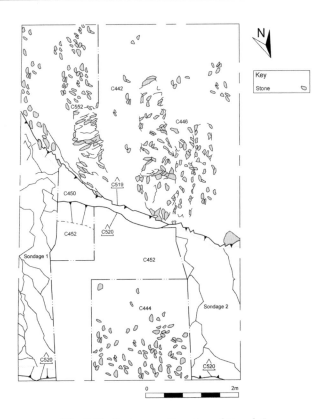

Fig. 3.31. Post-excavation plan of Trench 5.

which covered much of the area where the two ditches intersected. At the southern end of the trench bedrock was exposed, covered in places by C442, a deposit of clay mixed with charcoal and flecks of burnt bone.

3.3.3.1. The Southern Enclosure ditch

Running NNW/SSE across Trench 5 was C519, the ditch of the Southern Enclosure. This was very heavily truncated by the later ditch of the upstanding monument of Tlachtga (C520) and only a small portion of its southern edge remained. C519 was cut into the bedrock with an almost vertical edge ending at a flat base, which sloped slightly downwards to the north, similar in form to the ditch section previously seen in Trench 3. Only a very small portion of three fills of this ditch remained. C521 was a deposit of compact and smooth orange/grey clay with occasional small stones and flecks of charcoal. It lay directly against the rock-cut face and base of the ditch in the southeastern corner of Sondage 1 where the Southern Enclosure ditch C519 entered/exited the trench. A large fragment of animal bone was found within this deposit, lying directly on the base of the ditch. This was radiocarbon dated to cal AD 678–950 (UBA-32857; 1213±42 BP) with a 72.3% probability of being between cal AD 758–895. This is therefore contemporary with the main early medieval phase of Tlachtga rather than its construction dates and those of the Southern Enclosure.

Fig. 3.32. Looking south at Trench 5, in the foreground is the collapsed bank material C444. The cut of the enclosure ditch C519 is visible at both edges of the trench.

Fig. 3.33. Vertical cut in bedrock of C520, potentially part of an earlier feature.

Above C521 was C450, which extended north–northwest as a thin band, 0.06–0.08 m wide for a length of 4.24 m. It had a maximum depth of 0.30 m and comprised compact clay with charcoal and occasional small stones. The true extent of C450 is unknown as it was heavily truncated by the Tlachtga ditch (C520). The final deposit associated with C519 was C522, which primarily comprised large angular pieces of limestone in a matrix of dark grey silt. This only occurred over C450 in the southeastern corner of Sondage 1, where it was truncated by the later ditch, but it also extended over an area of bedrock outside the Southern Enclosure ditch.

The western extent of the Southern Enclosure was visible in the northern part of Sondage 2 where it was cut vertically into bedrock. The base of the ditch was flat but sloped slightly from east to west. The lowest fill within C520 was C547, a deposit of mottled compact clay with small stones and charcoal flecks. This deposit was located against the southern ditch edge in Sondage 2, filling a step in the bedrock at the base of the ditch (Fig. 3.33). A radiocarbon date from here returned a Bronze Age date of 1260–1051 cal BC (2950±30 BP; Beta-446132). While C547 was initially interpreted as a fill of the Southern Enclosure, it is possible that it belongs to an earlier phase of monument as the vertical cut into the bedrock of C520 marks a clear additional intervention within the base of the ditch.

3.3.3.2. The Tlachtga ditch

C520 was the second to outermost ditch of the upstanding monument and ran southeast–northwest across Trench 5, measuring 4.00 m wide by 0.64–0.74 m deep. For the most part only the southern edge of the ditch was visible as its northern edge lay beyond the northern limit of excavation.

C520 probably truncated the earlier ditch of the Southern Enclosure (C519), running along most of the same course from southeast to northwest across the ditch (Fig. 3.34). Where C520 entered the trench in the southeast (Sondage 1) the ditch edge was cut into C522, a localised fill of the Southern Enclosure. Moving northwest, C520 was cut into C450. This section of the ditch had a gradually sloped side; however, toward its northwest extent beyond the limit of C450 (Sondage 2), it was cut vertically into the bedrock.

Above C547, the first fill of C520 was C460, a substantial deposit of gritty clay with frequent small to medium sized stones and fragments of animal bone. C460 was 0.22–0.34 m deep and contained a small piece of struck flint (2015: SF096). Within Sondage 1 at the base of the deposit lying directly on the bedrock were several large fragments of animal bone, similar to those on the base of the Southern Enclosure ditch. Three later prehistoric bone scrapers (2015: SF125; 2015: SF129 and 2015: SF130; see Riddler and Trzaska-Nartowski, this volume) were recovered from this context. A crucible fragment (2015: SF105) found while cleaning the section of the ditch and originally attributed C460, is more likely to have originated from the overlying hearth feature (see below and O'Neill, this volume).

Overlying C460 were two very similar deposits C444 and C452, the boundary between which was virtually indistinguishable; however, small differences of composition suggest that they were two separate contexts. C452 extended across much of the width of the ditch (maximum width of 3.17 m) and comprised loose sandy silt with frequent charcoal inclusions, occasional stones and bone fragments. Finds from C452 included a partial later prehistoric bone scraper (2015: SF092) and a small piece of rock crystal (2015: SF093). Two small, isolated deposits of charcoal and burnt bone (C523) and charcoal with burnt clay (C546) were contained within C452. Partially overlying C452 was C444, which was concentrated at the northern end of the trench and measured 1.56 m wide and 0.40–0.82 m deep. This deposit comprised material from the largely levelled bank of Tlachtga and contained very frequent angular stones and fragments of bone.

Truncating C452 at the eastern edge of the trench in Sondage 1 was an irregularly shaped cut (C459), measuring 3.00 × 1.10 m, with a maximum depth of 0.12 m. This was filled with C453, a stony deposit that formed the base for a hearth. The hearth was set in a small circular cut (C454) with gradually sloping sides and a flat base. It was filled with three layers of charcoal and burnt clay (C549, C548, C451) with a combined depth of 0.17 m (Fig. 3.35). Two stakeholes C455 and C457 truncated the middle hearth layer. Finds from the uppermost fill of the hearth comprised a piece of struck flint (2015: SF087), a crucible fragment (2015: SF090) and a partial bone scraper (2015: SF092). Southwest of the hearth, truncating the stony deposit C453 was a small circular cut (C494) measuring 0.40 m diameter with a maximum depth of 0.18 m. This was filled with C493, a deposit of reddened clay, mid-way down within which was a layer of small flat stones. C493 was covered by the uppermost layer of the hearth C451.

Sealing the upper fill of the hearth and representing the final fill of the Tlachtga ditch C520 was C449 a deposit of loose silty clay with charcoal, bone and occasional stones.

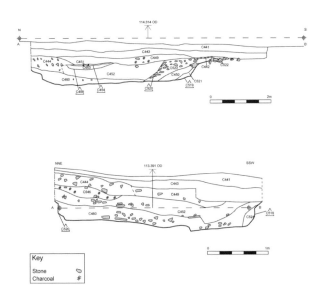

Fig. 3.34. East (top) and west (bottom) facing sections of Trench 5 showing the Southern Enclosure ditch C519 and fills C521, C522 and C450 truncated by the later Tlachtga ditch C520.

Fig. 3.35. The small hearth C454 mid-excavation showing fills of charcoal and burnt clay.

This underlay C448, a localised deposit of charcoal and burnt clay and C443, the topsoil interface.

3.3.4. Trench 7

Trench 7 measured 10.00 × 3.00 m and was located to the southeast of the upstanding monument, orientated NW–SE. It was positioned to investigate the innermost ditch of the monument of Tlachtga (*i.e.* the ditch beyond the central mound) in an area where the banks of the monument had already been levelled. The removal of topsoil produced a small quantity of animal bone and collection of post-medieval and modern finds including several sherds of pottery, pieces of glass and a horseshoe. A clay pipe stem engraved with the word 'Volunteer' on one side and 'Du...' on the reverse (2016: SF166; Fig. 3.36), dates to post-1850 and is likely related to a British army regiment, DU being short for Dublin (James Kyle, pers. comm).

Following removal of the sod and topsoil, bedrock was exposed at the northwest and southeast ends of the trench at a depth of only 0.20 m. Across the centre of the trench was a large ditch (C904) oriented northeast–southwest (Fig. 3.38; Fig. 3.39). Health and safety concerns regarding its depth meant it was excavated in steps, the southwestern and northeastern sides were excavated first and subsequently the central area was taken down to the bedrock (Fig. 3.39). C904 was cut into the bedrock and measured 3.65–3.85 m wide at the base, expanding to a maximum of 5.30–5.50 m at the top, and was 1.76–1.35 m in depth. It had a flat base of limestone bedrock from which extended steep almost vertical edges (Fig. 3.38).

At the interface of bedrock and the main ditch fill (C914) was C919. This thin layer (0.18–0.23 m) covered the base of the ditch and comprised coarse grained mid-yellow/brown silty sand with inclusions of angular stones and gravel. On the southeastern side of the ditch, above C919 was C920, a very similar deposit that covered the lowest portion of the ditch edge. Above C919, on the northwestern side of the ditch was C918, a clayey silt with angular stone inclusions, most likely fragments of quarried bedrock. This had a maximum depth of 1.68 m and included occasional flecks of charcoal and some animal bone. Above C920, extending east–west along the southern edge of the ditch with a maximum depth of 1.10 m, was C917 a loose dark grey/brown silty sand with abundant angular stone inclusions. This was originally interpreted as a secondary deposit, laid down after the initial removal of bedrock from the ditch; however, along with C918, C919 and C920 it is more likely to have been a primary deposit. These four deposits were truncated by a substantial re-cut C921, which measured 1.90 m wide at the base expanding to 3.20 m at its upper boundary. The cut for C921 reached the original ditch base and the sides were steeply sloped cutting through the four deposits described above (see Fig. 3.39). Hazel charcoal from C919 was radiocarbon dated to cal AD 416–538

10 mm

Fig. 3.36. Clay pipe stem engraved with 'Du...' and 'Volunteer'.

Fig. 3.37. Looking southeast at Trench 7 pre-excavation showing the large ditch C904 and upper stony fill.

(UBA-45318; 1610±23 BP) while *Prunus* charcoal from the recut (C914; see below) dated to cal AD 886–1023 (UBA-45319; 1071±21 BP).

The primary fill of the re-cut was C914 a coarse-grained deposit *c.* 80% of which comprised small (<0.10 m) pieces of shattered bedrock with some charcoal and animal bone. C914 had a depth of 0.20–0.98 m. Constant rainfall during the excavation of C914 caused the soil to clump and it was extremely difficult to remove and almost impossible to dry sieve. As a result, only *c.* 10% of this deposit was screened. C914 produced a small piece of decorated animal bone, subsequently identified as a partial casket mount (2016: SF296; see Riddler and Trzaska-Nartowski, this volume) and the shaft of a copper alloy ring pin (2016: SF255 – see Maguire, this volume).

At the base of C914 were two separate episodes of burning, C915 and C916. C915 was a spread measuring 0.90–0.95 m in length with a depth of 0.06–0.08 m. It again included sub-angular shattered pieces of bedrock, along with ash, charcoal and some animal bone. C916 was located on the eastern side of the trench where it extended for 1.00 × 0.75 m. This very dark coloured fill included charcoal flecks and calcined bone, but in profile was only *c.* 0.01 m deep. There was limited evidence for *in-situ* oxidation in both deposits and they are unlikely to represent hearths but were perhaps dumps of material from thermal episodes in the vicinity, similar to those seen in the outer ditches at Trench 1.

Above C914, on both sides of the re-cut was C912, which appears to have slumped into the ditch following its

Fig. 3.38. Looking southeast at Trench 7 post-excavation showing the bedrock cut ditch C904 and stony fills excavated in stepped sections.

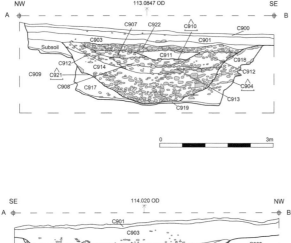

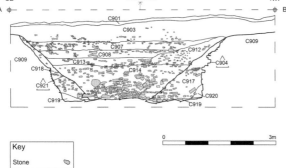

Fig. 3.39. Southwest facing (top) and northeast facing (bottom) sections through C904, the innermost ditch of Tlachtga.

re-cutting. This fill was again overwhelmingly dominated by angular pieces of fractured bedrock (*c.* 80%), and had a variable depth of 0.10–0.56 m. C912 yielded abundant animal bone and a heavily corroded copper ring (2016: SF257). This has been identified as a late Bronze Age hair ornament (K. Becker, pers. comm.; see Maguire, this volume). This is presumably redeposited from the underlying Bronze Age phase excavated in previous seasons. Also recovered from C912 was a broken basalt ingot mould (2016: SF252; Fig. 3.40). This has multiple casting matrices: the upper surface has three bar-shaped matrices, with a possible pin-shaped matrix on the reverse and a flattened, circular matrix on the unbroken end. The mould is of similar type to objects described recovered from a number of high-status sites in Cos. Meath and Westmeath, including Lagore Crannog (Comber 2004, appendix 3), Moynagh Lough, (Bradley 1991, 5), Knowth (Barton-Murray and Bayley 2012), and Ballinderry Crannog (Hencken 1942, 65, Fig. 32:368). However, these objects are almost all either of schist or sandstone. Basalt examples are very uncommon, although a single matrix basalt mould was catalogued by Heald (2005, 244) from Dunadd, Argyle.

Directly above the central part of C914 was C913. Measuring 0.11–0.28 m in depth, this deposit of soft, dark grey-brown silty sand was rich in charcoal and animal bone with inclusions of sub-angular to angular stones.

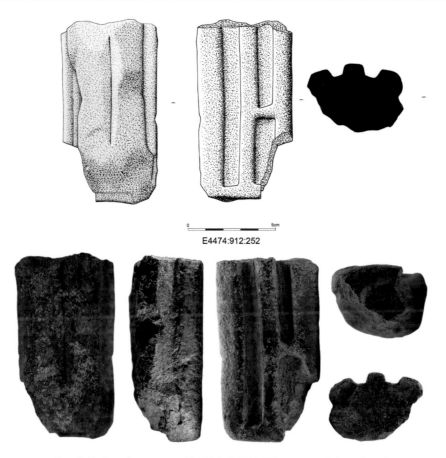

0   5cm

E4474:912:252

Fig. 3.40. Basalt ingot mould 2016: SF252 (Illustration: Johnny Ryan).

Large portions of cattle bone were recovered from C913 and this deposit has been interpreted as a possible layer of domestic refuse.

Above this was C908, a deposit of soft silty sand with a depth of 0.15–0.19 m. Once again this included shattered bedrock, charcoal and animal bone. A medium-sized mammal radius and ulna were recovered partially articulated with the distal epiphysis connected but unfused. A small quantity of probable furnace slag was recovered from this context (Brendan O'Neill, pers. comm.).

Overlying C908 was C907, a sandy layer (0.17–0.19 m) that again mostly comprised angular pieces of shattered bedrock (80%). Within this was a large quantity of animal bone and charcoal. C907 was the uppermost fill within the ditch and may represent the closing deposit. It was truncated by a small sub-circular cut (C910), with a gently concave base filled with C911. C911 was a firm silty deposit with charcoal inclusions and poorly sorted angular grit and gravel between 1.00–30.00 mm; it was covered by a final stony layer (C922) that likely represents a final ploughed out remnant of the Tlachtga bank. The last deposit that occurred within the very upper limits of the ditch was C903, a soft clayey silt with charcoal flecks and animal bone. This had a variable depth of 0.45–0.50 m and constituted the interface between topsoil and subsoil, showing clear evidence of bioturbation. Southeast of the ditch C904 was a plough furrow C905.

This ran northeast–southwest across the southern part of the trench and was 0.60–0.90 m wide with a maximum depth of 0.35 m. It was filled with C906, a firm mid-orange-brown silt, with occasional inclusions of poorly sorted stone and burnt bone.

3.4. Tlachtga: the central mound

3.4.1. Trench 6

Trench 6 was located at the northeastern half of the central platform of the upstanding monument, orientated north-northwest to south-southeast and sloping downwards towards the north. The initial cut measured 9.00 × 5.00 m, but the southern half was extended westwards by 0.50 m giving the trench a slight L-shape. A second small extension was located at the northwest corner.

The removal of sod and topsoil (C800) up to 0.25 m in depth produced a number of finds including a metal tunic button featuring a 'Prince of Wales' Feathers' design (Longford Militia; 2016: SF151 – *cf.* O'Carroll *et al.* 2016; Fig. 3.41), a flint barbed and tanged arrowhead chronologically attributable to the early Bronze Age (2016: SF170), and a cylindrical stone rod (2016: SF164), most likely part of a slate pencil (*cf.* Shaffrey 2022). A similar object recovered from excavations at Caherconnell, Co. Clare has been suggested to be 14th or 15th century in date (M. Comber, pers. comm.).

10 mm

Fig. 3.41. Longford Militia button 2016: SF151.

Fig. 3.42. Looking southeast at Trench 6 and the section through deposits C817 and C818.

Fig. 3.43. Burned deposit of C821 (C822) beneath C818.

Trench 6 was excavated down to bedrock, above which, unevenly distributed across the central area of the trench, was a very thin clay deposit (C823), entirely sterile in nature. This most likely represents a natural transitional deposit similar to those seen elsewhere on site. In the western area of the trench and in the northern trench extension a deposit of sterile yellow clay (C805) lay directly above the bedrock. Again, this did not appear to be anthropically disturbed and was most likely a natural deposit. The extension of the trench at the northern end clearly demonstrated that the central mound was not surrounded by an external ditch but was constructed on areas that were either wholly natural or overlying earlier cultural material.

Directly over C823 and spread across the central area of the trench, was C818, a dark grey clay with a variable depth of 0.08–0.10 m containing a high concentration of charcoal and animal bone (Fig. 3.42). Several pieces of struck flint were recovered from this context, including a bifacially worked plano-convex flint knife (2016: SF271) attributable to the late Neolithic/early Bronze Age. In the southern portion of the trench and beneath C818 was a shallow approximately circular cut (C821) with a diameter of *c.* 1.00 m and a single fill (C822) of charcoal-rich dark brown soil mixed with ash (Fig. 3.43). Charcoal from C822 provided a radiocarbon date of cal AD 260–530 (UBA-45317; 1665±25 BP; 84.9% probability of being between cal AD 337–435) while a fragment of cattle bone from C818 yielded a date of cal AD 895–1034 (UBA-32858; 1071±43 BP).

Directly above C818 several deposits were exposed across the trench. C817 covered an area of 3.60 × *c.* 1.20 m in the central area of the northern half of the trench. This shallow deposit (0.20 m deep) of bright red-brown oxidised material, had no obvious inclusions and yielded no finds. At first glance it appeared to be burned; however, this proved not to be the case. It probably represents the remains of a degraded organic deposit (*e.g.* wood – H. Lewis, pers. comm.), and constitutes the primary phase of mound construction. Also above C818, abutting C817 and extending southwards for 3.80 m, was C819, a thin deposit averaging 0.15 m in depth, of loose dark brown silt.

Evenly spread over C817 and C818 was C808, a deposit of reddish clay, 0.15–0.25 m deep, which extended into the central and southern area of the trench (Fig. 3.44). This deposit produced no finds or ecofacts. Slightly above C808, extending under the eastern baulk was C807 a thin brown/orange spread with an average depth of only 0.05 m. No finds were associated with this deposit and it is interpreted as another probable organic layer which began to decompose before burial. Patches of iron and manganese oxide were visible throughout.

Extending southwards for *c.* 2.00 m from the northern baulk, directly under the topsoil (C800), and above C805, C808 and C823 was C803, a grey clay deposit with some small stony inclusions. This sloped towards

Fig. 3.44. Looking east-southeast at Trench 6 showing the basal organic deposit C808 and the section through mound layers C815 and C810.

10 mm

Fig. 3.45. Possible iron key or awl (2016: SF222) post-conservation.

the northern part of the trench and measured 0.05–0.25 m in depth. C803 produced some animal bone and an iron object (2016: SF222), possibly a key or part of an awl (Fig. 3.45; see Delaney and Murphy 2022, 127), and a flake of struck quartz (2016: SF220). C803 also covered the limestone flags C809 (see below).

In the southwest corner of the trench was C820, a group of large, angular stone blocks. These appeared to be intentionally placed, but their purpose remains unclear and they did not form any sort of regular setting. The blocks of C820 were embedded in C816, a sterile grey layer concentrated in the southern part of the trench. Both were covered by C815, a deep and largely sterile

deposit that extended over the entire southern half of the trench. Comprising yellow/orange clay this was likely the primary construction material of the central mound. C815 had an average depth of 0.50 m increasing to 0.60 m towards the central area of the trench (Fig. 3.46). It produced a small quantity of burnt animal bone and a small fragment of burnt flint (2016: SF270), possibly a rejuvenation flake. The lack of stratigraphic layering, artefacts and animal bone suggests that this deposit was laid down rapidly.

Abutting C815, sloping towards the north was C812, a deposit of large and comparatively fine limestone flags (Fig. 3.47). These varied in size and shape and were laid as a lower revetment to contain C815. In the southwestern area of the trench C812 became visible only after removing a thick layer of comminuted shale (C814). This compact layer extended east–west across the trench with an average depth of 1.3 m. No finds were recovered from C814 and it covered both the flagstones of C812 and, in places, C810 and C811 (see below).

In the centre of the southern half of Trench 6, above the main mound material C815 and partially above the flags C812 was a deposit of grey clay (C811) which

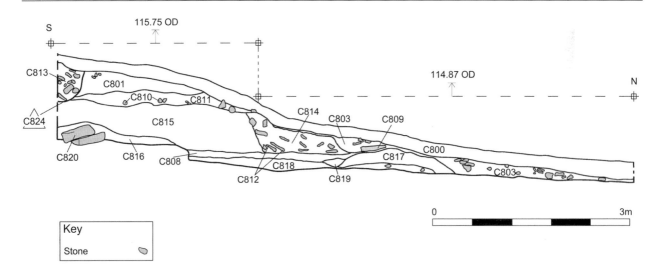

Fig. 3.46. East facing section through the layers of the central mound.

Fig. 3.47. Lower shaly flagstones C812 overlying decomposed organic deposit C808; in the background are the rounded cobbles of C810.

extended east-west for the entire width of the trench and to the north north-west for 2.7 m. C811 was 0.18–0.35 m in depth and included very frequent large, rounded stones (C810) which formed a capping for the central mound. The stones formed a capping for the central mound. A

small quantity of burnt animal bone and iron slag were recovered from this deposit. In the southwestern corner of the trench. C810 and C811 were truncated by a later cut (C824), the fill of which (C813), was a 0.50 m deep deposit of grey silty clay containing shattered limestone bedrock and a small quantity of animal bone.

Above C810 and C811, beneath topsoil, in the southern part of the trench was C801, a yellow clay deposit with small stone inclusions. This was a very firm layer 0.20–0.45 m in depth, which appears to have been an ancient soil horizon. Within C801 was found an oblique projectile point (2016: SF152) and a partially ground stone axe (2016: SF163), made from a sandstone cobble (see Mandal and Gilhooly, this volume). A small amount of animal bone was also retrieved from this context. C801, C810 and C811 were truncated by a later cut (C824), the fill of which (C813), was a 0.50 m deep deposit of grey silty clay containing shattered limestone bedrock and a small quantity of animal bone.

Abutting and partially overlapped by the stony capping of C810 and C811, was C809, a line of large, angular limestone flags, of variable size and shape but much more blocky than the flags of C812. C809 ran southwest–northeast across the entire trench (Fig. 3.48). These may have formed an upper revetment to the mound or could have functioned more as a path to allow movement over the freshly constructed mound prior to subsidence.

In the northeastern half of the trench, directly below the topsoil were C802 and C806 (Fig. 3.49). These combined extended for an area of 1.40 m × 1.40 m with a maximum depth of 0.60 m. C802 was composed of moderately fragmented shale, set in a loose grey matrix (C806). C806 produced a small quantity of flint debitage, a possible rubbing stone and a stone loom weight (Fig. 3.50 2016: SF267).

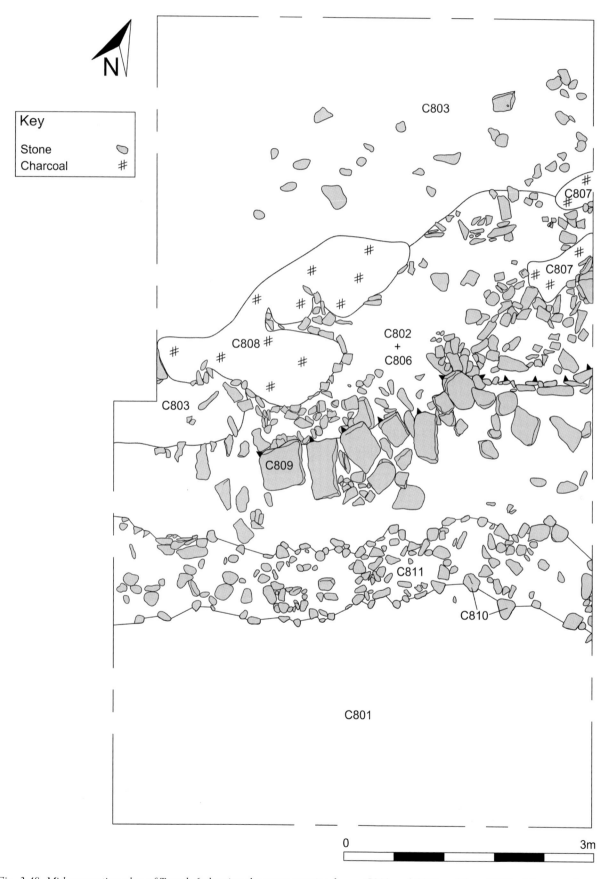

Fig. 3.48. Mid-excavation plan of Trench 6 showing the stony capping layers C810 and C811 and flags C809 of the central mound.

Fig. 3.49. Shale layer C802.

10 mm

Fig. 3.50. Stone loom weight 2016: SF267.

3.4.2. Test Pit 2

Test Pit 2 was located in the northern half of the central mound of the upstanding monument, just south of Trench 6. It centred on a large magnetic anomaly identified as a probable pit. The test pit measured 3.00 × 2.00 m and was orientated southeast–northwest. Following the removal of sod and topsoil to a depth of 0.30 m, a layer of sandy clay (C037) was exposed. This appeared to be an ancient soil horizon, similar to C021 in Trench 1 and was compact and stony. Given its close spatial proximity this is most likely also equivalent to C801/C804 in Trench 6. Excavation of Test Pit 2 revealed a cut C052, presumably the pit identified in geophysical survey. Complex stratigraphy and time constraints resulted in the decision to half-section the fill of C052, however, the depth of deposits present meant that the excavation did not reach the base.

The exposed portion of C052 revealed a cut oriented approximately north–south with a sharp break of slope

Fig. 3.51. Looking northwest at Test Pit 2 with timber C069 visible running north–south across the base, adjacent to various deposits of burnt clay and charcoal.

at the top and a vertical edge. The base of cut was not reached; however, the portion excavated was *c.* 1.90 m deep. C052 truncated two archaeological deposits, the lowest of which, C067, comprised compact silt with occasional inclusions of grit, decayed stone and flecks of burnt clay and charcoal. This was overlain by C066, a 0.70 m deep deposit of yellow/grey clay with inclusions of burnt clay, small stones and very occasional charcoal flecks.

The lowest deposits reached within C052 were C073 and C074, comprising significant layers of charcoal, ash and burnt clay. Overlying both of these was C069, the heavily charred remains of a moderately sized timber, oriented north–south (Fig. 3.51). Identified as oak, a fragment of this was radiocarbon dated to cal AD 1051–1270 (UBA-27558; 849±36 BP), with a 90% probability of being between cal AD 1154–1270; however, this could conceivably be impacted by old wood error and so date to somewhat earlier.

Adjacent to the timber and truncating C074 was C070, a small circular deposit of charcoal 0.20 m in diameter, which was probably the remains of an upright post. Overlying these remains were six layers (C051; C056; C057; C058; C062 and C068) of silty clay measuring between 0.07–0.18 m in depth and containing substantial quantities of ash, charcoal, burnt stone and grit. Much of this material comprised heat altered, partially vitrified clay

10 mm

Fig. 3.52. Refitted fragments of heavily burnt and vitrified clay from Test Pit 2 (Brendan O'Neill).

with inclusions of shale, quartz and mica. It was possible to refit a number of pieces of this burned material, which most likely formed part of an industrial structure such as a furnace (Fig. 3.52).

The burnt layers within C052 were overlain by C059 a deposit of compact clayey silt including some grit, burnt stone and charcoal, with frequent small stones. This was overlain by C065 a deep layer (0.60 m) of very loose stones between which were many voids and a small amount of soil infill, possibly from the overlying C038. C038 was the uppermost fill of C052 but extended beyond the edge of the cut to the northwest. It comprised a layer of loose silty clay with frequent angular stones, animal bone and occasional pieces of burnt clay and charcoal flecks. The animal bone assemblage from C038 included numerous pieces with evidence of butchery and burning (see Carden and Crowley-Champoux, this volume). This deposit produced three bone finds including a small piece of lightly-burnt, polished bone (2014: SF039), probably part of a larger object, a bone blade (2014: SF064) and a single pointed pin beater (2014: SF0068) – see Riddler and Trzaska-Nartowski, this volume. It is likely that C038 represents a mixed refuse deposit within the pit that was initially targeted.

3.5. The eastern complex – Trench 8

Trench 8 was located to the east of the upstanding monument, orientated northeast–southwest and was positioned in line with the possible entrance avenue of Tlachtga, and to investigate a complex series of anomalies identified by geophysical survey. Initially Trench 8 measured 8.00 × 3.00 m but during the course of the excavation was extended 1.00 m to the south. This small trench produced very complex archaeology. The features excavated in Trench 8 are described below moving from north to south in the order that best reflects the stratigraphic sequences and spatial distribution. Rock-cut ditches at each end of the trench form a point of reference for surrounding features.

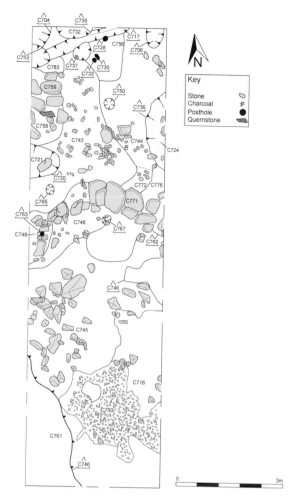

Fig. 3.53. Mid-excavation plan of Trench 8 showing clustered features at northern end and southern ditch.

Removal of the sod and topsoil (C700) up to 0.20 m in depth exposed no visible features and so the underlying plough soil C701, was taken down in 0.10 m spits for another *c.* 0.25 m yielding a few isolated finds including pieces of flint and chert debitage and an iron nail. C702, revealed at a depth of 0.45 m, was a compact layer of grey-orange-brown silty clay that covered the entire trench. This contained frequent flecks of charcoal and some fragmentary animal bone. In the northern half of Trench 8 the removal of C702 revealed a cluster of pits and an east–west aligned ditch C711 (Fig. 3.53; Fig. 3.54).

In the northwest corner of the trench, below C702, was a pit C704, which extended beyond the limit of excavation. Within the trench C704 was approximately oval and measured 0.60 × 0.32 m and was 0.15 m deep (Fig. 3.55). It had gradual sloping sides and a concave base and contained a single fill (C705) of loose, black/brown silty clay with frequent animal bone and lenses of burnt material.

C704 truncated an earlier pit, C753. Like C704 this too extended beyond the limit of excavation but within the trench was semi-circular and measured 0.44 × 0.35 m and was 0.20 m deep. C753 had a sharp break of slope at the top, moderately steep sides and an uneven, concave base which cut through C783, an isolated patch of compact

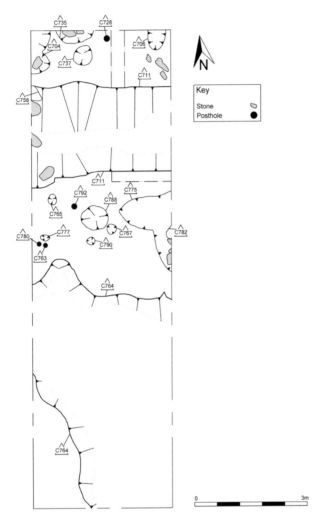

Fig. 3.54. Post-excavation plan of Trench 8 showing ditches C711 and C746 with pit and posthole clusters at the northern end.

yellow clay. C753 contained two fills – C754 and C755. The primary fill C755 was 0.06–0.10 m deep and comprised silty clay with a significant quantity of charcoal. The absence of burnt residue in the surrounding area suggests that this was redeposited burnt material rather than the result of *in-situ* burning. Above C755 was the secondary fill, C754, an orange-brown silty clay with inclusions of orange burnt clay and an average depth of 0.10 m. This upper fill was cut to the north by C704 and to the south by C717 (see below).

To the east of C704 just 0.40 m south of the northern trench limit, was C737, a shallow sub-circular pit with gently sloping sides and a concave base. C737 measured 0.37 × 0.27 m and was 0.06 m in depth. This was cut directly into natural subsoil and partially into C756 (see below). It was filled with C723, a layer of loose, reddish brown sandy clay with numerous inclusions of orange burnt/heated stone/clay (Fig. 3.56). C756, into which the pit was partially cut, was a compact layer of orange-brown sandy clay with fine inclusions of angular stones, charcoal flecks and heat affected material. C756 had a diffuse upper boundary and covered an area of 1.20 × 1.20 m and was 0.07 m in depth. It yielded a small quantity of iron slag and some burnt clay.

Above C723 but extending beyond the cut for the pit was C719, a small sub-rectangular spread of charcoal rich dark grey/brown silty clay which contained a quantity of possible furnace lining and a small amount of burnt clay. C719 also partially overlay C783, an isolated patch of compact yellow clay located in the northwestern side of the trench. This was located south of C717 and cut by pit C753.

East of C704 and cut into C737 was another pit (C735), which again extended beyond the limit of excavation and which contained fills indicative of localised burning activity. C735 was semi-circular and measured 0.74 × 0.32 m and was 0.30 m in depth. Cut into the subsoil and underlying bedrock, the sides of the pit were almost

Fig. 3.55. Pit C704 in the northwest corner of Trench 8 post-excavation.

Fig. 3.56. North facing section through pit C737, showing burnt fill C723.

vertical, and the base was concave. The primary fill was C740, a deposit of coarse sand with flecks of charcoal and occasional small stones. Above this was C739, an extremely loose clay-silt with some orange burnt inclusions and an ash-like texture. A tiny fragment of struck quartz (2016: SF288) was recovered from this context along with a small quantity of possible smithing slag. Above C739 was C738, an extremely soft grey clayey silt 0.06–0.08 m in depth with inclusions of stone charcoal flecks and yellow-burnt material. This contained no finds but included some animal bone. The upper fill of C735 was C732, a soft clayey silt with frequent inclusions of burnt material and flecks of charcoal. In the centre of pit C735, cutting both upper fills C738 and C732, was a shallow posthole C726. Measuring 0.13 × 0.25 m and 0.09 m deep, C726 was semi-circular and contained a single fill (C727), of silty sand with some oxidised subsoil and occasional charcoal and burnt stone.

Above C735 was a shallow, flat-bottomed cut (C717), that ran diagonally northeast–southwest. This linear feature, only 0.07 m deep, cut through the upper fills of pits C704 and C753. It had a single fill (C718) of loose silty clay with occasional small stones and may have been a flue associated with the metalworking feature of C735. The southern edge of C717 cut a posthole (C728), which measured 0.13 × 0.13 by 0.07 m deep. C728 had steep sides, a sharp break of slope and a U-shaped base.

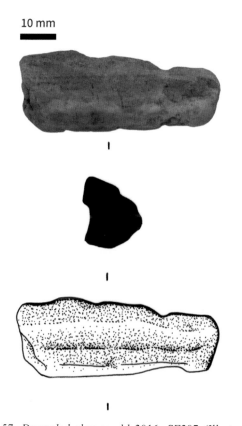

10 mm

Fig. 3.57. Degraded clay mould 2016: SF297 (Illustration: Johnny Ryan).

It contained a single fill (C729) of soft sandy clay with occasional angular stones.

In the north-eastern corner of the trench was another sub-circular pit (C706) with a very sharp upper edge and steep sides cut into subsoil. The primary fill of C706 (C708) was a 0.15 m deep stony layer of silty sand containing some burnt clay. Above this was C707, a 0.07 m deep layer of dark silty clay with red flecks, some charcoal, burnt clay and burnt stones. A degraded clay mould (Fig. 3.57; 2016: SF297) was recovered from this context.

In the centre of the trench at a distance of 0.60 m from the northern baulk were two postholes C730 and C733. Cut into bedrock and subsoil, C730 was oval and measured 0.13 × 0.07 m and 0.11 m deep. It had a single fill (C731) of firm silty clay with occasional light brown flecks. Immediately southwest of C730 was C733, also cut into the bedrock. C733 was circular and measured 0.08 × 0.09 m by 0.14 m deep, with a single fill (C734) of dark silty clay with occasional flecks of burned material.

Immediately south of this cluster of pits and postholes was an east–west orientated ditch C711, which corresponded to the anomaly suggested by the geomagnetic survey (the avenue). The ditch was revealed by removal of the overlying C702 (see above). C711 was cut into both the subsoil and underlying bedrock, it was 1.50 m in width and depth, with a sharp break of slope at the top and uneven sloped sides leading to a sharp break of slope at the base. The base was for the most part flat but somewhat irregular (Fig. 3.58).

The primary fill of C711 was C774, which had an average depth of 0.20 m and consisted of very soft and loose gritty sandy clay, with frequent small (0.10–0.20 m) pieces of broken bedrock and occasional flecks of charcoal. A partial lignite bracelet with incised decoration (2016: SF224 – see Stevens, this volume) and a small flake of struck chert (2016: SF284) were recovered from C774.

Overlying C774 was a deposit of dark brown sandy clay (C773), 0.20 m in depth. C773 contained abundant charcoal, oxidised clay, animal bones and occasional slag. It also contained a significant amount of heat affected stones and magnetic material including debris from a heavily degraded iron object and a quantity of furnace lining (Brendan O'Neill, pers. comm.). A small amount of hammerscale characteristic of secondary smithing, along with a diminutive 'whittle-tang' iron knife blade (Fig. 3.59; 2016: SF239) were recovered from this context. The presence of significant burning along with hammerscale strongly suggests that C773 was linked to ferrous metalworking.

Above C774 and abutting C773 was the main fill of ditch C711, C744. This light-brown sandy clay was 0.21–0.26 m deep and included frequent charcoal flecks and occasional small angular stones. A small amount of iron slag was recovered from this context. Overlying C744 was deposit C743, which ran north–south across the centre of the ditch covering an area of 1.20 × 1.10 m

Fig. 3.58. East–west orientated ditch C711 cut into subsoil and bedrock.

10 mm

Fig. 3.59. Iron 'whittle-tang' knife 2016: SF239 (Goodall 1990, Type C).

to a depth of 0.15 m. C743 was a loose layer of medium sized (<0.10 m) sub-angular to sub-rounded stones, in a matrix of dark silty clay. This was interpreted as a metalled surface created to enable crossing the soft underlying ditch fills. The stones were significantly different in character from those seen in bank construction, notably smaller and more water-rolled, rather than large, angular pieces. A small piece of iron slag was recovered from this context.

One of the upper fills of C711 was C772, which lay above both C743 and C773. This compact yellow-brown clay most likely represents a layer of redeposited subsoil. It appeared in pockets across the ditch area and was very similar to C787 (see below). C772 was truncated by C751,

a shallow sub-circular cut measuring 0.14 × 0.15 m and 0.06 m in depth. C751 had gradual sides and a concave base filled with C752, a soft sandy clay with flecks of orange burnt material and charcoal.

Three deposits, C742, C725 and C710, lay above C711 but are not interpreted as fills and appear to postdate the ditch. C742 covered an area of 1.50 × 1.10 m and was 0.07 m deep. Comprising dark brown silty clay with inclusions of frequent orange flecks and charcoal it suggested some local burning, though not *in situ*. A single flake of struck flint (2016: SF240) and a small piece of iron slag were recovered from this deposit. C725 extended beyond the eastern limit of excavation but within the trench measured 1.90 m north–south and 0.88 m east–west. Varying between 0.03–0.05 m in depth it comprised a layer of redeposited burnt orange clay with large inclusions of charcoal. Finally, C710 comprised loose sandy clay with charcoal flecks. This layer was most likely contemporary with C703 in the centre of the trench (see below) and extended across the entire width of the northern part of Trench 8.

Above the western end of C711, where the ditch exited the trench, the upper fills were covered by C759,

Fig. 3.60. Looking north at paving slabs C771 (foreground) and C759 (rear).

a roughly north–south orientated deposit of large stones. The stones covered a rectangular area of 1.30 × 0.70 m and were surrounded by C758, a soft dark greyish-brown sandy clay with very frequent orange flecks and lenses of charcoal, and small (<0.02 m) angular stones. One of the stones used in C759 (2016: SF244) was dressed and has been identified as a broken quernstone (N. Kelly, pers. comm.). The stones of C759 were set within a layer of dark brown sandy clay with occasional stones (C779). This directly overlay C773 within the underlying ditch, and contained pieces of furnace lining and magnetic material, including hammerscale from secondary smithing. C759 is interpreted as paving and may have been related to C743, the metalled surface, which lay immediately to the southeast. Combined with another area of paving (C771) and another metalled surface towards the southern end of the trench (C750), these stoney features may have formed a pathway. The presence of broken quernstones at early medieval settlement sites has been suggested to mark the abandonment of houses (O'Sullivan and Kenny 2008; O'Sullivan 2017, 112); however, the close spatial association between the broken quernstone and the probable blacksmithing area is curious given the potentially

gendered implications of both blacksmithing and cereal grinding (*ibid.*, 110–113).

In the approximate centre of Trench 8 was C771, an east–west orientated line of substantial limestone slabs, the largest of which measured 0.70 × 0.50 by 0.08 m thick (Fig. 3.60). The slabs were set horizontally, side-by-side and were poorly preserved and fragmented when lifted. The stones of C771 were set in C787, a layer of loose sandy clay containing occasional angular stones and flecks of charcoal.

Truncating the southwestern edge of the ditch C711, was C720, a semi-circular pit which extended beyond the limit of excavation. C720 was cut into the bedrock along the ditch edge and measured 0.61 × 0.59 m and was 0.18 m deep. The cut was somewhat irregular but contained two fills C722 and C721. The primary fill C722 was a clayey silt with frequent angular stones, charcoal and yellow and orange/red flecks, suggesting it was redeposited burnt material. It was overlain by C721 a fine-grained deposit with frequent flecks of charcoal and burned clay.

At the eastern edge of the trench, truncating the upper ditch fill C725 and an earlier pit C775 (see below), was pit C736. C736 extended beyond the limit of excavation but appeared to be sub-circular or perhaps oval and within the trench measured 1.50 m north–south and 0.40 m east–west. It had gently sloping sides and a concave base, and was filled with C724, a deposit of light brown sandy clay with abundant pebbles and sub-angular stones, 0.07–0.10 m deep. C724 also contained some animal bone and a single small flake of burned flint (2016: SF246). Immediately south of and partially below pit C736 was an earlier feature C775. This possible pit also extended beyond the excavation limit, but within the trench measured 2.20 × 0.50 m and was 0.20 m deep. C775 was irregular in shape with rounded corners, gradual concave sides and a concave base. The main fill was C776, a dark black-brown clay with frequent charcoal flecks. This was cut by pit C736 and posthole C762 (see below) and was located directly beneath slabs C771 and the stone setting C782 (see below).

Cut through the centre of C776 was a possible posthole C762, which again extended beyond the limit of excavation. C762 was 0.10 m in diameter and 0.15 m deep. It contained a single fill (C760) of a dark greyish-black friable coarse sand, with a large quantity of charcoal and occasional orange flecks. This deposit had a smooth texture and contained small pieces of highly fragmented animal bone and burnt clay.

Along the southern side of ditch C711 were several more postholes and small pits. Close to the western edge of the trench, just south of pit C720 was C765, another small circular pit or posthole measuring 0.30 × 0.37 m and 0.30 m deep. This was cut into the subsoil, with gradually sloping sides and a concave base. It contained a single fill (C766) of sandy clay with orange flecks and occasional flecks of charcoal. This feature lay beneath both deposits C710 and C702. To the southeast of C765 was a larger oval pit C788, which measured 0.50 × 0.60 m and was 0.30 m deep. C788 had a U-shaped profile with steep sides and a concave base. It was cut through natural subsoil and into bedrock, and held a single fill (C789) of sandy clay flecked with charcoal and occasional stony inclusions. It also included frequent chunks of redeposited subsoil and some fragments of burnt bone. The pit was sealed by one of the slabs of C771. Immediately south of C788 was another small pit or posthole C790. Roughly oval in shape, C790 measured 0.16 × 0.20 m and was 0.10 m in depth with gently sloping sides and a concave base. It contained a single fill (C791), of compact, stone-free silty sand with some charcoal flecks.

The area around and immediately south of these pits was dotted with small postholes and stakeholes (C763; C777; C780 and C792). These had an average diameter of 0.10 m and were filled with deposits of sandy clay flecked with appreciable quantities of charcoal. The cuts for C763 and C777 truncated C769, a layer of heat-cracked stones embedded in a sandy matrix, rich in charcoal and burnt material (C748). The fills of C777 and C763 were particularly charcoal rich and it seems that the stakes

Fig. 3.61. Posthole C767, mid-excavation showing the formal setting of packing stones C770.

in these holes may have burned *in situ*, with this event also causing the stones of C769 to shatter and resulting in the charcoal-rich C748. C748 was spread extensively above these features and extended to the southern end of the trench.

The final feature in this area was a slightly larger sub-circular posthole C767, which measured 0.22 × 0.20 m and was 0.23 m deep. The cut for C767 was well-lined with packing stones (C770), the smallest of which formed a rectangular setting in the centre of the feature (Fig. 3.61). C767 was filled with C768, a dark sandy clay with inclusions of charcoal and burnt clay. This deposit extended around the packing stones and, like all the other postholes in this area, produced no finds.

Just south of the centre of Trench 8 was ditch C746, which corresponded with a feature visible in the geophysical survey (see Carey and Curran, this volume). C746 was orientated approximately northwest–southeast but its edges – within the trench – were not parallel (Fig. 3.62). The southern edge of C746 was cut through the underlying subsoil and into bedrock; however, the northern edge was almost entirely cut into subsoil. It had a steep break of slope at the top, gradually sloping sides and a mostly flat base. C746 was quite shallow measuring just 0.24 m deep, and of variable width from 2.50–3.70 m across.

Laid directly on the bedrock at the base of the eastern part of C746, was an extensive metalled surface (C750). This covered an area of approximately 3.00 × 2.00 m and was composed of small water-rolled pebbles, *c.* 0.05 m in diameter, in a matrix of firm sandy clay with charcoal flecks and occasional pieces of animal bone. Directly above the metalled surface was a stony layer (C741) of large angular pieces of broken bedrock embedded in sandy clay with flecks of charcoal and orange clay.

The primary fill of the ditch was C745, a dark grey-brown sandy clay, which covered an area of 2.85 × 3.00 m and was 0.07 m deep. C745 contained frequent

Fig. 3.62. Looking north at ditch C746 post-excavation.

small stones, charcoal flecks, and traces of burning along with some larger limestone blocks, fragmentary animal bone and a small quantity of slag. It surrounded a layer of larger limestone cobbles (C757), possibly the remains of a collapsed wall, or perhaps associated with the paving stones of C771. Both C745 and C757 partially overlay the metalled surface C750.

In the eastern part of the trench C741 was overlain by C709 (also numbered C715 and C749 during the excavation), an upper fill of the ditch. This deposit of orange-brown sandy clay contained frequent inclusions of angular stone, burnt clay, charcoal and fragmentary animal bones. It varied from 0.05–0.25 m in depth and sloped downwards towards the southeast. C709 was rich in archaeological finds, and included a remarkable hoard of 22 complete and fragmentary Anglo-Saxon silver coins dating from the reign of Aethelstan (r. AD 927–939) to Eadgar (r. AD 959–975). These all pre-dated Eadgar's reform of English coinage in AD 973 and offer a *terminus ante quem* for the deposition of C709/C715 (see Woods, this volume).

In the western part of the trench the primary fill C745 was covered by C713, which extended beyond the western

10 mm

Fig. 3.63. 2016: SF231 Iron 'whittle tang' knife (Goodall 1990, Type A).

limit of excavation was C713. This dark grey charcoal-rich deposit of sandy clay covered an area of 3.60 × 1.70 m and was 0.15 m deep. C713 contained frequent small angular stones, abundant animal bone and charred cereal grain. Along the western side of the trench C745 and C713 were both partially covered by C748, a charcoal rich deposit, which also extended towards the northern end of the trench.

Also in the western part of the trench, above C713 and C709, and covering an area of 2.39 × 1.24 m and up to 0.08 m in depth was C712, a dark brown sandy clay rich in charcoal and animal bone, some of which was burnt and highly fragmented, in addition to a quantity of charred grain. An early medieval pig fibula needle was recovered from this deposit, broken in two pieces (2016: SF097 – see Riddler and Trzaska-Nartowski, this volume).

The uppermost archaeological layer exposed within the mid- to southern portion Trench 8 was C703. This was a transitional layer between the fills of C746 and the plough soil. C703 was 0.10–0.50 m deep and comprised sandy clay with frequent inclusions of angular stone, animal bone and occasional flecks of charcoal. It produced a small iron whittle-tang knife (Fig. 3.63; 2016: SF231) and a fragment of a possible grinding stone. A partial antler coronet-ring (2016: SF294) was recovered from the southern part of this deposit (see Riddler and Trzaska-Nartowski, this volume).

3.6. Dating Tlachtga (Stephen Davis)

A total of 22 AMS radiocarbon dates have been obtained from the site alongside the date ranges of the 22 Anglo-Saxon coins recovered (Table 3.6.1; Fig. 3.64; Fig. 3.65). These have been calibrated with OxCal 4.4.4 (Bronk Ramsey 2009), using the IntCal20 Northern Hemisphere calibration curve (Reimer *et al.* 2020). Where available $\delta^{13}C$ and $\delta^{15}N$ figures are reported.

One of the key initial aims of the excavation was to try to date the three major phases of the site observed in geophysical survey. Clearly the complexity of any site is not fully expressed by such surveys and some features would repay further dating.

The majority of the features excavated on site were ditches and ditch fills. While every attempt was made to date short-life material (either charcoal or animal bone) from primary contexts as a proxy for construction dates, the potential for cross contamination is always present. It is clear that in some locations recutting of ditches

occurred (*e.g.* Trench 4, inner and middle ditch) and that both Tlachtga and the Southern Enclosure despite secure early medieval dates are constructed adjacent to, and in part overlapping with a very large Bronze Age monument. This is evident in both the material culture (*e.g.* the hair ring in Trench 7 – Maguire, this volume) and the radiocarbon chronology (*e.g.* dates from Trench 5).

3.6.1. The Hillfort Phase

Fills from the three ditches of this phase excavated at Trench 4 all returned similar dates, with the inner ditch (1122–926 cal BC; Beta-420644; 2860±30 BP) slightly earlier than the middle (1014–836 cal BC; Beta-420643; 2790±30 BP; 83.8% probability of being between 1014–892 cal BC) and the outer (912–807 cal BC; Beta-410642; 2710±30 BP). These dates are very consistent with reported dates for the start of hillfort construction in Ireland (see O'Brien and O'Driscoll 2017, 321–341; Grogan 2005, 128–132). Two further Bronze Age dates were obtained on the site with similar date ranges: the fill of a post hole adjacent to Trench 3 returned a date of 1259–1015 cal BC (UBA-27559; 2937±38 BP), while a date from C547, an isolated basal fill of the second Tlachtga ditch returned a date of 1260–1051 cal BC (Beta-446132; 2950±30 BP). Together these suggest the earliest monumental activity recorded on the hilltop began no earlier than *c.* 1260 cal BC, with the construction of the hillfort a little later. This places it within the latter half of the middle Bronze Age (Ginn and Plunkett's 2020 'Settlement Phase 3') and closely contemporary with nearby Faughan Hill (Dowling and Shot 2023). While the dates for the three circuits overlap, the inner has a date range that begins

Table 3.6.1. AMS ^{14}C dates from the Hill of Ward, Co. Meath.

Lab no.	Context	Material	Trench	Brief description	Date	SD	Cal range (2-sigma)	$\delta^{13}C$ (‰)	$\delta^{15}N$ (‰)
UBA-27558	C057	Oak charcoal	TP2	Burned timber, Test Pit 2	849	36	cal AD 1051–1078 (5.5%) cal AD 1154–1270 (90.0%)	N/A	N/A
UBA-32858	C818	Cattle bone	6	Securely contexted deposit beneath central mound	1071	43	cal AD 895–924 (20.6%) cal AD 950–1024 (74.8%)	N/A	N/A
UBA-45319	C914	*Prunus* charcoal	7	Recut and main fill of inner Tlachtga ditch	1071	21	cal AD 895–924 (20.6%) cal AD 950–1034 (74.8%)	N/A	N/A
Beta-446131	C549	Pomaceous charcoal	5	Metalworking area within 2nd outer Tlachtga ditch	1150	30	cal AD 773–789 (7.5%) cal AD 824–988 (88%)	-24.9	N/A
UBA-45325	C745	*Salix* charcoal	8	Primary fill of southern ditch within Trench 8	1150	23	cal AD 773–788 (7.4%) cal AD 827–862 (11.9%) cal AD 868–978 (76.1%)	N/A	N/A

(Continued)

Table 3.6.1. (Continued)

Lab no.	Context	Material	Trench	Brief description	Date	SD	Cal range (2-sigma)	$\delta^{13}C$ (‰)	$\delta^{15}N$ (‰)
UBA-45326	C714	*Prunus spinosa* charcoal	8	Slump of construction material within ditch C746	1158	23	cal AD 772–790 (10.8%) cal AD 822–904 (48%) cal AD 912–976 (36.7%)	N/A	N/A
UBA-32857	C521	Probable cattle bone	5	Southern enclosure, intercut with Tlachtga ditch	1213	42	cal AD 678–749 (19.8%) cal AD 758–895 (72.3%) cal AD 924–950 (3.4%)	N/A	N/A
UBA-32234	C460	Horse bone	5	Basal date, 2nd outer Tlachtga ditch	1285	35	cal AD 660–776 (89.2%) cal AD 790–822 (6.3%)	N/A	N/A
Beta-388456	C063	Human rib	3	Infant burial, Trench 3	1580	30	AD 420–556	-21.7	10.8
Beta-386849	C026	Fox tooth	1	Basal date, penultimate Tlachtga ditch	1610	30	AD 412–542	-21.1	N/A
Beta-386850	C048	Cattle bone	3	Basal fill southern enclosure (cattle bone)	1610	30	AD 412–542	-22.5	N/A
UBA-45318	C919	*Corylus* charcoal	7	Basal date or inner Tlachtga ditch, original cut	1610	23	AD 416–538		
UBA-45317	C822	*Alnus* charcoal	6	Burned area within basal fill beneath central mound, securely contexted	1665	25	cal AD 260–279 (7.0%) cal AD 337–435 (84.9%) cal AD 465–474 (1.1%) cal AD 502–508 (0.6%) cal AD 516–530 (1.9%)	N/A	N/A
Beta-436097	C478	Grain (hulled barley)	4	Drying kiln outside BA enclosure	2030	30	146–140 cal BC (0.6%) 108 cal BC–cal AD 68 (94.8%)	-24.9	N/A
UBA-32235	C470	Horse bone	4	Main fill of inner ditch, BA enclosure	2248	53	400–176 cal BC	N/A	N/A
Beta-386851	C009	Cattle bone	2	Main fill of inner ditch, BA enclosure (2014)	2340	30	516–364 cal BC	-22.6	N/A
Beta-420642	C429	Human molar	4	Fill of outer ditch, BA enclosure	2710	30	912–807 cal BC	-21.4	13.7
UBA-32856	C402	Cattle tooth	4	Fill of recut of recut C475 (middle ditch)	2764	30	992–828 cal BC	N/A	N/A
Beta-420643	C427	Cattle bone	4	Base of middle ditch, BA enclosure	2790	30	1014–892 cal BC (83.8%) 881–836 cal BC (11.7%)	-21.8	5.4
Beta-420644	C479	Cattle bone	4	Base of inner ditch, BA enclosure	2860	30	1122–926 cal BC	-22.1	5.9
UBA-27559	C005	Hazel charcoal	3	Posthole outside southern enclosure	2937	38	1234–1015 cal BC (92.4%) 1259–1242 cal BC (3.1%)	N/A	N/A
Beta-446132	C547	Hazel charcoal	5	Bedrock infill, 2nd outer Tlachtga ditch	2950	30	1260–1051 cal BC	-24.2	N/A

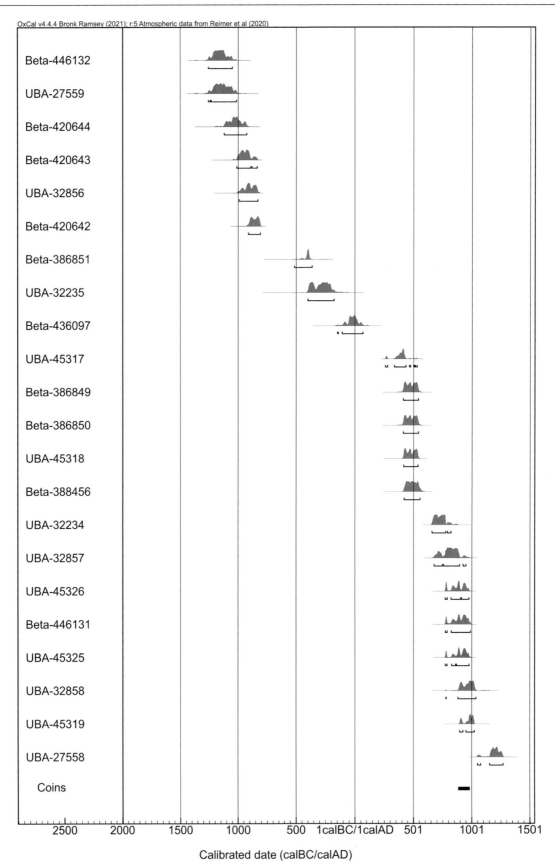

Fig. 3.64. Calibrated AMS radiocarbon dates from the Hill of Ward, Co. Meath. Calibration undertaken in OxCal 4.4.4 (Bronk Ramsey 2009) using the IntCal20 calibration curve (Reimer et al. *2020).*

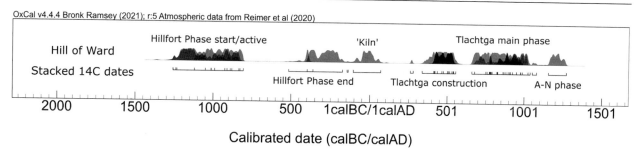

Fig. 3.65. Stacked AMS radiocarbon dates and site phasing from the Hill of Ward, Co. Meath. Calibration undertaken in OxCal 4.4.4 (Bronk Ramsey 2009) using the IntCal20 calibration curve (Reimer et al. 2020).

c. 100 years before the second ditch, while the third range begins another century later, with inner and outer ranges not overlapping.

Dates from the fills of the three hillfort ditches provide an incomplete picture of the monument through time. From the outermost ditch a human mandible was directly dated to 912–807 cal BC (UBA-32856; 2764±30 BP) while a recut of the middle ditch also returned a late Bronze Age date of 992–828 cal BC (UBA-32856; 2764±30 BP). These dates suggest the site was still in use at this time. The main fills of the inner ditch at Trenches 2 and 4 both returned much later dates: cattle bone from Trench 2 yielded 516–364 cal BC (Beta-386851; 2340±30 BP), while horse bone from Trench 4 provided a date of 400–176 cal BC (UBA-32235; 2248±53 BP). These are likely to date the final closing of this phase of the monument. Further dates from these fills would improve confidence in this latter suggestion; however, the fills appeared uniform in nature and selection of appropriate dating material is therefore not clearcut.

3.6.2. The possible kiln

The feature located outside of the Hillfort Phase, tentatively identified as a kiln, included plentiful securely contexted material for dating. Three grains of charred barley were dated to 146 cal BC–cal AD 68 (Beta-436097; 2340±30 BP), with a 94.8% probability of being between 108 cal BC–cal AD 68. This is as little as 30 years after horse bone was deposited in Trench 4, but most likely at least 70 years. This could potentially be seen as a continuation of the Bronze Age/Iron Age phase; however, no other dates overlapping this range have been obtained, so it is likely that this postdates the main phase of activity at the Hill of Ward at this time.

3.6.3. The Southern Enclosure

The dates for the Southern Enclosure were securely contexted on both the infant burial at cal AD 420–556 (Beta-388456; 1580±30 BP) and adjacent *in-situ* animal bone directly at the base of the rock cut ditch, immediately above bedrock at cal AD 412–542 (Beta-386850; 1610±30 BP). Short of a recut that removed the entire

fill of an earlier structure, these dates securely constrain the construction of this enclosure.

3.6.4. Tlachtga – construction phase (Early Medieval 1)

The basal dates for the innermost ditch (cal AD 416–538; UBA-45318; 1610±23 BP) and penultimate ditch (cal AD 412–542; Beta-386850; 1610±30 BP), as well as the securely contexted burned area beneath the central mound (UBA-45317; AD 260–530; 1665±25 BP; 84.9% probability of being between cal AD 337–435) closely correspond to those from the Southern Enclosure and fall within a very narrow date range (three dates between Tlachtga and the Southern Enclosure share an identical mid-point). This strongly suggests that these represent a genuine construction date for the site – statistically speaking the same date as the Southern Enclosure. As previously discussed, this is broadly contemporary with the earliest hypothesised construction dates for multivallate ringforts across Ireland (see O'Sullivan *et al.* 2021a, 64–70), and very much contemporary with the dates recently published for Garranes, Co. Cork (O'Brien and Hogan 2021, 94). The basal date from the second outer ditch in Trench 5 is somewhat later (cal AD 660–822; UBA-32234; 1285±35 BP). This is more likely as a result of the dated material having originated during the later use of the ditch than implying sequential construction.

3.6.5. Tlachtga – early medieval phase (Early Medieval 2)

The securely contexted metalworking hearth within the penultimate Tlachtga ditch (cal AD 773–988; Beta-446131; 1150±30 BP), a burned horizon within the main fill in Trench 7 (cal AD 886–1023; UBA-45319; 1070±21 BP) and the securely contexted sub-mound habitation debris of C818 (cal AD 895–1034; UBA-32858; 1071±43 BP) all returned dates within a similar range. Two further radiocarbon dates from ditch fills within Trench 8 also returned near identical dates between the late 8th century to late 10th century (cal AD 773–978; UBA-45325; 1150±23 BP for the primary fill with a probability of 76.1% of being between cal AD 868–978; UBA-45326;

AD 772–976; 1158±23 BP for slump of apparent construction material). The date from C818 provides a *terminus post quem* for the construction of the central mound.

This range of dates is also shared by the hoard of coins from Trench 8, which provide a *terminus post quem* for the closing of the southern part of Trench 8 of *c.* AD 973. It should be stressed that these represent only part of the overall sequence, even within the features excavated at Trench 8: they represent the terminal phase of a structure that might have been in use for decades or more previously. Taken together these suggest an earliest date for this phase of the late 8th century AD with the very latest possible date being early in the 11th century AD, but most likely in the late 10th century AD. This later phase of activity is not matched at Garranes (O'Brien and Hogan 2021) and perhaps suggests a phase of abandonment followed by a later, renewed settlement phase.

3.6.6. Tlachtga – early medieval to Anglo-Norman phase

Only a single date was obtained from this phase, represented by a series of heavily burned deposits identified on the summit of the central mound (UBA-27558; cal AD 1051–1270; 849±36 BP), including possible structural timbers and industrial material. There is a 90% probability that this date originated in the range cal AD 1154–1270. The only timber identified here was oak; however, the timber dated was clearly a large *in-situ* piece, potentially structural in nature, so it was felt this offered a better prospect for dating than the disarticulated animal bone above it. A second confirmatory date from shorter life material here might be beneficial to refine the overall chronology of this phase. This date provides a *terminus ante quem* for the completion of mound construction.

4

Interpreting the results: telling the story of Tlachtga

4.1. The Hillfort Phase

With the exception of isolated features in the area of the Southern Enclosure, the earliest monumental construction for which excavation evidence exists on site appears to be the large trivallate enclosure underlying the existing monument of Tlachtga. Geophysical surveys in the surrounding landscape (Carey and Curran, this volume) place this construction in the context of likely middle Bronze Age funerary monuments and field systems.

Suggestions of earlier activity are present, both in the form of the fragmentary pecked stone object (O'Sullivan, this volume), the lithics/polished stone artefacts and the two small fragments of middle Neolithic pottery recovered over the three seasons of excavation; however, these are all portable objects and not necessarily indicative of an earlier phase of construction at the site. As a parallel, the nearby Class 2 hillfort at Faughan Hill encloses elements of middle Neolithic date (*c.* 3600 cal BC) but lacks the very substantial early medieval phase seen at the Hill of Ward (Dowling and Schot 2023); this suggests the strong possibility for a now obscured Neolithic phase at the Hill of Ward that precedes the first trivallate enclosure.

The earliest visible large enclosure was of unusual form (closely spaced multivallate), but its size and hilltop setting argue in favour of it being classified as a hillfort. The classification of hillforts and hilltop enclosures is discussed extensively by Grogan (1995, 111–121) and Grogan *et al.* (1996), with more recent discussion in O'Brien and O'Driscoll (2017, 1–12). The internal area of this phase (*c.* 2.15 ha) closely matches the average area calculated by Grogan *et al.* (1996) for Class 2 (multivallate) sites. As previously noted, there are clear parallels with geophysical surveys at the Hill of Lloyd (Dowling 2015) and at Faughan Hill (Dowling and Schot 2023), the recently published dates from which closely match those

from the Hill of Ward enclosure (see below). It seems likely that this group of Class 2 hillforts which incorporate closely spaced multivallation represent a local tradition in this part of Meath.

The three ditches of the Hillfort Phase deepen from the outermost inward. The outer ditch was shallow and V-shaped, the middle deeper but more irregular and the innermost ditch very broad and flat-bottomed. Apart from the outermost ditch where the V-shaped cut essentially disregarded the form of the bedrock, the other two ditches made consistent use of the limestone bedding planes to form either a flat (innermost) or sloping (middle) base to the ditch. The inner ditch was exposed in two locations, at Trench 2 and Trench 4. The sequence at Trench 2 was significantly less complex than at Trench 4 – there was no obvious variation within the animal bone-rich fill, and no associated features beyond the cut of the ditch itself. At Trench 4 there were significant differences. On both sides of the inner ditch at Trench 4 there were a series of small rock-cut stakeholes. The most likely function of these was to assist in the construction of a bank, potentially providing an anchor for a stone and earthen construction. Similar concentrations of small stakeholes have been found beneath the bank at Rathnagree, Co. Wicklow (O'Brien and O'Driscoll 2017, 257). Although the exact function of these remains unclear, at Rathnagree they may have formed part of pre-bank palisade. The absence of matching stakeholes at Trench 2 is unlikely to be because of a genuine absence, as these could well have been cut into subsoil rather than bedrock and subsequently destroyed by agricultural activity. Both the middle and inner ditches within Trench 4 were subject to episodes of recutting, which were not apparent within the fill of Trench 2.

Basal dates for the three ditches at Trench 4 range from 1122–926 cal BC (Beta-420644; 2860±30 BP) for the inner ditch, to 1014–836 cal BC (Beta-420643; 2790±30 BP) for the middle ditch and 912–807 cal BC (Beta-420642; 2710±30 BP) for the outer ditch: the probable construction dates from the inner and outer ditch dates do not overlap. This potentially provides an approximate timeframe for the construction of the monument, a maximum span of a little over 300 years, a minimum of *c.* 120 years. While there is overlap between the dates of the two innermost ditches, a significant proportion of the 2-sigma range of the inner ditch is earlier than the dates from the other circuits. This implies that the inner ditch circuit was begun first, followed by the middle and the outer. The date from the outer ditch was from a human mandible, one of two partial burials recovered from the hillfort ditches (the other only as a single tooth). Cleary (2005, 34) discusses the presence of such deposits in such liminal spaces as serving to '[reinforce] the distinction between the settlement and the wider society'. It is also possible that these depositions marked important stages in the evolution of the monument (Brück 1999). As such these may represent final closing deposits for this stage of the monument.

There is little evidence as to the function of this monument: much of the interior is overbuilt by later features and while there is significant ecofactual evidence, especially in the form of animal bone (see Carden and Crowley-Champoux, this volume), no clear structural remains are present save for the enclosing ditches and associated stakeholes. As regards artefactual remains, a number of later prehistoric bone implements were retrieved, most of which find their clearest parallels in hide-working toolkits (*e.g.* Christadou and Legrand-Pineau 2005) or the spinning of yarn (spindle whorls). Meat was also clearly cooked and consumed at the site during this phase, and perhaps brought either as live animals or as prepared joints by different local groups in a similar way to that demonstrated at Navan Fort in the Iron Age (Madgwick *et al.* 2019; see Carden and Crowley-Champoux, this volume). A silver-gilt hair ornament was also recovered that is also likely to be contemporary with this phase of occupation and perhaps hints at high status occupation.

Two dates were obtained from fills of the inner ditch, one from Trench 2, the other from C470, which sealed the episode of recutting in Trench 4 and represents the closing of the ditch. The 2-sigma ranges of these two dates overlap, with the date from Trench 2 returning 516–364 cal BC (Beta-386851; 2340±30 BP) and that from Trench 4 400–176 cal BC (UBA-32235; 2248±53 BP). These dates suggest that the closing of the inner ditch took place in the early centuries BC, which is late for Irish hillforts, most of which appear to terminate at the end of the Bronze Age (O'Brien and O'Driscoll 2017, 321–341), and most likely later than the nearby site at Faughan Hill (Dowling and Schot 2023, 15).

While the nature of this closing event is unclear, the complete lack of topographic expression of this substantial rock-cut monument suggests that it may have been intentionally backfilled as part of its abandonment. In this it may demonstrate parallels with the formalised destruction by fire events noted at hillforts in Co. Wicklow (O'Brien and O'Driscoll 2017, 408–410) where the aim seems to be a performative obliteration of the site rather than just a partial destruction – the 'ritual dismemberment of a symbolic location' (*ibid.*, 410). This is suggested by the authors to have predominantly been the result of tribal conflict but could also represent the ritualised closing of a site, perhaps associated with major societal change (*ibid.*, 409–410).

Immediately outside the Bronze Age enclosure, excavation revealed a possible Iron Age cereal drying kiln, dating to between 146 cal BC–cal AD 68 (Beta-436097; 2030±30 BP), 94.8% probability of this being between 108 cal BC–cal AD 68. This is typical for its geographic location and period (*e.g.* Monk and Power 2012). Its location could imply that the people who constructed it were aware of the position of the Bronze Age enclosure although this is not necessarily the case.

It is unclear if or how the presence of the earlier enclosure influenced the builders of the later monuments of the Southern Enclosure and Tlachtga, if at all. Although the structures clearly overlap spatially, the Hill of Ward remains a strategic location and an obvious place to construct either a defensive earthwork or a ritual monument. There is apparent evidence in the deposition of prehistoric finds in later phases that the location was recognised in some way as having a longer history, but it seems likely that most or all of the Bronze Age structure was invisible to the later monument builders.

4.2. The Southern Enclosure

While only a small portion of the circumference of this feature was excavated, this resulted in the recovery of a complete infant burial of transitional late Iron Age to early medieval date. This burial was located immediately above bedrock within a semi-circular formal stone setting and overlain by a series of large slabs. A number of large pieces of cattle bone were placed alongside the burial on the base of the ditch. These may represent token burial offerings of some description, as discussed by McCormick (1985) from the perspective of Irish prehistoric monuments. Again, dating material from within the fill of a ditch cannot unequivocally date its construction; however, the animal bone and human skeletal material returned very nearly the same 2-sigma date range: cal AD 420–556 (Beta-388456; 1580±30 BP) for the burial and cal AD 412–542 (Beta-386850; 1610±30 BP) for the cattle bone. The relationship between this enclosure and the main enclosure of Tlachtga was unclear prior to excavation: with sites such as An Forrad/Teach Cormac at Tara there is an assumption that a later enclosure in some way drew power or influence from an earlier phase of monument ('sacral potency' – Dowling

2006). However, at the conjoined enclosure of Rathnew on the Hill of Uisneach, Schot (2006, 54–58) argues that both eastern and western enclosures were contemporaneous, in particular noting the absence of a clear fosse along the western perimeter of the eastern enclosure (*i.e.* where the enclosures are conjoined).

Excavation of the junction between the Southern Enclosure and Tlachtga at Trench 5 suggested either that the Southern Enclosure pre-dates Tlachtga or that the two monuments were contemporaneous in construction. Only a very small section of the Southern Enclosure ditch fills remained visible, and the fill had apparently been removed by the cut of the Tlachtga ditch. The dating evidence at this junction remains inconclusive: the bedrock infill of the second outer Tlachtga ditch returned a Bronze Age date (1260–1051 cal BC; Beta-446132; 2590±BP). This probably relates to residual charcoal from the earlier phase of monument construction. Two further dates were obtained from the intersection of the Southern Enclosure with Tlachtga and the Tlachtga ditch itself, returning cal AD 678–950 (UBA-32857; 1213±42 BP) and cal AD 660–822 (UBA-32234; 1285±35 BP) respectively (in the latter case 89.2% probability of being between cal AD 660–776), despite the stratigraphic relationship of these features being reversed. Given the slightly earlier dates obtained on the Tlachtga ditch elsewhere, this is likely to represent material incorporated into the ditch fill from later phases of construction. Although significant quantities of animal bone were retrieved from this phase of the monument it seems likely that its primary function was not settlement but ritual, perhaps as a foundation monument on the hill prior to the construction of Tlachtga. The use of this enclosure as a funerary monument is comparable to the situation at Mullamast Hill, Co. Kildare (O'Brien 2021, 51) where extended infant burials were encountered in association with significant quantities of cattle bone (Lenihan and Dennehy 2010, 46–47), albeit in a far smaller enclosing structure.

4.3. The main enclosure of Tlachtga

Tlachtga is a complex, multiperiod structure with construction and remodelling taking place over several centuries. A likely construction date was obtained from the outer bank-ditch circuit (Trench 1), which returned a 2-sigma range of cal AD 412–542 (Beta-386849; 1610±30 BP). The innermost Tlachtga ditch, excavated within Trench 7, also yielded a date of AD 416–538 (UBA-45318; 1610±23 BP). Both of these dates are directly comparable with the infant burial and cattle bone from the Southern Enclosure at Trench 3. A slightly earlier radiocarbon date was obtained for material directly beneath the central platform, which may record an initial preparatory stage in the construction of the monument (see below).

If we accept that neither of these dates represents residual material then the implication is that Tlachtga was

constructed at the same time as the Southern Enclosure, or at least the features were built within the same 2-sigma radiocarbon date range. The outermost enclosing element that returned this date is the same circuit that intersects the Southern Enclosure, and it seems likely that the concentric embankments were constructed at the same time. As with the Hillfort Phase, the outermost ditch was apparently more cosmetic in nature than genuinely defensive, being broad but very shallow, and apparently received little material from the main body of the site. The penultimate ditch was not fully exposed but appeared to be moderately shallow and rock-cut, again not of a comparable scale to the inner circuits.

The section of ditch excavated at Trench 5 was placed to attempt to disentangle the construction sequence of Tlachtga and the Southern Enclosure (see above). Even with excavation this proved difficult. Three further dates were obtained from Trench 5, all of which are firmly early medieval with overlapping 2-sigma ranges. These likely represent the most active phase of the site of Tlachtga itself, some centuries after its initial construction. Here, the Southern Enclosure ditch returned a date of cal AD 678–950 (UBA-32857; 1213±42 BP), substantially later than in the excavated section in Trench 3. Meanwhile, the Tlachtga ditch here returned a date of cal AD 660–822 (UBA-32234; 1285±35 BP) and a third date from a securely contexted metalworking hearth within the Tlachtga ditch, returned cal AD 773–988 (Beta-446131; 1150±30 BP), with an 88% probability of being between cal AD 824–988. Taken together these three dates suggest a peak in activity on site between the late 7th century and late 10th century AD. This phase of activity is also hinted at elsewhere (*e.g.* the central mound and eastern complex). Preliminary analysis of crucible fragments within the Trench 5 metalworking hearth suggests working of copper alloy (brass) and silver within the ditch circuit (O'Neill, this volume). A recut of the inner Tlachtga ditch at Trench 7 provided a date of cal AD 887–1023 (UBA-45319; 1071±21 BP), substantially overlapping the early medieval dates obtained from Trench 5, the third Tlachtga ditch, as well as the intercut with the Southern Enclosure and activity beneath the central mound (see below). It remains unclear whether there is continuity between the initial construction of the monument and the later phase of activity that is so clearly evident.

4.4. The central platform

Prior to excavation the central mound of Tlachtga was interpreted as an earlier feature (*e.g.* a mound barrow or possibly a megalithic tomb; see Halpin and Newman 2006, 358) that had been subsequently enclosed. Excavation in the first season revealed the presence of *in-situ* burned timbers (all oak) on the top of the mound. These dated to cal AD 1051–1270 (UBA-27558; 849±36 BP; 90% probability of between cal AD 1154–1270), or possibly

Fig. 4.1. Kilfinane Motte (LI056-024), looking north-northwest. Image copyright Neil Jackman, Abarta Heritage.

later given the potential for old wood error (the date was obtained on oak charcoal as this was the only *in-situ* material available). It was therefore, given the range of dates, unclear whether the burned structure on the mound represents a native Irish structure or an Anglo-Norman construction. Unfortunately, it was not possible to examine this feature further in subsequent seasons.

The central mound was most likely rapidly constructed in a single phase. The laying of a thick organic layer prior to the raising of the mound provided a very secure context, and a *terminus post quem* for the earliest phases of mound construction. This deposit also sealed a conspicuous burnt feature, marking a clear phase of pre-mound activity. Radiocarbon dates again closely fit the existing chronological framework seen elsewhere on site. The burning phase yielded a date of cal AD 260–530 (UBA-45317; 1665±25 BP), the greater part of this range overlapping with the dates seen for the earliest phases of Tlachtga and with the Southern Enclosure.

The main remaining phase of sub-mound activity (the culturally rich C818) dated to cal AD 895–1034 (UBA-32858; 1071±43 BP). This suggests that in its initial phase Tlachtga most likely took the form of conventional, if very large multivallate ringfort, enclosing an open central area rather than the mound evident in its present/final form. This spans the supposed 'destruction by fire' event noted in the Annals of Ulster/Annals of the Four Masters (see Bhreathnach, this volume), substantially overlaps with the dates seen in the secondary activity phase within the Tlachtga ditches and may also overlap with the date

obtained at the surface of the mound given the possible old wood error. The mound was, therefore, raised at the very latest early in the 11th century AD: as such, while it has clear similarities to later Anglo-Norman motte castles, it certainly pre-dates Anglo-Norman activity in Ireland and possibly the Norman invasion of Britain. Given the date, O'Keeffe (2021, 50) has argued that large mounds as that at Tlachtga and the strikingly similar site of Kilfinane, Co. Limerick (Fig. 4.1, LI056-024) might effectively represent pre-Norman mottes or at least 'power-display mounds' (see O'Sullivan *et al.* 2021a, 78–79). The final excavated stage at the site suggests that significant activity, perhaps industrial in nature, was occurring within the central portion of Tlachtga perhaps as late as the 13th century AD.

4.5. The eastern complex

For a small trench this area revealed some extremely complex archaeology, and exactly what these features represent remains somewhat unclear. The two ditches suggested by the geomagnetic survey were evident in excavation, although one side of the broad southern ditch was mostly beyond the limit of excavation. The strong magnetic signature of the northern cut in particular was explained by the presence of metalworking debris, including hammerscale. This indicates the presence of secondary smithing – *i.e.* blacksmithing. Some of this hammerscale was embedded within a burned matrix, possibly the remains of a clay floor. Around this a number of pits, postholes and stakeholes most likely indicate the presence of structural remains, but offer no clear pattern. Similarly, some of the stone tumble observed in the trench may be the remains of a wall, but there is no clear building form evident. Given its complexity, this area may require a larger trench to fully understand.

The discovery of a hoard of Anglo-Saxon coins offers a clear *terminus ante quem* for these features – the latest of the coins are Eadgar pennies of the late 10th century, none of which post-date the coinage reform of AD 973. To corroborate this, two radiocarbon dates were obtained from a slump of construction material and from the primary fill of the southern ditch. These returned near identical dates of cal AD 772–976 (UBA-45326; 1158±23 BP) and cal AD 773–978 (UBA-45325; 1150±23 BP) respectively. Most of this range pre-dates the latest of the coins, the implication being that the structural elements in Trench 8 pre-date the deposition of the hoard by as much as two centuries. Once again, these dates overlap with those for the early medieval floruit of the site and are very similar to the date obtained from beneath the central Tlachtga mound (cal AD 776–1036). It is unclear how activity at the eastern complex interacted with contemporary events at Tlachtga, or indeed with activity further east (see Carey and Curran, this volume); however, it seems likely that this was a subsidiary site — perhaps a specialist metalworking centre with associated settlement activity — that existed alongside Tlachtga in time and space.

4.6. Excavations at Tlachtga: refining the narrative and contextualising the site

The Hill of Ward has clearly seen repeated use as a symbolic and defensive location over millennia. During this time it has been home to multiple phases of enclosure, mostly hewn from the bedrock sitting just beneath the soil, and repeated remodelling, especially in its later phases. Towards the end of the 2nd millennium BC, construction of a large enclosure was begun, focused on the summit of the hill. Whether this enclosed a pre-existing monument is impossible to say, although some funerary structures or field systems were already present on the hilltop. Initially this large enclosure comprised a single substantial ditch circuit, followed in rapid succession by two further circuits, spaced closely together. The entrance to this enclosure is not clearly defined, but much of the monument is obscured by later phases of construction. A linear routeway approaching from the southeast is visible in the geomagnetic survey and may represent an early approach to the site. It is likely that this construction was contemporaneous with similar enclosures at Faughan Hill and perhaps the Hill of Lloyd.

This Hillfort Phase remained in use for several centuries; however, its primary function remains unclear, again owing largely to how little of the interior survives beyond the later phases of monumentality on the hill. It

was likely a focus of communal activity, perhaps related to food redistribution (primarily in the form of meat-based feasting – e.g. Hayden 2014, 233–295) with at least some emphasis seeming to have been on the working of hides and spinning of yarn. It is also important to note that this monument may have held a number of functions in a period of use that lasted almost 1,000 years.

At the end of this period – most likely in the early to middle Iron Age – the site was deliberately closed and abandoned. Why this occurred is unclear, but it post-dates the late Bronze Age abandonment phase usually encountered in Irish hillforts (see O'Brien and O'Driscoll 2017, 321–341) and pre-dates the so-called 'Late Iron Age Lull', an oft-cited but apparently asynchronous woodland regeneration phase noted across the island of Ireland in pollen diagrams from the late 1st millennium BC to the early centuries AD (Mitchell and Ryan 1997; Coyle-McClung 2013; Chique *et al.* 2017, 17). What took place on the hill from the end of this Bronze Age/Iron Age phase until the beginning of late Iron Age/early medieval construction is unclear; however, a possible cereal drying kiln dating to the middle Iron Age was identified beyond the outer ditch, demonstrating that the hill was still in use at this time and likely held at least some residual importance.

4.6.1. Building Tlachtga

A second major construction project began on the hill most likely in the 5th century AD. This consisted of two monuments constructed almost simultaneously: a 40 m diameter plectrum-shaped enclosure and a very large trivallate or quadrivallate ringfort. It is unknown whether the inner Tlachtga bank was constructed at this time (*i.e.* the original monument was trivallate) or if it is an original feature. It is not possible to understand the conception of these monuments in relation to earlier phases of activity, but the Southern Enclosure was wholly located within the interior of the Bronze Age phase, while Tlachtga itself avoided the summit of the hill and was instead located slightly to its northeast. Tlachtga overbuilt a significant part of the earlier monumental phase, its outer ramparts extending beyond the outermost earlier ditch to the northeast.

Excavation suggests that the Southern Enclosure was constructed first, but only just, then Tlachtga was constructed to conjoin with it, but not obliterate it – the overall plan of construction may well have been a unified design as described by Schot (2006) for Rathnew, Hill of Uisneach. Tlachtga initially took the form of a large ringfort with ditches deepening from outside inwards (see comparisons with Knockhouse Lower – Walsh 2020a; 2020b). Given its size and the number of vallations (at least three) this was most likely a very high-status defended settlement, potentially with royal associations (Grogan 2005, 130). Evidence of this first early medieval phase is sparse, in part because of subsequent remodelling; however, in the Southern Enclosure at least one infant was buried and cattle bones were laid at the base of the rock cut ditch in what appears to be a ritual manner.

The site most likely persisted in this form until at least the 8th century AD, after which significant changes occurred (although it is possible there was an intervening abandonment phase). In the period between the 8th and 10th centuries activity on the site peaked: ditches were recut, non-ferrous metalworking took place in the Tlachtga ditches and ferrous metalworking, including blacksmithing, took place off the hilltop to the east away from the core area of the site. The penultimate Tlachtga ditch yielded evidence for working of silver and copper alloy, and a basalt ingot mould again with possible traces of copper alloy casting was recovered from the innermost ditch. This activity was at least partially taking place within the ditches of Tlachtga itself – emphasising that these were important activity areas. At the eastern complex evidence suggests the presence of a building – a smithy or workshop, in which a hoard of Anglo-Saxon silver coins was concealed. While the quantities of non-ferrous metals recovered are small across the site there is evidence of these being exchanged (Trench 8), melted (Trench 5) and cast (Trench 7).

Also around this time the form of the site fundamentally altered and a mound was begun in the central portion of the enclosure. This may have required some initial levelling of pre-existing occupation debris: what remained was a largely inorganic and apparently structureless spread of material, which included a prehistoric tool – a high quality flint plano-convex knife, possibly deliberately placed. Above this was constructed a mound of organic material which in turn was covered, probably rapidly, by more clay-rich deposits. Two phases of revetment were then inserted, the first including a significant shale component both as debris and large slabs, the second comprising more substantial limestone blocks. While shale outcrops exist in the area, the hilltop itself is an outcrop of limestone, so the shale appears to have been brought to the site to serve a specific purpose. The mound was capped by a surface of rounded cobbles, again specifically gathered for the purpose, and a small collection of prehistoric tools ranging in date from the Neolithic to the early Bronze Age was placed within its uppermost layers as a talisman or good luck charm, a practice seen elsewhere in early medieval Ireland (see O'Sullivan 2017, 113–116).

The final phase encountered in excavation was the apparent destruction by fire of a timber structure that stood on the summit of the mound. This was only revealed in Test Pit 2 and produced a radiocarbon date that spans the period of the Anglo-Norman invasion of Ireland. The large deposits of intensely burned clay suggests there was ongoing industrial activity at this location, although no clear evidence of metalworking was encountered. After this burning the site is likely to have fallen out of regular use, although the latter end of the date range for this phase is within the 14th century AD.

4.7. Environment and economy at the Hill of Ward

4.7.1. Bronze Age to late Iron Age

Despite the excavation and flotation of a large volume of material from this phase of the site, very few plant remains were recovered. The inner ditch of the large enclosure yielded only 10 grains of barley at Trench 2 (seven of which were identified as hulled), while at the corresponding feature in Trench 4 a total of 11 charred seeds were recovered, only one of which was identifiable (again, hulled barley). The fills of the middle ditch were more productive, with the lowest fill (C427) yielding a moderate number of cereal grains (40), predominantly barley (hulled and naked), and free threshing wheat. The upper fill of this ditch (C461) produced a very small number of charred cereals including oat and rye, but no barley. No plant macrofossil remains were recovered from the fill of the outer ditch.

These low numbers of seeds recovered from Bronze Age levels are in contrast to the very large assemblage recovered at the similarly dated Haughey's Fort, Co. Armagh, where McClatchie (2014) identified a cache of over 10,000 whole and fragmentary cereal remains as well as the remains of wild plant species. While it is possible that cereal grains were genuinely a rarity at the Hill of Ward during this phase, it is more likely that this low visibility is a function of the small proportion of the site excavated: if cereal remains are present as large caches then encountering one of these is likely to be the exception rather than the rule. While the relative lack of charcoal also seen in the Bronze Age phase might argue for poor preservation, charred material of a similar nature was recovered from many similar, later contexts.

No identifiable charcoal was recovered from the inner ditch in 2014 (Trench 2). However, in the sections of ditch some was retrieved during the 2015 season. In the outer two ditches of the Hillfort Phase this mostly comprised scrubby species (*e.g. Prunus* spp.; hazel) and secondary woodland taxa (ash). Samples from the inner ditch included more oak, most of which was derived from trees more than *c.* 45 years old. This discrepancy may relate to the slightly earlier construction date *i.e.* oak being preferentially selected and felled early in the construction process. Alternatively this could relate to activities for which oak is a preferred fuel source, including metalworking or cremation.

The near basal date on the Jamestown Bog pollen diagram (Maguire, this volume) of 776–487 cal BC suggests the base of the core is likely to be near coincident with the early development of the site, or at least cover the period immediately post construction of the Bronze Age phase. One might reasonably expect this to be a period of significant activity within the local landscape. This does not especially appear to be the case at Jamestown Bog, in contrast to the hinterland of some other Irish hillforts (see O'Driscoll 2023). The pollen data suggest a moderately wooded landscape, perhaps with some remaining primary woodland dominated by oak and elm. No cereal cultivation is evident but a continuous *Plantago lanceolata* curve suggests likely ongoing pastoral agriculture in the area. The subsequent LPAZ2 sees a peak in charcoal but also rising proportions of both Cyperaceae and *Sphagnum* spores, suggesting a shift towards somewhat wetter conditions. This is also reflected in the recorded peat stratigraphy, with more poorly humified peat above this LPAZ boundary.

The animal economy at the Hill of Ward in the Bronze Age was overwhelmingly dominated by cattle, with some wild boar/pig, sheep/goat and dog. However, owing to preservation conditions much of the bone was very fragmented and so not identifiable to species through ordinary methods. This pattern is repeated across time and space at the Hill of Ward. Wild animals including fox, red deer, hare and woodmouse appear to be of very limited importance, echoing the findings at both Mooghaun, Co. Clare and Haughey's Fort, Co. Armagh (Murphy and McCormick 1996; McCormick and Murray 2006).

The overall pattern of livestock exploitation is also like that seen at Haughey's Fort, and to a lesser extent Mooghaun. In both cases there is a significant dominance of cattle (*cf.* McCormick and Murray 2007), as opposed to the assemblages seen at Bronze Age domestic sites (*ibid.*, 143), where pig appears to have been of greater economic significance, or, in the case of Dún Aonghasa, Co. Galway, sheep (McCormick and Murphy 2012). However, the element distribution at Haughey's Fort (Murphy and McCormick 1996, 48) is significantly different and includes a more diverse range of body parts than is evident at the Hill of Ward. This restricted range of skeletal elements, together with the cut mark and calcination data suggest that smaller animals were either brought to the site as disarticulated joints of meat while larger species (cattle) were more likely brought on the hoof.

Most of the material from this phase suggests specialised selection of joints and butchery practices that may be occurring offsite. Cattle skull fragments are over-represented in comparison to other phases, and in all domesticates lower forelimbs are the most common elements represented. While the assemblage from Trench 2 (C009) included only adult remains, the larger assemblages derived from the three ditches in Trench 4 include both adults and juveniles of cattle, pig and sheep/goat. There is some variation between ditches – for example the outermost ditch fill (C429) is dominated by ovicaprid bones – but the overall patterns remain similar. A significant number of animal bones from the Bronze Age phase have undergone further taphonomic alterations, in particular burning and carnivore gnawing. This suggests both the presence of appreciable numbers of carnivores on site (dog is present but not abundant within the bone assemblage), and that animal bones were probably disposed of directly into the open ditches.

The narrative usually suggested for hillfort societies is one of 'centralised and stratified' places (*e.g.* O'Driscoll 2017, 81), essentially operating as central places within a largely agrarian society, or as 'high-status residence, ceremony and assembly, and a visual expression of power' in the Bronze Age landscape (O'Brien 2017, 3). This may also have involved control of craftworking activities and expertise at some, but not all sites, such as is suggested by the metalworking and glassworking evidence uncovered by Barry Raftery's excavations at Rathgall, Co. Wicklow (*e.g.* Becker 2010). Plunkett (2009) discusses this in terms of the emergence of important food production centres, with hillforts controlling such production in the later 13th to 11th centuries BC. If this was the case, then it is certainly plausible that such 'community focused farming' would involve the 'redistribution of resources and the creation and maintenance of social ties through feasting' (O'Brien and O'Driscoll 2017, 416; Ginn and Plunkett 2020, 53). So far as is visible from the areas excavated and the pollen data, arable agriculture played a very limited role in the economy of the Hill of Ward at this time; however, the number of excavated comparator sites in Ireland is low. There are no published plant macrofossil remains (including wood/charcoal) from Mooghaun (Grogan 2005), while the assemblage from Dún Aonghasa numbers in the hundreds of charred cereal grains (Collins and Tierney 2012), unlike the enormous cache at Haughey's Fort. Meanwhile, the animal bone assemblage implies the movement of significant animal resources to the site, either post-slaughter (for smaller animals) or on the hoof (for cattle) for the purpose of communal feasting. Cattle skulls may perhaps have had some special significance in this activity, accounting for their over-representation, although these could hardly be considered as 'trophy' deposits (Rowley-Conway 2018).

4.7.2. Middle Iron Age

The only feature on site to date from this period was the possible cereal drying kiln (C481) to the south of the Bronze Age enclosure, which dates from 146 cal BC–cal AD 68. The feature contained two main fills, the lower of which included wheat, barley (both hulled and naked) and wild grasses, the upper of which lacked wheat and wild grasses but included oats. The clear differences between fills might imply re-use of the kiln perhaps by different social groups or for different harvests.

The cereal assemblage recovered is broadly typical of the period. In reviewing the evidence for middle Iron Age sites in southwest Ireland, Becker (2019) highlights material from Killow Pit 27a (Bermingham *et al.* 2012, 51) as well as Gortybrigane (Clark and Long 2010), which yielded assemblages dominated by (wild) oats and barley.

In their review of Iron Age drying kilns, Monk and Power (2012), highlight the mostly eastern nature of their distribution, albeit that their visibility has been significantly enhanced by road construction projects in the last two decades. As reported here, barley and wheat dominate the overall picture in such kilns, with oats less frequent. O'Sullivan and Kinsella (2013, 378) suggested that the abundance of drying kilns in this part of Meath could be linked to 'client-lord relationships and the food rents expected by the king of Tara'. Whether the Hill of Ward is considered within this hinterland or as an important elite site in its own right is debatable (*cf.* Newman 2005), but the idea of 'centralising control of crop processing in restricted locations', or perhaps significant locations makes a great deal of sense in this context.

4.7.3. Late Iron Age–early medieval period

Several areas excavated across the site have yielded dates that fall within the late Iron Age to early medieval period. Spatially these include the Southern Enclosure, the outer ramparts bank-ditch pair of Tlachtga, the inner ditch of Tlachtga and the burned area beneath the central mound. Once again, the small areas excavated must be borne in mind.

Plant macrofossil remains were very sparse across all features within this date range. At Trench 3 (Southern Enclosure) a total of four cereal grains were recovered, three of which were barley. The corresponding fill of the Southern Enclosure in Trench 5 contained a total of 25 cereal grains, with small numbers of identified wheat, barley and oats; however, these may relate to a later phase given the lack of clarity with regard to the dating of this trench. Despite the paucity of charred macrofossil remains, significant quantities of charcoal were recovered from some of these features, especially from Trench 3 (C018). This context is one of only three on site where the charcoal assemblage is dominated by alder, the other two being the fills of the possible drying kiln C481 (see above). This is interesting given the location of the infant burial within this trench, and suggests that alder has an association with death (*e.g.* Newman *et al.* 2007 at Raffin Fort, Co. Meath). Very little charcoal was recovered from the second section of the ditch exposed in Trench 5. Elsewhere, C822, located beneath the central Tlachtga mound, yielded a small but diverse charcoal assemblage dominated by ash, but no other ecofacts of any kind.

The two main fills from Trench 3, C006 and C018, both contained a large number of cattle bones, with some bones of pig and sheep/goat. These fills also contained elevated proportions of both horse (6.9%) and of red deer (8.05%), including 13 fragments of red deer antler. C018 contained the largest number of animal bones of any context excavated in 2014 (NISP=800), with the assemblage including 76 identified cattle bones, represented by pelvic bones, mandibles, and elements from both the fore- and hindlimbs. C006 was, however, dominated by long bones and also fore- and hindlegs. In contrast the two fills of the Southern Enclosure ditch exposed in Trench 5 produced very few animal bones with the same caveat as for the plant macrofossil remains: that the chronology within Trench 5 is somewhat confused. C063, the context from which the infant burial was recovered, yielded only one identifiable animal bone – from a woodmouse – while C919, the basal fill of Trench 7 produced little charcoal but a moderate assemblage of animal bone (NISP=324, of which 233 remain unidentifiable), dominated by cattle (NISP=15). Similarly, C026, the basal fill of the penultimate Tlachtga ditch excavated in 2014, yielded no charcoal and only 30 fragments of animal bone, only one of which was identifiable to taxonomic grouping (a fox tooth) that was subsequently radiocarbon dated. C048, a basal deposit within ditch C014 (Southern Enclosure), contained only two large pieces of cattle bone, one of which was also radiocarbon dated. This and the fox tooth from Trench 1 returned identical dates of 1610±30 BP (cal AD 392–538). This is broadly coincident with an uptick in early medieval settlement activity across Ireland and especially with construction dates of multivallate ringforts previously discussed.

While preservation across the site is generally good, the lack of abundant ecofactual remains suggests a relatively low level of activity in much of the site during this phase. The exception here appears to be the Southern Enclosure, which not only includes an exceptionally high number of fragmentary animal bones, but also an unusually high proportion of red deer antler.

LPAZ 5 within the regional pollen covers approximately this time period, with an upper date at the zone boundary of cal AD 219–364. This is coincident with a significant rise in charcoal as well as a slight decline in alder pollen. This represents a low period within the *Plantago lanceolata* pollen curve, suggesting a possible decrease in pastoral agricultural activity, and is potentially an expression of the 'Late Iron Age Lull', a period in which human activity within the Irish landscape appears to decline (Coyle-McClung 2013; Chique *et al.* 2017; O'Donnell 2018). Cereal pollen remains almost absent from the diagram, as is the case throughout: while this is clearly a regional rather than local sequence, it mirrors the lack of onsite cereal remains during this period.

4.7.4. Early medieval period

The greater part of the ecofactual assemblage from the Hill of Ward derives from the early medieval phase. This includes the main fills of Trench 7 (the inner Tlachtga ditch), the sub-mound deposit of C818, the Tlachtga ditch in Trench 5 and activity to the east of the site in Trench 8. The main deposits within the inner Tlachtga ditch (Trench 7) yielded a moderate number of charred cereal grains, with both oat and barley recorded. Of the two contexts examined here, C915 is the first instance where oat represents a significant component of the plant macrofossil assemblage, although the abundance of plant macrofossil remains recovered from the earlier phases is in general comparatively low. The charcoal assemblages from Trench 7 are mixed, but C915 and C916 are dominated by pomaceous fruitwood with smaller proportions of ash with oak and hazel.

Overall, Trench 7 included a large number of highly fragmentary animal bones. Excluding C919 (discussed above) these totalled over 4,300 fragments, of which the majority were unidentifiable. Of the bones that could be identified, cattle again dominated with strong representation of both sheep/goat and pig. In all domesticates the assemblage included both cranial and postcranial material with clear evidence of cut and chop marks, suggesting that whole animals are likely to have been brought to site for slaughter/butchery. Where age information was available, the animals appeared to mostly be subadult. The sheep/goat assemblage included one neonate, while the pig assemblage also included young animals, potentially as a high-status food item. Of the two horses identified within the assemblage one was again subadult, although there was no evidence of butchery in this case.

In Trench 6, the sub-mound material of C818 contained no plant macrofossils but produced a small quantity of charcoal. This was dominated by hazel with some ash, similar to the earlier and adjacent deposit of C822. This fill also included a moderate number of fragmented animal bones (NISP=318), most of which were unidentifiable to species. Where these were identifiable, they were dominated by cattle (principally teeth), along with some sheep/goat and one pig scapula. Cranial and postcranial cattle bones were recovered, suggesting on-site carcass processing, although the situation is less clear for the other common domesticates.

Several fills within Trench 5 also contained charred plant macrofossil remains. The hearth (C459) contained three fills with small numbers of cereals in differing proportions: the lowest fill (C549) contained mostly barley with some wheat but no oats. The middle fill (C548) was a mixed assemblage of barley and oats, while the upper layer (C451) contained mostly barley with some wheat, and again no oats. Neither of the lower fills yielded significant charcoal remains; however, the upper fill contained a mixed charcoal assemblage dominated by blackthorn and hazel. The lower fill included a moderate number of highly fragmented animal bones, including a small number of cattle bones and the pelvis of a large dog. The upper fill included a larger number of fragments (NISP=177), with pig/wild boar dominating, followed by cattle, sheep/goat and dog. No animal bones were recovered from the middle fill.

The primary fill of the second Tlachtga ditch (C460) yielded no charcoal or charred plant macrofossils. The other main fills of this ditch were likewise very poor as regards macrofossil preservation, with sparse grains of barley and oat, but did preserve a small amount of charcoal, especially in C452 where oak and hazel represent most identified fragments. Given the proximity to the hearth it is possible the presence of oak here might be related to the metalworking activity at this location.

The fills of the penultimate Tlachtga ditch contained a significant quantity of highly fragmented animal bone. Across the three contexts over 2,000 fragments were retrieved, although the majority could not be assigned to species. Material in the lowest fill (C460) included six horse teeth, perhaps from a single animal as well as bones from at least two cattle and a medium-sized dog. Other domesticates were also present, especially sheep/goat as well as pig/wild boar. The cattle bones included adult and juvenile specimens, as did the pig bones, while the dog and horse remains were from adult animals only. In the subsequent fills a similar pattern emerges, with cattle dominant, sheep/goat as a secondary species and pig/wild boar as the third most abundant domesticate.

Trench 8 included a wide range of contexts, some of which were clearly industrial and others which may relate to domestic refuse or cereal processing. The overwhelming majority of charred plant macrofossils from the site were recovered from here, with over 1,200 identified seeds and fruits, many from a single widely dispersed context. Most of these comprised unidentifiable charred cereals, but where they were identifiable, oat and barley were present in approximately similar quantities. Some contexts also contained significant numbers of wild grass seeds (*e.g.* C715). The charcoal assemblages from Trench 8 include one (C773) that was almost certainly industrial in nature and dominated by oak charcoal. Other assemblages were more varied, mostly comprising charcoal from scrubby species.

A large number of fragmentary animal bones were also recovered across Trench 8, comprising over 2,200 fragments. These were dominated by cattle, but with a significant proportion of sheep/goat and pig with smaller numbers of dog (NISP=7) and wild species (1 hare bone; 4 red deer bones). The sheep/goat remains included a range of body parts, suggesting primary processing of animals on site. The pig bones included one neonate, suggesting either piglets were transported to site for consumption or, more likely, that live pigs were kept on site at this time. Most of the pig bones were in this younger age category, possibly representing a high-status food item. The presence of both cranial and postcranial material in the assemblage again suggests onsite butchery and preparation of whole animals on the hoof. The overall increase in agricultural activity at this time is consistent with current narratives of food and farming in early medieval Ireland (McClatchie *et al.* 2015; O'Sullivan *et al.* 2021b), although the relative lack of charred macrofossils within the central monument of Tlachtga in comparison to the eastern complex is surprising.

4.7.5. *Early medieval to Anglo-Norman*

This phase relates to the structural remains excavated at Test Pit 2. All of the charcoal identified here was oak. This may relate to industrial activity in the area and/or to the presence of structural timbers. No charred plant macrofossils were recovered from Test Pit 2; however, C038 produced a moderate animal bone assemblage, which, unlike other phases of the site has a bias towards pig/wild boar bones, followed by cattle and sheep/goat. Sub-adult individuals were noted of all three main domesticates. The cattle bone assemblage included 23 fragments of cattle horncore in addition to seven of antler, suggesting the hornworking might have been an important craft activity on site at this time. This assemblage included more bones subject to carnivore gnawing than in any other context excavated (over 2%).

4.7.6. *Synthesis*

While the Hill of Ward remained a significant archaeological place over a period of over 2,500 years, many elements of the economy seem to have remained constant over this time. Few charred macrofossils were recovered from the Bronze Age phase; however, where these were retrieved, they were largely a combination of barley and wheat. Charcoal in these earlier features was also largely mixed, and there was no apparent strategy as regards procurement of timber resources. There were no features within this phase where a single species appears to have been selected for a specific function. The pollen diagram at this time suggests a moderately wooded landscape, with secondary woodland (ash dominated) and scrub dominating, but some remaining primary oak/elm woodland in the wider region. Meanwhile, the animal economy within this phase focused largely on cattle. Wild taxa were poorly represented, not only in this phase but across the entire sequence, with occasional finds of red deer, hare and woodmouse. Animal bone preservation within the recuts of the Bronze Age ditches was universally poor, and unfortunately provided very little information on whether there was any clear change between the primary fills and the recuts. However, the animal bones in the earlier phases seems to suggest an emphasis on meat consumption, with smaller livestock like sheep/goats and pigs transported to the site as joints of meat, rather than as complete animals. Evidence of axial elements from cattle, however, suggests that cattle were likely to have been walked to the site before being slaughtered and the high proportion of subadult individuals suggests that these individuals were raised for consumption (*i.e.* beef herding), perhaps locally; however, McCormick (2009) discusses the possibility that the slaughter of young animals may have had a significance beyond purely the economic. Cut marks to distal limb bones of cattle suggests that cattle hides were also processed on site, a craft also suggested by the bone implements recovered.

The only feature of middle Iron Age date is the possible kiln located immediately external to the Bronze Age enclosure. This was likely constructed within a century of the abandonment of this phase. No animal bones were preserved in this feature, but some variation was evident in the two layers from which plant macrofossils were recovered. In the lower deposit there was a preponderance of free-threshing wheat, while the upper fill was dominated by a mix of barley with oats but no wheat. This represents the first major appearance of oats on site, although there is the possibility that these represent wild oats at this early date (see Becker 2019, 52).

The late Iron Age/early medieval phase includes the primary fills of the Tlachtga enclosure ditches and the Southern Enclosure. Charred plant remains were again sparse and charcoal was again varied; however, some contexts within the Southern Enclosure specifically favour the use of alder. The section of this enclosure excavated in 2014 included a significant but highly fragmented animal bone assemblage alongside the infant burial. This was again cattle-dominated with lesser components of pig and sheep/goat, although it also includes a significant proportion of horse and red deer bone. In the Southern Enclosure, the pattern of element distribution was even more exaggerated than in the preceding phase, suggesting that beef too may have been brought to the site as disarticulated joints of meat or even, as suggested by the low levels of cut or butchery marks, as clean bones.

The later early medieval phase saw very little change in the overall composition of the animal bone assemblage, with cattle still being the most abundant domesticate present. Higher proportions of juveniles and neonates within the cattle assemblage, coupled with an intensification of butchery and a higher percentage of roasted bones, suggests that animals were born and raised quite close to the site and likely consumed as high-status meals. Arable crop remains are significantly better represented in this phase, with co-dominance between barley and oat. This is likely to relate to a period of increased arable production and move away from a cattle-dominated economy from the 8th century AD onwards (McCormick and Murray 2007; McCormick 2008; McCormick *et al.* 2014; O'Sullivan *et al.* 2021b, 210).

The animal bone assemblage from Trench 8 contained significantly more sheep/goat remains than encountered elsewhere at Tlachtga. This may relate to its position away from the central area of the site and so to its comparative status. Sheep were regarded as a lower status food item in early medieval Ireland and were frequently owned by commoners (Peters 2015), as opposed to cattle, and are generally 'absent from most discussions in the law tracts regarding the foods that commoners could request' (*ibid.*, 105). The overall impression is that the diet of those who lived in the area of Trench 8 was substantively different from those at the core of the site. This area showed clear evidence of ferrous metalworking and was also the location of the hoard of silver coins recovered in excavation (Woods, this volume). It is likely that while the association of this area with metalworking conferred a degree of status upon its occupants, this was at a different level to any inhabitants of Tlachtga itself where cattle continued to dominate.

The final phase of activity saw a move away from the cattle-dominated economy seen throughout all previous phases of activity towards a more pig-dominated economy. Again, a number of juvenile individuals were noted suggesting a producer-consumer site and the consumption of potentially high value animal resources. Despite cattle representing a smaller proportion of the total livestock at the site during this final period, the high number of juvenile cattle and low numbers of immature and subadult individuals point to dairying as a likely herd management strategy, though the high number of adult individuals indicates that beef remained an important food item at this time, most likely for high status consumption. No plant macrofossil remains were obtained from this area; however, cutmarks to distal limb bones and horn cores, and the presence of red deer antler from this phase also indicates that craftwork in animal products, such as hides (leather), horn, and antler was practiced on site at this time. Whatever activity was taking place on the mound at this time may well have required a very hot fire: the charcoal remains here that may represent structural or industrial features are entirely of oak. At this time the construction of the central mound must have fundamentally altered the nature of the site, perhaps heralding a change from a continuously occupied settlement site to a location of periodic feasting and gathering. This is also coincident with a major recorded downturn in activity on multivallate sites dating to *c.* AD 1000 and after (O'Sullivan *et al.* 2021a, 65).

Finds and ecofacts

5.1. Stone axeheads (Stephen Mandal and Bernard Gilhooly)

5.1.1. Introduction

This report is based on the macroscopic examination of two stone axeheads found during archaeological excavations at the Hill of Ward, Co. Meath. The purpose of the study was to record the axes using the Irish Stone Axe Project recording system (see Cooney and Mandal 1998, 4–27). This report identifies the rock type from which the stone axeheads were made and potential sources, and comments on their method of manufacture and function. It is important to note that macroscopic petrographical studies have been considered of limited value in comparison to microscopic analysis. On the other hand, macroscopic studies provide an excellent preliminary assessment tool and have proven to be of considerable value in petrographical studies (e.g. see Mandal 1997; Cooney and Mandal 1998).

Over 21,000 stone axeheads are known from Ireland (Sheridan et al. 1992, 391; Cooney and Mandal 1998, 4). They are regarded as one of the characteristic objects of the Mesolithic and Neolithic periods (e.g. Woodman 1978; 1987; Cooney and Grogan 1994). Since 1991, stone axeheads have been the focus of detailed research by the Irish Stone Axe Project (ISAP). Stone axeheads were both a symbol of prestige and an ordinary working tool for people for thousands of years. They served a wide range of functions in early prehistoric Irish society, including use in woodworking, in burial and ceremonial contexts and as symbols of power.

5.1.2. The Irish Stone Axe Project catalogue entry

A standard format was devised by the Irish Stone Axe Project for cataloguing stone axes. It has been abbreviated for this report and a sequence is used that is broadly similar to that in other Project reports (e.g. Mandal et al. 1992; Mandal and Cooney 1996). Locational and contextual details are followed by the petrographical identification. This is followed by details of the possible method of manufacture.

5.1.2.1. 2015: SF004; C401. Trench 4 (2015) (Bernard Gilhooly); Fig. 5.1.1

Find location: Hill of Ward, Co. Meath; O.S. 6-inch sheet 30.

Circumstance of discovery: In excavation, within topsoil or interface of topsoil and archaeological layers.

Petrology: Porphyritic dolerite

Adze: Flaked, ground and polished.

Face Shape: FS03 (straight splayed sides).

Cross Section: CS06 (oval, flattened sides).

Edge Shape: ES05 (curved, symmetrical).

Profile: P02 (symmetrical; medium).

Blade Profile: BP10 (symmetrical; no junction).

Butt Shape: BU04 (flat; flat).

Clear junction between blade and sides, with faces ground in at blade end. Sides taper to the butt and become more rounded. Both faces have clear junctions with the blade. The faces are not ground; they may have been pecked for a haft.

Dimensions: L. 42 mm W. 45.8 mm T. 26 mm

Weight: 69.9 g; blade angle: 64°

The axehead has a straight symmetrical blade, in both plan and profile. There is no junction between the blade and the body of the axe. Both the faces (in plan) and the sides are splayed. The former narrow as they approach the butt, while the latter widen as they near the back of

Fig. 5.1.1. Stone axehead 2015:SF004 C001.

the axehead. There is no sign of faceting on the sides. The junction between the faces and the sides are slightly rounded. Similarly, the intersection between the butt and the sides and faces are also slightly rounded. The butt itself is relatively flat.

Three ground down flake scars, which run in a line along the intersection between one of the faces and a side, along with a similar ground down flake scar at the junction between the opposite face and the butt, are all that remains of the primary manufacturing technique. All other evidence of knapping has been ground out. There are abraded points along the rest of the sides and around the butt. These could suggest the use of pecking during manufacture; however, it is more likely they are the result of taphonomic processes, particularly as the artefact was found in the plough soil; these coarser areas are themselves worn down, supporting the suggestion the axehead has been rolled/moved in the soil.

The blade edge is dull and rounded, although there are a number of worn nicks and chips along the edge. While these have been seen as evidence of use-wear it cannot be stated categorically that these features are indicative of use in this instance, owing to the influence of taphonomy. Nonetheless, it is likely they were caused through use. This is supported by the differential distribution of the chips and nicks on the blade edge. A higher proportion are found from the midpoint of the blade to one end. This is consistent with the use of stone axes, where contact is not even along the whole blade edge.

Although it is possible the axehead was manufactured/ re-manufactured from a larger example there is no evidence to support this; breaks during production or use can sometimes leave very observable damage on the faces, though this is not always the case. Some breaks can be very clean, leaving no evidence beyond the break itself. Similarly, an axehead constructed from an unworked piece of stone, may or may not display face damage. As such, it is just as likely the axehead could have been manufactured from previously unworked stone. Having said that, it is unusual to see such a short axehead, relative to its blade length; the blade is approximately 50 mm long, and could possibly suggest the re-use of an earlier axehead.

Hafting such a short axehead, especially with its splayed sides, may have proved difficult; both sides run outwards from the butt to the blade at an angle of 113°. It is likely the roughening on the sides discussed earlier could be hafting related. The coarse surface would have helped hold the axehead within the haft socket; there is currently no evidence in Ireland for the use of binding material or adhesives to secure stone axeheads in their sockets. They are held in place through friction alone. Alternatively, the axehead could have been secured within some form of a sleeve before this in turn was positioned within the haft socket (see Sheridan *et al.* 1992). However it was hafted, it is apparent that due to its size/length, this was not designed for robust use. It is more likely to have been used for fine carpentry. This is supported by the relatively light damage to the blade edge.

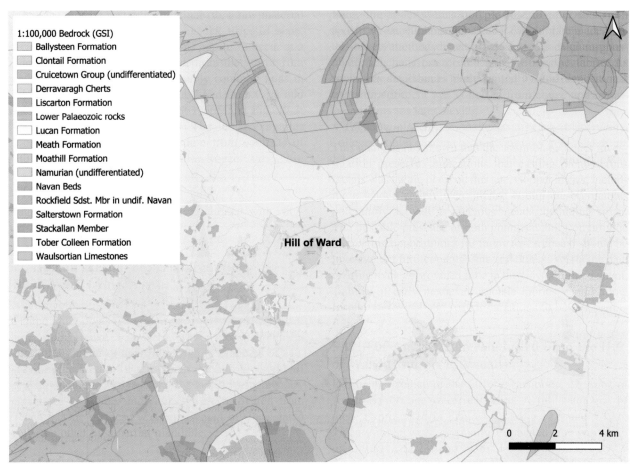

1:100,000 Bedrock (GSI)
- Ballysteen Formation
- Clontail Formation
- Cruicetown Group (undifferentiated)
- Derravaragh Cherts
- Liscarton Formation
- Lower Palaeozoic rocks
- Lucan Formation
- Meath Formation
- Moathill Formation
- Namurian (undifferentiated)
- Navan Beds
- Rockfield Sdst. Mbr in undif. Navan
- Salterstown Formation
- Stackallan Member
- Tober Colleen Formation
- Waulsortian Limestones

Hill of Ward

0   2   4 km

Fig. 5.1.2. The Geology of the Hill of Ward area, County Meath; 1:100,000 GSI bedrock data; OSM basemap.

This is quite an unusual axe in that it is very small in comparison to other axeheads made from dolerite/porphyry (see Cooney and Mandal 1998, fig. 4.10); however, the width of the blade and thickness of the axe relative to the length may indicate that this has been reworked from a larger axehead that was broken.

5.1.2.2. 2015:SF004: geology and potential sources

The predominant geology in the local area comprises shales and limestones (see Fig. 5.1.2). Dolerite and porphyritic dolerite account for a small but significant proportion of the petrographically identified stone axes in Ireland, with over 450 (about 3.5%) known. Interestingly, these are concentrated in the east of the country, with a source identified on Lambay Island, off the coast of north county Dublin for porphyry (see Mandal 1996; Dolan & Cooney 2010). The porphyritic dolerite axe found at the site does not appear to be of Lambay Porphyry type, though this would have to confirmed by thin section analysis. In terms of potential bedrock sources, the closest dolerite dyke swarms occur to the north in the Newry-Carlingford area and

to the south associated with the Leinster Granite. It is also important to note that this artefact may have been worked from a glacial erratic rather than from a primary bedrock source.

5.1.2.3. 2016: SF163; C801. Trench 6 (2016) (Steve Mandal) (Fig. 5.1.3)

Find location: The Hill of Ward, Co. Meath; O.S. 6-inch sheet 30.

Circumstance of discovery: Beneath topsoil in Trench 6, at summit of medieval central mound of the site, possibly deliberately redeposited.

Petrology: Sandstone – coarse grained yellow/red sandstone with irregular shaped quartz clasts up to 4 mm across.

Adze: Flaked(?) and ground.

Face Shape: FS03 (straight splayed sides).

Cross Section: CS07 (oval, flat sides).

Edge Shape: ES03 (gently curved, asymmetrical).

Profile: P05 (symmetrical; thick).

Blade Profile: BP04 (asymmetrical; no junction).

Butt Shape: BU11 (rounded; rounded).

Dimensions: L. 117 mm W. 63 mm T. 38 mm.

Clear junction between blade and sides, with faces ground in at blade end. Sides taper to the butt and become more rounded. Both faces have clear junctions with the blade.

This axe has been made from a water rolled cobble, which was naturally triangular in shape. The broad end has been ground to produce a blade. This process may have involved some flaking or pecking, but no evidence remains of this. The faces of this axehead are not ground but appear to have been pecked, presumably to provide grip for a haft.

5.1.2.4. SF163: geology and potential sources

The bedrock under the site consists of Lucan Formation, dark limestone (calp) and shale. The geology of the area is composed of formations from two distinct time periods: older Ordovician-Silurian rocks in the northern region with Lower Carboniferous Age rocks to the south.

The oldest dateable rocks in the area are the Ordovician White Island Bridge Formation (WI), consisting of tuff, tuffaceous siltstone and mudstone. There is a major unconformity between these rocks and the next oldest, of Ordovician-Silurian Age. These consist of the Clontail Formation (CL), calcareous red-mica greywacke; the Salterstown Formation (SA), calcareous greywacke and bedded mudstone; and the Rathkenny Formation (RK), black mudstone, siltstone and greywacke.

Another major unconformity separates these stratigraphically from the Lower Carboniferous Succession, the base of which is marked by the Old Red Sandstone (ORS), red conglomerate, sandstone and mudstone. The Lower Carboniferous is represented by a sequence consisting of: the Liscarton Formation (LC), laminated beds and muddy limestone; the Meath Formation (ME), pale grainstone; the Moatehill Formation (MH), mudstone, calcarenite and calcareous sandstone; the Ballysteen Formation (BA), dark muddy limestone and shale; the Waulsortian Limestones (WA), massive unbedded lime-mudstone; and the Navan Group (NAV), limestone, mudstone and sandstone. Finally, there is another gap in the sequence to the Lucan Formation (LU), (known as calp, the bedrock at the site).

The Ordovician to Ordovician-Silurian rocks represent tectonic activity, with volcanic activity and greywacke beds resulting from earthquake activity causing soft sediment slumps on the shallowly sloping seabed. The tectonic activity relates to the closure of the Iaepetus Ocean, a major ocean, which at its widest was probably greater than 3000 km across.

The Lower Carboniferous rocks, which also make up much of the Midlands of Ireland, represent the northward return of the sea at the end of the Devonian, *c.* 360 million years ago, owing to the opening of a new ocean to the south called the Palaeo-Tethys in what is

10 mm

Fig. 5.1.3. Stone axehead 2016: SF163 from the Hill of Ward.

now central Europe. The overlying tills of the area are derived predominantly from the underlying bedrock of calp limestone. The soils consist of grey-brown podzolics and brown earths.

The primary sources of sandstone, of which this axehead is made, are from within the Rathenny Formation, the Rockfield Sandstone Member and the Namurian (see Fig. 5.1.2). However, as noted in the description of the stone axehead above, it appears to have been made from a water rolled cobble and thus is from a secondary source (glacial tills, a riverine, lacustrine or seashore source). The tills at the site are predominantly derived from limestone, so are not a likely source, therefore it is reasonable to assume that the axehead was brought to the site. There are likely to be cobbles of this nature in riverine contexts in the rivers to the north of the site, where sandstones are more frequently occurring in bedrock.

Further examination (*e.g.* thin section and/or geochemical analysis) would not yield further information as to the source of the material used in the manufacture of this axehead, given that it is most likely a secondary source.

5.2. Pecked stone object (2014: SF005) (Muiris O'Sullivan)

5.2.1. Object description

This isolated stone object was recovered from the top of the denuded outer bank of the monument of Tlachtga. Its dimensions were a maximum of 125 mm (L) × 90 mm (W) × 28 mm (D). While the remains of the bank itself comprised a large quantity of fractured bedrock, this object was immediately apparent owing to its atypical geology.

On the flat or slightly concave face of a relatively small piece of sandstone, four near parallel grooves extend over the available surface. The grooves are V-shaped in section, approximately 10 mm across in each case and are apparently picked out artificially, with individual pick marks clearly visible. The granular texture of the stone makes it difficult to confirm that it has been truncated or worn post-picking but there is a strong possibility that it is a fragment of a larger decorated object. The nature of the picking is identical to that found in megalithic art and landscape rock art of the Neolithic and early Bronze Age period.

Arrangements of parallel or near-parallel lines occur in megalithic art in Ireland, notably at Knowth, Co. Meath (*cf.* Eogan and Shee-Twohig 2022), Loughcrew, Co. Meath (*e.g.* Shee-Twohig 1981, Fig. 243) and one or two orthostats at Knockroe, Co. Kilkenny (O'Sullivan 1987) but their occurrence on what might simply be a fieldstone at the Hill of Ward is intriguing. The reverse face of the stone is converse and, taken with the slightly concave obverse surface, might suggest that this is a fragment of a stone vessel such as the example reputedly from Knowth and displayed in the National Museum of Ireland. On the other hand, it would be unusual and technically difficult to decorate the inner side of such a stone vessel.

The most likely interpretation is that this is a fragment of a larger panel of megalithic art, perhaps part of a large concentric motif, such as is seen at Loughcrew Cairn U (Shee-Twohig 1981, Fig. 240 C3). The passage tomb cemetery at Loughcrew is clearly visible from the findspot at the Hill of Ward, and the possibility that this stone originated at a now destroyed cairn either at Loughcrew or at the Hill of Ward itself cannot be discounted.

5.3. Lignite/jet objects (Paul Stevens)

Over the course of three seasons of excavation fragments of two objects of jet/jet-like jewellery were recovered from the Hill of Ward. One object (2015: SF074) was recovered from a feature that post-dated the use of the innermost ditch of the Bronze Age enclosure (C469). This is likely to be late Iron Age or later in date. The other fragment (2016: SF224) was recovered from Trench 8 (C774).

10 mm

Fig. 5.2.1. Pecked stone object (Illustration: Conor McHale).

Both radiocarbon evidence and the Anglo-Saxon coins recovered from this trench suggest a date of mid- to late 10th century for these features.

In Ireland, jet-like bracelets and bangles occur from the early Bronze Age to the early medieval period, although finger rings are limited to the later 1st millennium (Lanigan 1964; Hunter 2008, 104–106; Hunter and Sheridan 2014, 320; Stevens 2017a, 251–258). Alongside examples in stone, glass, silver and gold, jet or jet-like material (*i.e.* lignite, oil-shale, fossil-wood and cennel coal) is the most common medium used in Irish early medieval arm jewellery (Doyle 2014, 67–68). Evidence from Viking graves in Scotland show arm bangles were worn by both sexes (*ibid.*; Hunter 2008, 104–106; Hunter and Sheridan 2014, 320). Unfortunately, there is an absence of documentary evidence for Irish jet or jet-like jewellery, although other sources do exist outside of Ireland, *e.g.* the Greek Classical writer Pliny the Elder, and the later medieval English monk, the Venerable Bede; however, both focus more generally on the medicinal and occult uses of the material (Rackham 1989, 141–142; Coulter 2015, 117; Stevens 2017a, 246–247).

Indigenous manufacturing of jet-like jewellery took place at various locations throughout Ireland, and from the beginning of the 5th century to the end of the 12th century (Stevens 2017a, 251–257). Irish material was apparently carved by hand, using a knife or gouge to remove a central biconical waste core or disc, followed by a smooth polishing stone to produce a high gloss lustre (*ibid.*, 243–246, Fig. 3a). This technique was universally adopted in Ireland and in parts of western Scotland alongside earlier native techniques (Hunter 2016, 294–298). However, jet/jet-like jewellery was not popular in Anglo-Saxon England, despite access to sources of the raw material, and was only reintroduced in York by the Scandinavians, who co-opted the material and following initial contact from Viking raids on Great Britain and Ireland, apparently adopted their own modes and style (Hunter 2008; Stevens 2017b, 255).

Scientific analysis of British archaeological material has identified a broad range of raw materials with similar properties that were used in the manufacture of hard black highly polished jewellery. Carboniferous organic and inorganic materials used include true-jet (including Whitby Jet), lignite, oil shales and coals, and although true-jet is not in the geology of Ireland, the remaining material types can be sourced in a limited number of outcrops and seams throughout the island of Ireland (Lanigan 1964; Patrick Orr, pers. comm.). Alongside visual assessment, scientific identification of this material was undertaken using non-destructive analytical techniques, including X-ray and FTIR, using a methodology well-established in Britain and Scandinavia (Hunter *et al.* 1993; Watts and Pollard 1998; Allason-Jones and Jones 2001; Allason-Jones and Davis 2002; Penton 2008; Plahter 2011).

5.3.1. Discussion

SF224 is possibly a rare fragmentary example of a decorated bracelet with extant terminal. Alternatively, the object may also be interpreted as a pendant, *i.e.* a broken bangle, reused and reworked into a decorative object – presumably worn hanging from a chain or string. The vast majority of jet-like arm jewellery is fragmentary, and evidence of a decorated terminal in early medieval jet-like jewellery is unique in an Irish context (Lanigan 1964; Stevens 2017a). An original terminal end would indicate this object was a penannular bracelet, rather than an annular bangle. Decoration of any kind is also rare, and this object has a coarse gauged line parallel to the terminal end. The line appears to be original, deliberate and purely decorative, albeit quite coarse. It does not form a complete circle on the interior (invisible) side, but would have completely encircled the width of the bracelet on the exposed exterior.

Only one other decorated jet or jet-like bracelet fragment has been recorded from early medieval Ireland, and was recovered from a pit during excavation of the ecclesiastical enclosure ditch at Cathedral Hill, Armagh (Gaskell-Brown and Harper 1984, 136–137, Fig. 13, Find 74). This object has a circular cross-section and key-pattern decoration at the (missing) terminal and was recently interpreted by the writer as Roman in origin (Stevens unpublished). Roman jet bracelets of this type are known throughout the Empire, from Roman Britain to Jordan, and often had gold embellishments adorning the terminals (Allason-Jones, pers. comm.).

Several examples of jet-like 'pendants' have been recovered from early medieval contexts, *e.g.* at Clonmacnoise, Co. Offaly, Cloughwater, Co. Antrim, Ballynagallagh (Lough Gur), Co. Limerick, and Woodstown, Co. Waterford (Stevens 2017a, 244, 248, table 1, 259–268). One early Iron Age 'claw-shaped pendant' was recorded from Dun Ailinne, Knockaulin, Co. Kildare (National Museum of Ireland Files, D38.4). However, broken bangles/bracelets have not been subject to a detailed analysis and may have been misinterpreted as reworked pendants in several cases.

The artefact is identified by its D-shaped cross-section as typical of the early medieval jet-like jewellery of Ireland. Most of the Irish literature relating to this type of jet-like arm ring jewellery lists the raw material as either 'lignite' or 'jet' (O'Sullivan *et al.* 2014, 407–408, 467–468; Stevens 2017a, 239–240). However, the raw material for these artefacts was identified as most likely to be oil shale, which may be imported or locally sourced. This object represents an important new addition to the corpus of jet-like jewellery in Ireland.

5.3.2. Catalogue of jet/jet-like jewellery
5.3.2.1. E4474:SF074 (2015). Bangle/bracelet fragment

Oval cross-section (Type A3) with one side partially flattened. Circular hoop, irregular in thickness and its circumference is slightly asymmetrical. Object was in very poor condition and heavily laminated and fractured along laminations. Snapped at both ends; one end snapped straight across, the other snapped partly diagonally and straight along a fissure. Interior and exterior are worn and roughly finished. Burnished, not polished, both exterior and interior, hand-carved with faint long transverse cuts still visible on the interior, and longitudinal gauge marks visible along the exterior and one side. L. 48.21 mm. W. 7.95–8.29 mm. Th. 5.64–6.10 mm. Estimated internal diameter 45 mm. Estimated external diameter 50 mm. 27.5% survives.

> **Material:** dark brown, laminar, crystalline structure and large visible fissure, hackly fracture. X-ray has a high opacity, especially given its thickness.

Due to chemical conservation treatment, no FTIR analysis was possible; Raw material likely to be oil-shale. Excavated in 2015 from Trench 4 (C469), the lower fill of re-cut (C491) inner enclosure ditch (C464), main fill dated to middle Iron Age. Recovered in association with flint/chert lithics and several worked bone awls.

Note: Object was analysed after treatment and chemical stabilisation, carried by Suzannah Kelly (Conservation Lab, UCD School of Archaeology).

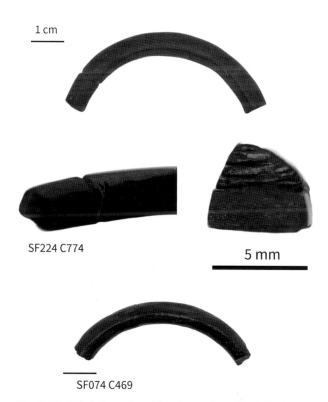

SF224 C774

SF074 C469

Fig 5.3.1. Oil shale and jet-like objects from the Hill of Ward. Top: 2016: SF224 showing decorated terminal and fracture at partially sawn end; Bottom: bracelet/bangle 2015: SF074.

5.3.2.2. E4474: SF224 (2016). Bracelet fragment with terminal

D-ovoid section, bi-conical interior, semi-circular exterior, circular hoop is irregular in thickness and circumference is asymmetrical, one extant terminal appears deliberately worked to a flatten rounded end, with a roughly transverse (decorative) line incised, set 9 mm back from the terminal end. Split lengthwise/longitudinally, one end snapped, straight across. Hand carved, long carve/slice cut-marks visible longitudinally throughout the interior, exterior marks obscured by polishing. Dull lustre and polish, particularly on the exterior, little evidence of internal polish. Slightly worn and some scratches from use. L. 75.28 mm. W. 5.4–5.9+ mm. Th. 6.7 mm. Est. Int. Diam. 57.28 mm. 33% survives.

> **Material:** black, fine laminations, hackly fracture. X-ray has a high opacity, especially given its thickness. FTIR analysis indicates absorption peaks at 3901–3566; 2365–7; 2010–9; 1733–1698; between 1652–1396 and 545–425; Raw material likely to be oil-shale. Excavated in 2016, from Trench 8 (C774) dated 8th to 10th century AD, by association with Anglo-Saxon coins and radiocarbon dating.

5.4. Lithic finds (Martha Revell with contributions by Mark Powers)

This report summarises an assemblage of 77 lithics recovered during excavations at the Hill of Ward, over three years of excavation (Table 5.4.1). This report combines previous analysis and reports that were produced separately over the three seasons in order to gather a more coherent picture of prehistoric activity at the site and lithic technologies employed. All stone finds deemed natural by the excavators were removed prior to this analysis, as such this report is concerned with the struck and retouched artefacts only.

All artefacts were visually analysed and catalogued using Microsoft Access. Each object was analysed looking at raw material, stage of reduction, condition of artefact, artefact type, presence of retouch and tool type as well as size and weight. These criteria are based on guidelines and terminology presented in Inizan *et al.* (1999). Typological names and language are based on those presented in Woodman *et al.* (2006).

5.4.1. Raw materials

Struck flint (53%) and chert (30%) make up the main portion of raw materials represented in the assemblage. A small number of siliceous limestone artefacts were recovered, which present very similarly to a fine chert or opaque flint. It is important to note that the removal of all natural material prior to this analysis somewhat limits our understanding of raw material procurement at the Hill of Ward.

Table 5.4.1 Lithic finds from the Hill of Ward.

SF#	Context	Raw Material	Removal: Blank	Burnt	Abraded	Patinated	Broken	Edge damage	Retouched	Typological name	l (mm)	w (mm)	t (mm)
2014: SF014	006	Chert	Flake	No	No	No	Yes	Yes	No	n/a	20	18	2
2014: SF023	024	Flint	Indet	No	No	No	Yes	Yes	No	n/a	8	6	1
2014: SF031	023	Quartz	Flake	No	No	No	No	Yes	No	n/a	39	32	12
2014: SF034	023	Flint	Indet	No	Yes	Heavy	Yes	No	No	n/a	9	5	2
2014: SF035	023	Flint	Indet	No	Yes	No	Yes	Yes	Yes	Convex scraper	10	11	4
2014: SF036	001	Flint	Flake	No	No	Light	No	Yes	Indet	n/a	15	15	2
2014: SF038	018	Siliceous limestone	Flake	No	No	No	No	Yes	No	n/a	32	31	9
2014: SF047	001	Chert	Flake	No	No	No	No	Yes	No	n/a	28	11	6
2014: SF048	026	Chert	Flake	No	No	No	No	Yes	No	n/a	13	9	1
2014: SF050	062	Siliceous limestone	Flake	No	Yes	No	No	Yes	No	n/a	41	27	10
2014: SF052	040	Chert	Blade	No	Yes	No	No	Yes	Yes	Edge-retouched blade	39	23	6
2015: SF001	401	Chert	Indet	No	Yes	No	No	Yes	Yes	Convex scraper	18	16	8
2015: SF002	401	Chert	Flake	No	Yes	No	No	Yes	No	n/a	12	14	4
2015: SF004	001	Flint	Indet	No	Yes	Heavy	Yes	Yes	Yes	Petit tranchet/ transverse arrowhead	12	14	4
2015: SF005	401	Flint	Flake	No	Yes	Light	Yes	Yes	Yes	Edge-retouched flake	19	18	3
2015: SF006	401	Quartz	Flake	No	No	No	No	Yes	No	n/a	20	16	6
2015: SF007	401	Quartz	Indet	No	Yes	No	No	Yes	No	n/a	37	28	3
2015: SF009	401	Chert	Flake	No	No	No	No	Yes	No	n/a	33	18	5
2015: SF012	001	Chert	Indet	No	No	No	Yes	Yes	Yes	Projectile	10	15	2
2015: SF016	401	Flint	Flake	No	Yes	No	Yes	Yes	Indet	n/a	13	10	2
2015: SF017	401	Quartz	Flake	No	No	No	No	No	No	n/a	15	10	3
2015: SF021	401	Flint	Flake	No	No	Heavy	No	Yes	Yes	Rejuvenation flake	15	12	4
2015: SF023	401	Siliceous limestone	Flake	No	Yes	No	Yes	Yes	No	n/a	40	32	16
2015: SF038	414	Chert	Flake	No	No	No	Indet	No	No	n/a	11	7	2
2015: SF046	431/417	Flint	Chunk	No	No	Heavy	Yes	Yes	No	n/a	11	8	6

(Continued)

Table 5.4.1 (Continued)

SF#	Context	Raw Material	Removal: Blank	Burnt	Abraded	Patinated	Broken	Edge damage	Retouched	Typological name	l (mm)	w (mm)	t (mm)
2015: SF047	414	Flint	Flake	No	No	No	No	Yes	No	n/a	15	10	2
2015: SF056	414	Chert	Flake	No	Yes	No	No	Yes	No	n/a	21	16	4
2015: SF060	431/417	Chert	Indet	No	Yes	No	No	Yes	Indet	n/a	14	14	4
2015: SF067	405	Chert	Flake	No	No	No	No	Yes	Yes	Double edge-retouched	31	19	4
2015: SF078	429	Flint	Flake	No	No	Light	No	Yes	No	n/a	12	8	3
2015: SF080	463	Flint	Flake	No	No	Heavy	No	Yes	No	n/a	21	9	6
2015: SF083	473	Flint	Flake	No	Yes	Heavy	Yes	Yes	Yes	Convex scraper	25	19	9
2015: SF087	451	Flint	Flake	Heavy	No	Heavy	Yes	Yes	No	n/a	17	11	3
2015: SF093	452	Rock Crystal	Indet	No	Yes	No	No	Yes	No	n/a	8	7	2
2015: SF096	453	Flint	Indet	No	No	Heavy	No	Yes	No	n/a	8	11	2
2015: SF099	469	Quartz	Flake	No	Yes	No	Indet	Yes	No	n/a	18	12	6
2015: SF106	441	Flint	Indet	No	No	No	No	No	No	n/a	7	6	2
2015: SF118	479	Chert	Flake	No	No	No	Yes	No	No	n/a	26	12	7
2015: SF119	402/428	Flint	Flake	No	Yes	Heavy	Yes	Yes	Yes	Convex scraper	21	27	6
2015: SF120	402/428	Siliceous limestone	Flake	No	No	No	Yes	Yes	No	n/a	41	31	10
2015: SF131	401	Chert	Flake	No	No	No	Indet	Yes	No	n/a	51	30	12
2015: SF132	401	Chert	Chunk	No	No	No	Yes	Yes	No	n/a	42	21	13
2015: SF133	401	Chert	Indet	No	Yes	No	No	Yes	Yes	Convex scraper	36	32	16
2016: SF152	801	Flint	Blade	No	No	No	No	Yes	Yes	Petit tranchet/ transverse arrowhead	50	15	5
2016: SF156	801	Chert	Flake	No	No	No	Yes	Yes	No	n/a	21	24	8
2016: SF156	801	Flint	Flake	No	Yes	No	Yes	Yes	No	n/a	13	8	3
2016: SF157	801	Flint	Chunk	No	Yes	Light	Yes	Yes	No	n/a	19	11	6
2016: SF159	700	Flint	Flake	No	No	Light	No	Yes	No	n/a	33	27	6
2016: SF160	800	Chert	Flake	No	No	No	No	Yes	No	n/a	27	23	6
2016: SF161	800	Flint	Indet	No	Yes	Light	Yes	Yes	No	n/a	15	16	4
2016: SF162	818	Chert	Indet	No	Yes	No	No	Yes	No	n/a	32	13	7
2016: SF170	800	Flint	Indet	No	Yes	Light	Yes	Yes	Yes	Barbed and tanged arrowhead	24	16	3

(Continued)

Table 5.4.1 Lithic finds from the Hill of Ward. (Continued)

SF#	Context	Raw Material	Removal: Blank	Burnt	Abraded	Patinated	Broken	Edge damage	Retouched	Typological name	l (mm)	w (mm)	t (mm)
2016: SF174	701	Flint	Indet	No	Yes	Light	Yes	Yes	Indet	n/a	30	21	4
2016: SF175	701	Chert	Flake	No	No	No	No	Yes	No	n/a	13	11	3
2016: SF176	701	Flint	Flake	No	Yes	Light	No	Yes	Indet	n/a	11	9	1
2016: SF203	802	Flint	Flake	Light	No	Heavy	No	Yes	No	n/a	24	20	5
2016: SF211	818	Chert	Flake	No	Yes	No	No	Yes	No	n/a	37	26	5
2016: SF217	818	Flint	Flake	Light	No	No	Yes	No	No	n/a	15	11	4
2016: SF220	803	Quartz	Indet	No	Yes	No	No	Yes	No	n/a	34	36	15
2016: SF225	801	Flint	Flake	Heavy	No	Heavy	Yes	Yes	No	n/a	10	7	2
2016: SF238	801	Flint	Chunk	No	Yes	Heavy	Yes	Yes	Indet	n/a	23	15	12
2016: SF240	742	Flint	Flake	No	Yes	No	Yes	Yes	No	n/a	32	23	4
2016: SF246	724	Flint	Flake	Heavy	Yes	Heavy	Yes	Yes	No	n/a	13	12	1
2016: SF247	715	Flint	Flake	No	No	No	Yes	Yes	No	n/a	12	8	3
2016: SF250	818	Flint	Flake	Heavy	No	Heavy	Yes	Yes	No	n/a	16	11	2
2016: SF253	818	Chert	Flake	No	Yes	No	Yes	Yes	Yes	scraper	24	19	8
2016: SF270	815	Flint	Flake	Heavy	No	Heavy	Yes	Yes	Indet	Rejuvenation flake	25	16	6
2016: SF271	818	Flint	Flake	No	Yes	Light	Yes	Yes	Yes	Plano-convex knife	69	26	8
2016: SF277	800	Quartz	Flake	No	Yes	No	No	No	No	n/a	21	15	4
2016: SF284	774	Chert	Flake	No	Yes	No	No	Yes	No	n/a	18	16	4
2016: SF285	709	Flint	Flake	No	No	Light	No	No	No	n/a	10	13	2
2016: SF286	818	Flint	Flake	No	Yes	Light	No	Yes	No	n/a	18	9	4
2016: SF287	801/804	Flint	Flake	No	No	No	No	Yes	No	n/a	15	13	3
2016: SF288	739	Quartz	Indet	No	No	No	No	No	No	n/a	8	6	1
2016: SF290	716	Flint	Flake	No	Yes	Light	No	Yes	No	n/a	19	15	3
2016: SF298	709	Flint	Indet	No	No	No	No	Yes	No	n/a	4	8	1
2016: SF299	818	Flint	Indet	No	Yes	No	Yes	Yes	No	n/a	16	11	2

5.4.1.1. Flint

Forty-one flint artefacts were examined. Flint was mainly grey, light grey or honey in colour. 54% of artefacts were tertiary and 37% were secondary reduction stages, indicating a later stage of production. There is a good size range of flint artefacts within the assemblage between 10–25 mm in length, with a few select artefacts being less than 10 mm in length or as long as 69 mm in length. The high percentage of flint artefacts compared with other lithologies in the collection is important given the limited natural sources for flint in Ireland and none within the local vicinity of the Hill of Ward. It is possible, however, that flint nodules were sourced from local glacial landforms (eskers). Twenty-six of the forty-one (63%) flint removals were flakes.

5.4.1.2. Chert

Twenty-three chert artefacts were examined. The chert utilised was almost entirely black in colour with only two dark grey artefacts recorded. Hard, fine-grained chert is native as laminations between planes of the limestone bedrock at the Hill of Ward, and small unworked pieces were frequently encountered during excavation. All bar one of the chert artefacts examined are removals, with the anomaly being an indeterminate piece, possibly a primary flake. Of the remaining 22 removals, 16 are flakes, four are indeterminate, one is a blade, and one is a chunk.

57% of chert removals are tertiary whilst 39% are secondary again showing a tendency towards latter stages of resource processing. There is a greater length range between flint and chert, with chert having a length range from 10–51 mm with far more size variation.

Four artefacts within the assemblage are of unusual geology: they are very similar to chert but have fine grained structure, possibly a chert variation or a siliceous limestone, these have been categorised separately for further consideration. Of the four artefacts of this geology all were regular flakes, two were grey and two dark grey. All bar one were tertiary removals with a high proportion of fine but clear edge damage.

5.4.1.3. Other materials

Eight quartz artefacts were present in the collection; all were white in colour bar one which is clear. Six of the eight artefacts are secondary removals whilst two are primary. One of these is the only core present in the assemblage (see below core technology description). Similarly, one primary rock crystal of less than 10 mm was retained. Due to the nature of the material and its size, it is unclear whether this is a true removal or struck piece.

5.4.2. Condition of material

Overall, there is little to no evidence of burning or patination across the collection; however, edge damage is common with 88% of material being affected. Broken artefacts are relatively evenly split with 43% having some level of breakage and 53% being intact. Similarly, levels of abrasion are relatively even with 48% abraded and 52% fresh. The significant proportion of edge damage over other markers of condition is important to note; this may be an indication of use rather than post-depositional factors and mirrors the high degree of fragmentation seen in the animal bone assemblage.

5.4.3. Assemblage composition

5.4.3.1. Cores

One possible quartz core (2015:007) was identified during analysis. Owing to the angular way quartz naturally forms and breaks it is not clear if this artefact is a core; however, there is one possible platform and a clearer prior removal scar suggesting working rather than a natural phenomenon.

5.4.3.2. Removals and retouched material

Of the 77 artefacts identified in the collection 67 (87%) were removals, with 15 (19%) being definitively retouched. Most removals were flakes, 51 in total. Retouch was identified on seven of these whilst four had indeterminate retouch. Only two blades were identified in the collection, both of which were retouched. Ten indeterminate removals were recovered, these artefacts are clearly struck pieces that are either retouched to an extent, which masks the original removal type, or that are broken obscuring the original removal form. Of these 10, two had no retouch, two had indeterminate retouch and six were retouched. Finally, four chunks were recorded; these are removals with clear platforms, but which are too substantial and irregular to be classified as flakes or blades. Three of these had no evidence of retouch, one had possible retouch evidence.

5.4.3.3. Scrapers

- 2014:035: C023 Convex scraper (proximal portion): Flint, grey, tertiary; edge damage, abraded, broken, 10 × 11 × 4 mm.
- 2015:001: C401 Convex scraper: Chert, black, tertiary; edge damage, abraded, 18 × 16 × 8 mm.
- 2015:083: C473 Convex scraper: Flint, light grey, tertiary; edge damage, abraded, heavily patinated, broken, 25 × 19 × 9 mm.
- 2015:119: C402/428 Convex scraper: Flint, cream, tertiary; edge damage, abraded, heavily patinated, broken (crushed platform and broken distal end), 21 × 27 × 6 mm.
- 2015:133: C401 Convex scraper: Chert, dark grey, Secondary; edge damage, abraded, 36 × 32 × 16 mm.
- 2016:253: C818 Convex scraper: Chert, black, secondary; edge damage, abraded, broken, 24 × 19 × 8 mm.

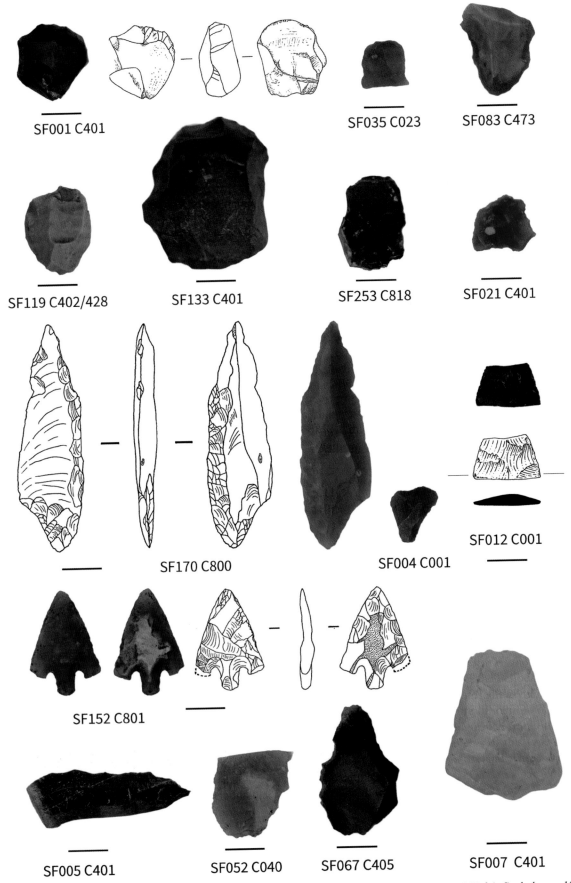

SF001 C401

SF035 C023

SF083 C473

SF119 C402/428

SF133 C401

SF253 C818

SF021 C401

SF170 C800

SF004 C001

SF012 C001

SF152 C801

SF005 C401

SF052 C040

SF067 C405

SF007 C401

Fig. 5.4.1. Lithics from the Hill of Ward. Illustrations by Mark Powers except SF012 (Conor McHale). Scale bar = 10 mm.

5.4.3.4. Edge retouched forms

- 2014:052: C040 Edge retouched blade: Chert, black, secondary; edge damage, abraded, 39 × 23 × 6 mm.
- 2015:005: C401 Edge retouched flake (proximal portion): Flint, light grey, secondary; edge damage, abraded, broken, 19 × 18 × 3 mm.
- 2015:067: C405 Double edge retouched form: Chert, black, secondary; edge damaged, 31 × 19 × 4 mm.

5.4.3.5. Rejuvenation flakes

- 2015:021: C401 Rejuvenation flake (from scraper?): Flint, red, secondary; edge damage, heavily patinated, 15 × 12 × 4 mm.

5.4.3.6. Projectile points

- 2014:004: C001: Petit-tranchet derivative arrowhead: Flint, honey, tertiary; edge damage, abraded, heavy patination, broken, 12 × 14 × 4 mm.
- 2014:012: C001: Arrowhead (diagnostic identification not possible medial portion of arrowhead form): Chert, black, tertiary; edge damage, broken, 10 × 15 × 2 mm.

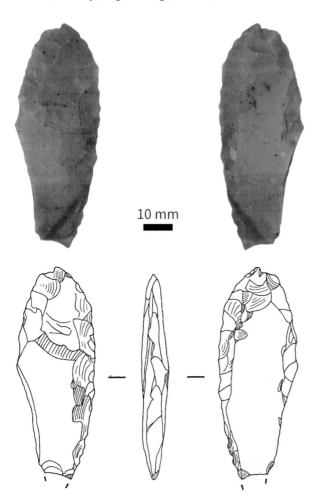

10 mm

Fig. 5.4.2. Bifacially worked plano-convex knife (SF271 C818) (Illustration: Mark Powers).

- 2016:152: C.801: Petit-tranchet derivative arrowhead: Flint, honey, tertiary; edge damage, 50 × 15 × 5 mm.
- 2016:170: C800: Barbed and tanged arrowhead (type B) (see Woodman *et al.* 2006, 139): Flint, light honey, secondary; edge damage, abraded, light patination, broken (very tips of tangs), 24 × 16 × 3 mm.

5.4.3.7. Knives

- 2016:271: C.818 Plano-convex: Flint, light grey, tertiary; edge damage, abraded, light patination broken (along parts of edges and distal end) 69 × 26 × 8 mm.

Although an important indication of material working and reuse, the rejuvenation flake 2015:021 is not diagnostic for a particular period. Similarly, the three retouched flakes and blades are not strong indicators of a particular period but would be more likely to appear from the Neolithic onwards. Stronger diagnostics of Neolithic activity are the six convex scrapers, whilst the petit-tranchet, oblique and barbed and tanged arrowheads and bifacially worked plano-convex knife indicate continued later Neolithic and potentially early Bronze Age activity.

5.4.3.8. Contexts

The most common contexts within the collection are: C401 at 31% of recorded material and C818 at 17% of material. Similarly when considering the diagnostic artefacts these two contexts are the only ones that appear multiple times, whilst most other contexts, for standard and diagnostic materials are more evenly split.

5.4.4. Summary

The Hill of Ward lithics assemblage is diagnostic of Neolithic, likely later Neolithic, activity with some early Bronze Age activity. It includes some particularly nice examples of petit-tranchet derivative, oblique and barbed and tanged arrowhead forms. This mirrors indications of Neolithic activity provided by the fragment of probable megalithic art recovered from the top of the bank at Trench 1 (O'Sullivan, this volume). Overall, the collection is in good condition, but edge damage is disproportionately high compared to other condition markers. This is likely owing to the rocky nature of many of the fills present on site leading to physical damage of objects. It is suggested that the higher proportion of removals and retouched tools over cores and the presence of scraper, retouched flakes and projectiles favours domestic or working/hunting activity at the site over more industrialised lithics production or quarrying. This is further supported by the lack of large removals and an indication of a reliance on smaller flint pebble source material from glacial deposits, and chert derived from between the planes of the limestone bedrock.

5.5. Animal bones (Ruth Carden and Erin Crowley-Champoux)

5.5.1. Introduction

During three seasons of excavation at the Hill of Ward a total of 18,408 animal bones were recovered from 113 excavated contexts within 10 areas: the topsoil, one test pit, and eight excavation trenches. The faunal assemblage (total weight 43,309.45 g) was identified to 18 taxonomic groupings.

5.5.2. Methodology

Bones were identified using a personal reference collection of domestic and wild faunal species; skeletal collections in the National Museum of Ireland, Natural History Division; a loan collection from the National Museums of Scotland, Edinburgh; and published literature (*e.g.* Silver 1963; Boessneck 1969; Pales and Lambert 1971; Schmid 1972; Hillson 1992; Cohen and Serjeantson 1996; Zeder and Lapham 2010).

Bone size characteristics were used only as a guide since these are problematic when dealing with differences between the ontogenetic (developmental) stages and male/female traits, where males are often larger than females within the same species. Age estimation was recorded per bone if suitable anatomical features were present as either adult (adult dentition, suture fusion stages), subadult, juvenile (immature) and neonate. Identification of bone fragments derived from species' juveniles were dependent on the appearance of the external bone morphology and the stage of the suture fusion of the epiphyses. Highly porous bone is indicative of young animals in accordance with actual bone development within various ontogenetic stages. Side element differentiation (left or right) was recorded as per characteristics associated with functional morphology and anatomical details of the animal bone.

5.5.2.1. Size classes

The number of long bone shaft fragments, bone fragments, vertebrae and rib fragments that could not be identified to species were grouped into body size classes of mammal or animal:

- Small-sized (*e.g.* mice, shrew, lemming, rat, vole, bat, stoat, frog, toad, lizard and some fish and bird species)
- Medium-sized (*e.g.* hare, rabbit, red fox, cat, badger, squirrel, otter, certain breeds of domestic dog and some fish, marine mammals and bird species)
- Medium/Large-sized (*e.g.* sheep, goat, deer (excl. red deer), pig/wild boar, certain breeds of domestic dog, wolf and some marine animals and bird species)
- Large-sized (*e.g.* cattle, horse, brown bear, red deer)

5.5.2.2. Taphonomy

Taphonomic processes such as natural weathering, sun bleaching, and plant root etching were noted where relevant. Locations and descriptions of cut marks were documented, if present. Where such modifications were preserved on bones, carnivore and rodent modifications (tooth pits and gnawing) to bones were recorded, including any that may have passed through the digestive tracts. Bones were examined for signs of burning, scorching and/or cremation; thus blackened, calcined and partially calcined bones were recorded. Such bones exhibit characteristic external and internal properties including certain types of surface fracture morphologies and colouring.

5.5.2.3. Unidentifiable bone and unidentified bone

The term *unidentifiable* was used when the bone fragment in question could not be identified to a skeletal element (whole or part thereof) or to a minimum taxonomic level. This was primarily due to lack of any recognisable morphological features on the bone fragment that allowed for identification other than mammal or animal bone, where 'animal bone' included any taxa (bird, amphibian, mammal, reptile etc).

The term *unidentified* indicates bones that eluded identification due to lack of distinguishing anatomical features and/or highly fragmentary state at the current time but may be identified in the future with additional time using different applied techniques and/or by a different animal osteologist or zooarchaeologist. Only four such unidentified bone fragments were of this type within this assemblage, three of which were partial neonatal mammalian bone shafts.

5.5.2.4. Recorded information

The following information was recorded for each bone or fragment where possible: context, minimum taxonomic unit, type of bone element, left or right side, whole or partial, the state of the bone fusion (descriptions and method after Carden and Hayden 2006), evidence of carnivore and rodent gnawing and digestive processes, evidence of human agency (worked, burned/heated, butchered), condition, evidence of bone arthropathies (or bone pathology), estimated age or developmental stage, weight (g) and other noteworthy observations. All data were recorded in an Excel workbook. Due to the nature of bone fragmentation in this assemblage, very few osteometrical data were recorded – no total lengths of long bones were recorded which would have allowed investigation of changes and comparison of estimated withers heights in cattle and the ovicaprids, or distal measurements that would have allowed sexing of the bones.

5.5.2.5. Life or developmental stage (age) estimation

Estimating developmental life stages of mammals is based on the fusion of epiphyses of the bones and the developmental tooth eruption patterns and subsequent wear pattern of teeth (*e.g.* Silver 1969). Fusion data may under-represent very young animals since immature and very young bones do not survive as well as those from mature individuals. Furthermore, fusion data are only useful until skeletal maturity is reached, which is attained prior to full mature body size. Teeth are more likely to survive within archaeological deposits than bone, but although there is less bias towards older animals, deciduous teeth from young animals may be missed owing to poor retrieval methods (O'Connor 1998). The degree of wear patterns on teeth is a direct reflection of the type of forage ingested by the animal, thus seasonal and geographic variations exist due to varying types of forage ingested throughout the year and between geographic regions. Inherent variability associated with timing of epiphyseal fusion (not only within each individual skeletal element within one animal, but also between males and females of one species and other geographic factors (Carden and Hayden 2006) and tooth eruption/wear patterns within species can make estimating age at death/slaughter difficult to determine. The highly fragmented skeletal remains did not allow for an in-depth estimation of age of the identified taxa since most of the teeth were loose. Therefore, the use of broad age classes, including neonate, juvenile, immature, subadult and adult developmental stages were used.

5.5.2.6. Palaeopathology

Identification of pathological modifications on bone includes the identification of arthropathies (osteoarthritis), osteomyelitis, fusion of separate bones, and the healing of misaligned bones (after a fracture). Osteological pathologies can be useful measures for the study of animal remains from archaeological sites as they provide information about how the animal lived, under what conditions, population health, and use for secondary products (*e.g.* arthropathies related to mechanical stress as a result of use in transportation or traction).

Only two skeletal fragments within the entire assemblage displayed palaeopathologies: a partial adult vertebra of a medium-sized mammal from C009 displayed evidence of bone pathology on the centrum body region of the bone. This extra bone deposition and morphology is usually associated in mature adult individuals where there is loss of intervertebral cartilaginous discs resulting in a degree of arthro-related pathologies (*e.g.* arthritis or infection related).

5.5.2.7. Number of identified specimens (NISP)

The number of identified specimens or bone fragments (NISP) by anatomical element and species was recorded for each context. The NISP is a fundamental broad general measure and simple unit by which faunal remains have been recorded and comprises all bone fragments that have been identified to some level of taxa (Lyman 1994; O'Connor 2008). NISP provides a simple overview or

description of the relative abundance of species and their identified skeletal remains whilst the minimum number of individuals (MNI) may provide an estimate of numbers of immature and adult individual animals (estimator of population) present within the assemblage based on the separation of left and right bones of the same skeletal element (Lyman 1994; O'Connor 2008).

5.5.2.8. Minimum number of individuals (MNI)

MNI was calculated examining the most commonly occurring skeletal element of a taxonomic grouping, whilst taking consideration of left (L) and right (R) sided skeletal elements and also accounting for the number of the skeletal element type within an individual species (*e.g.* one atlas cervical vertebra occurs in all animal species, whereas the number of teeth or metapodial bones differ between species and taxonomic groupings). The higher count was taken as the smallest number of individual animals within each excavated site and where appropriate if sufficient numbers of skeletal element were present, other counts were examined for the same identified species. Additionally, where lefts or rights of fragments were not available, the presence of adult and/or subadult/juvenile bones or adult and deciduous teeth were taken into account from the most commonly occurring skeletal element. One obvious issue when using MNI is where there are low numbers of identified bone fragments available (*e.g.* one bone fragment of a species is equal to one individual animal). Furthermore, if one individual animal is represented in multiple excavation trenches/areas within an archaeological site then it will be counted twice. Thus, caution must be emphasised when regarding the MNI data associated with the identified taxonomic groupings within this report. See Lyman (1994) and O'Connor (2008) for further issues and discussions of the use of NISP and MNI measures within zooarchaeological analyses.

5.5.2.9. Minimum animal units (MAU)

MAU is a proportion based on the expected value and the total number of possibilities. In the case of paired elements it divides the range in half, i.e. marks the average for the set of options. It is only influenced by the expected number of elements per individual. As the expected number increases, the MAU becomes a smaller value relative to all possible values. Because of the assemblage fragmentation and stratification, there were components of the site for which it was not possible to calculate MNI values. For this reason, MAU values were calculated.

5.5.3. Results and discussion

5.5.3.1. Overview

A total of 17,822 skeletal fragments were recovered from secure archaeological contexts and examined from 113 archaeological contexts. Nineteen taxonomic categories were identified from the assemblage (Table 5.5.1).

Table 5.5.1. Identified faunal taxonomic categories identified within the Hill of Ward faunal assemblage, vernacular and full taxonomic names used where possible. Unidentifiable mammal or animal bone fragments were grouped in the 'Unidentifiable' category.

Order	Family	Genus and Species	Vernacular name
Artiodactyla	Bovidae	*Bos taurus*	Cow
		Ovis aries	Sheep
		Ovis/Capra sp.	Sheep/Goat
	Cervidae	*Cervus elaphus*	Red deer
	Suidae	*Sus scrofa*	Pig/Wild boar
	Equidae	*Equus* sp.	Horse
	n/a	n/a	Ungulate/Large Ungulate sp.
Carnivora	Canidae	*Vulpes vulpes*	Red fox
		Canis familiaris	Domestic dog
	Felidae	*Felis catus*	Domestic cat
Rodentia	Muridae	*Apodemus sylvaticus*	Wood mouse
Lagomorpha	Leporidae	*Lepus* sp.	Hare
Body-size categories			Large mammal (LM)
			Medium mammal (MM)
			Small mammal (SM)
Possible identifications		?*Canis* sp.	?Dog/Canid sp.
		?*Cervus elaphus*	?Red deer
		?*Sus scrofa*	?Pig/Wild boar
			Unidentifiable (UNID)

Table 5.5.2. The distribution of faunal fragments per excavation trench.

Trench	Top	TP2	1	2	3	4	5	6	7	8	n/a	Total
Cattle	12	40	5	29	76	205	175	73	255	130	1	1001
Sheep/Goat	0	15	0	4	31	40	98	29	114	88	1	420
Pig/Wild Boar	5	50	0	9	11	71	73	33	131	64	1	448
Horse	0	1	0	0	7	16	10	2	15	6	0	57
Dog/Fox	0	1	1	2	2	10	18	1	5	7	0	47
Cat	0	0	0	0	0	0	0	1	3	0	0	4
Hare/Rabbit	0	1	0	3	0	4	1	0	1	1	0	11
Red deer	0	7	0	2	14	2	2	1	4	4	0	36
Birds	0	0	0	0	0	7	0	0	5	2	0	14
Fish	0	0	0	0	0	0	0	0	0	0	0	0
Rodent	0	0	0	1	1	2	1	72	0	0	0	77
Lg	12	134	38	130	277	473	429	126	506	225	3	2353
Md	0	116	0	32	33	53	108	14	73	148	4	581
Sm	0	1	0	0	0	3	0	0	0	0	0	4
UNID	28	225	122	159	968	3259	2387	928	3553	1680	46	13355
Total	57	591	166	371	1420	4145	3302	1280	4665	2355	56	18408

Of the recovered fragments, 12,947 were unidentifiable to species, family group, or size class (73%). Thus, only 27% (n=4,875) of the assemblage was able to be assigned a taxonomic category or size class. At least 18 taxonomic genera/species were identified within the

assemblage from 2,027 bone fragments (11%), and one additional category for unidentifiable or unidentified remains (UNID).

Of the 18 taxonomic genera/species identified only six wild species were identified (wood mouse, red

Table 5.5.3. The distribution of fragments by phase of occupation.

	Bronze Age/mid-Iron Age	Late Iron Age–early medieval	Early medieval	Later medieval	Total
Cattle	234	98	593	39	964
Sheep/Goat	44	36	307	15	402
Pig/Wild Boar	80	11	279	50	420
Horse	16	12	32	1	61
Dog/Fox	12	3	31	1	47
Cat	0	0	4	0	4
Hare/Rabbit	7	0	3	1	11
Red deer	4	13	3	7	27
Birds	7	0	7	0	14
Rodent	3	1	73	0	77
Lg	603	373	1,162	167	2,305
Md	85	36	335	83	539
Sm	3	0	0	1	4
UNID	3,418	1,265	8,039	225	12,947
NISP	407	174	1,339	107	2,027
NSP	4,516	1,848	10,868	590	17,822

Table 5.5.4. The percent of the number of identified fragments (%NISP) per taxa by period.

	Bronze Age/mid-Iron Age	Late Iron Age–early medieval	Early medieval	Later medieval	Total
Cattle	57.49	56.32	44.29	34.21	47.31
Sheep/Goat	10.81	20.69	22.93	13.16	19.83
Pig/Wild Boar	19.66	12.64	20.84	43.86	20.72
Horse	3.93	6.90	2.39	0.88	3.01
Dog/Fox	2.95	1.72	2.32	0.88	2.27
Cat	0.00	0.00	0.30	0.00	0.20
Hare/Rabbit	1.72	0.00	0.22	0.88	0.54
Red deer	0.98	8.05	0.75	6.14	1.33
Birds	1.72	0.00	0.52	0.00	0.69
Rodent	0.74	0.57	0.00	0.00	0.64
%NISP	9.01	9.42	12.31	18.35	11.37

Table 5.5.5. The percent of number of fragments among size classes and unidentified fragments for the entire assemblage per period.

	Bronze Age/mid-Iron Age	Late Iron Age–early medieval	Early medieval	Later medieval	Total
Large	13.35	19.16	10.69	28.64	12.87
Medium	1.88	1.95	3.08	14.24	3.04
Small	0.07	0.00	0.00	0.17	0.02
UNID	75.69	66.23	73.92	38.59	72.68
%NSP	25.34	10.37	61.02	3.27	100

fox, hare, crow, passerine and red deer). In contrast, four identified domestic species predominated, with skeletal fragments of cow (n=964, 47% of the NISP) being the most prevalent followed by fragments of sheep/sheep-goat (n=420, 21%), then pig/wild boar (n=402, 20%), and horse (n=61, 3%) (Tables 5.5.2 and 5.5.3). Three body-size categories were recorded, representing 16% (n=2,848) of the full assemblage: large mammal (n=2,305), medium mammal (n=539), and small mammal (n=4).

Wild and commensal/domestic mammals are indicated within Tables 5.5.3, 5.5.4 and 5.5.6 and Figure 5.5.1, 5.5.2

Table 5.5.6. The minimum number of individuals (MNI) per taxa per period and, where appropriate, the minimum animal units (MAU) per taxa.

	Bronze Age/mid-Iron Age	Late Iron Age–early medieval	Early medieval	9th–12th c. AD*	Later medieval	Total
Cattle	5	4	5	4.5	2	22.5
Sheep/Goat	2	2	6	3	2	16
Pig/Wild Boar	2	2	3	3.5	4	15.5
Horse	3	1	1	1	1	7
Dog/Fox	4	1	4	2	1	13
Cat	0	0	1	1	0	2
Hare/Rabbit	2	0	1	1	1	6
Red Deer	2	1	1	1	1	6
Birds	1	0	0	2	0	3
Rodent	2	1	45**	0	0	3
Total	23	12	22	19	12	94

*Elements from these features could not be sided. This represents the minimum animal units (MAU).
**These represent individuals from a single context or nest and were not included in the final MNI.

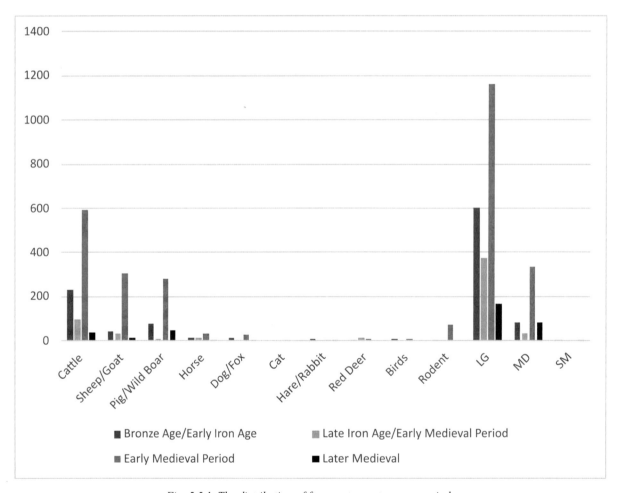

Fig. 5.5.1. The distribution of fragments per taxa per period.

and 5.5.3 provide a broad summary of the proportions of the recovered faunal remains identified to the taxonomic categories from the Hill of Ward.

The faunal assemblage was divided into four chronological periods based on the stratigraphic relationships between features and radiocarbon dating (see Figs 5.5.1,

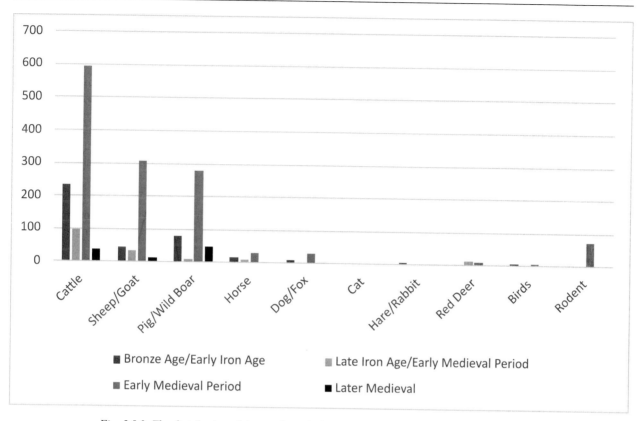

Fig. 5.5.2. The distribution of the number of identified specimens (NISP) per taxa per period.

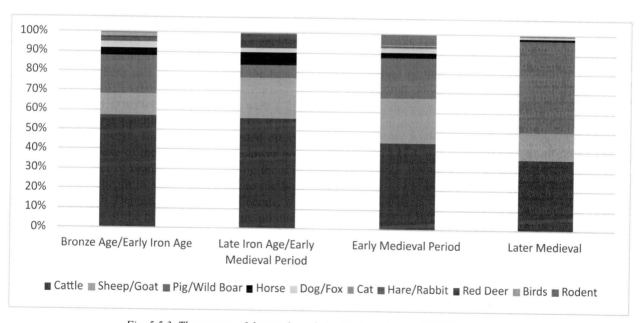

Fig. 5.5.3. The percent of the number of identified specimens (%NISP) per period.

5.5.2 and 5.5.3). These comprise the Bronze Age–early/developed Iron Age (13th to 4th centuries BC), the late Iron Age–early medieval transitional period (3rd to 6th centuries AD), the early medieval period (7th to 10th centuries AD), and the later medieval period (11th to 13th centuries AD). These occupational phases include the

construction and use of the Hillfort Phase (Bronze Age), the destruction of the Hillfort Phase (early/developed Iron Age), the construction and use of the Southern Enclosure and construction of the inner Tlachtga ditch (late Iron Age–early medieval transition), the construction and fill of the additional Tlachtga ditches (early medieval period),

Table 5.5.7. The number of fragments with representations of each type of modification.

	Bronze Age/ mid-Iron Age	Late Iron Age– early medieval	Early medieval	Later medieval	Totals
Burned	1248	329	527	81	2185
Carnivore Gnawing	266	48	302		616
Rodent Gnawing	18	1	36		55
Butchery (cut/chop)	76	29	190	4	299
Worked	3	7	15	3	28
Pathology	3		2		5
Root etching	118	9	120	2	249
Chalky and/or decalcified	393		104		497
Weathered	709		709		1418
Associated residue/crust	1				1
Fresh/Recent indentations	5	3	6	1	15

Table 5.5.8. The total percentage of the assemblage with each kind of modification.

	%NSP
Burned	12.26
Carnivore Gnawing	3.46
Rodent Gnawing	0.31
Butchery (cut/chop)	1.68
Worked	0.16
Pathology	0.03
Root etching	1.4
Chalky and/or decalcified	2.79
Weathered	7.96
Associated residue/crust	0.01
Fresh/Recent indentations	0.08

and the burning event on the top of the central mound (later medieval). With the exception of *in-situ* animal bones directly on the base of ditch deposits it was not possible to distinguish bones from the Bronze Age construction phase from those of the closing of the Hillfort Phase. Bones derived from topsoil were not included in these counts.

Across all periods, cattle were by far the most abundant identified species (47% of the identified specimens), followed by pig/wild boar (21%), then by sheep/goats (20%). The relative frequencies of identified species changed over time, with cattle being the most abundant in the Hillfort Phase (58%) and then becoming progressively less abundant from the late Iron Age through later medieval periods (from 56%–37%). Meanwhile, sheep and goats, which only represented 11% of the identified specimens from the Hillfort Phase, become more abundant during the late Iron Age through the early medieval periods (21%–23%) before becoming less abundant during the later medieval period (14%). Pigs/wild boar

had a greater amount of variance, representing 20% of the Hillfort Phase assemblage, then only accounting for 13% of the late Iron Age to early medieval transitional period assemblage, then 21% of the early medieval period/ Tlachtga monument assemblage, before representing 47% of the later medieval assemblage. These shifting frequencies represent differences in preference and practice over time, with cattle becoming less dominant over time and sheep/goat becoming progressively more common with pig becoming uncommon during the late Iron Age to early medieval transition and then becoming as common as sheep/goat before becoming quite abundant during the later medieval phases.

In addition to these major livestock species, the assemblage from the Hill of Ward also contains domestic horses, dogs, and cats and wild animals including red deer, hare/ rabbit, birds and rodents. The presence of postcranial elements of red deer from the Late Iron Age to early medieval transition suggests that some limited hunting may have taken place, though most of the red deer remains consist of antlers, which are shed annually and can be collected without injury of the animal.

The species frequencies for the Bronze Age to early/ developed Iron Age and early medieval periods are typical for other Irish sites of their respective time periods, with cattle dominating the assemblages and then lesser amounts of pig and sheep/goat (McCormick 2007). The high proportion of horse in the Late Iron Age to early medieval transition, high number of rodent remains in the early medieval period, and the high proportion of pigs in the later medieval period are somewhat unusual. These patterns may be a result of specialized activities at the site (with regards to the Southern Enclosure) or a matter of the material excavated (the high number of rodent remains mostly derived from a single deposit, a probable nest within the stone revetment of the central mound). It should also be noted that differences in total assemblage size per period can result in the relative abundance of some species being inflated.

5.5.3.2. Taphonomic agents

Many factors may affect the preservation and representativeness of the faunal assemblage. These include destructive human and animal activities upon the bones themselves and additionally natural pre- and post-depositional physical and chemical degradation, may affect the skeletal material differently. It is important to note that a single individual bone fragment may show multiple taphonomies. Of the total faunal assemblage, nearly a third (n=5,368, 30.12%) of the skeletal remains exhibited some taphonomic modification (Table 5.5.7 and 5.5.8).

Depending on the temperature, burned bones may show evidence of charring, partial burning or total burning (calcination) and are associated with colour changes to the outer and inner bone matrices (Table 5.5.9). These characteristics are affected by bone moisture content, temperature of the heat source and duration of exposure. Charred bone from roasting is generally black-blue-grey, whereas calcined bone is grey-white in colour. Calcination is associated with relatively clean bones (of meat) that have been disposed of in a fire in terms of refuse or cremation: sustained high temperatures for a long duration. The difference between weathered (exposed to environmental elements) and calcined bone is that a fine powder is produced when the bone surface is scratched with a fingernail in the case of calcined bone.

Additionally, very high temperatures (>420°C) associated with long burning duration causes distortion of the bone surfaces and micro-fractures within the bone and can lead to full decalcification and render the bone to a chalk-like substance and/or ash. These anatomical characteristics associated with short and long duration burning events may occur with cooking and the purposeful

Table 5.5.9. General descriptions of the colours of burned bone associated with varying temperatures (degrees Celsius, °C), after Gilchrist and Mytum (1986).

Temp. (°C)	Colour description
200	Very pale brown
300	Brown to dark reddish brown
350	Dark brown to black
420	Bluish grey
500	Light grey
600	Pinkish grey
700	White

burning of refuse within a fire (or in layers directly below a fire pit). Between 10% and 50% of bone when heated may be totally destroyed (Gilchrist and Mytum 1986) or become extremely fragmented (Knight 1985), which results in recovered bone pieces that are unidentifiable (Lyman 1994).

Within the Hill of Ward assemblage, a total of 12.26% of the fragments showed evidence of burning or subjection to high temperatures, mostly within Bronze Age and early medieval features (Table 5.5.10). Decalcified fragments were recorded in 2.76% (n=497) of the assemblage, calcined fragments, 11.80% (n=2,103) and burned/roasted fragments 0.46% (n=82) (some of these fragments showed evidence of both calcination and decalcification). Most burned fragments were unidentifiable.

After burning, weathering was the next most frequently observed taphonomic agent at 7.96% (n=1,418 fragments) (Table 5.5.8). Some fragments showed evidence of gnawing and tooth pit marks associated with carnivores (3.46%), especially within early medieval features. Very little evidence of plant root etching was observed on the bone fragments (1.40%). Butchery related cut/chop marks was infrequently observed too (1.68%); however, it must be noted that while butchery marks were infrequently visible, nearly 73% of the full assemblage was highly fragmented and just under 12% of the fragments were burned/subjected to high temperatures which may have obliterated other traces.

Gnawing/tooth pits from carnivores were identified on 3.46% (n=616) of the assemblage and gnawing damage from rodents was identified on 0.31% (n=55) of the assemblage. In addition to providing information about the nature of the assemblage and how it formed, carnivore gnawing also provides indirect evidence for the presence of carnivores and insights into the human–carnivore relationships. Carnivore impacts were observed on the remains of cow, pig/wild boar, sheep, sheep/goat, horse and hare. With regards to small mammals the carnivore remains could be attributed to the likes of a red fox in a classic predator–prey scenario, but coupled with burning and potentially cooking and consumption, such damage could be attributed to either dog and/or red fox. Both pits and gnawing marks were evident on fragmented remains also. It is possible that some bones with evidence of dog gnawing may be the result of dogs being deliberately provisioned. Gnawing damage caused by rodents, however, represents scavenging by rodents. Evidence of rodent gnawing indicates that the bones were exposed for some time before being buried. This was observed on bones

Table 5.5.10. Number of fragments that were calcined vs. roasted per period.

	Bronze Age/mid-Iron Age	Late Iron Age	Early medieval	Later medieval	Totals	%NSP
Calcined	1,235	324	514	30	2103	11.8
Roasted	13	5	13	51	82	0.46

from Bronze Age and early medieval features, but hardly any from Iron Age or later medieval features.

Overall, there was little evidence of direct butchery impact marks within the skeletal assemblage (n=299, 1.68%). While there is evidence of butchery in every phase of activity at the site, the greatest frequency of butchery marks was found within early medieval features. Even with the low incidence of butchery related marks, there is some evidence of butchering and processing of domesticates for meat acquisition and craft production. With evidence of roasted bones it is likely that a variety of culinary techniques were used at the Hill of Ward, including removal of meat before roasting or boiling, roasting meat on the bone, and boiling meat on the bone.

During the Hillfort Phase, while there is little evidence for butchery, what evidence there is, is more associated with only livestock species (cattle, sheep/goat, and pig). Among sheep/goat and pig, chop and cut marks are confined to meat-bearing elements, including scapulae, humeri and femora. For cattle, while there is evidence for butchery associated with disarticulation and butchery (cut marks on a mandible, scapula, humerus, radius and pelvis) the majority of modifications are associated with the distal limbs (astragalus, calcaneus, tarsals, metatarsals/metacarpals and phalanges). Cuts to these elements are associated with skinning practices and suggest hide preparation (Table 5.5.11). This is in keeping with the evidence of the bone tool assemblage (Riddler and Trzaska-Nartowski, this volume).

Elements from the Southern Enclosure, related to occupation during the late Iron Age–early medieval transitional period, demonstrate an unusual pattern of butchery (Table 5.5.12). In this phase butchery marks indicate meat removal (modifications on meat-bearing elements) as well as slaughter, including cut marks to a large mammal (cattle, horse, or red deer) cervical vertebra, associated with decapitation. From these contexts there is also a high proportion of modifications on horse remains (3) and red deer antler (4).

Butchery evidence from Tlachtga demonstrate a shift in butchery practices (Table 5.5.13). During this phase there is an increase in evidence for all stages of butchery, including slaughter, disarticulation and decapitation, and filleting. This intensification is also associated with increased evidence for craftwork, including cut marks to crania and distal limbs (metacarpals/metatarsals and phalanges) associated with skinning and hide preparation, and red deer antler.

There was very little evidence for butchery from Test Pit 2, associated with the later medieval period, just two unidentifiable medium mammal fragments with cut marks.

5.5.3.3. Skeletal element distribution

The proportion of each skeletal body part group was examined within each period of occupation to ascertain if there were any biases towards certain body parts that may be linked either to natural mortality or to or human activities.

Differences in by phased skeletal element distribution from the Hill of Ward (Figs 5.5.4, 5.5.5, 5.5.6 and 5.5.7) suggests differences in agricultural, craft activity and food practices. Overall, skeletal element distributions from the earlier phases of activity appear to suggest specialised selection and butchery practices, while assemblages from later periods appear to represent a greater degree of whole animal butchery. Sheep/goat and pig remains from the assemblage from the Hillfort Phase includes a higher proportion of meat-bearing bones (limb bones, pelves and mandibulae) and fewer axial elements (crania, vertebrae

Table 5.5.11. Cut mark data from the Hillfort Phase, indicating on which element cut marks occur for each taxon.

	Cattle	Sheep/Goat	Pig/wild boar	LM	LM-MM	MM	UNID
Mandible	1						
Scapula	1	1	1				
Humerus	1	1	1				
Radius	2						
Pelvis	2						
Femur		1					
Astragalus	2		1				
Calcaneum			1				
Tarsals	1						
Mt/MC	1						
1st Phalanx	3						
2nd Phalanx	2						
3rd Phalanx	1		1				
Limb bone				18	9	3	
UNID							6
Rib					2		

Table 5.5.12. Cut mark data from the Southern Enclosure, indicating on which element cut marks occur for each taxon.

	Cattle	Horse	Sheep/Goat	Pig/wild boar	Red Deer	LM	LM-MM	MM	UNID
Antler					4				
Cranium						1			
Mandible		1						1	
Scapula	2								
Humerus			1						
Radius	1			1					
Pelvis									
Femur	1								
Astragalus									
Calcaneum									
Carpals									
Mt/MC		1							
1st Phalanx									
2nd Phalanx		1							
3rd Phalanx									
Limb bone									
UNID						7			1
Rib							2		
Cervical vertebrae						1			
Caudal vertebrae						1			

Table 5.5.13. Cut mark data from the Tlachtga monument ditches, indicating on which element cut marks occur for each taxon.

	Cattle	Horse	Sheep/Goat	Pig/wild boar	Red Deer	LM	LM-MM	MM	MM-SM	UNID
Antler					1					
Cranium	1							2		
Mandible	6	1	2	1		1	1			
Scapula	4	1								
Humerus	5									
Radius	3					1				
Ulna	2									
Pelvis	8			1		2				
Femur				1					1	
Tibia	2		1	1		1				1
Astragalus	1		2	1						
Calcaneum										
Carpals	1									
Mt/MC	6	1								
1st Phalanx	2									
2nd Phalanx										
3rd Phalanx										
Limb bone						18	6			
UNID						11	6	1		26
Rib	1			1		19	2			
Cervical vertebrae	1									
Other vertebrae						4				
Atlas				1						

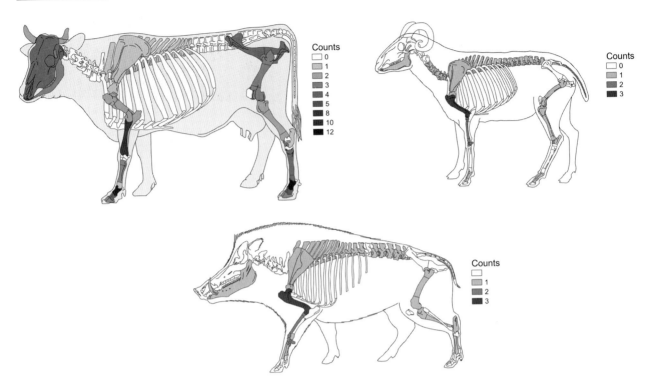

Fig. 5.5.4. Skeletal element distribution (by count) for the Bronze Age–Early Iron Age assemblage.

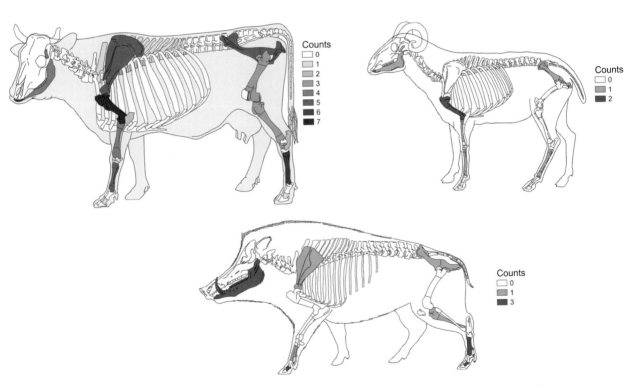

Fig. 5.5.5. The skeletal element distribution (by count) for the Late Iron Age–early medieval transitional period assemblage.

and ribs). This suggests primary and secondary butchery, related to filleting meat of transported elements (Tourunen 2008; Gifford-Gonzalez 2018). The cattle remains, however, with the higher proportion of crania, suggests slaughter and whole animal butchery. During the late Iron Age to early medieval period transition, the pattern of

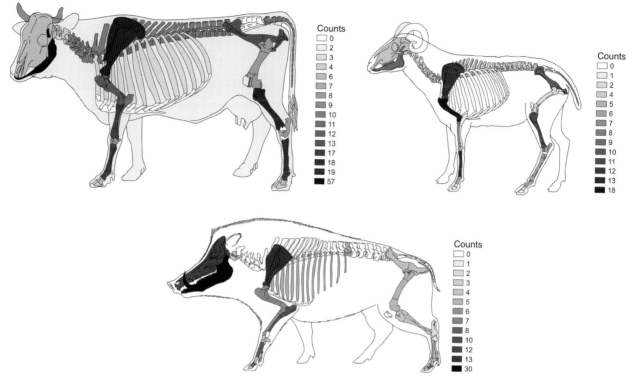

Fig. 5.5.6. The skeletal element distribution (by count) for the early medieval period assemblage.

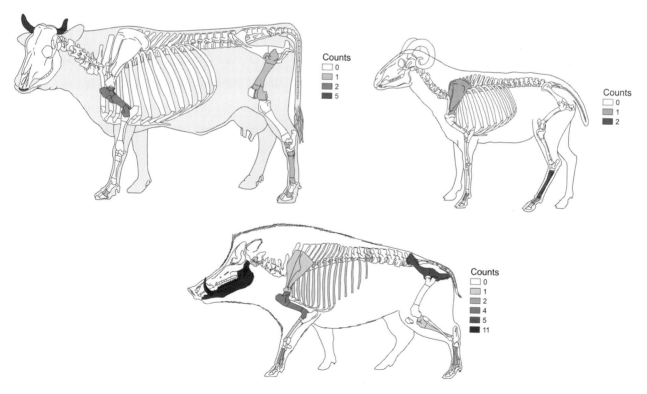

Fig. 5.5.7. The skeletal element distribution (by count) for the later medieval period assemblage.

transported sheep/goat and pigs persists, while cattle also appear to have been brought to the site as meat-bearing elements. At the Tlachtga monument (from the early medieval period through the later medieval period), there is evidence of slaughter, primary and secondary butchery or whole animal butchery.

There were, overall, few recorded vertebra or ribs, this may be due to the highly fragmented nature of the assemblage, resulting in vertebrae and ribs classified only by size class or as unidentifiable remains, or may be owing to a genuine absence from the assemblage. Coupled with the extensive burning, weathering and other taphonomic marks identified along with the butchery related marks, there is evidence of preparation and cooking of forequarters, some hind quarters, and cranial/skulls of domestic species (cow, sheep, sheep/goat, pig/wild boar and horse) at the Hill of Ward.

5.5.3.4. Demographics

Though the evidence for age related data was sparse at the Hill of Ward, understanding age distributions provides information about agricultural and consumption practices. Observation of gross bone shape (morphology) and measurement (osteometric) methods have been employed to determine age and sex. Age determinations are estimated in two ways: through analysis of epiphyseal fusion and tooth eruption and wear. Mandibular age estimations are more accurate in juvenile individuals by charting tooth eruption phases. Particularly useful are observations of the presence of and wear on the deciduous fourth premolar (dP4), eruption of the fourth premolar (P4), and wear on the first and second molars (M1 and M2).

Taphonomic issues must also be considered when determining mortality profiles. Small or juvenile bones are more prone to destruction by scavenger gnawing or by soil chemistry. Therefore, an underrepresentation of juvenile skeletal material may not be clearly indicative of certain animal husbandry practices, or a higher proportion of certain skeletal elements may not be indicative of a specialised butchery practice, but indicative of the taphonomic environment. At the Hill of Ward age estimation was established for cattle, caprovine and pigs by epiphyseal fusion and the presence of deciduous fourth premolars (Fig. 5.5.8).

Cattle dominate the assemblage from the Hillfort Phase. The bone fusion data indicate a high percentage of subadults with equal proportions of immature and adult individuals but an absence of juvenile or neonates. Among the teeth, there were five mandibular M1/2 (indicating individuals >7 months old) and one deciduous fourth premolars (indicating individuals <33 months old), suggesting a bias towards older individuals and supporting the fusion data. Herds with a high proportion of subadults and adults and low proportion of juveniles are more often associated with beef herding, though with small assemblages, this is difficult to say with any certainty. Sheep/goat data, on the other hand, with a high proportion of juveniles and adults (based on fusion data and supported by five M1/2 and one deciduous fourth premolar) are suggestive of a dairy herd; however, again, with a small assemblage, this is uncertain, as meat from juvenile sheep/goats may have been preferable. Pigs during the Hillfort

Phase were slaughtered at all ages, though there is a high proportion of adult individuals. However, the presence of neonatal pig remains suggests that they might have been raised on site or nearby. Finally, neonatal horse remains were also included in the assemblage from this period, further suggesting that animal husbandry took place either on site or nearby.

In the Southern Enclosure cattle continue to dominate, and the age-related data indicates a high proportion of adult individuals, based on the bone fusion data (Fig. 5.5.9). These data are supported by presence of four mandibular M1/2 and one deciduous fourth premolar. This suggests beef husbandry; however, with few individuals, it is difficult to draw conclusions about agricultural practices, rather these individuals may have been specially selected for activities associated with these features. The high proportion of adults in the assemblage might also represent the accumulation of cattle in a system of cattle wealth. In such a system, cattle accumulation is the objective over primary and secondary products and, as a result, individuals are kept for longer than would be expected for meat consumption (Russell 2011). All of the aged sheep/goat and pigs from the assemblage were identified as either subadults or adults.

The faunal assemblage from the main early medieval phase suggests a mixed agricultural economy with dairying, beef herding, and sheep raised for wool on site. A higher proportion of juvenile cattle (and evidence of neonatal cattle) suggests that dairy was one product produced at the Hill of Ward or its immediate environs; however, the presence of a high proportion of older individuals suggests that some of the cattle were also likely raised for beef consumption, traction or herd maintenance. The sheep/goat assemblage contains a high proportion of juveniles and subadult individuals (Fig. 5.5.10). This also resembles the demographic profile for dairy production (Payne 1973) but may also represent raising sheep for wool production and the consumption of lamb.

Being quite small, it is difficult to say for certain how the later medieval assemblage from the Hill of Ward reflects animal economies at the site. However, the high proportion of adult individuals for both cattle and sheep/goat suggest meat consumption and the presence of a number of juvenile pigs suggests that pigs were being raised near to the site (Fig. 5.5.11).

5.5.4. Discussion

The faunal assemblage from the Hill of Ward provides key insights into the different aspects of community and agricultural practices in eastern Ireland from the 13th century BC to the 12th century AD. Faunal remains were found in all components of the site, with varying degrees of preservation. The primary species represented in the assemblage comprised cattle, sheep/goat and pig. There was also evidence of horse, dog, cat, hare, wild birds, red deer, fox and rodents.

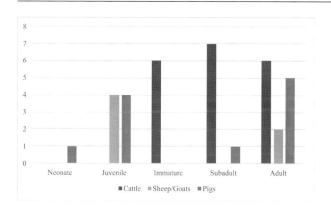

Fig. 5.5.8. Bronze Age–Early Iron Age age estimates for cattle, sheep/goat and pig.

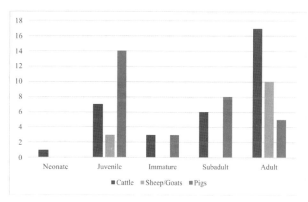

Fig. 5.5.10. Early medieval period age estimates for cattle, sheep/goat and pig.

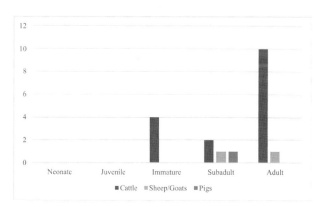

Fig. 5.5.9. Late Iron Age–early medieval transitional period age estimates for cattle, sheep/goat and pig.

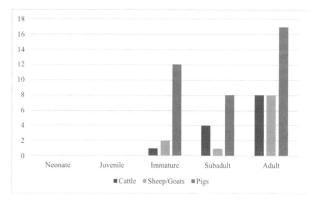

Fig. 5.5.11. Later medieval period age estimates for cattle, sheep/goat and pig.

Material from Trench 4 returned dates from both the Bronze Age and early/developed Iron Age, suggesting that, while the Hillfort Phase features were constructed during the Bronze Age, there was continued activity into the early/developed Iron Age. This may be related to continued practice or to reoccupation of the site. For this study, the faunal remains were counted together due to the difficulty of discriminating between these two periods stratigraphically. During this broad phase, cattle dominated, representing 57.49% of the identified faunal material. After cattle, pig/wild boar was the most commonly identified taxa, representing 19.66% of the assemblage, followed by sheep/goat at 10.81%, then horse (3.93%), dog and fox (2.95%), with marginal contributions from hare, red deer, birds and rodents. Except for a neonatal horse, there were few young individuals, and there were no neonatal or juvenile cattle. Material from this phase had significant evidence of burning with 1,235 of the 4,516 fragments showing evidence of calcination. Similarly common was evidence of carnivore gnawing, rodent gnawing and weathering, suggesting that animal bones from this phase of activity at the site were left exposed for a long period of time before being buried. Finally, a relatively high frequency of cut marks and butchery marks

indicates that butchery took place on site with a preference for domesticated meat (e.g. beef, mutton and pork) over wild game (e.g. venison), and evidence for skinning and the preparation of cattle hides. This is also supportive by an assemblage of 13 whole and fragmentary awls and scrapers of later prehistoric date (see Riddler and Trzaska-Nartowski, this volume). Skeletal element distributions of the major livestock species during this period suggest that these butchery practices are likely related to feasting activities with animal remains brought to the site either as disarticulated meat-bearing elements, or as whole animals for slaughter and consumption (cattle).

The late Iron Age–early medieval transitional period material from the Southern Enclosure, while quite small at 174 identifiable fragments, reveals interesting changing patterns in activity at the site. While cattle continue to dominate at 56.32%, sheep/goat become the next most prevalent taxa at 20.69% ahead of pigs at 12.64%. There is an increase in the relative proportion of horse at 6.9% and red deer at 8.05% (represented by 13 antler fragments and one patella), and marginal contributions from dog and rodent. The assemblage from these contexts continue to demonstrate a high level of burning but less evidence of butchery and carnivore gnawing. The butchery evidence demonstrates a focus on meat removal (*e.g.* cut marks on meat-bearing elements) and craftwork. None of the remains from this period show evidence of weathering, suggesting that the remains were covered soon after deposition. Further, the skeletal element distributions of the major livestock species suggest that elements from this phase were likely brought to the site disarticulated. This may relate to specialised feasting and depositional practices as elements from the basal fills were found in association with an infant burial.

The faunal material from the early medieval period, represents the greatest proportion of the assemblage, at 10,875 fragments, of which 1,339 were identifiable to at least family group. During the early medieval period, the dominance of cattle was reduced to 44.29% and sheep/goat and pigs were nearly equivalent in their proportions (22.93% and 20.84%, respectively). These proportions represent the expected distribution of fragments, in comparison with other early medieval sites (McCormick and Murray 2007). The next most common taxa was horse at 2.39%, with marginal contributions from canids (dog/fox), cat, hare, red deer, birds and rodents. While there were a high number of fragments of rodents in the assemblage (73) they all derived from a single context and likely represent a nest. This provides a unique insight into the depositional and agricultural practices, as very few of the fragments from this period demonstrate evidence of rodent gnawing (n=36). Rodents are attracted to human settlements by food remains and, if faunal remains were available, as suggested by the high number of weathered fragments (n=709) and those with carnivore gnawing (n=329), then the rodents may have been attracted by additional food sources, such as grain. Further modifications suggest that consumption was especially important, with 190 fragments with butchery marks. While some bone implements were recovered these were less abundant than from earlier phases of the site and included at least two objects that were decorative rather than functional (a 'coronet ring' SF2016:294 and a partial casket mount SF2016: 296). The butchery evidence from this phase of activity reflects all levels of butchery, from slaughter to filleting, as well as skinning and craftwork. The intensity of butchery evidence demonstrates a shift in, or an industrialisation of agricultural practices (Seetah 2005). The skeletal element distributions from this phase of occupation indicates whole animal butchery (including slaughter on site, disarticulation and filleting), suggesting that animals were either raised in the immediate environs of the site or were all brought to the site for slaughter. The demographic data also supports the interpretation that the community at the Hill of Ward enjoyed a meat-rich diet, or high status feasting, as the age evidence indicates that most individuals were at or nearing adulthood at the time of slaughter, which is indicative of meat consumption.

Finally, the later medieval phase of occupation, represented by Test Pit 2 produced the smallest assemblage at only 107 identifiable fragments. This small assemblage had a relatively high proportion of pigs, including juveniles (representing 46.73% of the identifiable remains). This dominance of pig remains is likely a representation of sampling bias. That is to say that pigs would likely have represented a smaller proportion of the faunal assemblage, if more features dated to this phase had been excavated. However, a low proportion of the assemblage (14%) was burnt, with the majority of the burnt remains showing evidence of roasting meat on the bone, rather than complete calcination. These piglets therefore probably represent the remains of specialised feasting. The relatively high proportion of cattle horn core from this phase might also indicate high status craft activity.

5.6. Bone objects from the Hill of Ward (Ian Riddler and Nicola Trzaska-Nartowski)

Over the three seasons of excavation a small collection of bone implements was recovered from the Hill of Ward. These can be separated into a group of Bronze Age date, and a second early medieval group. As an assemblage there are some clear indications of fabric processing such as spindle whorl 2015: SF114 and a range of awls. This may relate to wool working (*e.g.* Cleary *et al.* 2003), which is thought to have become important in Ireland at around this time. Processing of hides is also suggested by a number of implements from the earlier phase.

5.6.1. Later prehistoric implements (Fig. 5.6.1)
5.6.1.1. Small spatulate awls (Trench 2; Trench 3)
Two small bone implements (2014: SF058 and 2014: SF069) were identified as 'small spatulate awls'. The term has been used to describe them here in order to distinguish them from implements of a later date, which are known as 'small pointed blades'. The two awls are small, between 43 mm and 50 mm in length, and they taper on two faces towards one end to form sharp spatulate points. In one case (2014: SF069) it is possible that the opposite end of the implement, part of which has fractured away, was also tapered to a point. The form of the implement is a simple one and it is their size, the deliberate choice of a splintered segment of bone midshaft as their raw material and the short, spatulate nature of their pointed terminals that enable them to be distinguished from other forms of bladed point. Small implements of this type are characteristic of the Bronze Age in Ireland. There are a number of examples from Dún Aonghasa, in particular, mostly recovered from stratified contexts of late Bronze Age date (Mullins 2012, figs 8.88.1555; 8.89.2214, 8.90.2309; 2435 and 2491; 8.91.2667 and 8.92.2997 and 4012). Two examples from Chancellorsland Site A were retrieved from contexts of middle Bronze Age date (FitzGerald 2008, 317 and Fig. 2.5.4:1). Several were recovered from sites at Lough Gur, most of them from contexts that were not

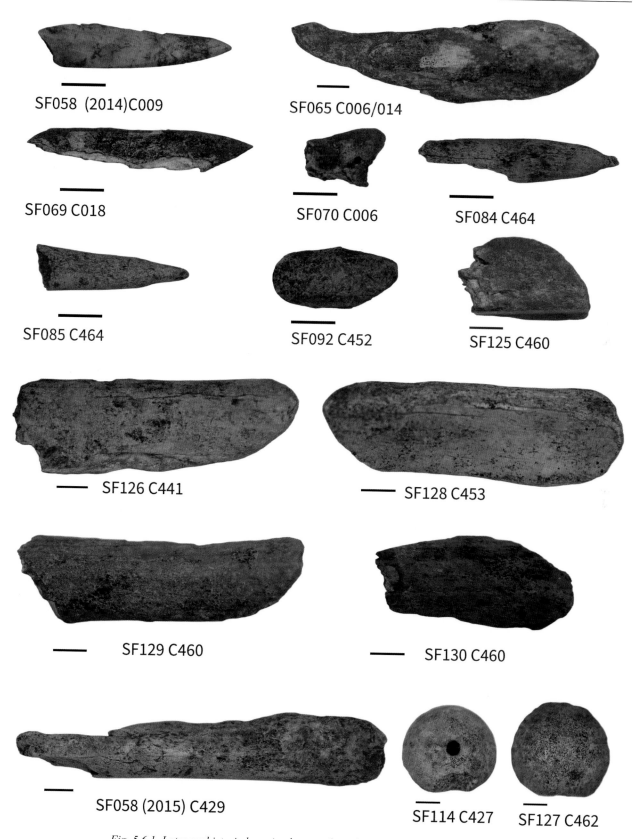

SF058 (2014)C009

SF065 C006/014

SF069 C018

SF070 C006

SF084 C464

SF085 C464

SF092 C452

SF125 C460

SF126 C441

SF128 C453

SF129 C460

SF130 C460

SF058 (2015) C429

SF114 C427

SF127 C462

Fig. 5.6.1. Later prehistoric bone implements from the Hill of Ward. Scale = 10 mm.

closely dated (Ó Ríordáin 1954, Fig. 26.2 and 5, plate XL.7–9 and 18–20; Grogan *et al.* 1987, Fig. 25.2890). Small spatulate awls would have been suitable for delicate work with soft materials. The pointed terminals are sharp but are quite wide and short, and are better suited to marking a surface, rather than perforating it.

2014: SF058 Trench 2 C009

Complete bone awl, cut from a splinter of bone midshaft from a medium- to large-sized mammal, tapering to a short, stub point, with the inner surface of the bone channel visible on one side. Polished throughout, more apparent on the outer surface.

2014: SF069 Trench 3 C018

Fragmentary awl, cut from a splinter of bone midshaft from a medium to large-sized mammal, trimmed on two edges to a sharp point at one end, rectangular in section and slightly curved in profile, possibly tapering to a second point at the other end. Some traces of fire blackening on both sides.

5.6.1.2. Possible Awls (Trench 3)

A segment (2014: SF065) fractured from a cattle-sized piece of long bone, possibly the upper part of a tibia, survives in degraded condition. The edges of the bone appear to have been deliberately rounded and smoothed, and taper to a point. The pointed terminal is almost triangular in shape as it survives, which would be very unusual for a prehistoric implement, but the outer surface of the bone has laminated and this has probably obscured the original shape of this part of the implement. It can be compared with a bone implement of the same size and section from Dún Aonghasa (Mullins 2012, Fig. 8.87.1315). That implement, which comes from a late Bronze Age context, has a sharper terminal and was probably used as an awl. A small fragment of bone (2014: SF070) from the same context at the Hill of Ward has a rounded terminal and resembles a feature seen on another large bone awl from Dún Aonghasa, which has a side projection close to the terminal (Mullins 2012, Fig. 8.91.2739).

2014: SF065 Trench 3 C006

Near complete bone implement, surviving in degraded condition, cut from a cattle-sized long bone midshaft, possibly the upper part of a tibia. The edges of the upper part of the implement are rounded and it tapers to a point that is almost triangular in shape.

2014: SF070 Trench 3 C006

Small fragment of bone with a rounded terminal, curving away to the side, where it has fractured.

5.6.1.3. Splinter Awl (Trench 4)

A fragmentary bone splinter awl (2015: SF084) has been cut from an ovicaprid long bone, almost certainly the midshaft of a metatarsus, and tapers at one end to an indented point. It can be identified as part of a splinter awl, partly on the basis of its indented point, which distinguishes it from small pointed blades such as those seen at Lough Gur (O'Ríordáin 1954, Fig. 26.16–20), and partly because small pointed blades include the proximal or distal articulation of the bone. In this case, although the object is not complete, it is likely that it consisted merely of a section of midshaft. An example from a late Bronze Age context at Dún Aonghasa presents a good parallel (Mullins 2012, Fig. 8.85.779). In both cases the tip of the indented point has fractured and has not been repaired or reshaped.

2015: SF084 Trench 4 C464

Fragment of one end of a bone splinter awl, cut from an ovicaprid metatarsus and fractured across the midshaft with the inner bone channel visible, sliced diagonally towards the terminal, which ends in a fractured, indented point. Slight traces of polish, mainly around the point.

5.6.1.4. Awl (Trench 4)

A bone awl (2015: SF085) has fractured close to the tapered terminal, which has a lightly indented and rounded tip. The thickness of the bone in cross-section suggests that it was cut from a cattle-sized long bone. The manner in which the rounded terminal is distinguished from the shaft of the awl is characteristic of this specific object type. A number of complete examples can be seen at Dún Aonghasa (Mullins 2012, Fig. 8.85.1105a–f). These large awls, made from cattle-sized bone midshafts, can be readily distinguished from smaller splinter awls and they tend to have blunt, rounded points. Most of them have been cut from sections of midshafts and they now lack any trace of the proximal or distal articulations of the bone. The presence of rounded points is intriguing, since these would be of little use in perforating materials and this example is lightly indented, so that it could only extend some 9–10 mm into a surface. Accordingly, it may have been used to widen perforations already made with another implement.

2015: SF085 Trench 4 C464

Fragment of one end of a bone awl, cut from a cattle-sized long bone and rectangular in section with some cortile tissue surviving on the inner surface. The shaft taper to a lightly indented, short, rounded point. Polished at the point and fractured along the midshaft, seemingly in antiquity.

5.6.1.5. Scrapers

Two different forms of scraper were recorded. They vary in the choice of bone and, correspondingly, in their size. A small bone scraper has been cut from an ovicaprid long bone, whilst a series of four larger scrapers, and a fifth example that may be unfinished, have been made from the midshafts of cattle long bones. A small section of midshaft (2015: SF092), cut from an ovicaprid long bone, has been trimmed to a rounded terminal at one end and a broad, tapered point at the other end. Both surfaces are polished, probably from handling. It is a rare example of a small bone scraper, intended for precise work. It fits well into the hand and the broad tapered end, which has a flat terminal, can be drawn across surfaces. There are faint traces of wear across the terminal, confirming that this is the principal working area. It is possible that originally the tapered end was shaped to a sharp point, much like a small bone splinter awl from the Broch of Ayre in Scotland (Sutherland Graeme 1913–1914, Fig. 8). Equally, however, the object may well be complete and intended to be a small, delicate scraper.

A group of four further large bone scrapers can also be identified. They include one near-complete example (2015: SF126), as well as three fragments, arising from two different contexts. They consist of sections of midshaft cut from cattle long bones; most of the fragments are difficult to identify to bone type. The near-complete example has been cut from a cattle metatarsus, whilst another example comes from the lower part of a cattle metacarpus. In each case the medial or lateral side of the bone forms the main part of the implement, which has been neatly rounded at one end. The opposite end narrows in section to form a broad, flat blade. In use, the rounded end would have been held by the fingers, its deliberately smoothed terminal fitting well in the hand, with the thumb located along the inner bone channel. The blade could then be pulled across surfaces and used to scrape away debris. Only one of these objects is nearly complete and it has been damaged in antiquity across the blade. The other examples include modern breaks along the midshaft, as well as fractures that probably occurred during the period of their use. This is not a common implement type for Ireland, but it is attested in England. A complete example came from a middle Iron Age context at Harston Mill, Cambridgeshire (Crummy 2016, 64 and Fig. 3.36.14).

A closely related implement (2015: SF128) has been cut from one side of the midshaft of a cattle long bone and has a rounded terminal at one end. The opposite end has been cut diagonally, but has not been further worked, and it is possible that this is an unfinished example of the object type.

2015: SF092 Trench 5 C452

Small piece of modified bone, a section of midshaft from an ovicaprid long bone, trimmed to a neat curve at one end and to a broad, triangular point at the opposite end. Slight polish on the interior face, more extensive polish on the outer surface.

2015: SF125 Trench 5 C460

Fragment of one end of a bone implement, cut from the midshaft of a large ungulate, the terminal neatly curved on both sides. Sliced through one side of the bone to expose

the inner channel, fractured at the opposite end. Exterior surface is slightly degraded, no trace of any wear or polish.

2015: SF126 Trench 5 C441 (topsoil)

Complete bone scraper, cut from the medial or lateral side of a cattle metatarsus and trimmed to a rounded terminal at one end. Roughly trimmed along the sides and cut laterally with a blade at the opposite end. The bone tapers in section at this end to form a rough edge, part of which has been damaged.

2015: SF128 Trench 5 C453

Complete bone implement, probably an unfinished scraper, cut from the medial or lateral side of a cattle long bone and shaped to a rounded terminal at one end. The opposite end has been cut diagonally but has not been further shaped. Slightly degraded exterior surface, polished throughout and on the long edges.

2015: SF129 Trench 5 C460

Bone scraper, a fragment of the lower part of a cattle metacarpus, sliced along the bone so that only the medial or lateral face remains, which has been trimmed to a rounded terminal at one end. The bone has fractured at the opposite end. Exterior surface is slightly degraded and laminating; no trace of any wear or polish.

2015: SF130 Trench 5 C460

Fragment of a bone scraper, cut from the midshaft of a large ungulate, with a curved section. The terminal at one end has been neatly rounded; the opposite end has fractured, with a modern break. Slight polish on the exterior surface.

5.6.1.6. Large pointed blade (Trench 4)

A large pointed blade (2015: SF058) has been cut from the upper part of the midshaft of a cattle radius, and the lower part of the bone shaped to a rounded point. The object has fractured to either side of the terminal and a diagonal slice across the bone at this point is now incomplete. The bone has the appearance of having broken in the course of the manufacturing process, during the fashioning of its terminal. It shows no sign of being utilised.

2015: SF058 Trench 4 C429

A fragmentary bone large pointed blade, cut from the upper part of a cattle radius midshaft, from the medial or lateral side, and shaped to form a blunt, rounded terminal at the lower end. Part of the terminal has fractured away on both sides, possibly during manufacture.

5.6.1.7. Spindle whorls (Trench 4)

Two bone spindle whorls have both been cut from the proximal articulations of cattle femurs. One is complete and the other is near-complete but unperforated. The complete bone spindle whorl (2015: SF114) is pierced axially by a perforation roughly 6 mm in diameter. Walton Rogers (2007, 23–24) has noted that Iron Age spindle whorls tend to have spindle holes mostly of 4–6 mm in diameter, whilst early medieval spindle holes are broader, at 6–9 mm in diameter. It is likely that the same distinction applies in Ireland as well. Comparable spindle whorls have been found in Iron Age contexts at Freestone Hill, Co. Kilkenny and at Dún Ailinne, Co. Kildare (Raftery 1969, 50, 83–84 and Fig. 13.E61:8 and E61:188; Crabtree and Campana 2007, 125–126). Four spindle whorls of this type from Dún Aonghasa were thought to be of late Bronze Age date (O'Brien and FitzGerald 2012). The diameters of their axial perforations were not published but three of them are around 5–6 mm, to judge from their illustrations (*ibid.*, fig 8.104). The spindle whorls from Freestone Hill and Dún Ailinne have spindle holes that also lie within this range, with the exception of one of the whorls from Freestone Hill, whose spindle hole is around 7 mm in diameter (Raftery 1969, Fig. 13.E61:8).

The weight of a spindle whorl is also an important indicator of its precise use but unfortunately the weights of most whorls have not been supplied in publications. In this case the finished whorl has a weight of 19.4 g. Henry (1999, 72) established that for the early medieval period in England, spindle whorls could be separated into three groups by weight. The lightweight group weighed 10 g or less, the median group extended from 11 g to 29 g and the heavy group weighed over 30 g. Femur caput spindle whorls are likely to have a restricted range of sizes and, correspondingly, a small range of weights, and virtually all of the 73 whorls of this type from Ipswich lay within the median group by weight (Riddler *et al.* forthcoming).

2015: SF114 Trench 4 C427

Complete bone spindle whorl, produced from the articular end of a cattle femur. The bone has fused and has been cut roughly across the base with a blade, and perforated axially. The bone is otherwise unmodified.

2015: SF127 Trench 4 C462

Near complete, sliced proximal articulation from a cattle femur, cut laterally across the bone. Slight damage on one side. The object has not been perforated. Slight polish on the upper surface.

5.6.2. *Early medieval implements (Fig. 5.6.2)*

5.6.2.1. *Pin-beater (Test Pit 2)*

This complete bone pin-beater (2014: SF068), found in two pieces, was rectangular in section and tapers at one end to a rounded point. Single pointed pin-beaters are associated with the vertical two-beam loom, which was widely used during the Roman period and was reintroduced to northern France during the 7th century (Walton

Rogers 2001). From there it was disseminated to England during the 8th century and may have arrived in Ireland at around the same time, or possibly a little later, during the course of the 9th century. The vertical two-beam loom was made entirely of wood and required no loom weights, and it is the dating and distribution of single pointed pin-beaters that provides an index of its use. Outside of Dublin, where over 70 examples have been identified, antler and bone single pointed pin-beaters are still comparatively rare finds in Ireland and usually occur as single finds, as at Carraig Aille, Co. Limerick, Cloghermore Cave, Co. Kerry or Knowth and Lagore in Co. Meath (Ó Ríordáin 1949, 83 and Fig. 14.11; Connolly and Coyle 2005, 109–110 and 188–189; FitzGerald 2012, 559). The object type continued in use until the 12th to 13th century and was eventually supplanted with the advent of the horizontal loom. Single pointed pin-beaters from Cork and Waterford came from 13th-century contexts and are amongst the latest examples to have been discovered in Ireland (Hurley 1997a, 671 and Fig. 17.5.8; 2003, 331 and Fig. 8.1.5).

2014: SF068 Test Pit 2 C038

Complete bone single pointed pin-beater, cut from the midshaft of a cattle-sized long bone and rectangular in section, tapering at one end to a rounded point. Polished throughout with some finishing marks visible.

5.6.2.2. *Large pointed blade (Test Pit 2)*

A complete bone implement (2014: SF064) has been fashioned from the upper part of a cattle radius and retains part of the proximal articulation. The bone has been fractured and lightly worked to form a blunt, rounded point at its terminal. There are traces of polish around the edges of the point and slight polish on the surface of the bone. The implement forms a large pointed blade. Whilst small pointed blades are well-defined and cover a limited range of bone types and implement forms (Britnell 2000, 183), large pointed blades vary widely in the choice of cattle bone. They are much less common than small pointed blades, as a simple comparison of two English late prehistoric sites shows. At Danebury just two of the 38 pointed blades were made from cattle-sized bones, and at Fiskerton only one of 55 bladed implements had been made from cattle bone (Sellwood 1984, 385; Olsen 2003, table 5.1).

There are several broadly comparable implements from Irish and Scottish contexts, mostly of early medieval date. Crabtree and Campana (2007, 129) noted that a cattle tibia from Dún Ailinne had been sawn close to the proximal end and the resulting midshaft tapered to a rounded terminal, producing a large blade of similar dimensions to this example. Similarly, a large blade cut from one side of a cattle metatarsus from Knowth retains part of the proximal articulation and ends in a blunt, rounded terminal, much as with the Hill of Ward example (Barton-Murray 2012, 670 and Fig. 7.8:1.455). The Knowth implement can be compared with a similar example from Pool, Sanday, Orkney (Smith 2007, 497 and Fig. 8.819.PL0342). Large pointed blades occur in later prehistoric contexts but are also found in early medieval deposits and, given the wide variety of objects within the category, it is difficult to date them closely. The blade of this implement is blunt and rounded, and it shows little sign of use. The object sits well in the hand and it could have been used either as a burnisher or as a scraper, depending on how it was held in the hand.

2014: SF064 TEST PIT 2 C038

Complete bone large pointed blade, cut from a cattle radius with part of the proximal articulation still

present. The lower part of the midshaft has been lightly trimmed to form a blunt, rounded terminal. Its edges are polished, and there is slight polish across the bone surface.

5.6.2.3. Bone fragment (Test Pit 2)

A small fragment of bone (2014: SF039) from Test Pit 2 shows no overt signs of working but has a polished surface and several thinly incised longitudinal lines along one side, which represent finishing lines, the vestiges of the final polishing process. It is likely, therefore, that this fragment comes from a worked bone object. It is lightly curved in section and is noticeably thin, and it has the texture of bird bone, although the diameter of the curved section is larger than would be expected from most avian bones. It has also been lightly burnt.

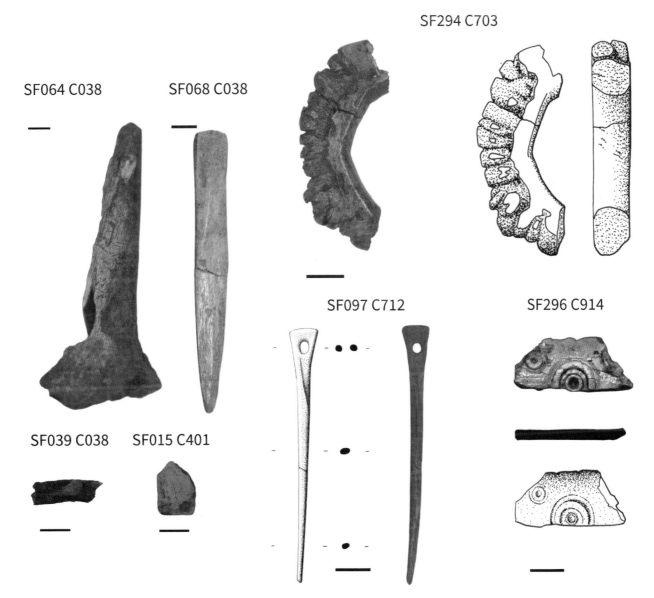

Fig. 5.6.2. Early medieval bone implements from the Hill of Ward. Scale = 10 mm.

2014: SF039 TEST PIT 2 CONTEXT 038

Small fragment of bone, slightly curved in section and relatively thin, possibly from an avian bone. Lightly burnt on both sides with some polish visible on the exterior surface, alongside several diagonal finishing lines.

5.6.2.4. Worked bone fragment (Trench 4)

A small fragment of worked bone (2015: SF015) has been neatly sawn at one end and has fractured along its sides. It is possibly a small piece of an object, like a bone cylinder, but it is more likely to represent waste from bone working. The neatly sawn edge is indicative of an early medieval or later date.

2015: SF015 TRENCH 4 C401

Small fragment of bone, from the midshaft of a large mammal long bone, cleanly sawn in a single direction at one end and fractured along the sides. Either waste material from bone working or possibly part of an object like a cylinder.

5.6.2.5. Needle (Trench 8)

A complete bone needle (2016: SF097) has been cut from a pig fibula, with the distal end of the bone forming the head, which has a slightly rounded apex and a prominent knife-cut perforation. The form of the head allows it to be assigned to Type 4 for Dublin, within a typological scheme that is broadly applicable to Ireland as a whole (Riddler and Trzaska-Nartowski forthcoming). Eva Andersson placed bone needles from Birka into three groups, depending on whether the head was flat, rounded or pointed (Andersson 2003, 83–87 and 127–130). The same groups can be utilised for early medieval Ireland, where bone needles with flat heads are the most common, ahead of those with rounded heads, with pointed heads relatively scarce. Bone needles generally have broad heads, much wider than contemporary needles of metal. They could be produced quite easily and simply, with pig fibulae used for the majority of them. Although described as needles, it is better to view them as weaving implements that could have been used for a variety of purposes.

2016: SF097 TRENCH 8 C712

Complete pig fibula needle, broken in two at mid-point. With rounded apex and knife-cut perforation.

5.6.2.6. Coronet ring (Trench 8)

A fragmentary antler coronet ring (2016: SF294) retains the natural tissue surrounding the burr of the red deer antler (the coronet) and the sides of the object have been lightly trimmed to flatten them. Coronet rings are comparatively rare finds within early medieval Ireland. Around 20 examples were found in the National Museum's excavations within Dublin and small numbers have been recorded from outside of Dublin, notably at

Clones, Lagore, Lismullin 1, Oughtymore and Rathgureen (D'Arcy 1900, 228; Hencken 1950, Fig. 108.120; Mallory and Woodman 1984, Fig. 4.6; Comber 2002, Fig. 18.71; Riddler and Trzaska-Nartowski 2009). This is a welcome addition to a small corpus. The coronet ring from Oughtymore came from a context with a radiocarbon date suggesting occupation between the 7th and 9th centuries, whilst the example from Lismullin 1 came from a context within a group of pits located near to a souterrain, other pits in the group returning radiocarbon dates largely of *c.* 770–970 (Mallory and Woodman 1984, 56; O'Connell 2009, 65–66). Their origins may lie in the 8th century, the Dublin sequence suggesting that they continued into the 10th century, and possibly a little later.

These rings retain the outer coronet but the central part of the burr was hollowed out and the inner part of the ring normally shows traces of extensive wear, as is the case here. In terms of their function, they can be compared with the series of coronet rings found in graves mainly of the 4th and 5th century in northern Germany and Anglo-Saxon England (Bode 1998, 95; Riddler and Trzaska-Nartowski 2013, 99–103). These are found largely in the graves of females and examples from inhumation graves indicate that the rings were fastened at the waist and used to suspend objects on straps made from organic material. A similar function can be suggested for the Irish series. With the coronets retained as the outer parts of the rings, it would have been obvious that they had been fashioned from red deer antler, and they may have been imbued with a symbolic value. Deer shed their antlers each year, growing a new set in a remarkably short space of time. Thus, antlers are symbols both of regeneration and of fertility. Ursula Koch has suggested that the related sequence of antler burr discs found in early medieval graves in southern Germany also reflect a cycle of life, with growth towards a position of strength and display, followed by a waning before they are discarded, and the process begins again. There is a possibility that the women buried with these amulets had either not reached adulthood or, if they had, they had not become pregnant; and the discs would have acted as symbols of the hope of fertility, given to them at puberty (Koch 2001, 199). The humbler coronet rings may not have been quite as symbolic as the later series of burr disc rings (*ibid.*, 222), but at least some of the same symbolism may have applied, indicating that they were more than just suspension rings.

2016: SF294 TRENCH 8 C703

Partial antler coronet ring fashioned from basal part of red deer antler. Some evidence of internal wear. Approximately 40% remaining.

5.6.2.7. Casket mount (Trench 7)

A small fragment of a rib bone casket mount (2016: SF296) is decorated with single- and double ring-and-dot designs. Mounts from early medieval caskets are largely made from sections of animal rib, a raw material that would provide reasonably long, flat strips of bone. Rectangular rib bone casket mounts appear to occur at a comparatively late date in Ireland, from the 9th or 10th century onwards. They are reasonably common finds in Dublin and over 40 have been published from Cork and Waterford (Hurley 1997a, 658, 663–665 and Fig. 17.3; 1997b, 261–263 and Fig. 105). The latest examples of casket mounts of this type come from contexts of 13th-century date (Riddler and Walton Rogers 2006, 276).

2016: SF296 Trench 7 C914

Fragmentary bone casket mount, decorated with ring-and-dot design.

5.7. Human skeletal material from the Hill of Ward (Abigail Ash)

Over the course of the three seasons of excavation remains of three individuals were recovered (B1–3). The first of these, from Trench 3 in 2014, was a mostly complete burial of an infant of approximately 3–5 months of age, placed at the bottom of a rock-cut ditch to the south of the main monument. Subsequently, in 2015, fragmentary remains of two other individuals were recovered from Trench 4. One of these was represented by an isolated tooth, the other by a partial mandible.

5.7.1. HOW14-B1 (2014)

Trench 3 was opened to investigate a smaller enclosure to the south of Tlachtga (the 'Southern Enclosure'). Towards the northern part of the trench, at the base of the ditch the articulated remains of an infant were discovered (designated HOW14-B1). The remains were supine and extended along a southwest–northeast axis with the head to the southwest. The upper body rested directly on the bedrock base of the ditch while the lower body lay on a thin layer of orange clay, suggesting the ditch had had time to begin to sediment up before the body was deposited in it. Deposition appeared deliberate, with careful placement of the body within a cavity produced through the natural fracture pattern of the bedrock and the posture of the body being characteristic for an infant laid on its back; arms by the sides and the legs slightly flexed at hip and knee so that the knees were apart, but the feet were together. No artefacts were associated with the burial; however, a group of stones appeared to delineate a space around the remains, and it is possible that larger stones were also lying on top of the skeleton forming a rudimentary cist.

5.7.1.1. Recovery of remains

Excavation of the remains was conducted using small metal tools, bamboo picks and soft brushes. Sediment was carefully removed to reveal the remains and to allow the burial to be recorded visually. Once recording had taken place, the bones were lifted and packaged. Due to the small size of the bones and their fragile nature, several sections of the body were lifted as blocks. Soil samples were collected from the areas of the hands and feet to ensure any small bones missed initially could be recovered later and sediment was collected from above and below the remains for later sieving.

Cleaning of the bones took place in a lab at University College Dublin. Sediment was carefully removed from the bones, again using small metal tools and bamboo picks with the aid of a soft brush. The adhering sediment remained moist and was relatively easy to remove. A small amount of water was brushed onto the diaphyses of the long bones and the right orbital roof to clean these surfaces, but the bones were not washed due to their fragility. Bones were then allowed to dry slowly, which improved the stability of the material.

5.7.2. Osteological assessment

5.7.2.1. Preservation and completeness

The skeleton was mostly complete, although the preservation of individual elements was variable. Using the damage scale suggested by the British Association for Biological Anthropology and Osteoarchaeology (McKinley 2004), the long bones showed Grade 2–3 surface erosion, possibly through the action of water, while the small bones, ribs and cranial surface were better preserved (Grade 1–2). As the ribs appeared well-preserved, several fragments were removed for radiocarbon dating (see Section 3.6).

Within the burial environment the cranium had been crushed and compacted and this had been removed as a single mass. During cleaning the different elements of this cranial block were carefully teased apart and although highly fragmented, most of the cranial bones were represented, including the small bones of the inner ear (see Fig. 5.7.1). The ribs and small bones of the spine were well preserved although the lumbar and sacral regions were underrepresented and the pelvis was poorly preserved with only a fragmentary portion of each ilium present. Long bone diaphyses were mostly complete although the metaphyses were damaged, and no epiphyses were recovered. This is unlikely to be the result of the excavation process as precautions were taken to recover small bones, rather the young biological age of HOW14-B1 (see below) indicates that many of the epiphyses had not yet begun to ossify and the low mineral content of those that had begun ossification would significantly reduce the likelihood of survival (Brickley 2004a). Four metatarsals and a possible calcaneus from the right foot survived and fragments of metacarpals were recovered from the sieved samples. Mineralising deciduous dentition was found both loose within the burial environment and within crypts in the maxillae and hemi-mandibles. Almost all of the teeth were represented, with excellent preservation of the enamel surface and these provided an assessment for the biological age of the individual.

5.7.2.2. Age at death

Initial assessment from the size of the remains suggested that the individual was very young at death, and this informed the laboratory procedures that were subsequently performed. Biological age[1] may be estimated from juvenile remains through the analysis of both dental and long bone development, although dental development often provides a more accurate estimate as it is less affected by

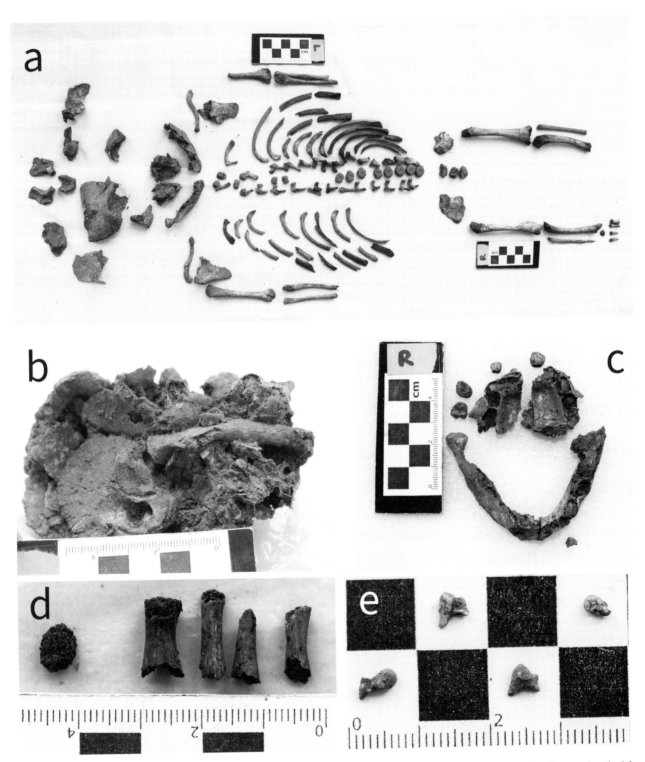

Fig. 5.7.1. The remains of HOW14-B1 are almost complete and in excellent preservation. The full skeleton (a) with inset detail of the compacted cranium during cleaning (b), maxillae and hemi-mandibles after cleaning revealing the deciduous dentition (c), metatarsals (d) and ossicles of the inner ear (e). All scales are in mm. (Photographs copyright A. Ash).

environmental conditions, such as malnutrition, which can disrupt long bone growth (Brickley 2004a).

Maximum length measurements were taken from the long bones where preservation allowed (see Table 5.7.2) and used to estimate biological age through comparison to modern growth standards (Scheuer and Black 2000) and the calculation of age regression formulae (Scheuer *et al.* 1980; see Table 5.7.2). Both methods suggest a relatively young age for HOW14-B1; however, as the regression formulae become inaccurate after one month postpartum (Scheuer *et al.* 1980) and comparison to modern growth standards suggests this individual was probably older than that, regression results must be discounted here. Age estimations were also calculated using measurements taken from the scapula and *pars basilaris* portion of the occipital bone (Scheuer and MacLaughlin-Black 1994; Rissech and Black 2007), which indicated a slightly older age than suggested by the long bones (see Table 5.7.2).

Presence of deciduous dentition within the jaw indicated that eruption of any tooth had probably not yet occurred and loose dentition allowed the direct assessment of dental mineralisation. When compared to dental charts (Ubelaker 1999; Al Qahtani *et al.* 2010) the dental development of HOW14-B1 lay between birth and six months of age with an error margin of two months. Comparison of loose teeth to developmental trajectory charts (Moorrees *et al.* 1963) again suggested a biological age of less than six months, while measurements of crown length were used in regression equations (Liversidge *et al.* 1998; see Fig. 5.7.2), which produced an estimated age of between 3.8 to 4.8 months. Taking these individual estimates into account and allowing for some error and variation in the development of juveniles between modern and ancient population, a conservative estimate of three to five months of age is suggested.

5.7.2.3. Sex determination

Due to the young age of the individual it is not possible to determine sex through osteological examination with any degree of accuracy or replicability (Brickley 2004b). One technique for determining the sex of juveniles based upon the morphology of the mandible and ilia was investigated (Schutkowski 1993) but results were mixed; some morphological features being more masculine and others more feminine. Definitive sex determination may be possible if DNA can be recovered from the remains (Skoglund *et al.* 2013) and with this in mind the right petrous portion of the temporal bone was removed before cleaning and stored separately. DNA analysis was undertaken by Dr Lara Cassidy, Trinity College Dublin, and demonstrated that the biological sex of the infant was male (see Cassidy, this volume).

5.7.2.4. Pathology

Pathological analysis of HOW14-B1 proceeded through assessment of the bones by eye and with the aid of a hand

lens. There was no evidence of cutmarks or rodent gnawing on any bones suggesting that the body was interred whole and immediately covered. Some porosity was noted on the cranium and long bones; however, given the age of the individual this porosity is more likely to be due to the normal reactive bone forming process of skeletal growth than to any pathology. A possible exception is an area of marked porosity with a more molten appearance on the right proximal radius (see Fig. 5.7.3), which may be pathological although normal bone growth cannot be ruled out. The same area on the left radius cannot be assessed due to taphonomic damage. The left distal humerus also appears to be slightly larger than the right, which might indicate some disruption to the growth of the right arm; however, damage to the right humerus may be causing an exaggeration of any difference. No other pathologies were evident and there were no signs of trauma to the bones; all damage appears to be post-mortem.

5.7.2.5. Interpretation

Osteological examination of the infant excavated at the Hill of Ward indicated that it had died at between three

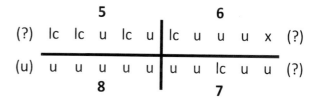

Key

u	unerupted but visible in crypt
lc	loose crown
x	lost post-mortem
?	unobservable

Fig. 5.7.2. Dental chart for HOW14-B1 following the Fédération Dentaire Internationale *system of recording. Symbols in brackets indicate the development of the first permanent molars of which only one was visible in the mandible. Table 5.7.1 presents the linear measurements of crown development for three of the loose teeth and estimations of age from these measurements using the regression formulae of Liversidge* et al. *(1998).*

Table 5.7.1. Estimations of age from crown development using the regression formulae of Liversidge et al. *(1998).*

Tooth	Length (mm)	Age estimate	Error
Upper left central incisor	7.34	4.80 months	±2.28 months
Upper right lateral incisor	6.14	4.32 months	±2.04 months
Lower left canine	4.62	3.84 months	±2.64 months

Table 5.7.2. Linear measurements from HOW14-B1 and estimations of biological age from these measurements (Note: Scheuer et al. 1980 estimates are in weeks since conception).

Bone	Side	Metric	Measurement (mm)	Age estimation	Method
Radius	Right	Maximum length	59.10	42.3 weeks (±2.29)	Scheuer *et al.* 1980
				1.5–3 months	Scheuer and Black 2000
Ulna	Left	Maximum length	68.08	42.4 weeks (±2.2)	Scheuer *et al.* 1980
Humerus	Right	Maximum length	76.51	43.7 weeks (±2.33)	Scheuer *et al.* 1980
				1.5–3 months	Scheuer and Black 2000
Femur	Right	Maximum length	91.40	43.7 weeks (±2.08)	Scheuer *et al.* 1980
				1.5–3 months	Scheuer and Black 2000
Tibia	Left	Maximum length	76.78	43.8 weeks (±2.12)	Scheuer *et al.* 1980
				1.5–3 months	Scheuer and Black 2000
Clavicle	Left	Maximum length	46.06	<7-12 months	Black and Scheuer 1996
Scapula	Right	Middle diameter of glenoid surface	6.70	4.10 months	Rissech and Black 2007
Pars basilaris of occipital		Maximum width basilaris	18.35	>3–5 months <8 months	Scheuer and MacLaughlin-Black 1994
		Sagittal length basilaris	13.82		
		Maximum length basilaris	18.64		

10 mm

Fig. 5.7.3. Detail of proximal radius showing marked porosity on shaft. Owing to young biological age and location of porosity at attachment of biceps brachii *muscle normal bone modelling cannot be ruled out.*

to five months of age. No signs of physiological stress or trauma were evident on the remains and placement of the body suggested the infant had been carefully and respectfully interred.

While there is a long tradition of infant burial in Ireland, especially as regards cillíni – burial grounds traditionally associated with unbaptised infants – the dating of these remains problematic. However, Finlay (2000, 411) highlights the potential association of such sites with important places, including those of pre-existing archaeological significance. The Hill of Ward burial would certainly belong to this category, although it is unclear from the small area excavated whether this represents an isolated feature or one of a number of interments. Similarly, O'Sullivan *et al.* (2021b, 293) suggest that pre-Christian burials may have been focused on pronounced topographical locations, especially those 'imbued with significant mythological, ancestral and political meanings', again a not inaccurate description of the Hill of Ward, even prior to the construction of Tlachtga. Assuming any prior knowledge of the earlier Bronze Age phase at the Hill of Ward would certainly have increased the likelihood of the site being reused for burial in the early medieval period (*ibid.*, 300).

In discussing the apparently long-lived practice of infant burial at Mullamast Hill, Co. Kildare, O'Brien (2021, 42) speculates that these infants may represent a form of fertility ritual, possibly comprising the offering of living infants, mirrored in the later tithing of infants to the early church. Like Mullamast, the Hill of Ward represents an important pre-Christian ritual centre, and the infant burial may represent a similar ritual deposition. The most obvious comparison as an isolated burial would be the infant deposition from the boundary ditch of Raith na Rig at the Hill of Tara (Roche 2002), although this is likely to predate the example from the Hill of Ward by up to 300 years and is firmly dated to within the Iron Age (Cahill-Wilson and Standish 2016). Here again, O'Brien suggests the potential for this to be a sacrificial offering, perhaps a foundation sacrifice (O'Brien 2021, 42) and makes explicit comparison to the Hill of Ward burial. In conclusion, while there are no clear indications as to the cause of death of the Hill of Ward infant, a deliberate deposition or sacrifice cannot be discounted as beyond cultural norms.

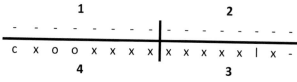

Key

o   observable in alveolar
l   loose tooth
c   possible congenital absence
x   lost post-mortem
-    unobservable

Fig. 5.7.4. Dental chart for HOW15-B2 following the Fédération Dentaire Internationale *system of recording.*

5.7.3. HOW15-B2 (2015)

This specimen comprises a fragmentary mandible and three mandibular teeth recovered from context C429 in Trench 4 of the 2015 excavations at the Hill of Ward, the fill of the outer ditch of the large Bronze Age enclosure (Fig. 5.7.4; Fig. 5.7.5). This was directly radiocarbon dated to 912–807 cal BC (Beta-420642; 2710±30 BP). Cortical and cancellous bone exposed through fragmentation of the specimen is of similar colouration to the external surface of the bone suggesting that most of the damage occurred either prior to deposition or within the burial environment itself. Edges of the breaks are, however, ragged indicating that they were dry bone fractures occurring post-mortem. The cortical surface of the bone is roughened due to taphonomic processes but there are no signs of rodent gnawing or other scavenger activity, which would suggest deposition soon after death rather than prolonged exposure.

The right lower third molar was not present and no crypt in the alveolar bone was observed distal to the second molar. The tooth may not have erupted prior to death; however, it is also possible that it was congenitally absent. The left side of the mandible was broken mesial to the second molar so comparative remarks are not possible. Although the lower left second premolar is missing and the lower left first molar has become dislodged from the mandible, refitting of the molar indicates an exaggerated gap between the two teeth. Post-mortem damage makes assessment of the alveolar bone in this area difficult, however, a bony lump may be observed on the lingual surface of the mandible inferior to the empty root cavities of the left premolars (see Fig. 5.7.6), which is not mirrored on the right side. This may be due to non-eruption of the second premolar and retention of a deciduous molar within the jaw or, alternately, the presence of an apical abscess. However, no other pathologies were apparent on the specimen.

Mild symmetrical wear was apparent on the molars with exposure of the dentine in small areas where the cusps had worn away. Wear to the cusp of the second premolar was minor. This level of dental wear would indicate that the individual was probably in their mid- to

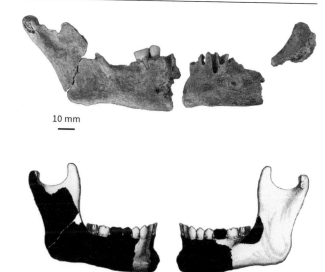

Fig. 5.7.5. Inventory for HOW15-B2 showing portions of the mandible that were present (shaded areas).

late 20s (Brothwell 1981; Lovejoy 1985). The robust morphology of the mandible, including a pronounced keel at gnathion and flaring at the gonial angle, would suggest that this was a male individual. aDNA extraction was attempted on the dislodged first molar but unfortunately no suitable DNA was obtained (see Cassidy, this volume).

5.7.4. HOW15-B3 (2015)

Specimen comprises a single isolated tooth also recovered from Trench 4, but from context C473 (within the inner ditch). Significant waisting at the cemento-enamel junction and flaring of the roots suggest this is a deciduous tooth, while size and morphology indicate that it is most likely a mandibular second deciduous molar (see Fig. 5.7.7). The colour of the enamel suggests eruption was complete at the time of deposition, although minimal wear to dental cusps would indicate either a soft diet or that little time had elapsed between eruption and deposition. Root formation was at least three quarters, and possibly entirely, complete. The tips of the roots were broken post-mortem and are not missing due to resorption or formation processes. Presence of the roots suggests the tooth was not found in isolation as a result of natural exfoliation. Based on the development of the tooth, the individual is estimated to be greater than two years of age but less than seven or eight years old (Moorrees *et al.* 1963; Ubelaker 1999). Dental wear would place the age towards the lower end of this spectrum. No pathologies were observed.

5.7.5. Discussion

For both HOW15-B2 and HOW15-B3 insufficient body parts remain from which to draw many conclusions. However, the presence of directly dated uncremated

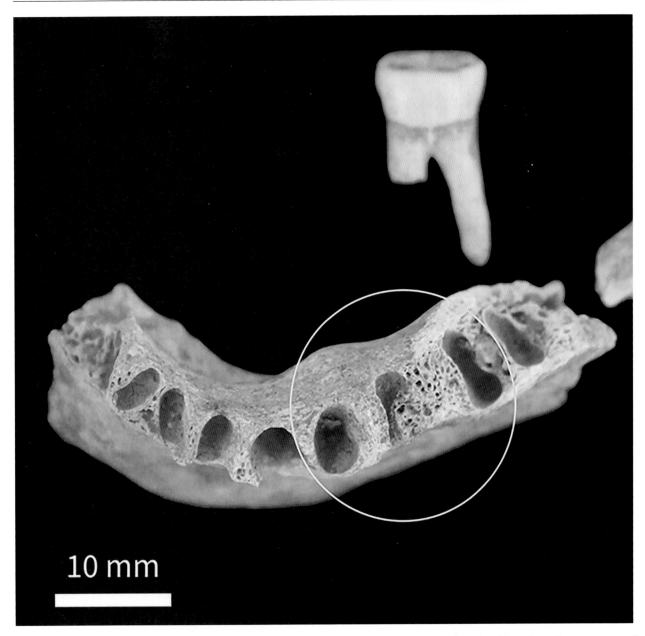

Fig. 5.7.6. Fragment of mandible from HOW15-B2 highlighting bony lump inferior to premolars (circle) and gap between roots of the second premolar and first molar (bracket) (Photograph copyright A. Ash).

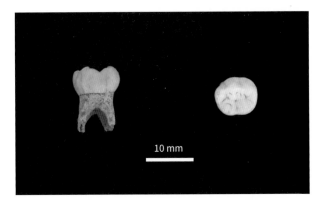

Fig. 5.7.7. HOW15-B3, showing size and morphology of crown and roots (all scales in millimetres, photographs copyright A. Ash).

remains of this date is of some interest and is unusual. The presence of the Hill of Ward remains within the fills of the enclosure ditches is unlikely to be accidental and is most likely linked to major changes within the lifecycle of the monument (Brück 1999).

5.8. Ancient DNA analysis of the human remains from the Hill of Ward (Lara Cassidy)

Ancient DNA analysis was carried out on two samples recovered from the Hill of Ward, Co. Meath. The first was the right petrous bone of an infant (Lab ID: HW14), dating to the very start of the medieval period (cal AD 420–556; Beta-388456). The second was a tooth (Lab ID: HW15) taken from a late Bronze Age mandible (912–807 cal BC; Beta-420642). DNA extraction and library creation was carried out as described in Cassidy *et al.* 2020.

5.8.1. *Sequencing statistics*

Each sample was first subject to shallow shotgun sequencing on either an Illumina MiSeq platform (HW14) or NovaSeq6000 (HW15) to estimate human DNA content. HW14 gave an excellent endogenous yield of 46.77%, while HW15 had little to no surviving human DNA (0.11%). HW14 was subsequently sequenced to a deeper coverage of 1.25X on an Illumina HiSeq2500 to allow for genotype imputation and haplotype-based analyses. No further downstream sequencing or analysis was carried out on HW15.

5.8.2. *Molecular sexing*

Molecular sexing was carried out following previously described methods (Skoglund *et al.* 2013; Cassidy *et al.* 2020). HW14 was found to be a male infant with an XY karyotype. No evidence of aneuploidy was found for the sex chromosomes or autosomes.

5.8.3. *Uniparental markers*

The mitochondrial (mtDNA) haplotype of HW14 was characterised using Haplogrep software (Weissensteiner *et al.* 2016) following the pipeline outlined in Cassidy *et al.* 2020. HW14 belongs to mtDNA haplogroup K1c1, with additional mutations 709A and 9962A. K1c1 has been observed across Europe from the Copper Age onwards. This includes a number of English Bronze Age, Iron Age and medieval sites (Gretzinger *et al.* 2022; Patterson *et al.* 2022), as well as two unpublished samples from Bronze Age and medieval Ireland. However, the specific K1c1 haplotype of HW14 is very rare. To the author's knowledge, no ancient K1c1 individual with the 709A and 9962A mutations has been previously identified and these are not listed in the large public genealogical database from Yfull (www.yfull.com; v11.04.00).

To determine the Y chromosome haplogroup of HW14, the allelic state at each SNP in the ISOGG database of Y chromosomal markers was assessed (Version: 15.73, Date: 11 July 2020), as described in Cassidy *et al.* 2020. HW14 was found to belong to an uncommon Y chromosome haplotype. The dominant lineage observed in Ireland from the early Bronze Age to the present-day is R1b-L21, which is one of the many descendant lineages of the upstream R1b-L151 haplogroup. HW14 does not belong to L21, but can be placed within R1b-L151. HW14 cannot be placed in any downstream sublineage of R1b-L151, either due to a lack of site coverage or because HW14 belongs to a haplotype not characterised in modern populations.

5.8.4. *Genomic affinities*

Haplotype-based analyses were used to identify the ancient and modern populations to which HW14 bears most affinity (Lawson *et al.* 2012; Browning and Browning 2013). Diploid genotypes were imputed in HW14 using GLIMPSE software and recommended pipeline (Rubinacci *et al.* 2021). These data were merged with imputed genotypes from a dataset of approximately 1100 published (Martiniano *et al.* 2016; Schiffels *et al.* 2016; Brunel *et al.* 2020; Margaryan *et al.* 2020; Dulias *et al.* 2022; Fischer *et al.* 2022; Patterson *et al.* 2022) and unpublished samples from western Europe, spanning the Bronze Age to medieval period. The unpublished data included 101 Irish Iron Age and medieval genomes available from the host laboratory.

First, Beagle5 and refinedIBD (Browning and Browning 2007; 2013) were used to identify long genomic segments shared between HW14 and other ancient samples in our dataset, which are indicative of relatively recent genealogical links (identical-by-descent or IBD segments). After filtering for a LOD score of 10 and a genomic segment length of 3 cM, HW14 was found to share two or more segments with only 14 samples. Of these, eight were from the English Iron Age and none were from Ireland. To explore further, the total length of IBD segments HW14 shared with different Iron Age and medieval populations (n>20) was calculated and then normalised by the population size. The highest value was seen for the English Iron Age, followed by the Scottish Iron Age and Irish medieval populations (Fig. 5.8.1).

We then used ChromoPainter to 'paint' the HW14 genome as a mosaic of haplotypic chunks donated by modern individuals from Ireland and Britain (Leslie *et al.* 2015; Byrne *et al.* 2018), grouped into regional genetic clusters based on Byrne *et al.* 2018. Each chunk is donated by the modern individual who shares the most recent common ancestry with the ancient sample at that genomic region. Modern individuals were also painted against one another and this matrix was used to generate an 'ancestry profile' for HW14 through non-negative least squares (nnls) regression (Leslie *et al.* 2015). Population-level profiles were also generated for published English Iron Age and medieval genomes (Martiniano *et al.* 2016; Schiffels *et al.* 2016), as well as a dataset of unpublished Iron Age and medieval genomes from Ireland, including individuals from the medieval cemetery at Ranelagh, Co. Roscommon, previously subject to preliminary investigation in (Delaney and Murphy 2022).

The ancestry profile of HW14 had only a small contribution from modern Irish populations (Fig. 5.8.2). Instead, the majority of contributions come from English populations. This stands in contrast to the population-level profile seen for Irish genomes of a similar time depth to HW14. The English Iron Age population shows a similar profile to HW14, with approximately a third of contributions coming from Irish and Scottish populations, and the remainder from English populations, with the largest single contribution coming from a genetic cluster associated with modern-day Devon (light purple).

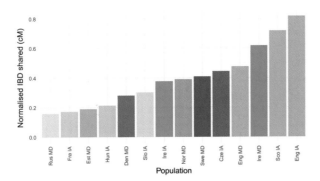

Fig. 5.8.1. IBD Sharing between HW14 and Iron Age and medieval populations. The total amount of IBD shared (cM) with HW14 was divided by the population's size to get the normalised value. Iron Age (IA) and medieval (MD) populations were grouped by country (three letter codes).

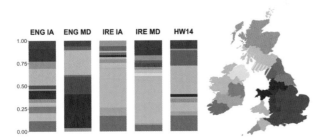

Fig. 5.8.2. Ancestry profiles generated through NNLS. The ancestry of each population or HW14 is described as a mosaic of contributions from modern British and Irish genetic population clusters, which associate strongly with geography. The geographic distribution of each modern cluster is shown on the map. The Irish IA population consists of unpublished samples dating to the same time depth as HW14 (Late Iron Age–early medieval transition). The Irish MD population consists of samples from Ranelagh, Co. Roscommon, dating from the early to late medieval period.

These results, taken together with the uncommon Y chromosome haplotype of HW14, suggest that all or a substantial portion of the ancestry of HW14 may in fact derive from Britain. It cannot be said whether this infant's parents migrated during their own lifetime or if they came from an established British community living in Ireland. Further genomic sampling from Ireland and Britain across the period of AD 200–600 may better help establish this infant's ancestral origins.

5.8.5. Inbreeding

When two related individuals have a child together, this child will inherit identical genomic segments from both parents, resulting in runs of homozygosity (ROH). The more long ROH an individual has in their genome, the more closely related their parents. Using refinedIBD no ROH over 3 cM in length were identified in the genome of HW14. Thus it can be concluded his parents did not share any recent ancestry with one another. This argues

against them coming from a small population or endogamous community.

5.8.6. Phenotypic predictions

Imputed genotypes were used to predict the appearance of the infant using HIrisPlex-S software (Chaitanya *et al.* 2018), bearing in mind that pigmentation can change with age and these predictions are for the adult phenotype. The individual was most likely brown-eyed with light brown hair and pale to intermediate skin tone. HW14 was found to have two copies of the derived allele at rs4988235, indicating that the individual would have been lactose tolerant had he reached adulthood.

5.9. 2016: SF257 Hair ring (Rena Maguire)

Hair, or lock rings are small circlets of metal, mostly dating from the late Bronze Age, and are found across Britain, Europe and Ireland. Some of the Irish specimens are solid gold, but many were made of copper alloy or lead, and they sometimes even had clay cores, covered by gold or electrum sheet metal (Eogan 1997, 308). Early finds clustered in Munster made Eogan initially theorise that they had been first introduced and manufactured there (Eogan 1968, 98), having been based on European prototypes. However, further analysis during the 1990s demonstrated a more widespread distribution of around 160 examples across the island (Eogan 1997, Fig. 1). Despite the nomenclature of hair rings, they remain of unknown function. The hypothesis that they secured the long plaits of 8th and 9th century BC elites is as valid as Armstrong's (1933, 33) theory that they were a form of currency. Eogan (1997, 318) had suggested their presence in Ireland, and the rest of Europe, indicated a shift in the social order, with new material expressions of status.

The ring found at the Hill of Ward (2016: SF257) was recovered from within C912, one of the fills of the inner Tlachtga ditch. It measures 13.2 mm in outer diameter, 4.1 mm inner diameter and weighs 1.9 g. It is made of either silver-gilt, or possibly electrum alloy (see Table 5.9.1). Silver-gilt is unusual in Irish antiquity, being more associated with the arrival of the Vikings. In Ireland and Britain, the use of silver-gilt is more common from the 6th century AD onwards (Speed 2020), the 'Tara' brooch being a fine example of this (Whitfield 2008). However, silver 'military' pins dating to the late Iron Age have been identified and discussed by Gavin (2013) and the Coleraine Hoard, also late Iron Age, contains silver artefacts (Crawford 2014).

One of the earliest methods of silver-gilding entailed pressing gold foil to the surface and holding it in place by bending the edges of the foil round the edges of the object, or by slotting the edges of the foil into notches cut into the surface. The gold would be burnished down and gently hammered into position. Once the gold foil was in contact with the silver substrate, it was heated to

5 mm

Fig. 5.9.1. Probable late Bronze Age hair ornament (2016: SF257).

Table 5.9.1. pXRF readings (pers comm. V. Orfanou).

	Al concentration	P concentration	Cu concentration	Ag concentration	Au concentration
Reading 1	2.11408	4.09668	5.95115	11.48939	61.90506
Reading 2	2.60162	4.45666	6.46562	10.83793	59.62773
Mean	2.35785	4.27667	6.20839	11.16366	60.76640

a temperature below the melting point of silver, but which would still allow adhesion of the two metals to take place. This method of gilding can be traced back to the 3rd millennium BC (Oddy 1993). However, two gilt-bronze torcs from Snettisham, Britain, dating to the pre-Roman British Iron Age indicated the use of the more complex mercury gilding, where gold is dissolved in mercury for application to a silver or copper-alloy object (Oddy 1993, 180). This gives a signature of mercury within the alloy composition. This is absent in the pXRF reading (Table 5.9.1) for 2016: SF257, although that absence could simply indicate that the makers employed the more basic kind of gilding.

The lack of mercury (Hg) in the specimen is more likely to identify the alloy as a form of electrum. Early medieval Irish texts note that electrum was indeed worked and may have been called *findbruidne* although in the *Cath Catharda* it is named as 'electarda' (Scott 1981, 243 footnote 8, 244–245). The author of the *Cath Catharda* was unclear of the alloy composition apart from it containing precious metals. Electrum alloy is a pale white metal, which can be either naturally occurring or manufactured. It is enduring and hard-wearing, which made it a popular choice for coin manufacture in the ancient world.

In the modern world, the alloy is categorised as 20% silver (Ag) and 80% gold (Au), but no such standardisation existed in the ancient world, as demonstrated by natural ores at Dolgellau in Wales (Forbes 1868). As scrap metals

were melted and recycled to make new objects, the result would not be the standard composition of electrum we understand today, although some kinds of regional ratios had been achieved in the Mediterranean, when using the alloy for coins.

The chronology of the lock ring found at Hill of Ward must remain uncertain, as it could extend from the late Bronze Age to the last phases of the Iron Age. This lock ring may even be a British or European import, as we do not yet know the full extent of the use of either early gilding or electrum in Ireland. It does emphasise, however, the need to further examine small metal objects to create a better understanding and differentiation of metalworking techniques in Ireland's past.

5.10. 2016: SF255 Copper alloy ringpin (Rena Maguire)

Copper alloy pins are a relatively common find in habitation sites such as ringforts, raths and crannogs. They are mostly associated with the early medieval period, but earlier examples do exist. They were used to fasten clothing, with ornate specimens presumably reserved for elites. The plainest varieties may have been used to secure shrouds, where ornate filigree on display was not important.

The simple copper alloy pin (2016: SF255) was found at the Hill of Ward in C914, the main fill of the inner

10 mm

5 mm

Fig. 5.10.1. 2016: SF255. Copper alloy ring pin from Hill of Ward, Co. Meath.

Tlachtga ditch. It is of simplistic design, yet does not fully conform to any of the Viking-era pins detailed in Fanning (1994). It is 115.4 mm in length and 3.7 mm wide, with the head 5 mm at its widest point. The perforation is 1.4 mm in diameter (Fig. 5.10.1). It has a slight bend in the shank, which may be the result of holding fabric together, as it is something that is commonly observed on these objects. The patina has a greenish tinge, indicating that the alloy used is rich in copper that has oxidised.

Despite the undecorated head there are some indications it may not have been as plain and basic as it is in its present form. The decorative rings of ringed pins were fitted through transverse perforations. The Hill of Ward pin has instead a small sagittal perforation (Fig. 5.10.1) through the widest part of the pinhead. Of course, this could also be human error, in the metalworker placing the perforation the 'wrong' way round. This indicates that it held some kind of decorative feature in place, most likely a ring. The tip of the pin head has a cast groove, suggesting something may have fitted into it.

The pin has more in common design-wise with bone and antler pins which often have sagittal piercings (Boyle 2009). In her corpus of work on early medieval dress, Doyle (2014, illus. 6, 73) analysed over 2,200 pins and found that 65% were metal, with others made of other materials. It is not unfeasible that there were crossovers of style between materials.

The closest parallel with this pin is held in a private collection but recorded and registered in the National Museum of Ireland as IA/140/71, and was found in Ballycasheen, near Inchiquin, Co. Clare. It too has the sagittal piercing at the widest point of the pinhead, although has a ridged neck, which is lacking in the

Hill of Ward example. It is classified as having an earlier date range, *c.* late 4th to 6th century AD. Another reasonably close parallel was found in a Late Roman burial at Colchester (Crummy 1983, no. 490, Fig. 29, 29). It is almost impossible to precisely date the Hill of Ward pin, but the lack of similarity to any examples in Fanning may well suggest an early medieval date like that from Ballycasheen.

5.11. Analysis of crucible fragments from the Hill of Ward (Brendan O'Neill)

5.11.1. Introduction

Three crucible fragments were discovered in and around a burnt feature excavated during the 2015 Hill of Ward excavations. Although fragmentary, these pieces appear to be from 'pyramidal' (Edwards 1990, 90; Kerr *et al.* 2013, 38) or 'triangular' (Tylecote 1986, 97; Comber 2004, 33) crucibles, almost certainly dating them within the early medieval period (Fig. 5.11.1). These are typically thin-walled vessels, conical in plan with a triangular mouth opening. Additionally, they are generally vitrified on their exterior surface with residues on the interior walls. Access to this material and the possibility to obtain detailed elemental data from a securely dated feature allows us to explore specific questions such as:

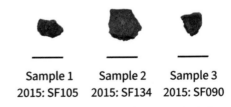

Sample 1   Sample 2   Sample 3
2015: SF105   2015: SF134   2015: SF090

Fig. 5.11.1. Hill of Ward crucible fragments. Scale bar = 10 mm.

- Are there any detectable residues present on either the interior or exterior surfaces of the crucible fragments to provide detail on craft practices on this site?
- Can a clear identification of the clay type be made?
- Can a likely composition for the crucible's fabric be reconstructed?

5.11.2. Methodology

Data capture was undertaken using a Hitachi TM-1000 Tabletop Microscope with Swift-ED EDX system at University College Dublin's School of Earth Sciences. Under Scanning Electron Microscopy (SEM) residues appeared as localised regions on the crucible surface, which had noticeably different textures and forms to the surrounding ceramic fabric. The crucible walls were dynamic and undulating, with many small cracks running over their internal surfaces. Residues collected against high points, along the edges of cracks and on rough surfaces. Initial scans of these substances, using Energy Dispersive X-ray Spectrometry (EDX) suggested that they have different elemental compositions to the fabric and so a programme of elementally mapping areas of interest was conducted. When suitable sites were identified, SEM backscatter images and EDX scans were taken at 60 (Area Scan), 500 (Area Scan), 1,500 (Area Scan) and 10,000 (Point Scan) times magnification. This allowed the specific composition of given areas to be observed in relation to their immediate surroundings.

Once data capture was completed the raw information was processed. Initially, the unedited data from each sample was prepared by dividing spectra (scans) into specific 'Scan Area Groups' and removing failed spectra (Tables 5.11.1, 5.11.2 and 5.11.3; Figs 5.11.2 and 5.11.3). These data were then analysed to ensure that the elemental progression was consistent throughout the various scales in all areas. Following this, the general fabric composition for each sample was ascertained by extracting all 10,000 times magnification fabric scans from each sample and calculating their average. Using these data, residues were detected by overlaying 10,000 times magnification residue scans over the average fabric with sharp divergences taken to be evidence for the presence of residues.

In order to compare the individual clay compositions, average readings for each sample were graphed together to show similarities and differences while data from individual scans was overlaid onto this to examine more specific trends (Fig. 5.11.4). Finally, the fabric composition was determined by extracting the specific clay signals from residues leaving only additional elements.

5.11.3. Description and analysis

In terms of answering the first question relating to interior and exterior residues, all three crucible fragments display evidence for internal residues while no identifiable residue location was identified externally.

- Sample 1 (2015: SF2015 – Fig. 5.11.5; Table 5.11.2) had the major element silver (Ag) (and sulphur (S) = silver sulphide?) with minor amounts of gold (Au) and copper (Cu) also present. There were also trace readings for chlorine (Cl) which may be contamination from washing in tap water.
- Sample 2 (2015: SF134 – Fig. 5.11.6; Table 5.11.3) had a major reading for lead (Pb) with trace amounts of titanium (Ti) and arsenic (As). As with Sample 1 there was a chlorine (Cl) signal.
- Sample 3 (2015: SF090 – Fig. 5.11.7; Table 5.11.4) had major amounts of iron (Fe) and zinc (Zn) with trace readings for tin (Sn) and copper (Cu). The zinc (Zn), tin (Sn) and copper (Cu) readings together may be from the melting of a zinc (Zn) infused copper alloy (i.e., gunmetal). The positive detection of iron (Fe) appeared in several locations and was well adhered to the inner surface.

5.11.4. Interpretation

The presence of silver (Ag) and sulphur (S) together on Sample 1 in the same scan area has been interpreted elsewhere (Photos-Jones 2005, 138) as evidence for a silver sulphide residue. In anaerobic environments silver residue on the inner surface of the vessel reacts with sulphur present within the depositional context to produce a sulphide compound. The signal for gold (Au) only appears in one scan area at one scale (spectrum 11 × 10,000) but is sufficiently strong to suggest this metal was indeed present. That said, it is not clear whether this was a result of casting objects in gold (or a related alloy) or whether it was imparted as an impurity in one of the other metals present (most likely the latter).

Sample 2 is more straightforward in that its only major element is lead (Pb), which is spread over large areas of the internal surface contaminating even visually clear areas of the fabric. Experiments examining technical ceramics (Kearns *et al.* 2010) have demonstrated that lead, due to its high volatility, tends to infuse the inner surface of crucibles and is therefore overrepresented in analysis of this kind. It seems likely that other residues are also present on this crucible, but it is not possible to detect them due to the dominance of lead.

Sample 3 is the most complicated of the fragments tested due to the identification of multiple elements, including very high detections for iron. The spatially related (Residue 2) copper (Cu), tin (Sn) and zinc (Zn) readings seem likely to represent the melting of a gunmetal copper alloy, a variable mixture of these three metals. That the zinc signal relates to an alloy and not contamination is inferred by its relatively high detections compared to copper and tin, both much less reactive metals. At the temperatures needed to melt copper alloys, zinc becomes gaseous and impregnates the majority of the internal surface of silicate crucibles. Iron (Fe) was also detected

Table 5.11.1. Sample 1. EDX data (2015: SF2015).

Name	Area description	Backscatter scale	Na	Mg	Al	Si	P	S	Cl	K	Ca	Ti	Fe	Cu	Zn	Br	Ag	Au
Spectrum 1	1st Internal Fabric	×60			8.2	51.7	9.9			8.3	10.7	1.8	9.5					
Spectrum 2	1st Internal Fabric	×500			10.4	53.1	8.3			5.7	9.3		13.2					
Spectrum 3	1st Internal Fabric	×1500			8.1	50	8.2			5.3	9.8		18.6					
Spectrum 4	1st Internal Fabric	×1500			8.3	50.5	10.6				6.1		24.5					
Spectrum 7	1st Internal Residue	×60		1.2	9.6	43.8	9.8		1.2	5.9	8.1	0.8	12		4		3.7	
Spectrum 8	1st Internal Residue	×500	1.7		8.1	27.1	4.5		1.8	3.6	7.7		13.4		3.5		28.5	
Spectrum 9	1st Internal Residue	×1500			4.8	9.3	2.6		2.9		5.1		8.4	1.2			65.7	
Spectrum 10	1st Internal Residue	×10000			4.9	4.6	2.2		2.7		4.5		4.8	0.4			75.7	
Spectrum 11	1st Internal Residue	×10000		1	2.3	2.6	2.2		1.2		2.9	1	2.9	0.3			75	9.6
Spectrum 12	2nd Internal Fabric	×60		1.6	10.5	47.8	8.6		1.4	5.2	6.5		12.4		4.9			
Spectrum 13	2nd Internal Fabric	×500	1.3	1	7.8	57.3	6.6			8.7	5.4		7.7		0.6		3.7	
Spectrum 14	2nd Internal Fabric	×1500	1.8	1	7.4	60.4	3.3			12.4	5.3	0.8	5.9		1.6			
Spectrum 15	2nd Internal Fabric	×10000		1.3	6.8	62.9	1.9			13.7	3.4		3.3		6.8			
Spectrum 24	2nd Internal Residue	×60		1.4	8.7	44.6	9.8	1.8	1.2	3.8	8.7		11.1		3		5.7	
Spectrum 25	2nd Internal Residue	×500			7.1	60.5	5.2			3	4.5		8.3		4.1		7.1	
Spectrum 26	2nd Internal Residue	×1500		1.2	7.1	31.3	5.9	4		1.8	6.1		15		1.2		26.2	
Spectrum 27	2nd Internal Residue	×10000			4.1	17.7	2.2	4.1			4.7		10.1				57.1	
Spectrum 28	2nd Internal Residue	×10000			4.7	22.5	3.1	2.6			4.6		15.2				47.2	
Spectrum 29	1st External Fabric	×60	2.2	2.1	8.4	57.2	3.5			13.1	7.6		5.8					
Spectrum 30	1st External Fabric	×500		1.3	9	59.4	5.2			7.3	8	1.6	8.4					
Spectrum 31	1st External Fabric	×1500			9.5	64.1	4.8			6.7	8.1		6.7					
Spectrum 32	1st External Fabric	×10000		1	7.5	78	2.9			3.5	2.8		4.4					

Table 5.11.2. Sample 2. EDX data (2015; SF134).

Name	Area description	Scan type	Backscatter scale	Mg	Al	Si	P	S	Cl	K	Ca	Ti	Fe	As	Pb
Spectrum 1	1st Internal Fabric	Area	×60	1.2	9.8	49.2	5			2.9	3		5.8		23
Spectrum 2	1st Internal Fabric	Area	×500	1.2	10.7	67.6				3.7	2.3		6		8.5
Spectrum 3	1st Internal Fabric	Area	×1500	1	11.7	67.4	3.9			4.3	2.4		9.2		
Spectrum 4	1st Internal Fabric	Point	×10000		6.8	83.1	3.6			2.3	1.4		2.9		
Spectrum 5	1st Internal Residue	Area	×60		4.3	12.6	9.7		3.6		7.1		2.2	0	60.5
Spectrum 6	1st Internal Residue	Area	×500		4.5	4.5	11.4		3.6		8.8		2.3	0.4	64.5
Spectrum 7	1st Internal Residue	Area	×1500		4.4	3.9	11.7		3.7		8.3		2	0.6	65.3
Spectrum 9	1st Internal Residue	Point	×10000		1.5	2	12.2		4.9		13.6		1.1	0	64.7
Spectrum 10	2nd Internal Fabric	Area	×60		10	47.4	5.9			3.1	3.6		7.3		22.7
Spectrum 11	2nd Internal Fabric	Area	×500		11.2	60.1	5.2			5.2	3.8		10.7		
Spectrum 12	2nd Internal Fabric	Area	×1500		10.7	71.4		3.8		4.4	2.9		10.6		
Spectrum 13	2nd Internal Fabric	Point	×10000	0.9	9.6	78.6				4.6	1.3		5		
Spectrum 14	2nd Internal Residue	Area	×60		9.7	43.8	7.6			2.9	3.9		5.1		27
Spectrum 15	2nd Internal Residue	Area	×500		3.6	11.3	9.3		3.5		6.3		2.6		63.5
Spectrum 16	2nd Internal Residue	Area	×1500		2.8	12.1	9.1		2.8	1.6	5.9				65.7
Spectrum 17	2nd Internal Residue	Point	×10000		3.4	13.9	8.3		3.5		5.7	3.8	2.6	0.6	58.3

Table 5.11.3. Sample 3. EDX data (2015: SF090).

Name	Area description	Scan type	Backscatter scale	Na	Mg	Al	Si	P	K	Ca	Mn	Fe	Cu	Zn	Br
Spectrum 1	1st Internal Fabric	Area	×60		1.6	11.4	59.3	6.4	4.4	8.8		8			
Spectrum 2	1st Internal Fabric	Area	×500		1.1	12.6	56	6.9	4.6	11.4		7.4			
Spectrum 3	1st Internal Fabric	Area	×1500		1.5	11.6	48.5	9.5	4	17		8			
Spectrum 5	1st Internal Fabric	Point	×10000		1.6	12.3	53.7	11.8	3.7	12.2		4.7			
Spectrum 6	1st Internal Residue	Area	×60				59.1	5.4	4.3	5.6		9.2			16.5
Spectrum 7	1st Internal Residue	Area	×500			9.6	53.3		5.7	1.4		30			
Spectrum 8	1st Internal Residue	Area	×1500			7.3	30		2.2	1.6		58.8			
Spectrum 9	1st Internal Residue	Point	×10000				10.4		0.6			84.3			4.8
Spectrum 10	2nd Internal Residue	Area	×60			10.6	61.5		4.6	8.3		14.9			
Spectrum 11	2nd Internal Residue	Area	×500			9.7	55.6	8.6	3.4	8.6		14.1			
Spectrum 12	2nd Internal Residue	Area	×1500		1.8	9.3	44.6	5.4	2.5	8.2		23.9		4.2	
Spectrum 13	2nd Internal Residue	Area	×5000		3.2	6.6	17.4	4.7		6.2		47.7	3.9	10.4	4.8
Spectrum 14	2nd Internal Residue	Point	×10000		2.6	3.1	12.5	4.5		3.8		44.9	4.5	19.3	
Spectrum 15	3rd Internal Residue	Area	×60			7.1	57.1	6.6	5.2	8.5		15.5			
Spectrum 16	3rd Internal Residue	Area	×500		1.8	9.2	53.9	7.3	3.2	10.3	2.2	12.2			
Spectrum 17	3rd Internal Residue	Area	×1500		1.4	6.8	58.3	9	2.1	9.1		13.4			
Spectrum 18	3rd Internal Residue	Point	×10000		3.8	6.5	14.2	2.1	3.4	2.7		23		33.2	
Spectrum 20	2nd Internal Fabric	Areal	×60		1.6	11.8	57.3	5.1	3.4	9.9		10.8	0		
Spectrum 21	2nd Internal Fabric	Area	×500		1.4	12.7	61.2	5.5	4.3	6.2		8.7			
Spectrum 22	2nd Internal Fabric	Area	×1500		1.4	12.8	63.7	4.6	4	5.7		7.9			
Spectrum 23	2nd Internal Fabric	Point	×10000			12	43.8	4.6	2.7	29.6		7.2			
Spectrum 24	1st External Fabric	Area	×60	1.5	1.7	9.9	50.1	6.7	11.2	12.1		6.9			
Spectrum 25	1st External Fabric	Area	×500		1.7	13.8	51.8	8	8	8.2		8.4			
Spectrum 26	1st External Fabric	Area	×1500		1.5	10.6	44.1	14	6.5	14.6		8.7			
Spectrum 23	2nd Internal Fabric	Point	×10000			12	43.8	4.6	2.7	29.6		7.2			

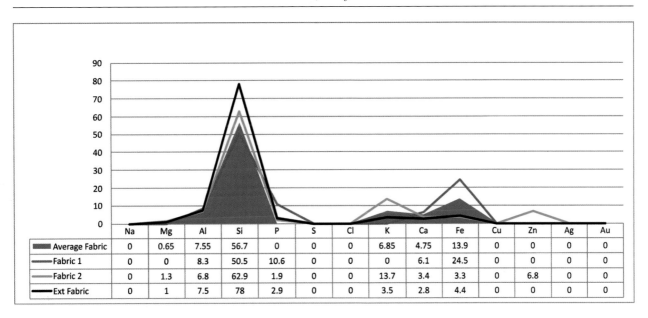

Fig. 5.11.2. Sample 1 Average Fabric Composition. Overlaid are first and second fabric readings as well as a reading for the external surface fabric.

	Na	Mg	Al	Si	P	S	Cl	K	Ca	Fe	Cu	Zn	Ag	Au
Average Fabric	0	0.65	7.55	56.7	0	0	0	6.85	4.75	13.9	0	0	0	0
Fabric 1	0	0	8.3	50.5	10.6	0	0	0	6.1	24.5	0	0	0	0
Fabric 2	0	1.3	6.8	62.9	1.9	0	0	13.7	3.4	3.3	0	6.8	0	0
Ext Fabric	0	1	7.5	78	2.9	0	0	3.5	2.8	4.4	0	0	0	0

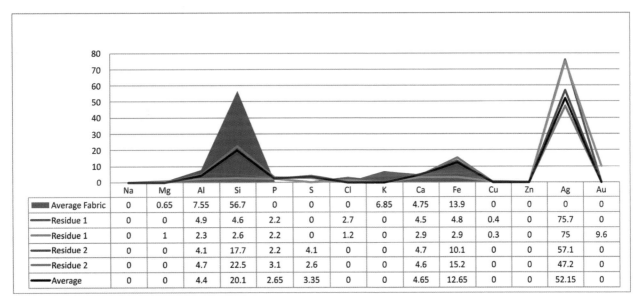

Fig. 5.11.3. Sample 1 Residue signals overlaid onto the Average Fabric Composition. An average for the residue signal for Sample 1 is also provided to assess deviations.

	Na	Mg	Al	Si	P	S	Cl	K	Ca	Fe	Cu	Zn	Ag	Au
Average Fabric	0	0.65	7.55	56.7	0	0	0	6.85	4.75	13.9	0	0	0	0
Residue 1	0	0	4.9	4.6	2.2	0	2.7	0	4.5	4.8	0.4	0	75.7	0
Residue 1	0	1	2.3	2.6	2.2	0	1.2	0	2.9	2.9	0.3	0	75	9.6
Residue 2	0	0	4.1	17.7	2.2	4.1	0	0	4.7	10.1	0	0	57.1	0
Residue 2	0	0	4.7	22.5	3.1	2.6	0	0	4.6	15.2	0	0	47.2	0
Average	0	0	4.4	20.1	2.65	3.35	0	0	4.65	12.65	0	0	52.15	0

in numerous scans on the internal surface of this fragment. It is tempting to think of this as evidence for the melting and casting of iron but currently there is too little evidence to support this interpretation. Lagore Crannog in Co. Meath is the only other site where this has been suggested (Hencken 1950, 237–239; Scott 1991, 3) but supporting evidence is lacking and no subsequent proof has emerged. Given the qualitative nature of these results it is not possible to definitively determine this, but it seems more likely that this detection represents contamination of some kind.

The results from the fabric scans strongly suggest that the clay used to create these crucibles was illitic,

evidenced by the consistent readings for silica (Si), aluminium (Al) and potassium (K). This interpretation is strengthened by the generally higher readings for aluminium (Al) compared with potassium and the trace presence of magnesium (Mg) (Welton 2003, 47). Illite is very common and widely spread over most of the surface of Ireland during and following the last glacial maximum and so these results are not surprising. No determination of source or number of crucibles can be made based on this factor. Comparing the residues, however, it seems that this assemblage represents the remains of three different crucibles used to melt different metals. This is based on the fact that the majority residue in each example (Sample

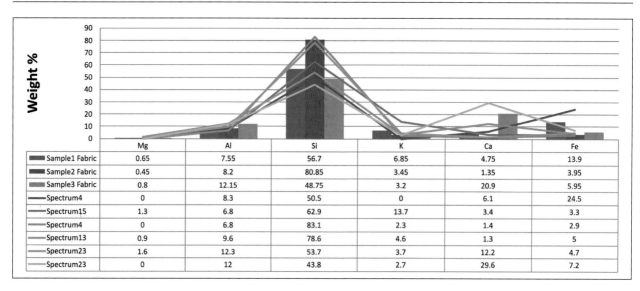

	Mg	Al	Si	K	Ca	Fe
Sample1 Fabric	0.65	7.55	56.7	6.85	4.75	13.9
Sample2 Fabric	0.45	8.2	80.85	3.45	1.35	3.95
Sample3 Fabric	0.8	12.15	48.75	3.2	20.9	5.95
Spectrum4	0	8.3	50.5	0	6.1	24.5
Spectrum15	1.3	6.8	62.9	13.7	3.4	3.3
Spectrum4	0	6.8	83.1	2.3	1.4	2.9
Spectrum13	0.9	9.6	78.6	4.6	1.3	5
Spectrum23	1.6	12.3	53.7	3.7	12.2	4.7
Spectrum23	0	12	43.8	2.7	29.6	7.2

Fig. 5.11.4. Comparison of all sample's fabrics, average and specific.

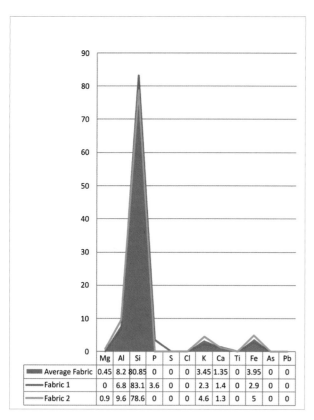

	Mg	Al	Si	P	S	Cl	K	Ca	Ti	Fe	As	Pb
Average Fabric	0.45	8.2	80.85	0	0	0	3.45	1.35	0	3.95	0	0
Fabric 1	0	6.8	83.1	3.6	0	0	2.3	1.4	0	2.9	0	0
Fabric 2	0.9	9.6	78.6	0	0	0	4.6	1.3	0	5	0	0

Fig. 5.11.5. Sample 2 Average Fabric Composition. Overlaid are first and second fabric readings as well as a reading for the external surface fabric.

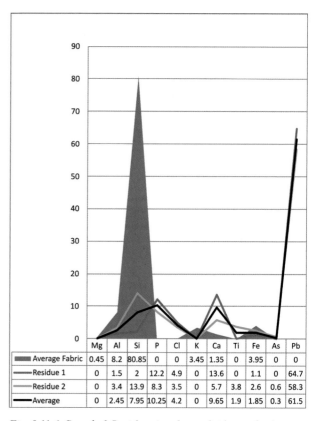

	Mg	Al	Si	P	Cl	K	Ca	Ti	Fe	As	Pb
Average Fabric	0.45	8.2	80.85	0	0	3.45	1.35	0	3.95	0	0
Residue 1	0	1.5	2	12.2	4.9	0	13.6	0	1.1	0	64.7
Residue 2	0	3.4	13.9	8.3	3.5	0	5.7	3.8	2.6	0.6	58.3
Average	0	2.45	7.95	10.25	4.2	0	9.65	1.9	1.85	0.3	61.5

Fig. 5.11.6. Sample 2 Residue signals overlaid onto the Average Fabric Composition. An average for the residue signal for Sample 2 is also provided to assess deviations.

1 – Silver; Sample 2 – Lead; Sample 3 – copper alloy) tends to be spread over wide areas on their respective interior surfaces. Also, there is very little overlap of residue signals between samples, with the exceptions of zinc and copper, which are both present on Samples 1 and 3. Correspondingly, it would appear that these are three different crucibles, possibly made from the same clay source, used to melt a range of different metals.

Interpreting the presence of elevated phosphorus was most complicated and yielded no conclusive results. There does appear to be a general trend linking phosphorus to the crucible's fabric and specifically not the metal residues although little more can be said based on these results. Elsewhere similar signals have been interpreted as a bone ash 'strengthener' (Photos-Jones 2005, 138), deliberately added into the clay before the crucible was formed and

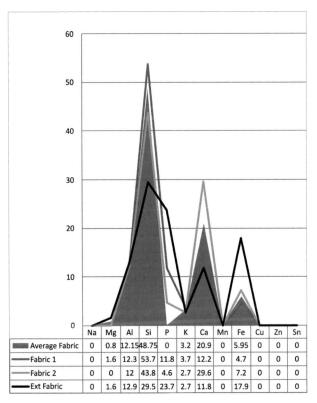

Fig. 5.11.7. Sample 3 Average Fabric Composition. Overlaid are first and second fabric readings as well as a reading for the external surface fabric.

	Na	Mg	Al	Si	P	K	Ca	Mn	Fe	Cu	Zn	Sn
Average Fabric	0	0.8	12.15	48.75	0	3.2	20.9	0	5.95	0	0	0
Fabric 1	0	1.6	12.3	53.7	11.8	3.7	12.2	0	4.7	0	0	0
Fabric 2	0	0	12	43.8	4.6	2.7	29.6	0	7.2	0	0	0
Ext Fabric	0	1.6	12.9	29.5	23.7	2.7	11.8	0	17.9	0	0	0

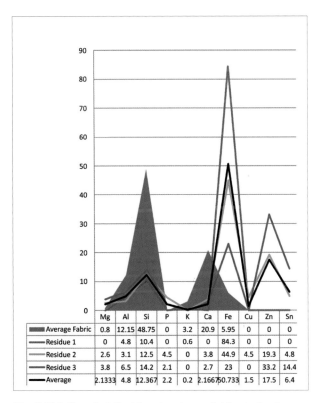

	Mg	Al	Si	P	K	Ca	Fe	Cu	Zn	Sn
Average Fabric	0.8	12.15	48.75	0	3.2	20.9	5.95	0	0	0
Residue 1	0	4.8	10.4	0	0.6	0	84.3	0	0	0
Residue 2	2.6	3.1	12.5	4.5	0	3.8	44.9	4.5	19.3	4.8
Residue 3	3.8	6.5	14.2	2.1	0	2.7	23	0	33.2	14.4
Average	2.1333	4.8	12.367	2.2	0.2	2.1667	50.733	1.5	17.5	6.4

Fig. 5.11.8. Sample 3 Residue signals overlaid onto the Average Fabric Composition. An average for the residue signal for Sample 3 is also provided to assess deviations.

fired. Importantly, it is not possible to infer this from spectrum data alone and instead it can only be made with the observation of distinct inclusions of calcium-phosphate rich bone (-ash) embedded within the fabric. As such, this detection is likely caused by post-depositional contamination.

5.11.5. Conclusion

This analysis has shown that the assemblage under investigation preserves indications that casting of numerous metals was taking place on this site. Copper alloys, including a leaded variety were melted within these crucibles potentially as well as precious metals, including silver. The possible presence of both gunmetal and iron provide interesting opportunities for future research and should be investigated further on this site and others. While the data relating to clays provided little in the way of refined detail, a study of early medieval crucible fabrics would allow for chronological and spatial variations to be assessed.

5.12. The Anglo-Saxon coin hoard from the Hill of Ward (Andrew R. Woods)

During the course of the 2016 excavations, 22 coins of Anglo-Saxon age were recovered. A full catalogue of these is presented in Figures 5.12.4, 5.12.5 and 5.12.6. Twenty-three were originally excavated but two fragments (2016: SF235 and 2016: SF236) were subsequently found to represent a single, broken coin. The coins were dispersed over a small area and represent a single hoard, slightly scattered through post-depositional activities. The composition of the hoard would certainly support this interpretation. The coins were examined by the author, with identifications aided by digital imagery. All of the coins are in good condition making identification to standard reference works possible. The coins are summarised in Table 5.12.1 with identifications utilising types and terminology from *Coinage in Tenth-Century England* (Blunt *et al.* 1989). The identification of mints rests upon stylistic analysis as well as moneyers and follows the suggestions of Bunt, Lyon and Stewart as well as Pagan (Blunt *et al.* 1989; Pagan 2008).

All of the coins are silver pennies struck in England. They were struck in the 10th century for six rulers, five rulers of southern or all England and one ruler of Anglo-Scandinavian York, as is summarised in Table 5.12.2. There is a single coin that is 'imitative', meaning that it is a contemporary copy of the other silver pennies. Its iconography would suggest a date that is broadly contemporary with the other coins within the hoard. The latest coins are those of Eadgar. He 'reformed' the English coinage during the early years of the 970s, significantly altering iconography and consistently adding named mints and moneyers (Naismith 2017, 260–261). All of Edgar's coins within this hoard are a part of the 'pre-reform' coinage meaning that they are likely to have

Table 5.12.1. Catalogue of coins from the Hill of Ward.

SF	King	Type	Mint	Moneyer	Condition notes	Weight (g)	Die axis	Obverse legend	Reverse legend
187	Athelstan	BC	Norwich	Eadger		1.56	240	+AEDELSTAN REX	+EADGAR MO NORDPNT
200	Athelstan	BC	London	Grimwald	Small chip	1.46	180	+AEDELSTAN REX	+GRIMPALD MO LONDLI
208	Athelstan	HT1 (NEI)	East Mids./ York?	Lytelman	Chipped and broken	1.24	180	+AEDELSTAN [ ]	UTILMAN
254	Athelstan	CC	York	Regnald		1.25	300	+EDEL'STAN REX TO BR	+REGNALD MO EFORPIC
188	Edmund	BC	Norwich	Eadgar	Incised cross on reverse	1.46	180	+EADMVND REX	+EADGAR MO NORDPI
196	Eadred	HR2	Chester	Frard	Bent and straightened	1.48	0	+EADRED REX	FRARD MON
292	Eadred	HT1	East Mids.	Theodmaer	Small chip	1.31	90	+EAD'RED' REX	DEODMAER M
293	Eadwig	HR1	Derby	Dunnes		1.07	180	+EADPIG REX	DVNNES MOT
189	Eadgar	BC		Baldwin	Cracked; incised cross on reverse	1.36	0	+EADGAR REX	+BALDVVIN MONETA
235/236	Eadgar	CC	Chester	Freothric	Two conjoined fragments	132+0.5	270	+[ ]ADGAR REX [ ]+0 PI	FR[ ]DER[ ]IC MON
258	Eadgar	CC	Chester	Freothric	Slight chip	1.22	270	+EADGAR REAX TO PI	FREODERIC MON
177	Eadgar	HT1 (NE V)	East Mids.	Manna		1.19	270	EADGAR REX	MANAN NO
234	Eadgar	HT1 (NE V)	East Mids.	Ive		0.99	0	+E'ADGAR RE+	IVE MONET
237	Eadgar	HT1 (NE V)	East Mids.	Unbein	Cracked	0.87	270	+E'A'DG'A'R REX:	VNBEIM MO
241	Eadgar	HT1 (NE v)	East Mids.	Unbein		0.98	90	E'A'DG'A'R RE+	VNBEIN HO
233	Eadgar	HT1	York	Durand		1.09	180	+EADGAR RE:C	DVRAND MO
207	Eadgar	HII	York	Heriger		1.14	0	+EADGAR REX	HERIGER MO
262	Eadgar	HT1	York	Heriger		1.16	330	+EADGAR REX	HERIG'ER MO
232	Eadgar	CC	York	Herolfes	Small chip	1.22	0	+EADGAR REX ANGL	HEROLF(I?) ES MO TERM
263	Eadgar	CC	York	Durand		1.25	0	+EADGAR REX'A'	+DVRANDES MOT
256	Imitation	CC	Copy	Copy	Cut	0.56		FONO	ALFOC
186	Eric Bloodaxe	Sword	York	Ingelgar		1.20	180	ERIC REX	INEELGAR I0

been struck in the 960s or early 970s. Edgar's reform of the coinage appears to have removed a significant proportion of these older coins from circulation. As such, it is likely that the coins of Eadgar within the Hill of Ward hoard left England shortly after they were struck.

The coins were struck at a range of different mints within England. Overwhelmingly they are drawn from the northern parts of England, with a particular focus on Chester, York and the East Midlands. The exception to this is those struck in Norwich and London (2016: SF187

Table 5.12.2. Summary of issuers represented in the Hill of Ward hoard.

Issuer	Regnal dates	Number	Percentage of total
Athelstan	924–939	4	18%
Edmund	939–946	1	5%
Eadred	946–955	2	9%
Eadwig	955–959	1	5%
Eadgar	959–975	13	59%
Eric Bloodaxe	952–954	1	5%
Imitation		1	5%
Total		22	100%

and 2016: SF200). To these can potentially be added a third, the *Bust Crowned* type of Eadgar struck by moneyer Baldwin (2016: SF189), the origin of which is likely to be southern England. While the focus of the coins on northern England is as would be expected, there are a greater proportion of coins from the northeast than the northwest. Those from the northeast outnumber the northwest 14 to 3. This is unusual as the ratio is usually roughly equal (Bornholdt-Collins 2003, 265–274; Blackburn 2008, 120). This may reflect statistical chance given the small numbers of coins involved. However, a potential explanation is that a parcel of coins had recently travelled from the northeast of England to enter the currency pool from which the hoard was drawn.

Between the coins being struck in England in the 10th century, and their deposition they are likely to have circulated both in England and in Ireland, as well as conceivably other points around the Irish Sea. The combination of different issuing authorities is typical for Ireland where hoards often contain coins that were struck some decades before their eventual deposition (*cf.* Kenny 1987; Krogsrud 2012). This is illustrated in Figure 5.12.1, where the proportions of coins issued by the various Anglo-Saxon rulers are summarised (data draws from Hall 1974; Kenny 1987 and forthcoming work on the NMI numismatic collection). Hoards from 950 to the reform of the coinage are plotted. These show a steady, although quite uneven, replacement of older currency with newer coins during the middle decades of the 10th century. The most likely explanation for this is regular, peaceable contact across the Irish Sea, which brought in parcels of currency on a regular basis (Blackburn 2008, 122; Woods 2015). The Hill of Ward hoard sits comfortably within the proportions that are typical for other Irish hoards. It finds closest parallels in three hoards that similarly have a majority of Edgar coins, but with a significant minority of earlier rulers – Smarmore, Co. Louth, Dalkey, Co. Dublin and Derrykeighan, Co. Antrim. There are a small number of hoards that are composed exclusively of coins of Edgar. The fact that a minority of other rulers are found in the Hill

of Ward hoard suggests that it was deposited at a slightly earlier point than these other hoards. While a broad date of deposition in the window 960 to 980 is possible, it is likely that the hoard was deposited in the years around 970 rather than closer to 980.

There are three coins of numismatic interest within the hoard. The first (2016: SF186) is a rare coin of Eric Bloodaxe's *sword* type. This is the 23rd known example of this unusual coin type (corpus to 1989 in Blunt *et al.* 1989; seven further coins have been found in the interim). It was struck for the moneyer Ingelgar who was the most prolific of Eric's moneyers. The connection between York and Ireland is emphasised in the distribution of coins of Eric with others found in Irish hoards at Killyon Manor, Smarmore and Lough Lene. The second coin (2016: SF256) is an imitative type with garbled legends, much of which are inverted or retrograde. This coin is from a reasonably sizable group of imitations that were struck in the time of King Edgar (Blunt *et al.* 1989, 209). The third (2016: SF262) is an unusual coin of King Edgar. It is a die-duplicate of that illustrated on plate 22, no. 302 of *Coinage in Tenth-Century England* (Blunt *et al.* 1989). What makes it unusual is the title 'RE+ ANGL' on the obverse and the 'MOT'ERM' on the reverse, following the moneyer's name. The annulet in the field on the reverse is also exceptional.

The presence of the hoard in the Irish midlands is not unexpected as there are significant numbers of hoards in this area from the 10th and 11th centuries (Gerriets 1985; Kenny 1987; Blackburn 2007, 126–130; Krogsrud 2012). The site was within the control of the Clann Cholmáin, a part of the southern Uí Néill, and the connection between this group and Dublin has been suggested as a reason for the presence of the large number of silver hoards that cluster in the Midlands (Kenny 1987; Purcell and Sheehan 2013; Sheehan 2018). This scholarship has emphasised the importance of Dublin as the likely entry point for most coinage into Ireland, even if it swiftly made its way further inland and into Irish hands where it was used, lost and deposited. Michael Kenny has argued convincingly on the basis of coin hoards that coinage was being used by Irish people between 30 and 70 miles from the Kingdom of Dublin (Kenny 1987). The author has argued for something similar on the basis of excavated and chance 'single finds' and more recent hoard finds, although with a slightly different shape for the 'coin-using' area suggested (Woods 2014). It is highly likely that the Hill of Ward coins were being used by Irish people who were economically connected to the coin-using population of Dublin. While impossible to determine the nature of the exchange relationships, it is most likely that this was peaceful contact – trade, tribute or gift exchange – rather than raiding.

It has been suggested that a 'dual economy' existed in the Irish Midlands during the 10th century with people comfortable using coin or bullion for a range of exchange relationships (Blackburn 2007). This manifests in a range of hoards that include mixed media (Sheehan 2007; Born-holdt-Collins 2010). While the Hill of Ward hoard does not contain anything other than coins, there is evidence that something of the metal-weight mentality that underpinned a dual economy continued to exist. This can be seen with 2016: SF256, the imitative coin (Fig. 5.12.2). It has been cut, leaving perhaps two thirds of the original coin. The score mark for this cut can be seen on the bottom of the Figure 5.12.2. The coins may have been altered because it was recognised as unusual, with a cut to ensure that it was genuine silver rather than plated. Regardless of why the cut occurred it appears to have continued to circulate as a piece of bullion, presumably valued according to its weight, rather than as a whole coin. There are also two coins (Fig. 5.12.3) where small, incised crosses have been scratched into the surface. This is clearer on 2016: SF188 but there is also a smaller cross on 2016: SF189. The meaning behind this action is uncertain but it finds its most ready parallels on silver ingots from the Bedale hoard from North Yorkshire (Griffiths 2012). This suggests that these crosses may represent a way of testing silver or perhaps as a guarantee of fineness. At the least, it suggests that there was a common approach to both coined and non-numismatic silver. More broadly, the addition of crosses to silver, although more usually at the point of production, has been recently discussed by Sheehan who has suggested that it is likely to denote silver, which had a connection to ecclesiastical circles (Sheehan 2018, 117–118).

The presence of the hoard in the vicinity of met-alworking evidence might also support a view that emphasises a continued metal-weight mentality. While the stratigraphy does not allow for the coins to be defin-itively connected with the metal-working evidence, it would not be unusual to find coins in such a context. For example in 10th-century York, a number of coins have been found in the same building as significant metal-working evidence (Pirie 1986; Hall *et al.* 2014), something that is also true of 11th-century Christchurch Place in Dublin (Woods 2013). Silver was a metal that was frequently adapted and transformed in the 10th century, as can be seen by the range of forms of silver in hoards (Sheehan 2007; 2018). Silver took the form of ingots, jewellery and coinage. Hoards that mix these media suggest that silver was changed with apparent regularity. It may be that the Hill of Ward hoard was a portion of raw material before it was transformed into

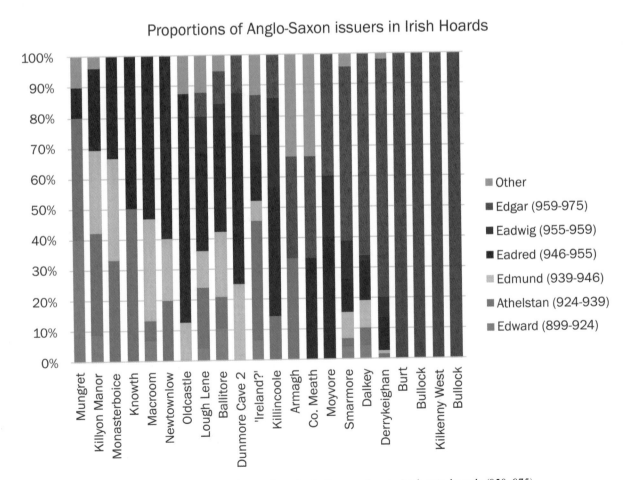

Fig. 5.12.1. Proportions of coins from Anglo-Saxon rulers in Irish coin hoards (950–975).

another form. This being said, it should be emphasised that this small number of coins, with a weight below 30 g, would only have formed a small ingot or jewellery element. Similarly, it should be stressed that in general coinage was likely predominantly used as a means of exchange, even if in this case there may also be a suggestion of another use.

A small point to note in the context of the prehistoric aspects of the site is that there is good evidence for the

re-use of large prehistoric monuments during the Viking Age. There are a number of other Irish coin hoards – Knowth, Fourknocks and Ballycastle – that have been placed in prehistoric monuments (*cf.* Hall 1974). It is more likely that the Hill of Ward hoard is to be associated with the near-contemporary early medieval activity at the site, but there remains a possibility that it was deposited because of the visible features within the landscape.

Fig. 5.12.2. Enlarged image showing cut imitative coin 2016: SF256. Scale bar = 5mm.

Fig. 5.12.3. Enlarged image showing incised cross on 2016: SF188 and 2016: SF189. Scale bar = 5 mm.

5.13. Plant macrofossils (David Stone and Nikolah Gilligan)

This report presents the results of analysis of 59 flots deriving from environmental bulk samples recovered during three seasons of excavations at the Hill of Ward, Co. Meath. Plant macrofossil remains for 2014–2015 (Trenches 1–5) were examined by Nikolah Gilligan (NG) while the remaining samples from 2016 (Trenches 6–8) were examined by David Stone (DS). In total, 1768 carbonised remains of cultivated cereals, wild/weed species and fruit/nut species were identified, the bulk of which (84%) came from the 2016 season.

5.13.1. Archaeobotanical analysis: methodology

Bulk soil samples were processed using the flotation method, one of the most important methodological developments in archaeobotanical research worldwide (Ford 1988; Wagner 1988; Wright 2005). The aim of using the flotation method is the recovery of seeds, animal bone and other small cultural remains that are overlooked or lost during the normal soil screening processes on archaeological sites.

Flots were 100% analysed using a Leica 9SD stereomicroscope with magnification between ×6.3 to ×50. The archaeobotanical material extracted was initially classified according to gross morphology and then identified by comparison to reference materials and images from various key publications (Clapham *et al.* 1962; Martin and Barkley 1973; Berggren 1981; Anderberg 1994; Gale and Cutler 2000; Cappers and Bekker 2013; Neef *et al.* 2012). All botanical and common names follow the order and nomenclature of Stace (2010). Nomenclature for cereals and other cultivars follows Zohary *et al.* (2013).

To assess the representativeness of remains discovered in archaeological sites it is necessary to consider the processes that took place during their creation, with taphonomy being of fundamental importance (Jones 1987; Miksicek 1987; van der Veen 2007). All material recovered at the Hill of Ward samples was preserved by carbonisation. Carbonisation is related to several factors, such as the temperature, length of exposure, moisture content and type of fuel used (Jacomet 2007, 2387; Turney *et al.* 2005, 930). Carbonised plant remains can only become preserved through virtue of having been in contact with fire (Fuller *et al.* 2014, 175–176). Hence,

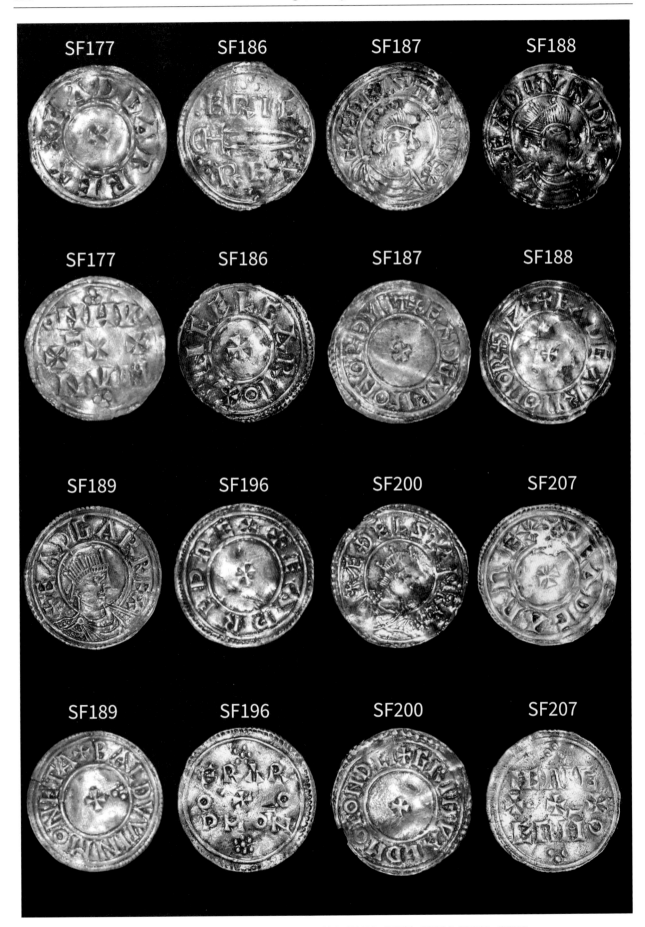

Fig. 5.12.4. Hill of Ward coins SF177; SF186; SF188; SF189; SF196; SF200; SF207.

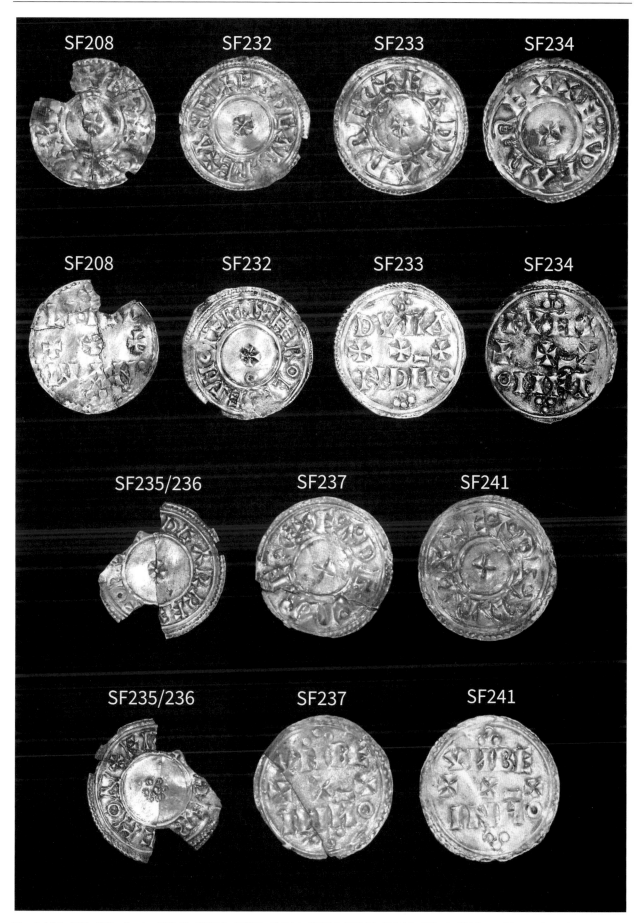

Fig. 5.12.5. Hill of Ward coins SF208; SF232; SF233; SF234; SF235; SF236; SF237; SF241. SF235 and SF236 have been digitally refitted.

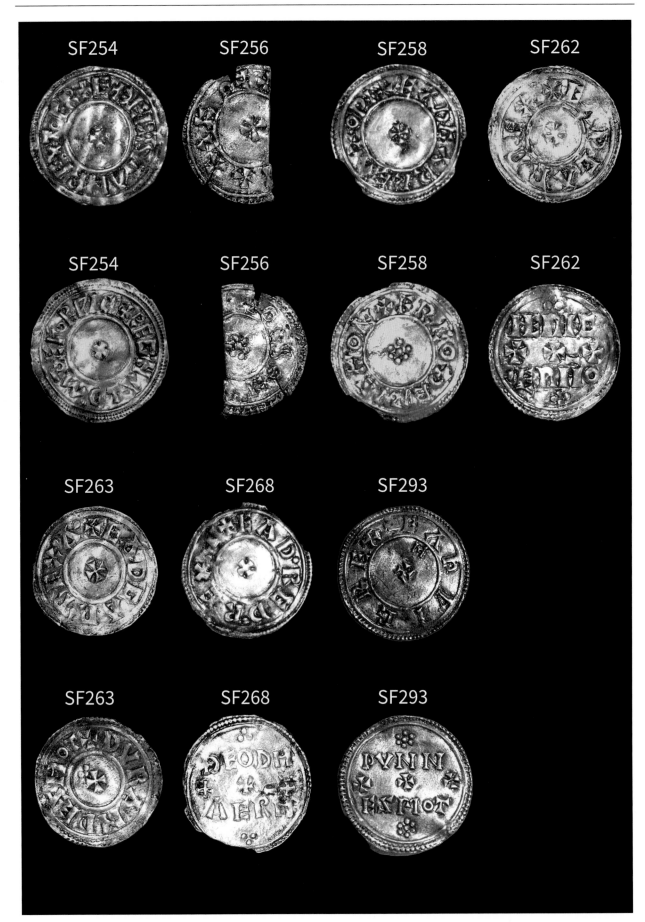

Fig. 5.12.6. Hill of Ward coins SF254; SF256; SF258; AF262; SF263; SF293.

the taphonomic processes experienced by carbonised only plant assemblages differ greatly from those of waterlogged or mineralised assemblages. These taphonomic processes are reasonably well understood and plant material can enter the archaeological record through several different routes (van der Veen 2007, 978). Carbonisation of plant remains usually occurs through three circumstances (van der Veen and Jones 2006, 221–222).

- When by-products of grain processing and cleaning are burned as fuel or waste;
- Accidentally during food preparation;
- The accidental burning of stored products.

Carbonised assemblages tend to be relatively homogeneous with samples mostly comprising cereal grains, cereal chaff, weed seeds and to a lesser extent pulses, nutshells, and wild plants (mostly arable weeds) (van der Veen 2007, 977). This bias mainly results from the processing cereals must go through before they are consumed and the differential survival of plant parts during burning (Boardman and Jones 1990; Fuller *et al.* 2014). In a typical charred assemblage, a relatively limited range of plant species is encountered, with approximately 35% of the range of edible plants documented in waterlogged samples (Colledge and Conolly 2014, 194).

Several activities/actions have been identified as potential routes to carbonisation. Hubbard and Clapham's (1992) three class system is used here to categorise different taphonomic processes that lead to the entry of remains into a charred assemblage within the archaeological record (Jacomet 2007, 2394). This classification system is useful in analysing the Hill of Ward assemblage as materials collected originate from varied contexts, representing all the three classifications.

- Remains charred within the context from which they were recovered (unambiguous origins).
- Secondary deposits where assemblages from a single burning event have been moved to the context from which they were excavated (single discrete event).
- Assemblages formed from the deposition of many successive charring events, possibly representing several different activities (multiple different events).

Reliable reconstructions of agricultural practice and diet are dependent on the quality of the datasets generated. So, in archaeobotanical analysis, the representativeness of the materials recovered and their potential to answer palaeoeconomic questions is important. The representativeness of an assemblage is influenced by a number of important factors including sampling strategy, sample processing, preservation, context and the chronological distribution of samples. Samples analysed by trench and by time period showed a high degree of variability; however, this is a reflection of both the number of discrete

contexts within some trenches and of the presence of plant macrofossil remains within either flot or residue of processed samples.

5.13.2. Archaeobotanical results by trench

In total, the flots analysed produced a large carbonised assemblage of 1,767 specimens, containing cereal, fruit/nut and wild/weed species. This assemblage was dominated by cereals (79.4%), with smaller quantities of wild/weed species (19.2%) and occasional fruit/nut species (0.2%). A minor component (1.2%) of the assemblage could not be identified and was recorded as 'unknown'.

5.13.2.1. Trench 2
Only one sample from Trench 2, the inner ditch of the Bronze Age monument, yielded any plant macrofossil remains.

- **C009:** Seven caryopses of hulled symmetrical barley were present; two were tentatively identified as germinated grains. A grain and a fragment of an unidentifiable barley species were also recovered.

5.13.2.2. Trench 3
Again, only one sample from this trench provided any plant macrofossils for analysis. This contained four carbonised specimens of cultivated cereals (Table 5.13.1).

- **C006:** This context contained a very small amount of barley; a hulled symmetrical caryopsis, a hulled caryopsis and a fragment of a barley species. A fragment of an unidentifiable cereal grain was also present.

5.13.2.3. Trench 4
Eight samples from the possible kiln, deposits, ditch and furrow features were examined from Trench 4, covering the three ditches of the Bronze Age monument. These contained 110 carbonised specimens which included cereal and wild/weed species (Table 5.13.1).

KILN (POSSIBLE) C481
The kiln contained three fills – C465, C478 and C472, all of which yielded plant macrofossils. Charred barley grains from the middle fill C478 were dated and place this feature in the Iron Age (146 cal BC–cal AD 68; Beta-436097). The lower fill C472 was recorded as natural clay but contained a number of charred seeds, including wheat, barley and possible rye. It also contained a number of weed seeds. Seeds within this layer may have been originally incorporated into the middle fill, but were impressed into the base of the feature.

- **C465:** A small quantity of cereal grain was recovered from this context including two barley grains (*Hordeum* sp.). A further grain was recovered but was too distorted or fragmented to identify to species level.

- **C478:** This context contained the largest quantity of carbonised specimens comprising 30 cereal grains. As with sample 97, barley was the dominant grain recovered and included a number of varieties including three naked two-rowed (*Hordeum vulgare var. nudum* subsp. *distichum*), two naked six-rowed (*Hordeum nudum*), and hulled six-rowed (*Hordeum vulgare* subsp. *vulgare*) (Table 5.13.1). Six oat (*Avena* sp.) grains were also recovered but could not be identified to species level as their floret bases were absent. A single of both wheat (*Triticum* sp.) and a possible example of rye (*Secale cereale*) was also recovered. A further seven cereal grains were recovered but were too distorted or fragmented to identify to species level and are recorded as 'Cerealia' in the taxonomic table.

- **C472:** A moderate quantity of carbonised remains were recovered from this sample. Barley was the dominant grain recovered and included a number of varieties including three naked two-rowed (*Hordeum nudum*), two naked six-rowed (*Hordeum nudum*), and hulled six-rowed (*Hordeum vulgare*) (Table 5.13.1). Naked wheat (*Triticum aestivum/durum/turgidum*) was also recovered in small quantities, along with a single possible rye (*Secale cereale*). A further two cereal grains were recovered but were too distorted or fragmented to identify to species level and are recorded as 'Cerealia' in the taxonomic table. Three wild grass (Poaceae indet.) seeds were the only non-cereal specimens recovered.

DEPOSITS:

- C461: This deposit sealed ditches C427 and recuts C402 and C476 and represented the interface with topsoil at this location. It produced a small quantity of carbonised material including three oat (*Avena* sp.) and a single rye brome (*Bromus secalinus*) grain. Two further seeds were recovered but could not be identified to species level.

DITCH FILLS:

- C463: A single carbonised grain of a hulled six-rowed barley (*Hordeum vulgare*) was recovered from this sample.
- C427: Three species of cereals were represented within the fill; 10 caryopses of free-threshing wheat were present, 12 caryopses of barley, including hulled and naked grains were identified. Four fragments of oat grains were noted and a number were assigned to wheat/barley fragments. One fragment of a hazelnut endocarp was also noted. C427 was dated to the Bronze Age (1014–836 cal BC; Beta-420643) by a fragment of animal bone.

- C473: Although 10 specimens were recovered from this sample, none were identifiable to species level and were recorded as 'unknown' in the taxonomic table.

FURROW:

- C431: A single grain of a hulled barley was the only material recovered in this sample, which is most likely medieval in date.

5.13.2.4. Trench 5

Thirteen samples from Trench 5 yielded plant macrofossil remains. In total 159 carbonised specimens were recovered from these samples including cultivated and wild/weed species. These are mostly likely to date to the latter part of the early medieval period, although the presence of a residual Bronze Age date within this trench raises the possibility that some Bronze Age plant remains might be incorporated into these later features.

- **C442:** A small quantity of carbonised grain was recovered from across two samples. One hulled barley grain (*Hordeum vulgare*) and two oats (*Avena* sp.) were the only specimens identified to species level. Three further cereal grains were recovered but were too distorted or fragmented to identify to species level and are recorded as 'Cerealia' in the taxonomic table, while three further seeds were too poorly preserved to identify and are recorded as 'unknown'.

- **C446:** A small quantity of carbonised cereal and wild/weed species was recovered from this sample, representing the possible fill of a plough furrow. Barley was the dominant grain (three cereals) with examples of both hulled and naked varieties present. Two naked wheat grains (*Triticum aestivum/durum/turgidum*) were also recovered. Other cereal grains were recovered but were too distorted or fragmented to identify to species level and are recorded as 'Cerealia' in the taxonomic table. One wild grass seed (Poaceae indet.) was the only non-cereal material recovered.

- **C448:** This context contained 15 carbonised seeds including cereal and wild/weed species. The cereal component included four oat (*Avena* sp.) and a single hulled barley (*Hordeum vulgare*) grain. Five wild grass (Poaceae indet.), and three dock fruits (*Rumex crispus*) were also recovered, and were the only non-cereal species identified. A further 3 specimens were extracted but could not be identified to species level and are recorded as 'unknown' in the taxonomic table.

- **C449:** Two barley grains (*Hordeum* sp.) were the only macrofossils identified.

- **C450:** A moderate volume of carbonised material was recovered from this sample. The cereal component of the assemblage included naked wheat (*Triticum aestivum/durum/turgidum*), naked and hulled barley (*Hordeum nudum*), and oat (*Avena* sp.). A number of grains were too distorted or fragmented to identify to species level and were recorded as 'Cerealia' in the taxonomic table. No non-cereal species were present.

- **C451:** A moderate volume of carbonised material was recovered from this sample, comprising cereal and wild/weed species. Hulled barley (*Hordeum vulgare*) was the dominant grain (16 grains) recovered with a smaller quantity of naked wheat (*Triticum aestivum/ durum/turgidum*), and oat (*Avena* sp.) recovered. A further 3 cereals were extracted but could not be identified to species level and were recorded as 'Cerealia' in the taxonomic table. Wild grasses (Poaceae indet. and *Bromus secalinus*) were the only non-cereal species identified.

- **C452:** A small quantity of carbonised cereal was recovered from this sample. One oat (*Avena* sp.) grain was the only species identified. Two further cereal grains were recovered but were too distorted or fragmented to identify to species level and are recorded as 'Cerealia' in the taxonomic table.

- **C493:** Two carbonised cereal grains were recovered. One was identified as barley (*Hordeum* sp.), with the other too fragmented or distorted to identify to species level and is recorded as 'Cerealia' in the taxonomic table.

- **C521:** A single barley grain (*Hordeum* sp.) was the only material identified.

- **C546:** A small quantity of carbonised cereal and wild/ weed species were recovered from this sample. Five barley (*Hordeum* sp.) and five oat (*Avena* sp.) were identified along with a small quantity of grains that were either too fragmentary or distorted to identify. Two small wild grass seeds (Poaceae indet.) were the only non-cereal material identified.

- **C548:** A moderate quantity of carbonised cereals and wild/weed species were recovered from this sample. Barley (*Hordeum vulgare*) was the dominant grain with 16 grains identified, followed by oat (*Avena* sp.) (13 grains) and two examples of naked wheat (*Triticum aestivum/durum/turgidum*). Two further cereal grains were recovered but were too distorted or fragmented to identify to species level. Four fat hen (*Chenopodium alba*) seeds and one of a rose family member (Rosaceae indet.) comprised the non-cereal component of the assemblage.

- **C549:** A moderate quantity of carbonised cereals and wild/weed species were recovered from this sample. Cereals recovered included two- and six-rowed barley (*Hordeum vulgare/Hordeum distichum),* naked wheat (*Triticum aestivum/durum/turgidum*), and one possible rye (*Secale cereale*). Two further cereal grains were recovered but were too distorted or fragmented to identify to species level and are recorded as 'Cerealia' in the taxonomic table. Three seeds of a wild grass (Poaceae indet.) species were the only non-cereal remains identified.

5.13.2.5. Trench 6
Trench 6 was placed to investigate the central area of Tlachtga. Despite a large amount of material being processed from both within and beneath the central mound no charred macrofossil remains were recovered.

5.13.2.6. Trench 7
Trench 7 investigated the innermost ditch of Tlachtga, with the bulk of the material excavated derived from the fills of a large, rock-cut ditch. Two features within Trench 7 produced a large archaeobotanical assemblage of carbonised material.

- **C915:** This context comprised an extensive but shallow spread of burned material only a few centimetres deep. A single sample collected from this context produced remains of 120 carbonised cereal grains and wild/weed species. Oat was the dominant grain (18.3%) followed by barley (5%) and wheat (5%). A large quantity of cereal grains (70%) recovered were too badly distorted to identify to species level and are recorded as 'Cerealia' in contingency tables. A single grain each of dock (*Rumex* sp.) and goosefoot/orache (*Chenopodium/Atriplex*) were the only non-cereal species recovered.

- **C916:** This context was located on the east side of the trench and comprised a thin layer (10 mm thick) of apparently burned material including burned bone and plant remains. Two samples from within this context produced a large quantity of carbonised material. A total of 138 seeds were recovered of which 44.2% were unidentifiable cereal ('Cerealia') remains. A further 28.2% comprised hulled barley and 13.0% naked barley. Oat was the next most abundant cereal grain (8.7%) while a very small number of wheat grains were also recovered (2.2%). A small proportion (3.6%) of wild grass seeds (Poaceae indet.) were also identified.

5.13.2.7. Trench 8
Trench 8 was positioned to investigate the eastern complex of anomalies identified by geophysical survey. A hoard of coins and two radiocarbon dates provided a *terminus ante quem* for these features of the late 10th century. Thirty-one samples deriving from Trench 8 were analysed and contained a large quantity of carbonised material).

Deposits/Spreads:

- **C703:** This context consisted of a dark greyish brown layer of loose sandy clay was a transitional layer between the fills of the southern ditch and topsoil. Twenty-one carbonised cereal grains and weeds species were recovered from this context. Barley (31.3%) was the dominant grain (35.3%) followed by wheat (18.8%) and oat (6.3%). 43.76% of grain was too badly damaged or distorted for identification. Five wild grass seeds (Poaceae indet.) were also recovered, representing the only non-cereal species recovered.

- **C707:** This was one of two fills of a sub-circular pit (C706). A single sample from this fill produced a small quantity of carbonised plant remains for analyses comprising nine carbonised cereal grain seeds. Two barley grains comprise the only species identified in this sample. The remaining seven grains were too badly distorted to identify to species level and are recorded as 'Cerealia' in contingency tables.

- **C709:** (Equivalent to C715 and C749): This context comprised an archaeologically rich layer from which a hoard of Anglo-Saxon coins was recovered (Woods, this volume). This context was equivalent to C715 on the western side of the baulk, and to C749 in the northern half of the trench. 486 charred seeds were recovered from this context, of which the most abundant were 166 unidentifiable cereals (34.2%) – 'Cerealia' – followed by a significant number (134) of oats (27.6%). Both hulled barley (7.4%) and *Hordeum* sp. (6.4%) were present at lower levels, and a very small proportion of wheat (2.5%). Wild grasses (Poaceae indet.) were very well represented (18.1%) along with a small assemblage of agricultural weed seeds, in particular *Polygonum* sp. (7), *Chenopodium album* (6) and *Rumex* sp. (3).

- **C715:** (Equivalent to C709 and C749): Located on the eastern side of the baulk, this is almost certainly the same deposit as C709. Eight samples produced a large quantity of carbonised material. The extensive sampling of this context was in part owing to the recovery of Anglo-Saxon coins from within it (Woods, this volume). As for the equivalent C709, 'Cerealia' were the most common remains encountered at 40.9% (166 grains). Oat (*Avena* sp.) was less abundant than on the eastern side of the baulk, comprising 11.7% of the assemblage (47 grains). Barley was present at a similar proportion to oats, with 11.2% not identifiable beyond *Hordeum* sp., with 4% hulled barley (*Hordeum distichon*). Wheat was a minimal component of the assemblage with only 13 grains (3.2%). Wild grass seeds were present in similarly high proportion to in C709 (21.3%) with a range of agricultural weed seeds again recorded. These include *Rumex* sp. (15 fruits), *Polygonum* sp. (7 seeds) and *Chenopodium album* (6 seeds).

- **C749:** (Equivalent to C709 and C715): It was not possible to clearly define the boundary between this deposit and C709/C715. It is likely that C749 represents a continuation of the same layer, but in the northern half of the trench. As in C709 and C715, a large quantity of carbonised material was recovered from this context. In the single sample examined, 149 carbonised cereal grain and wild/weed species were recovered. Barley was the dominant grain (19.7%) followed by oat (5.5%) and wheat (4.7%). 70.1% of grains recovered were too badly distorted to identify to species level and are recorded as 'Cerealia' in contingency tables. 18 wild intermediate sized grass (Poaceae indet.) seeds, two dock (*Rumex* sp.) fruits and a single seed each of knotweed (*Polygonum* sp.) and fat-hen (*C. album*) comprised the non-cereal material recovered.

- **C712:** This context was located to the west of the central baulk and was located directly above C709. Three samples from this context were analysed producing a moderate quantity of carbonised material. The most abundant remains encountered within this sample were oats (*Avena* sp.), represented by 11 grains (28.2%). A similar proportion of unidentifiable cereals ('Cerealia') were also encountered (25.6%). Barley, both *Hordeum distichon* (15.4%) and *Hordeum* sp. (12.8%) were the next most common remains, with a number of weed seeds also encountered. The most abundant of these were *Rumex* sp. (4 fruits) and *Polygonum* sp. (3 seeds).

- **C719:** This context consisted of a sub-rectangular spread of dark greyish material including possible industrial debris. A single sample from this context contained a moderate quantity of carbonised material. This comprised 16 carbonised cereal grains, weeds and nut species. Barley was the only cereal identified in the samples. A large proportion of cereal grains (50%) recovered were too badly distorted to identify to species level and are recorded as 'Cerealia' in contingency tables. Three hazelnut fragments (*Corylus avellana*) were recovered representing the only fruit/nut species. Wild intermediate sized grass (three grains) was the only non-cereal species recovered in the sample.

- **C725:** This consisted of an extensive spread of material, extending under the eastern baulk. A single sample from this context produced a small quantity of archaeobotanical material comprising 3 carbonised barley grains (*H. vulgare*).

- **C741:** This context consisted of a stony layer directly above metalled surface C750 in the southern half of the trench. Two samples from this context produced a moderate quantity of archaeobotanical material for analyses. Unusually, these comprised mostly wild/weed seeds. Only one carbonised barley (*H. vulgare*) grain was recovered along with 14 carbonised wild/weeds species. Seven wild intermediate sized grass (Poaceae indet.), Two knotweed (*Polygonum* sp.) and dock (*Rumex* sp.) fruits, and a single seed each of fat hen (*Chenopodium album*), and ryegrass (*Lolium* sp.) were recovered.

- **C742:** This comprised a discrete deposit of burned material within ditch C711. A single sample recovered from this context produced a moderate quantity of carbonised material (24 cereal grains). Barley was the dominant grain (41.7%) followed by oat (4.2%). 54.2% of grains recovered were too badly distorted to identify to species level and are recorded as 'Cerealia' in contingency tables.

POSTHOLES:

- **C721:** This comprised a discrete probable posthole cut into the fill of ditch C711. A single sample produced a small quantity of carbonised material for analyses comprising 19 carbonised cereal grains and weeds species. Barley was the dominant grain (36.8%) followed by oat (5.3%). A moderate volume of cereals recovered were too badly distorted to identify to species level and are recorded as 'Cerealia' in contingency tables. A small quantity of wild intermediate sized grass, knotweed (*Polygonum* sp.) (three seeds each), and a single dock (*Rumex* sp.) fruit was also recovered.

- **C727:** This context was the single fill from posthole C726, located within pit C735. A single sample was analysed from this feature which produced only a single hazelnut fragment (*C. avellana*).

- **C760:** This sample consisted of the single fill of a possible posthole (C762). It produced a moderate quantity of carbonised material for analyses totalling 15 carbonised cereal grains and wild/weed species. Three barley (*H. vulgare*) grains were the only cereal species identified. A further five grains recovered were too badly distorted to identify to species level and are recorded as 'Cerealia' in contingency tables. Seven wild intermediate sized grass (Poaceae indet.) seeds were the only non-cereal material recovered.

5.13.3. Discussion

The assemblage from all periods at Hill of Ward were dominated by carbonised cereals. These suggest that what arable economy existed was based on the cultivation of cereals, especially barley, oat and naked wheats.

Barley (*Hordeum* spp.) comprised over half the identified cereal remains at Hill of Ward (51%). It is one of the earliest domesticated arable crop species, and is one of the best adapted crop plants to a broad diversity of climates and environments, thriving in a greater variety of conditions including drier and colder environments, poorer soils, and more saline sediments (McClatchie 2018; Riehl 2019). In Ireland, barley has been cultivated since the early Neolithic and was most often grown as a spring-sown crop for both human and animal consumption (Murphy and Potterton 2010). Barley flour produces a heavy, dense loaf and is often considered to be 'inferior' to wheaten bread by those of higher status and consumed by lower-status members of society. Barley was also an important cereal particular because of its use in the malting process and was the most frequently used as it produced the best malt. An important factor affecting the size, shape and uniformity of barley kernels is the number of rows of kernels on the barley spike (Ayoub *et al.* 2002). Barley spikelets can be two-rowed or six-rowed and if preservation conditions are conducive to good survival of morphological characteristics these can be differentiated. While both species overall morphology

is quite similar, six-rowed barley (*Hordeum vulgare*) has an asymmetrical (twisted) grain, while two-rowed barley's (*Hordeum distichum*) is symmetrical (straight), most obviously affecting the ventral groove. All grains that were sufficiently well preserved were of the symmetrical variety and represent the presence of both six and two-rowed naked and hulled varieties. The dominant barley variety in early Bronze Age Ireland appears to have been naked barley, with hulled varieties becoming more ubiquitous towards the end of the late Bronze Age (McClatchie 2014).

Oat (*Avena* spp.) comprises 39% of all identified cereal remains at the Hill of Ward. While oat has been identified in Neolithic and earlier Bronze Age deposits in Europe these identifications are thought to represent arable weeds rather than representing oat as a crop (McClatchie *et al.* 2009; McClatchie 2018). In Ireland oat has been recovered in the prehistoric period but again, may have comprised a weed that was used for food rather than a crop in itself. The cultivation of oat appears to occur in the early 1st millennium when a significant increase in its size occurs. In the early medieval period oat was considered a low status grain, equated with the commoner in the *Bretha Déin Chécht* (McClatchie *et al.* 2009). Oat was (and still is) used in many foods including flat breads and biscuits, porridges, gruels, and many other vessel-based preparations, including alcoholic drinks (McClatchie 2018). The grains of common oat (*Avena sativa*) display morphological similarities to a variety of wild and weedy oat species, and it is difficult to identify them to species level without well-preserved floret bases (Jacomet 2006, 52).

Wheat comprises little over 10% of the identified cereal remains at the Hill of Ward. While wheat (*Triticum* sp./*T. aestivum/durum/turgidum*) has been discovered in Ireland from as early as the Neolithic. Early species, such as emmer wheat (*T. dicoccum*) typically had caryopses that were tightly enclosed by glumes (bracts). It is not until after the Anglo-Norman invasion, that free-threshing varieties become the dominant species (Monk 1986). Wheat can be used in stews, pottages or gruels but is most often used in the production of luxury breads that were of superior quality, with a lighter and finer texture than those made of barley or oat. Wheat may have also been used to make other foodstuffs such as ale. Wheat species at Hill of Ward were far less abundant than either barley or oat, representing only 3% of the identified grain. The identification of wheat species by grain alone is generally unreliable (Hillman *et al.* 1996) and with no chaff material recovered it is not possible to definitively identify the type of wheat present. Chaff fragments of wheat species are often much more easily identifiable to species level than the cereal grains (van der Veen 1992, 23). However, despite the lack of identifiable chaff many of the grains displayed morphologies consistent with that of naked wheat varieties (asymmetrical profile, with a rounded to angular dorsal ridge, concave to flat to rounded-convex ventral surface) and recorded as *T. aestivum/durum/turgidum* in Table 5.13.1.

The possible identification of three grains of rye at the Hill of Ward in Trench 4 and 5 was noted by NG. This crop is able to grow in poor soils and was listed as second highest of the cereals in the early medieval law texts (Kelly 2000, 219). It is suitable for growing over winter and can therefore produce grain at a time when other crops are only ripening. The crop has been found in prehistoric and early medieval sites in Ireland, although it is not as ubiquitous as the other cereals.

5.13.4. Diachronic changes in cultivars at the Hill of Ward

5.13.4.1. Cereal grains

Analysis of the plant macrofossil assemblage at the Hill of Ward highlights a number of general diachronic trends in the relative frequencies of cereal species (Figs 5.13.1 and 5.13.2). As previously stated, barley (*sensu lato*) was the dominant species of cultivated grain across all time periods excavated at Hill of Ward. However, when the varieties of barley are considered, variations over time are indicated. While naked barley (*Hordeum nudum*) was identified in small numbers within the Bronze Age and Iron Age samples, it is almost absent from later periods. Significantly more hulled barley was recorded from the later deposits in comparison to naked varieties. It should be noted that a large proportion of barley was impossible to identify beyond *Hordeum* sp., with no differentiation between naked and hulled varieties possible.

Differences in the proportion of oat (*Avena* spp.) recovered are also apparent through time. In the Bronze Age, oat comprises a relatively small proportion of the cereal assemblage (16.6% identified grain). The proportion of oat remains approximately stable in the Iron Age contexts but rises dramatically to 42.4% by the Early Medieval 2 period. Concurrently to the increase in oat over time, the proportion of wheat (*Triticum* sp./*Triticum aestivum/durum/turgidum*) declines. At Hill of Ward, wheat makes up 23.8% in the Bronze Age samples reducing over time to 12.8% in the Iron Age and comprising just 9.2% by the later early medieval period. The factors influencing these changes at the Hill of Ward could be cultural, environment or a blend of both. The decrease in wheat and the subsequent increase in oat and hulled barley might suggest environmental factors. As oat and barley can tolerate poorer conditions, the decrease in wheat may be as a result of sub-optimal conditions for its cultivation, possibly linked to a climatic downturn after the late 8th century AD (*e.g.* Kerr *et al.* 2009; Coyle-McClung and Plunkett 2020, 21–22).

5.13.4.2. Wild/weed species

A small quantity and narrow range of wild/weed species were recovered at the Hill of Ward. The majority of these are typical of those that grow either in or around fields or waste places. Arable or field weeds were present, with wild intermediate sized grass (*Poaceae* sp.) the most common species encountered, with small quantities of bedstraw (*Galium* sp.) also recovered. Species of wet/damp places were encountered in low numbers, mainly comprising members of the Polygonaceae (*F. convolvulus*; *Rumex* sp.; *Persicaria* sp.). A small quantity of fat hen and goosefoot/orache (*Chenopodium album/Chenopodium/Atriplex*) comprised the remainder of the assemblage. The weed flora recovered from this assemblage is impoverished and does not represent the full flora present during the period; however, it is possible that this reflects an assemblage derived from a mixed cultivation system, where the wild grasses were harvested and subsequently consumed alongside cereals (Behre 2008). This is particularly of note as regards Trench 8, where the proportion of wild grasses is elevated in comparison to the same phase of construction elsewhere at the site (Fig. 5.13.3).

5.13.4.3. Crop processing

The composition of the archaeobotanical assemblage from the Hill of Ward appears to have been substantially affected by crop-processing activities. Crop processing is a multi-stage process where a harvested crop is cleaned and prepared for consumption by threshing, winnowing, and sieving the crop to remove straw, chaff, weed seeds and other detritus (Hald 2008). The identification of crop-processing activities associated with cereals has become an established component of archaeobotanical research (Knörzer 1971; Dennell 1972; Hillman 1973; 1981; 1984; Körber-Grohne 1981; Jones, G. 1984; 1987; Jones, M. 1985; Miksicek 1987; Boardman and Jones 1990; Reddy 1991; 1997; 2003; Thompson 1996; Lundström-Baudais *et al.* 2002; Harvey and Fuller 2005). These studies have highlighted that crop-processing techniques create taphonomic biases that need to be considered when analysing assemblages as they have a major influence on the components recovered in the archaeobotanical record. Each distinct phase of crop processing produces a unique suite of products and by-products that can be differentiated in the archaeobotanical record (Hillman 1981). Each stage alters the composition of the crop assemblage, creating a product for retention and an unwanted by-product. The by-products of these stages have been grouped and classified according to the seeds physical characteristics, such as big-heavy-headed (BHH), big free-heavy (BFH), small headed-heavy (SHH), small-free-heavy (SFH), and small free-light (SFL) (after Jones 1984). Identification of materials from distinct stages allows archaeobotanists to identify to what extent the grain was processed before its deposition in the archaeological record. The identification of the level of processing is extremely important when making inferences of agricultural practices and

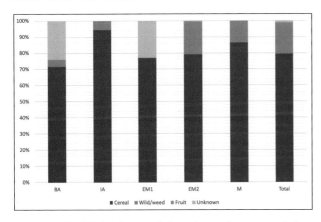

Fig. 5.13.1. 100% columns of the relative frequency of plant categories by period, highlighting the dominance of cereal grain.

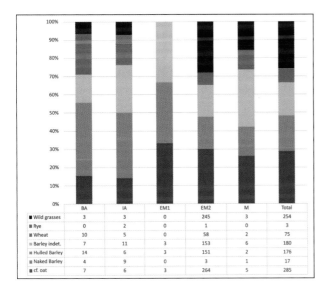

Fig. 5.13.2. 100% columns depicting the relative frequency of cereal species by period, indicating diachronic changes in cultivation over time.

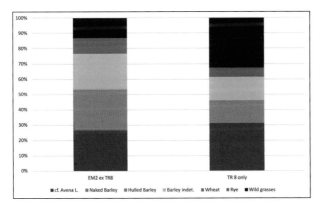

Fig. 5.13.3. Comparison between Trench 8 and early medieval phase 2, excluding Trench 8 showing increased representation of wild grasses.

when using the assemblage to understand social organisation in the past (Jones and Halstead 1995). All wild/weed species present at the Hill of Ward are categorised as BFH weeds, consistent with species usually associated with late stage processed cereal grains. The lack of small weeds and chaff also suggests that cleaning activities (threshing, winnowing, sieving) were not undertaken in the areas excavated and may have occurred outside the site.

5.13.4.4. Fruit/Nut species

Fruit/nut species were a very minor component of the Hill of Ward assemblage. Hazelnut (*Corylus avellana*) was the only species recovered with a small number of shell fragments present. Charcoal analyses by Lorna O'Donnell (O'Donnell, this volume) indicate a range of pomaceous fruit trees including crab apple (*Malus sylvestris*), pear (*Pyrus pyraster*), hawthorn (*Crataegus monogyna*), mountain ash/rowan (*Sorbus aucuparia*) and blackthorn (*Prunus spinosa*) wood burned at the site which likely grew in the local vicinity. These species would have produced a range of edible fruits for consumption or utilised for medical reasons. The lack of fruit is therefore likely a result of this taphonomy rather than an exclusion of fruits or nuts from the diet of the inhabitants of Hill of Ward as many can be eaten raw, and therefore have a much lower chance of becoming carbonised and entering the archaeological record.

5.13.5. Conclusions

Samples from the Hill of Ward produced a rich assemblage of 1,768 carbonised plant macrofossil remains from a range of cultivated, wild/weed and fruit/nut species. The assemblage details the arable economy between the Bronze Age and early medieval periods, highlighting interesting diachronic differences in cereal cultivation. Bronze Age samples produced a small range and quantity of species, but allowed the identification of the range of cultivated cereals present at the site. During this period barley (*Hordeum nudum/Hordeum vulgare*) and wheat (*Triticum aestivum/durum/turgidum*) and oat (*Avena* sp.) were all recovered with a preference for hulled barley (*H. vulgare*) and wheat (*T. aestivum/durum/turgidum*) apparent. Oat (*Avena* sp.) appears to have been a minor component and may have been a weed of the other cultivated plants. The Iron Age assemblage was equally impoverished with a small quantity and range of species. During this period barley was dominant, increasing in proportion in comparison to the preceding Bronze Age. The trends apparent during the prehistoric period continue into the Early Medieval 1 phase with very few seeds recovered, but with barley dominating. The later early medieval phase (8th to 11th century) yielded by far the most macrofossil remains. Here, hulled barley is abundant and the proportion of oat in particular increases

Table 5.13.1. Hill of Ward, Co. Meath plant macrofossil data.

Trench	2	3	4	4	4	4	4	4	4	5	5	5	5	5	5	5	5	5	5	5
Context	009	006	427	461	463	465	472	473	478	431	442	446	448	449	450	451	452	493	521	546
cf. *Avena* L.	7		4	3					6		2		4		1	3	1	1		5
Hordeum distichon L.		1	3							1		1				7				
Hordeum vulgare L.		1	3		1		2		4		1				1	3				
Hordeum nudum L. 2-row			1				3		2			1			2					
Hordeum nudum L. 6-row			3				2		2				1							
Hordeum sp.	3	1	4			2	2		7			1		2	1	6			1	5
T. aestivum/ durum/turgidum			10				4					2			4	2				
Triticum sp.									1											
Secale cereale L.							1		1											
Cerealia		1	6			1	2		7		3	1			6	3	2	1		2
Corylus avellana L.																				
cf. *F. convolvulus* L.																				
Persicaria sp.																				
Rumex sp.																				
Rumex crispus L.													3							
Polygonum sp.																				
Chenopodium album L.																				
Chenopodium/Atriplex																				
Galium sp.																				
Lolium sp.																				
Bromus secalinus L.				1												7				
Poaceae indet.			2				3					1	5			8				2
Rosaceae indet.																				
Unknown			4	2				10			3		2							
Total	**10**	**4**	**40**	**6**	**1**	**3**	**19**	**10**	**30**	**1**	**9**	**7**	**15**	**2**	**15**	**39**	**3**	**2**	**1**	**14**

(Continued)

Table 5.13.1. (Continued)

Trench	5	5	7	7	8	8	8	8	8	8	8	8	8	8	8	8	8	8	8
Context	548	549	915	916	703	707	709	712	713	715	719	721	725	727	741	742	749	760	773
cf. Avena L.	13		22	12	1		134	11	6	47	1	1				1	7		
Hordeum distichon L.		3		39			36	6	0	16	1	2			1	10	25		
Hordeum vulgare L.		1																	
Hordeum nudum L. 2-row																			
Hordeum nudum L. 6-row																			
Hordeum sp.	16	2	6	18	5	2	31	5	8	39	1	5	3					3	1
T. aestivum/durum/turgidum	2	3		0	3		4			9							6		
Triticum sp.			6	3			8		5	3									
Secale cereale L.		1																	
Cerealia	1	2	84	61	7	7	166	10	6	165	8	5				13	89	5	3
Corylus avellana L.											3			1					
cf. F. convolvulus L.										1									
Persicaria sp.										2									
Rumex sp.			1				3	4	7	8		1			2		2		5
Rumex crispus L.																			
Polygonum sp.							7	3		7		3			2		1		
Chenopodium album L.	4						6	1	1	5					1		1		
Chenopodium/Atriplex		1					1												
Galium sp.							1												
Lolium sp.															1				
Bromus secalinus L.																			
Poaceae indet.		3		5	5		88		4	82	3	2			7		18	7	
Rosaceae indet.	1																		
Unknown															1				
Total	**37**	**15**	**120**	**138**	**21**	**9**	**486**	**39**	**37**	**384**	**16**	**19**	**3**	**1**	**15**	**24**	**149**	**15**	**9**

significantly. Wheat remains a minor part of the overall assemblage. At Trench 8 (the Eastern Complex) grassy weeds are far more common than elsewhere on site.

Despite a range of fruit producing trees and shrubs present as charcoal, an extremely small range of wild fruit and nut species was recovered. Hazelnut trees likely grew in the vicinity and provided an important supplement to the grain diet. A similarly impoverished range of wild/weed species was recovered. The species recovered are common and likely grew on the edges of arable fields, streams or in the local vicinity of the ringfort. The weed component of the assemblage comprised a small quantity and range of species. Wild grasses (Poaceae indet.) were dominant with smaller quantities of bedstraw (*Galium* sp.), black bindweed (*Fallopia convolvulus*), docks (*Rumex* sp.), knotweed (*Persicaria* sp.), fat hen (*Chenopodium album*).

5.14. Charcoal remains (Lorna O'Donnell)

5.14.1. Introduction

This report discusses charcoal analysis from 66 samples from the Hill of Ward, Co. Meath. The aim of the charcoal analysis was to isolate suitable short-lived taxa for dating, to investigate local woodland cover in the area when the site was in use and to examine any contextual related variability within the samples.

5.14.2. Methodology

5.14.2.1. Processing

Samples were processed by flotation at the School of Archaeology, University College Dublin. Individual samples were poured into a flotation machine with a mesh measuring 300 microns. The flot was collected and dried. The retent was passed through sieves of 1 mm to 2 mm and was dried and separately bagged.

5.14.2.2. Charcoal identification

It was aimed to identify 50 charcoal fragments randomly per sample (McClatchie *et al.* 2015). If 50 fragments are not present in the sample, then all fragments possible are identified. Each piece of charcoal was examined and orientated first under low magnification (10–40×). They were then broken to reveal their transverse, tangential and longitudinal surfaces. Pieces were mounted in plasticine and examined under a metallurgical microscope with dark ground light and magnifications generally of 200× and 400×. Charcoal was identified by comparing relevant characteristics to keys (Schweingruber 1978; Wheeler *et al.* 1989; Hather 2000) and a reference collection supplied by the National Botanical Gardens of Ireland, Glasnevin. Nomenclature follows Schweingruber (1978). It was not always possible to separate *Prunus avium/padus* and *Prunus spinosa*, thus some identifications are classed as *Prunus* spp.

Each charcoal taxon group was weighed in grams to two decimal places. The general age group of each taxon per sample was recorded, and the growth rates were classified as slow, medium, fast or mixed. Ring curvature of the pieces was also noted – for example, weakly curved annual rings suggest the use of trunks or larger branches, while strongly curved annual rings indicate the burning of smaller branches or trees (Marguerie and Hunot 2007, 1421, Fig. 3). Tyloses in vessels in species such as oak can denote the presence of heartwood. These occur when adjacent parenchyma cells penetrate the vessel walls (via the pitting) effectively blocking the vessels (Gale 2003, 37). Insect infestation is usually identified by round holes caused by burrowing insects. Their presence might suggest the use of degraded wood, which may have been gathered from the woodland floor or stockpiled.

5.14.3. Results

5.14.3.1. Overall results

In total, 1,898 charcoal fragments were identified. It was necessary to subsample 26 samples to 50 fragments (Table 5.14.1). Thirteen native Irish tree and shrub taxa were identified. The most frequent was oak (*Quercus* spp.), which represented 30% of the identifications and was recorded in 36 samples, although it was rarely dominant. Hazel (*Corylus avellana*) comprised 25% of the overall results and was recorded in 37 samples. Ash (*Fraxinus excelsior*) represented 17% of the results and was noted in 32 samples. Alder (*Alnus glutinosa*) formed 12% of the results and was recorded in 23 samples. The pomaceous fruitwood type includes crab apple (*Malus sylvestris*), pear (*Pyrus pyraster*), hawthorn (*Crataegus monogyna*) and rowan (*Sorbus aucuparia*), these cannot be differentiated through wood anatomy. This grouping represented 9% of the overall results and was noted in 24 samples. Noted in lower amounts were birch (*Betula* spp.), blackthorn (*Prunus spinosa*), wild/bird cherry (*Prunus avium/padus*) willow (*Salix* spp.), ivy (*Hedera helix*), yew (*Taxus baccata*) elm (*Ulmus* spp.) and holly (*Ilex aquifolium*) (Figs 5.14.1, 5.14.2 and 5.14.3).

5.14.4. Contextual results

5.14.4.1. Trench 1

Charcoal was examined from four contexts. C023, C024, C027 and C039 were all fills from the outer ditch (C029). Hazel was important in most of the fills (Fig. 5.14.4). Pomaceous fruitwood was a common component in three fills (C023, C027 and C039), while ash was frequently noted in C024.

5.14.4.2. Test Pit 2

Charcoal was examined from five fills within pit C052 (C058, C068, C069, C070 and C074). A high level of oak only was identified from these five contexts, suggesting that they were the remains of structural oak timbers and/or industrial activity. The charcoal from pit C052 represents fairly large chunks to up to 40 mm in size, with ring

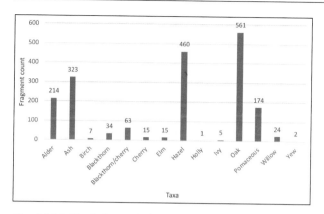

Fig. 5.14.1. Total charcoal identifications, fragment count, Hill of Ward charcoal assemblage.

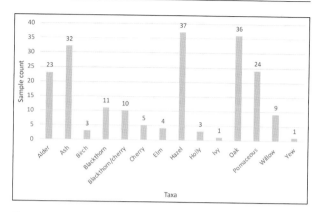

Fig. 5.14.3. Charcoal sample counts, Hill of Ward charcoal assemblage.

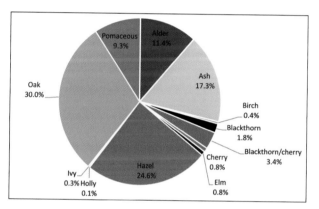

Fig. 5.14.2. Percentage fragment count, Hill of Ward charcoal assemblage.

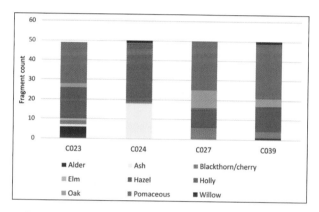

Fig. 5.14.4. Charcoal results from Trench 1, Hill of Ward.

counts ranging up to 45 (Table 5.14.1). Oak from C069 has been radiocarbon dated to cal AD 1051–1270 (849±36 BP; UBA-27558), the early medieval/medieval period.

5.14.4.3. Trench 3

Charcoal was analysed from five contexts. This includes samples from four fills from ditch C014 (C018, C048, C050 and C006). The primary fill was C018. Alder was the dominant taxa from C018 with ash also present. Also examined from ditch C014 were C048 and C050. Alder, ash, elm and pomaceous fruitwood were identified from C048, while alder and pomaceous fruitwood were recorded from C050. The final fill examined from this ditch was C006 from which mainly alder with hazel, ash, pomaceous fruitwood and blackthorn/cherry (Table 5.14.1; Fig. 5.14.5). One sample was examined from Bronze Age posthole C010 (C005) with ash, alder and pomaceous fruitwood recorded (Table 5.14.1).

5.14.4.4. Trench 4

Charcoal was analysed from nine contexts from this trench (Fig. 5.14.6). C475 re-cut ditch C428 and was filled with C402. Hazel, oak and ivy charcoal was recorded from

this fill. Charcoal was identified from the fills of the three Bronze Age ditches (C404, C428 and C464) and varied between the ditches (Fig. 5.14.6). While C429, the fill of C404 was dominated by hazel and ash, C427, the assemblage from C428 was diverse, with five wood taxa identified. Meanwhile, oak dominated the fills examined from the innermost ditch C464 (C463 and C473).

C469 post-dated the use of the Bronze Age phase and sealed C471, the uppermost fill of the inner ditch. The level of charcoal here was low, but five taxa were identified: oak, pomaceous fruitwood, ash, hazel and alder. This indicates that similar wood taxa continued to grow in the area after the site went out of use.

Pit C467 (filled with C468) is one of few pit samples from this phase. A wide variety of taxa were identified from here including alder, hazel, ash, pomaceous fruitwood, *Prunus* and oak. Alder and oak were the main two wood taxa present.

Possible kiln C481 has been radiocarbon dated to the late Iron Age 146 cal BC–cal AD 68 (2030±30 BP; Beta-436097). Two samples were examined from here. The main fill (C478) contained mainly ash with *Prunus*, hazel and alder. C465, the upper fill yielded mostly alder with some ash (Table 5.14.1; Fig. 5.14.6).

5.14.4.5. Trench 5

Charcoal was analysed from seven contexts within this trench. C448 was a burnt layer within ditch C520; while the level of charcoal was low, it was diverse with seven taxa identified. These included alder, ash, hazel, oak, birch, cherry, and yew (Table 5.14.1). A further fill (C452) ditch C520 yielded only three taxa, dominated by oak. A deposit of mixed clay with a small amount of burnt bone (C442) contained two wood taxa only, hazel and alder with hazel the most abundant (Fig. 5.14.7; Table 5.14.1).

Three samples were examined relating to hearth C454 (C451, C548 and C549). Seven wood taxa were identified from C451, dominated by blackthorn/cherry and hazel while alder, ash, pomaceous fruitwood, oak and willow were also recorded. Alder and oak were recorded from C548. Cherry, oak, hazel, ash and pomaceous fruitwood were identified from C549. The level of charcoal was higher in C451 than the other fills. Overall, eight taxa identified from the hearth C454 with blackthorn/cherry and hazel being the most frequently noted (Fig. 5.14.7). A cut (C494) recorded southwest of hearth C454 (fill C493) yielded charcoal of blackthorn and oak (Table 5.14.1; Fig. 5.14.7).

5.14.4.6. Trench 6

Above bedrock towards the centre of the mound was a small charcoal-rich spread of material (C822) beneath a much more extensive cultural deposit (C818). In the centre of the southern half of the trench above C815 and partially above C812 was a deposit of grey clay C811. Charcoal was analysed from these three contexts.

Willow and hazel only were recorded from C811. Four taxa were identified from C818, the most frequent being hazel and ash while smaller quantities of oak and pomaceous fruitwood were also recorded. Ash and hazel were also important in the earlier C822. Pomaceous fruitwood was also significant while a low level of oak and alder were also noted (Fig. 5.14.8; Table 5.14.1).

5.14.4.7. Trench 7

Charcoal was analysed from seven contexts from within Trench 7 (C910, C911, C913, C914, C915, C916 and C919), six of which were discrete layers within ditch C904. At the interface between the bedrock and the main ditch fill was C919. One fragment of hazel only was identified from here. C914 represents the main fill of the ditch, with oak and cherry charcoal recorded. Two areas of burning were evident at the base of C914 (C915 and C916). Mainly pomaceous fruitwood, ash and oak were recorded from C915, while low levels of blackthorn and hazel were also evident. C916 was dominated by pomaceous fruitwood while ash and hazel were also present. C913 was located above C914, with mainly oak with hazel recorded from this context (Fig. 5.14.9; Table 5.14.1). C910 represented a possible hearth, the fill of which was C911. Blackthorn only was identified from this context (Fig. 5.14.9; Table 5.14.1).

5.14.4.8. Trench 8

Charcoal was analysed from six contexts from Trench 8: C714, C741, C742, C745, C760 and C773. Hazel, oak, and ash were identified from C742, which was a deposit located above ditch C711. C773 was one of the fills of

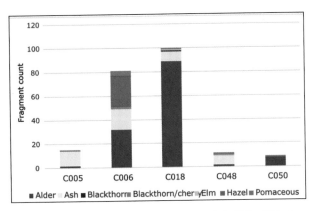

Fig. 5.14.5. Charcoal results from Trench 3, Hill of Ward.

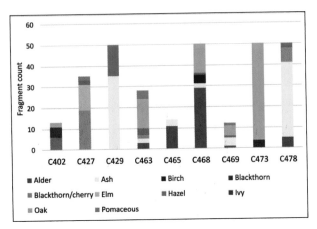

Fig. 5.14.6. Charcoal results from Trench 4, Hill of Ward

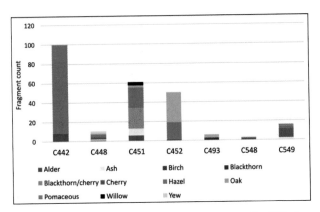

Fig. 5.14.7. Charcoal results from Trench 5, Hill of Ward

ditch C711 was probably related to metalworking. Mainly oak was recorded from this fill, while a low level of alder, ash, blackthorn, pomaceous fruitwood and birch were also recorded (Fig. 5.14.10).

C745 was the fill of ditch C746. Mainly hazel with ash, alder, oak and willow were recorded from here. C714 was an upper fill of C746. A low level of blackthorn only was identified from this context.

C741 represents a stony layer above the metalled surface C750. A range of eight taxa were identified from this context including hazel, oak, alder, ash, blackthorn, pomaceous fruitwood, cherry, and willow. Results were comparable between the three samples examined from C741, with most taxa being recorded in two samples. Ash and cherry were only identified in one of the three samples. C760 was the fill of possible posthole C762 and contained mainly ash with hazel, oak, cherry, and willow (Fig. 5.14.10; Table 5.14.1).

It was possible to phase 41 samples to a time period (Fig. 5.14.11). Ash was the main taxon dating to the middle/late Bronze Age, although this only was represented by a single sample so must be interpreted with caution. More varied taxa were noted from the late Bronze Age with oak, hazel, ash and blackthorn/cherry being important. Ash becomes dominant during the late Iron Age while oak and alder remain noteworthy. By the late Iron

Age/early medieval period, alder was the dominant taxon, with ash, hazel and oak being also important. Hazel and pomaceous fruitwood were the main taxa from the early medieval period while oak dominates the results from the early medieval/medieval period. There may be some bias in this though given the probable structural nature of the oak in Test Pit 2 where the early medieval/medieval samples were derived from.

5.14.5. Ring growth and form
The annual ring curvature in the birch, hazel, ivy, holly, cherry, blackthorn, willow and yew were mainly strongly curved, indicating the burning of smaller branches or twigs of these trees. The mixed ring curvature in the alder, ash, pomaceous fruitwood, oak and elm indicate that smaller to larger branches of these trees were burnt. Ring counts range from 1–45 and growth was mainly medium (Table 5.14.1).

5.14.6. Discussion
At the Hill of Ward, ash, oak and hazel are the main taxa dating to the Bronze Age. Ash, alder and oak are important during the Iron Age (Fig. 5.14.11). Charcoal results from the settlement site at Kilmainham, Kells, Co. Meath north of the Hill of Ward indicate that oak,

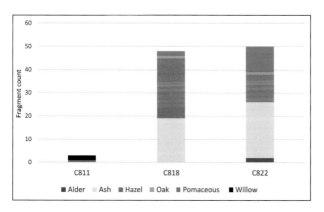

Fig. 5.14.8. Charcoal results from Trench 6, Hill of Ward.

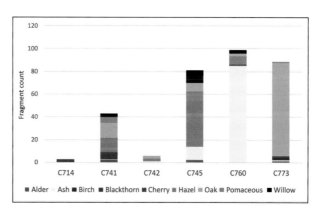

Fig. 5.14.10. Charcoal results from Trench 8, Hill of Ward.

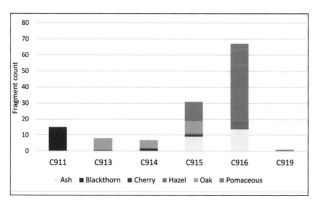

Fig. 5.14.9. Charcoal results from Trench 7, Hill of Ward.

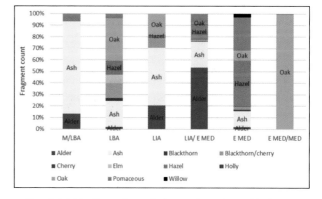

Fig. 5.14.11. Chronological charcoal results, Hill of Ward.

hazel, and alder were also the dominant taxa here during the Bronze Age. During the Iron Age oak and hazel were the dominant wood taxa at Kilmainham (O'Donnell *et al.* 2021). By the early medieval period at the Hill of Ward, hazel became the dominant taxon, followed by ash and pomaceous fruitwood, suggesting open canopy woodland or isolated areas of scrub (Fig. 5.14.11), implying clearance of primary woodland has likely taken place.

Oak is a hard, dense wood and has been used as a structural wood in Ireland from the Neolithic period to the post-medieval (O'Donnell 2007). Its apparent selection at the Hill of Ward for structural timbers in Test Pit 2 was probably a result of its durability, although it is unclear how available oak was in the landscape at this time. There is also a possibility that this context represents industrial burning as the burned residues recovered suggest a very intense firing. Ash, hazel, blackthorn/cherry and alder were the main woods identified from the Iron Age potential kiln C481 at the Hill of Ward. Oak and hazel were the main fuels noted from Iron Age kilns at Kilmainham, Co. Meath, although a variety of other taxa were also recorded (O'Donnell *et al.* 2021). Generally, a variety of wood types were used in the Irish Iron Age and early medieval kilns from Meath (O'Donnell *et al.* 2021). Pollen data from Jamestown, Co. Meath dating mainly to the Iron Age demonstrates the importance of hazel alder, and oak in the landscape at this time (Maguire, this volume). Plant macrofossil analysis does not demonstrate any evidence for woodlands in the vicinity of the site (Stone and Gilligan, this volume).

Charcoal from the early medieval period at Kilmainham (including kiln, pit and ditch fills) was dominated by hazel, alder, birch, oak and ash. The highest levels of hazel were noted during this period from Kilmainham, indicating that the tree grew prolifically in the area during this time (O'Donnell *et al.* 2021). This compares well to the charcoal results from the Hill of Ward, which suggests that hazel was likely the most common woodland species in the area during the early medieval period.

Charcoal has also been analysed from Knowth, at Brú na Bóinne, Co. Meath, to the northeast of the Hill of Ward. Of particular interest are two sub-circular ditches of 6th to 10th century in date. Here, nine wood taxa were identified, the most common of which were hazel and elder (Johnston and O'Donnell 2008). In comparison to the Hill of Ward, this indicates the prevalence of scrub in parts of Meath, dominated by hazel during this time, again highlighting the probable early clearance of old growth woodland. In contrast, charcoal from Killeen Castle, Co. Meath, to the southeast was dominated by ash and oak during the early medieval period. The amount of oak is noticeable and probably is representative of the high levels of metal working at the site during this time, presenting a somewhat biased result. Charcoal from the medieval period was also dominated by ash followed by oak. A variety of scrub-like

trees including cherry, hazel and holly were also identified from the site (O'Donnell 2009).

From Clonee, Co. Meath, charcoal from domestic contexts from the early medieval period was dominated by alder followed by hazel. Also present were ash, blackthorn, cherry, oak, pomaceous fruitwood and willow (O'Donnell 2021). Overall, charcoal results from early medieval sites in Co. Meath are indicative of fairly open canopy, secondary woodlands with a well-established shrub layer. Pollen analysis from Jamestown Bog also indicates some woodland clearance during the Iron Age/ early medieval period (Maguire, this volume). In most Irish metalworking and charcoal production contexts, the main tree identified is oak, suggesting that this was deliberately selected for this purpose (Kenny 2010; OCarroll and Mitchell 2016). This compares well to results from the Hill of Ward.

5.14.7. Local Meath woodlands

At the Hill of Ward the main canopy trees were ash and oak. Ash trees prefer moist, well drained and fertile soils. It is very intolerant of shade (Lipscombe and Stokes 2008, 188). Ireland has two native oaks, *Quercus robur* (pedunculate oak) and *Quercus petraea* (sessile or common oak) (Wyse-Jackson 2018, 35). Pedunculate oak grows best in deep fertile clays and loams but will tolerate a wide range of soils (Lipscombe and Stokes 2008, 156). Sessile oak prefers areas of high rainfall and grows best in deep, well-drained clays and loams (Lipscombe and Stokes 2008, 202).

The range of smaller shrub and scrub trees present in the samples suggests that local woodlands were not very open during the early medieval period. Blackthorn, cherry, hazel and the pomaceous fruitwood type will all grow well on woodland margins or as understorey in woodlands with a relatively open canopy. These fruit trees would have been a valuable source of wild food foraging, producing hazelnuts, cherries, sloes and crab apples. A large assemblage of plant macrofossil remains from the site were suggestive of an agricultural landscape in the area during the early medieval period, with oat and barley fields locally, and to a lesser extent wheat (Stone and Gilligan, this volume). This compares well to the wood results, which were suggestive of stands of open, secondary woodlands with a well-established shrub layer, although wild plant resources were almost absent from the plant macrofossil assemblage.

The presence of alder, willow and to an extent birch are suggestive of local wetland source close to the site. Ireland's native alder is *Alnus glutinosa* or common alder. It often grows on streams, rivers, lake shores and banks, thriving in boggy soils and moist woodlands (Wyse-Jackson 2018, 43). In comparison, willow will also grow in wet areas. The main Irish native willows are grey willow

Table 5.14.1. Charcoal counts from the Hill of Ward, Co. Meath.

Context	Identification	Weight (g)	Fragment count	Ring count	Size (mm)	Ring curvature	Growth
005	*Alnus* sp. (alder)	0.03	2	2	3	SC	M
005	*Fraxinus excelsior* L. (ash)	0.11	12	2–4	2–5	SC	M
005	Maloideae	0.03	1	2	2	SC	M
006	*Corylus avellana* L. (hazel)	2.59	50	5–12	4–9	SC	M
006	*Corylus avellana* L. (hazel)	0.72	9	3–6	4–6	SC	M
006	*Fraxinus excelsior* L. (ash)	0.39	9	4–7	3–5	SC	M
006	Maloideae	0.24	4	2–5	4–6	SC	M
006	*Prunus* L. (blackthorn/cherry)	0.02	1	4	4	SC	M
006	*Alnus* sp. (alder)	0.99	20	3–6	5–10	SC	M
006	*Alnus* sp. (alder)	0.15	12	3–5	2–4	SC	M
006	*Fraxinus excelsior* L. (ash)	0.13	8	4–6	3–7	WC	M
018	*Alnus* sp. (alder)	6.96	47	4–6	5–14	SC	F
018	*Fraxinus excelsior* L. (ash)	0.53	2	3–4	3–6	SC	M
018	*Prunus spinosa* L. (blackthorn)	0.12	1	6	3	SC	M
018	*Alnus* sp. (alder)	8.98	42	4–6	4–8	SC	M
018	*Fraxinus excelsior* L. (ash)	1.25	6	3–10	5–10	SC	M
018	Maloideae	0.32	1	4	10	SC	M
018	*Ulmus* sp. (elm)	0.39	1	4	18	WC	M
023	*Corylus avellana* L. (hazel)	0.5	15	3–6	4–10	SC	M
023	Maloideae	1.02	15	5–10	4–7	SC	M
023	*Prunus* L. (blackthorn/cherry)	0.21	2	3	4	SC	M
023	*Ulmus* sp. (elm)	0.05	1	3	4	MC	M
023	*Corylus avellana* L. (hazel)	0.06	1	3	3	SC	M
023	Maloideae	0.1	6	2–4	2–5	SC	M
023	*Alnus* sp. (alder)	0.17	6	2–6	2–5	WC	M
023	*Quercus* sp. (oak)	0.1	2	4–5	4	WC	M
023	*Fraxinus excelsior* L. (ash)	0.03	1	1	2	MC	M
024	*Corylus avellana* L. (hazel)	2.23	29	5–10	4–10	SC	M
024	Maloideae	0.18	1	3	4	SC	M
024	*Prunus* L. (blackthorn/cherry)	0.04	1	2	3	SC	M
024	*Salix* sp. (willow)	0.03	1	2	2	SC	M
024	*Fraxinus excelsior* L. (ash)	0.61	18	3–8	4–7	WC	M
027	*Corylus avellana* L. (hazel)	1.31	9	4–6	4–8	SC	M
027	*Ilex aquifolium* L. (holly)	0.03	1	3	4	SC	M
027	Maloideae	5.26	25	5–20	4–15	SC	M
027	*Prunus* L. (blackthorn/cherry)	1.01	6	3–6	3–5	SC	M
027	*Quercus* sp. (oak)	0.66	9	4–8	3–6	WC	M
039	*Alnus* sp. (alder)	0.12	1	5	5	SC	M
039	*Corylus avellana* L. (hazel)	0.93	13	5–15	5–10	SC	M
039	Maloideae	1.7	28	5–10	4–10	SC	M
039	*Prunus* L. (blackthorn/cherry)	0.32	3	10	6	SC	M
039	*Salix* sp. (willow)	0.15	1	4	3	SC	M
039	*Quercus* sp. (oak)	0.5	4	4–6	4–8	WC	M
048	*Ulmus* sp. (elm)	0.03	1	1	2	Indet	M
048	Maloideae	0.04	2	2–3	2–4	MC	M

(Continued)

Table 5.14.1. Charcoal counts from the Hill of Ward, Co. Meath. (Continued)

Context	Identification	Weight (g)	Fragment count	Ring count	Size (mm)	Ring curvature	Growth
048	*Alnus* sp. (alder)	0.03	2	2	2–4	SC	M
048	*Fraxinus excelsior* L. (ash)	0.19	7	1–3	2–5	SC	M
050	*Alnus* sp. (alder)	0.34	8	2–4	3–9	SC	F
050	Maloideae	0.02	1	3	2	SC	M
058	*Quercus* sp. (oak)	16.96	50	5–25	4–40	WC	M
067	Maloideae	0.34	2	7	7	SC	M
067	*Quercus* sp. (oak)	2.5	48	5–15	5–10	WC	M
068	*Quercus* sp. (oak)	4.35	50	4–15	4–20	SC	M
069	*Quercus* sp. (oak)	10.33	50	15–45	15–32	WC	M
070	*Quercus* sp. (oak)	4.22	50	5–15	5–15	WC	M
074	*Quercus* sp. (oak)	25.13	50	5–45	15–36	WC	M
402	*Corylus avellana* L. (hazel)	0.12	6	2–4	2–3	SC	M
402	*Hedera helix* L. (ivy)	0.05	5	2–4	2–3	SC	M
402	*Quercus* sp. (oak)	0.03	2	2–3	2	SC	M
427	*Corylus avellana* L. (hazel)	0.06	2	3	4	SC	M
427	*Prunus* L. (blackthorn/cherry)	0.13	2	4	4	SC	M
427	*Ulmus* sp. (elm)	1.5	12	4–6	5–12	SC	M
427	Maloideae	0.11	2	1–2	2–3	SC	M
427	*Prunus* L. (blackthorn/cherry)	0.52	17	2–5	3–6	SC	M
427	*Corylus avellana* L. (hazel)	2.23	48	3–15	4–8	SC	M
427	*Fraxinus excelsior* L. (ash)	0.51	2	20	7–8	WC	M
429	*Corylus avellana* L. (hazel)	0.86	15	5–8	5–10	SC	M
429	*Fraxinus excelsior* L. (ash)	0.27	35	2–7	3–5	WC	S
442	*Alnus* sp. (alder)	0.16	8	4–5	4–6	SC	M
442	*Corylus avellana* L. (hazel)	0.6	42	4–7	3–6	SC	M
442	*Corylus avellana* L. (hazel)	6.85	50	5–15	5–20	SC	M
448	*Fraxinus excelsior* L. (ash)	0.05	1	2	6	MC	F
448	*Betula* sp. (birch)	0.03	1	2	2	MC	M
448	*Quercus* sp. (oak)	0.03	1	2	3	MC	M
448	*Corylus avellana* L. (hazel)	0.04	3	3–4	3–4	SC	M
448	*Prunus avium* L.; *P. padus* L. (cherry)	0.02	1	3	3	SC	M
448	*Taxus baccata* L. (yew)	0.02	2	2–3	2	SC	M
448	*Alnus* sp. (alder)	0.04	1	3	3	WC	M
451	*Fraxinus excelsior* L. (ash)	0.15	7	5	3–5	WC	M
451	*Corylus avellana* L. (hazel)	0.4	20	3–6	3–6	SC	M
451	Maloideae	0.02	1	3	2	SC	M
451	*Prunus* L. (blackthorn/cherry)	0.63	22	3–7	3–6	SC	M
451	*Quercus* sp. (oak)	0.06	2	3	3	SC	M
451	*Salix* sp. (willow)	0.02	3	1	2	SC	M
451	*Alnus* sp. (alder)	0.12	6	3–5	2–5	SC	M
452	*Corylus avellana* L. (hazel)	0.81	18	5–15	4–8	SC	M
452	*Prunus spinosa* L. (blackthorn)	0.19	1	15	8	SC	M
452	*Quercus* sp. (oak)	0.74	31	5–13	4–12	WC	M
463	*Alnus* sp. (alder)	0.08	3	3–5	2–6	SC	M

(Continued)

Table 5.14.1. (Continued)

Context	Identification	Weight (g)	Fragment count	Ring count	Size (mm)	Ring curvature	Growth
463	*Corylus avellana* L. (hazel)	0.1	3	2–4	3–5	SC	M
463	*Fraxinus excelsior* L. (ash)	0.02	2	4	2–3	SC	M
463	Maloideae	0.17	4	2–5	3–4	SC	M
463	*Prunus* L. (blackthorn/cherry)	0.03	2	3	3–4	SC	M
463	*Quercus* sp. (oak)	0.21	14	3–6	4–8	SC	M
465	*Alnus* sp. (alder)	0.24	11	2–5	2–6	WC	F
465	*Fraxinus excelsior* L. (ash)	0.02	3	1–2	2	SC	M
468	*Betula* sp. (birch)	0.19	4	4–5	3–4	SC	F
468	*Alnus* sp. (alder)	1.14	29	2–6	2–7	SC	M
468	*Corylus avellana* L. (hazel)	0.02	1	4	3	SC	M
468	*Fraxinus excelsior* L. (ash)	0.07	2	4	7	SC	M
468	*Quercus* sp. (oak)	0.83	14	5–10	6–10	WC	M
469	*Alnus* sp. (alder)	0.01	1	2	2	N/A	N/A
469	*Corylus avellana* L. (hazel)	0.01	1	1	2	N/A	N/A
469	Maloideae	0.21	1	6	6	SC	M
469	*Fraxinus excelsior* L. (ash)	0.04	4	2–4	2–4	WC	M
469	*Quercus* sp. (oak)	0.16	5	1–6	3–4	WC	M
473	*Prunus spinosa* L. (blackthorn)	0.26	4	4	4	SC	M
473	*Quercus* sp. (oak)	0.39	46	2–4	4–6	WC	M
478	*Alnus* sp. (alder)	0.39	5	3–5	4–6	SC	M
478	*Corylus avellana* L. (hazel)	0.09	2	2–5	3–5	SC	M
478	*Prunus* L. (blackthorn/cherry)	1.12	7	3–6	4–5	SC	M
478	*Fraxinus excelsior* L. (ash)	2.81	36	2–4	2–10	WC	M
493	*Quercus* sp. (oak)	0.05	3	2–8	2–3	WC	S
493	*Prunus spinosa* L. (blackthorn)	0.08	3	2–3	3–5	SC	M
548	*Quercus* sp. (oak)	0.01	1	1	2	SC	M
548	*Alnus* sp. (alder)	0.08	2	3–4	4	WC	M
549	Maloideae	0.03	1	2	2	SC	M
549	*Corylus avellana* L. (hazel)	0.04	3	2–3	3	SC	M
549	*Fraxinus excelsior* L. (ash)	0.06	2	2–3	3–4	SC	M
549	*Prunus avium* L.; *P. padus* L. (cherry)	0.14	9	3–6	3–5	SC	M
549	*Quercus* sp. (oak)	0.05	1	1	2	SC	M
714	*Prunus spinosa* L. (blackthorn)	0.27	3	3–10	3–5	SC	M
741	*Prunus spinosa* L. (blackthorn)	0.26	3	4–5	5–7	SC	M
741	*Salix* sp. (willow)	0.07	1	2	3	SC	M
741	*Corylus avellana* L. (hazel)	0.28	7	3–4	3–5	SC	M
741	Maloideae	0.06	1	3	3	SC	M
741	*Quercus* sp. (oak)	0.14	6	2–5	3–5	WC	M
741	Maloideae	0.2	3	3–5	4–7	MC	M
741	*Prunus spinosa* L. (blackthorn)	0.03	1	1	2	MC	M
741	*Alnus* sp. (alder)	0.07	2	2	4–5	SC	M
741	*Quercus* sp. (oak)	0.29	7	3–6	5–10	SC	M
741	*Prunus avium* L.; *P. padus* L. (cherry)	0.04	2	2–3	3	SC	M

(Continued)

Table 5.14.1. Charcoal counts from the Hill of Ward, Co. Meath. (Continued)

Context	Identification	Weight (g)	Fragment count	Ring count	Size (mm)	Ring curvature	Growth
741	*Salix* sp. (willow)	0.11	2	2–3	4–5	SC	M
741	*Fraxinus excelsior* L. (ash)	0.1	1	3	3	SC	M
741	Maloideae	0.08	1	2	6	MC	M
741	*Alnus* sp. (alder)	0.1	1	6	4	SC	M
741	*Corylus avellana* L. (hazel)	0.96	6	6–12	4–8	SC	M
742	*Quercus* sp. (oak)	0.06	2	5	2–3	WC	M
742	*Corylus avellana* L. (hazel)	0.08	3	4–5	3–4	SC	M
742	*Fraxinus excelsior* L. (ash)	0.03	1	6	2	SC	M
745	*Corylus avellana* L. (hazel)	3.25	46	4–10	5–8	SC	M
745	*Salix* sp. (willow)	0.11	1	3	3	SC	M
745	*Fraxinus excelsior* L. (ash)	0.45	3	6–7	5–9	SC	M
745	*Alnus* sp. (alder)	0.18	2	4–5	4	MC	M
745	*Quercus* sp. (oak)	0.16	7	1–2	2–4	MC	M
745	*Corylus avellana* L. (hazel)	0.05	3	3–4	5–14	SC	M
745	*Fraxinus excelsior* L. (ash)	0.33	9	4–7	4–8	SC	M
745	*Salix* sp. (willow)	2.25	10	5–14	4–18	SC	M
760	*Corylus avellana* L. (hazel)	0.1	8	3–4	4–5	SC	M
760	*Prunus avium* L.; *P. padus* L. (cherry)	0.03	1	3	4	SC	M
760	*Quercus* sp. (oak)	0.12	2	2–3	4	SC	M
760	*Salix* sp. (willow)	0.11	3	2–3	5	SC	M
760	*Fraxinus excelsior* L. (ash)	0.73	35	2–4	4–7	WC	M
760	*Fraxinus excelsior* L. (ash)	12.56	50	5–13	5–25	SC	M
773	*Betula* sp. (birch)	0.03	2	3	3	SC	M
773	*Quercus* sp. (oak)	2.09	22	2–7	5–23	WC	F
773	Maloideae	0.06	1	4	6	SC	M
773	*Quercus* sp. (oak)	0.03	6	1–2	2–3	WC	M
773	*Quercus* sp. (oak)	0.88	48	3–10	4–7	WC	M
773	*Fraxinus excelsior* L. (ash)	0.05	1	2	3	SC	M
773	*Prunus spinosa* L. (blackthorn)	0.21	1	7	5	SC	M
773	*Quercus* sp. (oak)	0.26	6	2–4	4	SC	M
773	*Alnus* sp. (alder)	0.04	1	4	4	SC	M
773	*Prunus spinosa* L. (blackthorn)	0.03	1	3	4	SC	M
811	*Corylus avellana* L. (hazel)	0.35	1	6	6	SC	M
811	*Salix* sp. (willow)	0.05	2	2	3	SC	M
818	*Corylus avellana* L. (hazel)	0.63	8	3–7	5–26	SC	M
818	*Fraxinus excelsior* L. (ash)	0.02	1	5	2	MC	M
818	*Corylus avellana* L. (hazel)	0.74	15	3–8	6–9	SC	M
818	*Fraxinus excelsior* L. (ash)	0.59	18	2–6	2–5	SC	M
818	Maloideae	0.1	2	4–5	6	SC	M
818	*Quercus* sp. (oak)	0.1	1	3	5	WC	M
818	*Corylus avellana* L. (hazel)	0.11	3	4–6	4–5	SC	M
822	*Corylus avellana* L. (hazel)	0.29	12	3–6	4–7	SC	M
822	Maloideae	0.24	11	2–5	2–6	SC	M

(Continued)

Table 5.14.1. (Continued)

Context	Identification	Weight (g)	Fragment count	Ring count	Size (mm)	Ring curvature	Growth
822	*Fraxinus excelsior* L. (ash)	0.75	24	1–17	3–11	SC	S
822	*Quercus* sp. (oak)	0.03	1	1	4	MC	M
822	*Alnus* sp. (alder)	0.1	2	2–3	3	SC	M
911	*Prunus spinosa* L. (blackthorn)	1.15	15	3–11	4–7	SC	M
913	*Quercus* sp. (oak)	0.07	7	1–2	1–2	MC	M
913	*Corylus avellana* L. (hazel)	0.02	1	3	3	SC	M
914	*Quercus* sp. (oak)	0.02	2	14	2–4	MC	M
914	*Prunus avium* L.; *P. padus* L. (cherry)	0.03	2	2–3	2–4	SC	M
914	*Quercus* sp. (oak)	0.06	3	4–5	4–5	WC	M
915	*Fraxinus excelsior* L. (ash)	0.01	2	1–2	3	SC	M
915	Maloideae	0.39	12	2–6	2–4	SC	M
915	*Quercus* sp. (oak)	0.02	4	1–2	2–4	WC	M
915	*Corylus avellana* L. (hazel)	0.02	1	12	2	SC	S
915	*Fraxinus excelsior* L. (ash)	0.56	7	-6	1–2	MC	M
915	*Prunus spinosa* L. (blackthorn)	0.05	1	3	3	SC	M
915	*Quercus* sp. (oak)	0.1	4	1–2	1–3	WC	M
916	*Fraxinus excelsior* L. (ash)	0.12	1	2	4	SC	M
916	Maloideae	1.74	48	3–7	3–6	SC	M
916	*Corylus avellana* L. (hazel)	0.11	1	3	4	SC	M
916	*Fraxinus excelsior* L. (ash)	0.12	13	3–2	2–6	MC	M
916	*Corylus avellana* L. (hazel)	0.26	4	4–5	5	SC	M
919	*Corylus avellana* L. (hazel)	0.01	1	3	3	SC	M

(*Salix cinerea*), goat willow (*Salix caprea*) and eared willow (*Salix aurita*).

5.14.8. Conclusion

Charcoal results from the Hill of Ward indicate a fairly open landscape, with mainly secondary woodland taxa represented including ash and hazel. Some context related variation was apparent in Test Pit 2 where oak appears to have been used for timbers or possibly metalworking and also in Trench 8, a fill within ditch C711 where oak appears to have been selected for metalworking. However, much of the wood selection on site may well have been opportunistic except where specific properties were required.

5.15. Pollen analysis from Jamestown Bog (Rena Maguire)

Jamestown Bog, Bohermeen, Co. Meath (Fig. 5.15.1) is located between the significant archaeological sites of Tlachtga and Faughan Hill in Co. Meath. The study represented an opportunity to assess human interactions within an important prehistoric landscape and coincided with the archaeological excavation of the nearby site of Tlachtga by University College Dublin, and subsequent

excavations at Faughan Hill by the Discovery Programme (Dowling and Schot 2023). Importantly, understanding the past vegetation history of the area has significant potential for understanding the economic and settlement context of these sites, especially in an area of Ireland, which, despite its archaeological significance, is severely lacking in detailed palaeoecological sequences.

5.15.1. Site description: Jamestown Bog

Jamestown Bog (Figs 5.15.1 and 5.15.2) is a small raised mire of some 37 ha, located close to the border of Cos. Meath and Westmeath, Ireland. It is located *c.* 5 km from Navan, and *c.* 4.5 km from Athboy at 53°38'37.5"N 6°49'08.3"W. In 2005 it was listed as National Heritage Area (NHA 001324) to restrict further damage by commercial peat cutters (Irish National Statute Book 2005); however, since this time peat harvesting has continued. The bog is currently in a degraded condition, with large amounts of cutover peat evident along the southern perimeter and clear evidence that the extent of the site was formerly much greater. There are two areas of bog separated by an area of cut peat and managed coniferous plantation forestry; it is possible that these represent the remains of two original basins.

The current bog surface comprises of *Calluna vulgaris, Eriophorum* and various bog mosses such as *Sphagnum capillifolium, S. magellanicum, S. cuspidatum* and *S. papillosum*, all of which flourish best in acid conditions. *Narthecium ossifragum* (bog asphodel) was also observed on the uncut peat dome. This is a plant that thrives in wet boggy conditions on acid soils (Summerfield 1974). *Cladonia* lichen is also present at the higher parts of the bog (Derwin *et al.* 2002). The presence of *Calluna vulgaris* suggests the surface of the bog may be drying although the numerous species of bog moss indicate there is still considerable latent moisture remaining. The hydrology of the bog has not been fully analysed, despite occasional flooding events from the two tributaries of the Boyne, which converge 1.3 km southeast, near the hamlet of Ongenstown.

Co. Meath, like most of the Irish midlands, is a result of geological processes caused by deglaciation some 10,000 years ago. Jamestown Bog is a remnant of the great prehistoric wetlands of the east midlands of Ireland. The bog itself was one of many glacial lakes in the region, formed by meltwaters filling shallow depressions left by the retreating ice. It is believed to have a lacustrine clay base level (Meehan and Warren 1999, 24). Climatic changes during the early Holocene period resulted in increased amounts of vegetation growing around the

edge of the lake, gradually decreasing the depth of the water. The ongoing accumulation of decaying vegetation created fenland peat deposits, which built up into a dome of a raised bog, where the vegetation cover was no longer influenced by the mineral soils (Pilcher and Hall 2001, 55).

The underlying geology of the Jamestown area is mostly carboniferous 'calp' limestone, overlain by a flat till plain. Soils south of Navan are sandy or silty tills with relatively poor drainage. The bedrock of limestone (Ashton *et al.* 1986, 243) shows the presence of faulting and folding, possibly sometime during the Lower Carboniferous period, some 340 million years ago. The joints of the faults are heavily mineralised with lead and zinc deposits such as sphalerite and galena as well as smaller deposits of silver (Anderson *et al.* 1998, 535).

5.15.2. Jamestown Bog and its historical environment

Jamestown Bog is less than 1.5 km from Faughan Hill, and just under 5 km from Tlachtga/Hill of Ward. Both of these are multi-period sites, with activity from the middle Neolithic (Dowling and Shot 2023) to the medieval period (Davis *et al.* 2017). Faughan Hill rises up to the north of Tlachtga and south of Tailteann, offering a view of the

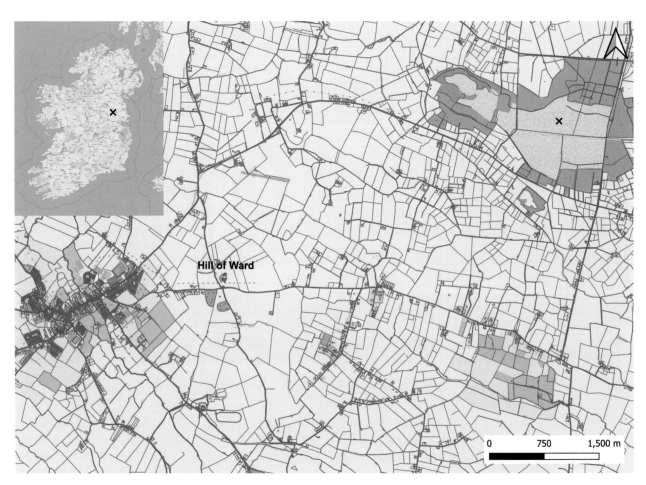

Fig. 5.15.1. Jamestown Bog location, regionally and nationally. Coring location marked.

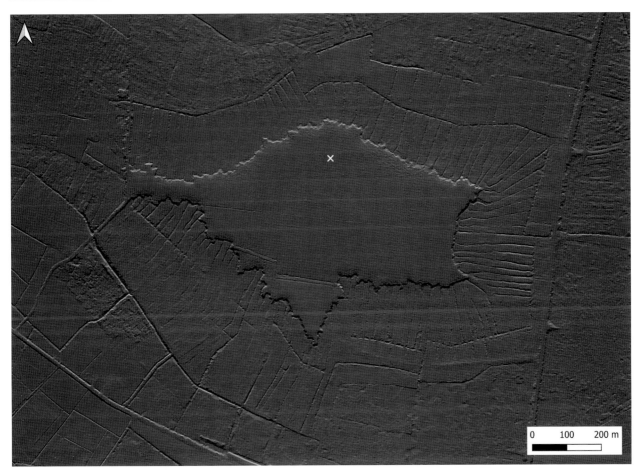

Fig. 5.15.2. Lidar 16-direction hillshade, Jamestown Bog, Co. Meath showing coring location and peat cuttings.

other hills of the Irish midlands. Little remains visible at the summit, although antiquarians of the late 19th and early 20th century regularly attempted to find the cairn that supposedly marked the burial place of the 5th century AD king, Niall of the Nine Hostages who was reputedly interred on the summit of Ochan, widely believed to be Faughan Hill (Walsh 1916; Swift 2000, 27). Morris (1926) records that the slopes of the hill were once covered in woodland, with a mound where a large totemic ash tree, known as the Mullyfaughan Tree, had once stood. Morris considered both Faughan Hill and Tlachtga to be part of the funerary procession path of Niall Niogiallach (Morris 1926, 33). The old name of Jamestown, Bohermeen, is derived from the Irish words Bóthar Mín, which translates as the 'Fine Road'. It is not known when the route dates to, although Morris suggested that it was at least contemporaneous with the Slíghe Mór, one of the five great roads of the early medieval period (Morris 1926, 33), or possibly even before (Maguire 2021, 67). Niall's burial and monumental cairn (Morris 1926, 38) would have been one of the few high places on the plains of Meath, where the hills of Tara and Tlachtga can be seen, effectively allowing him to continue overlooking his past kingdom. The Discovery Programme carried out a programme of geomagnetic survey on the summit of Faughan Hill

(Dowling and Cahill-Wilson 2014, 21; Dowling 2015) showing a wide range of multi-period features. These were followed by recently published small scale excavations (Dowling and Schot 2023).

The area around Faughan Hill and Jamestown Bog, then, appear to have become part of a landscape of meaning, which may have served as a reinforcement of identities by its very nature of continuity, serving as a commemorative 'memoryscape' (Thomas 1996, 86), perhaps in a similar way to the modern Mount Vernon Highway in the United States, which provides a functional road, representing technological achievements, but that road deliberately passes through sites connected with the founding fathers of the United States War of Independence (Davis 2001, 131–150), demonstrating that the past and present are linked by shared ideals, work accomplishments and identity. Swift (2000, 27–28) states that the course of the Blackwater River is marked with Uí Néill clan monuments, reinforcing the claims of their ancestor Niall.

5.15.3. The archaeology and folklore of Jamestown Bog

The site occupied by today's Jamestown Bog has been a wetland from the earliest phases of the Holocene, progressing from fenland to raised bog through prehistory. Folklore for the area abounds, very much in keeping with the belief of bogs as liminal spaces between worlds where nothing is quite what it appears to be. Folklore anecdotes from the 1940s and 50s mention children taken by the 'fairies' on Jamestown Bog, their bodies replaced with brooms (Marsh 2013, 107). It is clear from the narratives that the children were acknowledged to be dead, but their remains could not be referred to as human any more after their demise within the bog. European folklore also advises caution on bogs and mires, where supernatural transmogrification is a theme shared with Ireland and the United Kingdom (Pungas and Vosu 2012, 94).

If Niall Noígiallagh was indeed interred on Faughan Hill, the bog below would have formed a natural boundary between the world of the living and dead. The wetland itself has sufficient archaeological features and finds to suspect its status as a depositional site over an extensive period of prehistory. Kelly (2006, 26) has hypothesised that traditional boundaries were also foci for votive depositions, so a bog on the border of several townlands would perhaps have a more meaningful status. This practice was not exclusive to Ireland but appears coterminous with European practices. The pre-Roman European Iron Age already had established boundaries of marshes, forests and rivers, and it was around these features that cult centres developed (O'Riain 1972, 16). While many modern Irish townland boundaries date to the 12th century AD, others are likely to follow the ancient *tuath* borders of later prehistory and early historic periods (Ní Ghabhláin 1996, 37–61), which were defined by natural markers, including rivers, spring sources, certain kinds of forests, stones and marshy places (Power 1947, 220). These criteria would suggest that at some point in the past, Jamestown Bog and Faughan Hill above it may have carried a meaningful position within the landscape.

A drainage and cutting enterprise in 1848 led to the discovery of timber and wattle constructions within the bog itself, which Wood-Martin considered evidence of a crannog (Wood-Martin 1886, 72), although in the absence of more detail this could equally have been a platform or togher across the bog. Wetland sites have been used as votive platforms and habitations, or perhaps both, during the Iron Age (Fredengren 2007, 32), reminding us that the difference between sacred and profane sites may have been fluid, with the supernatural being part of daily life. Several bronze pins and a Roman patera, or libation ladle, were also found at this time. There are no details of the pins except that Wood-Martin (1886, 72) described them as 'beautiful'.

The patera most likely dates to the 2nd century AD (Ó Ríordáin 1945, 61; Warner 1976, 275). It lacks the hole at the base of the handle that Roman Army skillets had, to attach to backpacks. Instead, it has prongs projecting from the handle, similar to many specimens found in Romanised Europe (Ó Ríordáin 1945, 60–61). Warner

(1976, 275) mentions that the object was found at the convergence of tributary rivers beside the boundaries of Jamestown Bog.

During the late 19th century, a socketed bronze Class 2 axe head was found within the bog at a depth of 1.8 m (Eogan 2000, 109). A full report of the National Museum of Ireland's acquisitions of 1970 mentions a 'dagger' found between Greetiagh and Onganstown in 1935 (Lucas 1973, 183). Measuring over 30 cm it is a fine example of a middle Bronze Age rapier (Burgess and Gerloff 1981, 2–3; see image in Dowling and Schot 2023). Wood-Martin (1886, 171) mentions and illustrates a bronze sword found in Jamestown Bog, which he refers to by its traditional name of Bohermeen. Eogan (1965, 25; plate 37) could find no details of it but includes it within his corpus of work on Bronze Age swords.

5.15.4. Fieldwork and sample collection

Two overlapping cores, 4 m in depth, and a distance of 1 m apart, were taken from the peat dome on the southeastern edge of the bog at co-ordinates of 53°38'37.5"N 6°49'08.3"W (Fig. 5.14.2), and an elevation of 64.4 m OSL. The peat layers extended deeper than 4 m, but there was a silty, clay-like material below that depth.

A conventional Russian peat corer was used, with a cylinder length of 50 cm and barrel diameter of 5 cm. The samples were photographed in the field; it was noted the samples were uniformly composed of well-humified *Sphagnum* and *Eriophorum* peat. The cores were allocated identifying codes of JT1 and JT2, then wrapped in clingfilm to preserve moisture. Each 50 cm core was labelled with depth and core code, sealed with tape, and placed in protective half-pipes for transportation back to the laboratory at the 14CHRONO Centre, Queens University Belfast.

The descriptions in Table 5.14.1 display the categories of humification of all of the core segments, using Rydin and Jeglum's adaptation (2006, 86) of the von Post (1924) and Troels-Smith (1955) classification systems. The peat was almost uniformly dark in colour and well humified, with no obvious stratification; the composition of the peat occasionally changes, with fragments of *Calluna* and seed-like material.

5.15.5. Radiocarbon dating

Two subsamples were taken from the selected cores for radiocarbon dating at depths of 170 cm to 250 cm, which were estimated to be closest to the Iron Age/Bronze Age transition period. The depths also were synchronous with the pollen samples taken from the cores, which extended into the Late Iron Age/early medieval period. Both peat samples were processed according to the 14CHRONO Centre's laboratory protocol of AAA pre-treatment and graphitisation process based on Vogel *et al.* (1987). The resulting dates were calibrated using CALIB 7.0.1 (Stuiver

Table 5.15.1. Humification and lithology of cores 0–381 cm.

Depth (cm)	Description	Humification
0–8	*Sphagnum* and living plant materials. *Turfa*	H4
8–59	Dark brown peat. Well humified with slightly decomposed remains of *Eriophorum* spp. Mostly *Turfa bryophytica*	H5
59–243	Black-brown peat. *Turfa bryophytica* mixed with *Detritus lignosa*. *Calluna* twigs with *Eriophorum* fibres.	H6
243–320	Very black-brown peat. Well humified. *Turfa bryophytica*	H6
320–345	Dark brown/black peat. Twigs present. Very humified *Turfa bryophytica/Detritus lignosa*	H7
345–381	Dark brown/black in colour. Very humified *Turfa bryophytica* and *Detritus lignosa* with high amounts of *Eriophorum* fibres	H7

Table 5.15.2. Radiocarbon dates for 170 cm and 250 cm depth.

Lab ID Number	Sample ID	Sample type	Material type	Conventional age BP	StDev ±	$\delta^{14}C$	Calibrated date (2-sigma)	Probability
UBA-26266	JT170–171 cm	Plant macrofossil	Peat	1771	31	0.8021	AD 138–201	0.118
							AD 205–304	0.882
UBA-26267	JT250–251 cm	Plant macrofossil	Peat	2493	31	0.7332	783–513 BC	1.0

and Reimer 2013) using the IntCal20 calibration curve (Reimer *et al.* 2020).

The creation of a site chronology was of considerable importance, for without it, there effectively is no context or historical framework to place the results of the study. There is a level of uncertainty within the radiocarbon dates due to the deepest point being within the Hallstatt Plateau (*e.g.* Hamilton *et al.* 2015), so introducing the potential for significant dating error. Radiocarbon results and calibrated age ranges from samples taken for Core JT1 at 170 cm and 250 cm are given in Table 5.15.2.

5.15.6. Tephra sampling and results

The surface of the peat cores that had been in contact with the clingfilm was removed to eliminate possible contamination. The first 7 cm were removed from the core, which included the surface layer of the bog, as the peat contained considerable amounts of roots and organic material. Sub-samples of 1 cm³ were taken at 1 cm interval from 7–8 cm depth to 250–251 cm. Each of these were weighed and placed in crucibles and dried for 48 hours. The crucibles containing the peat samples were then combusted for four hours at 550°C. The peat ash samples were weighed to calculate loss on ignition (LOI), to assist with any calculation of tephra concentration, and act as a potential indicator of soil erosion.

After the LOI process, the ash was added to 35 ml of HCl at a 10% concentration, to clean the material of any remaining organic material. This was centrifuged for three minutes at 3000 rpm. The tubes with the ash residue at the bottom were then filled with 35 ml of distilled water to clean all remains of the acid and centrifuged at 3000 rpm for three minutes. Slides were made for each sub-sample, dried on a hotplate, then mounted with a drop of Histamount to secure the material. These slides were inspected for tephra using an Olympus CX41 biological microscope at a magnitude of 400×. Tephra shards were counted for each sample to produce a tephrastratigraphy for the site. Identification of contained tephra referenced well established tephrastratigrapies in Ireland (Hall and Pilcher 2002).

Three discrete layers of cryptotephra were detected within the core JT1 although tephra was at no point abundant in the peat.

- *Hekla AD 1104: 61–62 cm*: This slightly pinkish coloured tephra has been identified through numerous bogs in Ireland, particularly in the midlands and west of the island (Hall 2003, 8). It has been noted it is more plentiful in Ireland than across mainland Europe (Wastegård and Davies 2009, 505) and has been used as a reliably dated historical tephra within chronologies (Hall 2003, 8).

- *AD 860: 88–89 cm*: This colourless tephra has been found throughout Irish bogs such as Sluggan in Antrim and Barnsmore, Donegal (Pilcher *et al.* 1996, 491) and is one of the first cryptotephras recognised in early studies (Pilcher *et al.* 1995). It has been found in bogs on the eastern side of Ireland, such as at Clara Bog, Co. Offally (Connolly 2000). It would appear it has also been identified in Newfoundland, calling into question previous beliefs that it had originated in Iceland. It can be utilised to build accurate chronologies in North

America as well as Atlantic Europe (Jensen *et al*. 2014). Based on recent NGRIP studies it is believed to date to AD 847 (Coulter *et al.* 2012, 3)

- *GA4-85: 94–95cm:* Recently identified, this distinctive brown coloured vesicular tephra is believed to be of Icelandic origin and was originally considered to date to between AD 700 and 800 (Hall and Pilcher 2002, 225–228; Wastegård *et al.* 2003, 279). However, it is now believed that it dates more accurately to AD 800, with an error margin of ±30 years (G. Plunkett 2014, pers. comm.).

5.15.7. Pollen extraction and results

Sub-samples of 1 cm were taken at increments of 4 cm for pollen preparation, and placed in centrifuge tubes that had been previously weighed. Two tablets of *Lycopodium* spores were added to each tube, to act as markers for the calculation of subsequent pollen concentrations within each treated sample (Stockmarr 1971). These tubes were then filled with 30 ml of HCl, at a concentration of 10%, to break down the sodium bicarbonate binders in the tablets. The material was then decanted and 10 ml of KOH was added to each sample to assist deflocculation and break down some of the dense humic peat.

This solution was left to stand overnight, then filled with 45 ml of deionised water, and centrifuged at 3000 rpm for seven minutes. The supernatant was decanted off and the sample agitated on an orbital shaker. This material was then sieved and washed with deionised water through 120 μm and 6 μm meshes to remove organic debris. The peat was still exceptionally fibrous, so the decision was made to utilise acetolysis to eliminate the superfluous organic materials. The protocol followed was based on that of Erdtman (1943).

Each subsample of acetolysed peat was counted for a minimum of 300 Total Land Pollen (TLP). Identification was performed by referring to Faegri and Iverson (1989) and Reuille (1995). Selected testate amoeba and fungal spores were counted and categorised as NPPs – Non-Pollen Palynomorphs. Charcoal particles were also counted. These figures were then entered for percentage calculation to the Tilia software programme, version 1.7.16 (Grimm 1992). Local Pollen Assemblage Zones (LPAZ) were calculated using CONISS (Grimm 1992).

The pollen diagram (Fig. 5.14.3) represents the percentage curves of the vegetation around Jamestown Bog during the later prehistoric period. The 'best date' of the age-depth models' interpolated calculations was chosen as the start and finish points of each zone, due to the uncertainty within the calibrated radiocarbon dates. Charcoal and non-pollen palynomorphs (NPPs) are included in the results. The range of NPP can offer some indication of the variations of wetness within the bog, although those that survived the acetolysis process may be unrepresentative of the assemblages contained within the unprocessed peat. Tolonen (1991, 26) recommended that charcoal particle counts be incorporated as a vital part of any pollen analysis as they complement the natural vegetation patterns. This is indeed the case in this diagram, where charcoal offers evidence of fire events within the study area.

5.15.8. Results: zone by zone description of Jamestown Bog pollen diagram

5.15.8.1. LPAZ JT1 (258–232 cm)

Late Bronze Age–Iron Age transition; pre-700 BC to *c*. 437 BC

The trees and shrubs of the area remain reasonably steady throughout the period represented here, with a continual presence of *Fraxinus*. *Ulmus* is at its most abundant within the entire diagram in this zone while *Quercus* fluctuates. The slightly raised *Alnus* percentage suggests the presence of waterlogged soils. *Corylus*-type and *Alnus* peak within this zone, while *Salix* is present in very small amounts. As *Hedera* survives on woodland edge habitats (Vincent 1990, 82) and by climbing tall trees to gain sufficient light to flower (Pilcher and Hall 2001, 26) it is most likely that the area was dominated by hazel scrub.

A variety of herbaceous taxa are present, such as Chenopodiaceae, Brassicaceae and Asteroideae, suggesting disturbed ground; *Plantago lanceolata* and *Rumex* reinforce the likelihood of agricultural activity such as grazing and arable farming (Doorenbosch 2013, 21). Poaceae and Cypereaceae both decline, while *Calluna* increases, suggesting drier areas on the bog that could be linked to the charcoal peaks. *Pteridium*, often associated with fires (Ingrouille and Eddy 2006, 214), is also present. There is a strong representation of *Gelasinaspora* sp., which is often linked to burning activity (Zak and Widman 2004, 310) so it is not surprising there is a sharp and brief rise in numbers of these spores coinciding with the high charcoal counts. *Meliola* spores are likely to be from *M. ellisii*, which is a parastic growth on *Calluna* (Chambers *et al.* 2011, 10) The steady counts of Copepodal spermatophore structures indicate there were pools of water within the bog – Copepoda are minute aquatic crustaceans which can live in a variety of conditions, but require submergence in water (Heuschele and Selander 2014). *Typha* and *Sparganium* tolerate root submergence in water, often displacing grasses and sedges (Keddy 2010, 148), while the testates *Amphitrema wrightiana*, *Amphitrema flavum* and *Arcella discoides* type all suggest very wet conditions, although *Assulina muscorum* implies drier areas within the bog (Swindles 2003).

5.15.8.2. LPAZ JT2 (232–192 cm)

Early to commencement of late Iron Age; *c.* 437 BC to *c.* AD 16

This phase sees considerable variety and abundance of all the dryland vegetation – Chenopodiaceae, Asteroideae, Brassicaceae, Lactuceae, Ranunculaceae, *Rumex* and

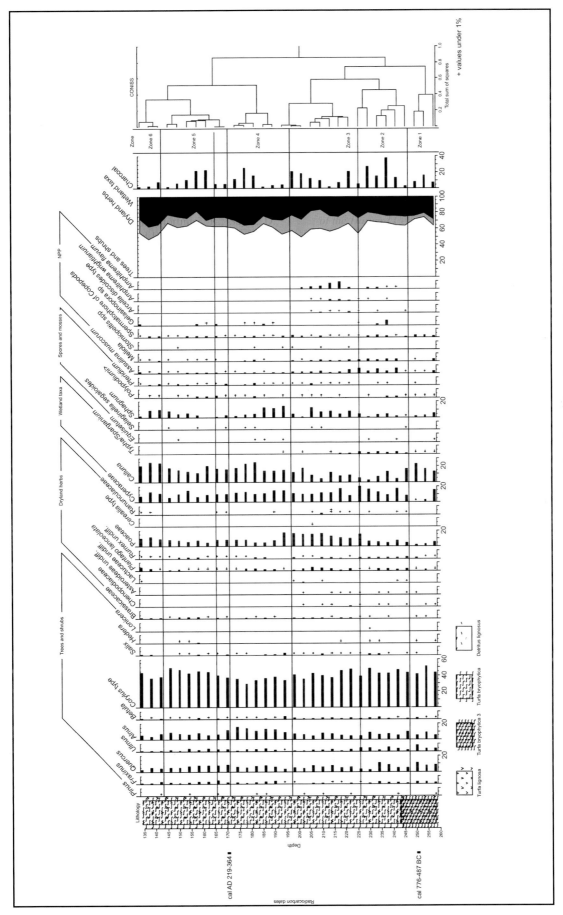

Fig. 5.15.3. Percentage pollen diagram (selected taxa) from Jamestown Bog, Co. Meath.

Plantago lanceolata – considered to be indicators of anthropogenic activity. Perhaps most important, at 206 cm depth, *c.* 140 BC there is a small representation of Cerealia-type pollen. Agricultural activity must have been occurring close to the bog, as cultivated cereal pollen is heavy, self-pollinating, and does not tend to travel far from where the plant is growing (Edwards 1988, 260). Both Cyperaceae and Poaceae increase, but it is Poaceae that is more abundant. The taller canopy trees of *Quercus*, *Ulmus* and *Fraxinus* all decline in representation. There is an increase in *Salix* at the closing of this zone. There is a small and prolonged increase in *Betula* suggesting the absence of shade-creating taller trees, as *Betula* flourishes in cleared areas (Pilcher and Hall 2001, 12). The continued representation of *Hedera* and the addition of *Lonicera periclymemum* indicate that despite the reduction of tree pollen, woodlands were still part of the landscape, although these plants will exist in hedgerows in the absence of forest (Pilcher and Hall 2001, 27). The sustained presence of *Polypodium* spores suggests tree cover, as it is an epiphyte, requiring arboreal hosts to grow upon (Ingrouille and Eddie 2006, 286). Both *Corylus* and *Alnus* remain at steady, though reduced, levels. There are two substantial peaks oof charcoal. The presence of *Selaginella selaginoides* offers more detail as to the nature of the mire. *Selaginella* growth is associated with discharges of springs and groundwater, requiring a stable hydrological system, neutral to alkaline soils, as well as cooler temperatures (Heidel and Handley 2006). The decline of *Calluna*, with a raised amount of *Sparganium* pollen suggests a wetter bogland, with a considerable rise in *Amphitrema flavum*, *Arcella discoides* type and spermatophores of Copepoda. *Stomiopeltis*, a fungus thriving in decaying matter (Yeloff *et al.* 2007) is also present. *Gelasinospora* spp. decline along with charcoal fragments, and *Assulina muscorum* and *Meliola* spp. both decline, suggesting the continuation of the previous zones wet bogland.

5.15.8.3. LPAZ JT3 (192–172 cm)
LATE IRON AGE: *c.* AD 16 TO *c.* AD 240

This zone differs considerably from the previous in that the taller trees show regeneration. *Quercus*, *Fraxinus*, *Alnus* and *Ulmus* all show higher representation than in the previous zone. *Corylus*-type remains steady but in lesser amounts than previous zones, while *Betula* also declines compared to JT2. Salix shows a brief rise in numbers before decline. Both Poaceae and Cyperaceae are present in reduced amounts. The herbs suggesting human activity decrease considerably. *Calluna* percentages fluctuate, as does *Sphagnum*, albeit briefly, before diminishing again by the upper section of the zone. There is a continued presence of *Selaginella selaginoides*. *Pteridium* percentages increase with the charcoal peaks between 185 cm and 174 cm. *Gelasinaspora* spp. increases slightly within this zone, while the testates and fungi which flourish in

very conditions all but vanish, replaced with prevalence in *Meliola* spp. and *Assulina muscorum*.

5.15.8.4. LPAZ JT4 (172–144 cm)
LATE IRON AGE LULL: *c.* AD 240 TO *c.* AD 446

It is likely this zone represents the fully developed 'Late Iron Age Lull' in the Jamestown area. *Quercus*, *Fraxinus*, *Ulmus*, *Corylus*, and even *Salix* increase within this zone. *Betula* rises sharply for a brief period before declining again by around 155 cm depth. *Alnus*, however, decreases slightly. *Hedera* and *Polypodium* are both present in small but steady amounts, suggesting increased arboreal growth. Brassicaceae and *Rumex* are present, although *Plantago* shows a slight decline. Poaceae and Cyperaceae are both reduced compared to the previous zone, although Cyperaceae shows more fluctuations. *Selaginella selaginoides* continues a small but regular presence within the zone. The charcoal peaks are matched with an increase in *Gelasinospora* spp. fungi. The testates and fungi that prefer drier environments increase marginally – *Assulina muscorum* and *Meliola* spp. are the most prevalent, while there is <1% of decay-loving *Stomiopeltis*. Small amounts of spermatophores of Copepoda indicate the presence of some pools of water. Charcoal particles indicate there were still burning events on or around the bog, although these decrease from 154 cm, *c.* AD 370.

5.15.8.5. LPAZ JT5 (144–134 cm)
EARLY MEDIEVAL TRANSITION PERIOD: *c.* AD 446 TO *c.* AD 516

The landscape changes within this zone indicate the clearance of trees, with decreases in *Ulmus*, *Fraxinus*, *Betula* and a smaller decline in *Quercus*. *Alnus* generally declines but with more fluctuation than other trees or shrubs in this zone. *Plantago lanceolata* increases dramatically by 134 cm, while Brassicaceae and Ranunculaceae offer further indications of agricultural activity. Both Poaceae and Cyperaceae increase slightly compared to the previous zone although Poaceae percentages are slightly higher. *Calluna* proportions increase, as do those of *Sphagnum*, which had declined in the previous zone. *Pteridium* and *Polypodium* are present, but in decreased amounts. The testates and fungi are similar to the previous zone, with representation of *Meliola* spp. and *Assulina muscorum* indicating a drier environment, while presumably the presence of spermatophore of Copepoda indicates pools within the bog.

5.15.9. Age-depth modelling
All dates obtained from tephra analysis and radiocarbon dating was entered into Clam software (Blaauw 2010) to create the age depth model for Jamestown Bog, with the radiocarbon dates shown in 5.14.2 and the tephra dates of AD 1104, 860 and 800. It runs to a depth of 250–251 cm

as this is where the basal sample taken for radiocarbon dating came from. A surface error of ±1 was used within the programme, allowing for the fact the cores were taken early in the year and most organic deposition would belong to the previous year. The peat accumulation rate is reasonably steady with no indications of bog bursts, although peat accumulates more rapidly through the early medieval period, perhaps due to wetter conditions *c.* AD 400–900 (Plunkett *et al.* 2013, 23).

5.15.10. Discussion

The late prehistoric period around Jamestown Bog is a time of subtle changes. While there is evidence of persistent woodland throughout the period covered in the pollen diagram, there are indications of limited clearances and subsequent reforestation. The late Bronze Age landscape of LPAZ JT1 (700 BC–440 BC) appears to be one of possible but quite subtle human activity and open woodland. The herbs that suggest anthropogenic activity are already present within JT1, which would suggest the agricultural increase of the late Bronze Age mentioned by Hall (2011, 104). Evidence of cultivation increases in LPAZ JT2 with a variety of weeds and herbs such as Chenopodiaceae, Asteroideae, *Rumex* and Lactuceae.

There may have been increased human activity or perhaps relocation of settlements to an area closer to the bog. The small but significant presence of *Cerealia*-type pollen in LPAZ JT2, at 204 cm, corresponds to dates *c.* 212–44 BC. While not a significant amount, it still indicates arable farming within the vicinity of the bog. The upper section of LPAZ JT2 shows some clearance of woodlands, decreased *Quercus*, although *Fraxinus* and *Ulmus* almost vanish from the record at around 202 cm. This opening of the land must have been to facilitate agricultural expansion. It could be suggested that as *Ulmus* in particular prefers good soils, intensive farming activity could have exhausted the soil and made it difficult for *Ulmus* to regenerate. As the landscape was being cleared, *Ulmus* may have been over-exploited for cattle fodder or simply part of the decline in the tree which Mitchell noted during later prehistory (Mitchell 1986, 165).

LPAZ JT3 (AD 16–AD 242) shows the gradual return of the woodland. *Poaceae* and *Plantago lanceolata* both fluctuate in amounts by the upper section of Zone 3, suggesting that grazing land was slowly becoming covered with small trees or shrubs such as *Corylus* type or *Alnus*. The diversity of herbs decreases to only *Rumex* and Brassicaceae from the upper section of JT 3 into JT4, plants that will grow in 'wasteland' conditions. This zone may represent the first phase of the 'Late Iron Age Lull' in the area around Jamestown, as JT 4 (AD 242–AD 446) would appear to be the 'real thing', although it is a somewhat low-key affair.

It is in JT4 that the trees listed in the 8th century AD law text the '*Bretha Comaithchesa*' as 'the lords of the forest' or *airig fedo* (Kelly 1999, 41) – reclaim the landscape. These trees are *Quercus, Fraxinus, Ilex, Corylus, Malus, Pinus* and *Taxus,* which all contributed to the early medieval economy, although it is unusual that *Pinus* is mentioned when it is believed to have been either extinct or barely present in Iron Age and early medieval Ireland (Hunt 2013, 41). The clearance of the early medieval period, at LPAZ JT5 (AD 446–AD 516) may be correlated with increasing importance of cattle within the economy (McCormick 2013), and the gradual introduction of intensive arable cultivation from monastic settlements (Doherty 1980). Zone LPAZ JT5 shows the beginning of the land clearances of the early medieval period, punctuated by a surge in *Plantago lanceolata* and Poaceae.

An Lóch Mór, on the west coast of Ireland has shown a marked forest regeneration through the 'Late Iron Age Lull', and a dramatic clearance at the advent of the early medieval period (Molloy and O'Connell 2004). Jamestown lacks this decisive landscape change. The pollen diagram shows no dramatic changes through the period assessed (similar to diagrams in Plunkett 2009), although that lack of change could be considered a palaeoenvironmental story in its own right. There was agricultural activity within the area from the early phases of the Iron Age, although with the mix of weeds and herbs it is difficult to assess if arable or pastoral farming was most prevalent. While there is an indication of clearance for farming in LPAZ JT2, and a regular presence of anthropogenic indicators such as *Plantago lanceolata* and *Rumex* spp., there are always indications of woodland coverage of the land until what appears to be a decline at the beginnings of the early medieval period.

There are few regional comparators for the work at Jamestown Bog, the closest comparator site being Emlagh Bog, Co. Meath (Newman *et al.* 2007). Emlagh is an atypical site in that it is one of the few known areas where cereal production continued throughout the Iron Age Lull (*ibid.*). Research comparing 39 sites and their estimated entry into the Lull suggests that evidence of reforestation around Emlagh commenced *c.* 150 BC, ending close to AD 200 (Coyle-McClung 2013, 75). Jamestown entered this 're-wilding' phase much later, at around the first decade AD, with the process continuing well into the last stages of the Iron Age *c.* AD 404, at depth 150 cm.

There is no firm indication why there were regular burning episodes in the environment of Jamestown Bog. It is unlikely that the bog was being burnt back for rough grazing. We could offer the hypothesis that if Wood-Martin's (1886, 82) crannog theory is correct, the charcoal may be connected to metalworking on site.

5.15.11. Conclusion

The pollen diagram from Jamestown Bog covers a period of tremendous significance in the archaeological development of the Hill of Ward and nearby Faughan Hill. Starting in the late Bronze Age, when the Hillfort

Phase was still open, the sequence spans the closing of this phase, the intermediary period (including the period in which the drying kiln was constructed), and on beyond the foundation of Tlachtga, although it is likely that it ends prior to the major change in Tlachtga in the 9th to 10th centuries.

If anything, the period immediately following the Hillfort Phase (LPAZ JT2) shows evidence of agricultural intensification, albeit on a minor scale. Charcoal remains high, as does *P. lanceolata*, and grasses significantly increase in representation. Towards the end of this LPAZ there is the suggestion of a (late) 'Late Iron Age Lull' with declining charcoal and grasses, along with increasing arboreal pollen. However, *P. lanceolata* remains a constant presence in LPAZ JT3 only showing significant decline only in LPAZ JT4. The presence of testate amoebae such as *Amphitrema* spp. and especially *Arcella discoides* suggests the bog was especially wet towards the middle of LPAZ JT3 (most likely the 1st century AD). LPAZ JT4 marks the least agriculturally active zone within the diagram and occupies much of the period between the construction of the corn drying kiln and the construction of Tlachtga. Archaeologically it is unclear what is occurring at the Hill of Ward at this time, but it appears to be between major monumental phases. The uppermost section of the diagram (LPAZ JT4), while short, covers the initial construction period of Tlachtga. This seems to coincide with increasing *P. lanceolata* (the highest in the entire core) and declining tree pollen, although no significant peak in charcoal is evident. In general, while at no point are the changes in this diagram dramatic, they correspond well to the known archaeological narrative on the Hill of Ward.

Note

1   The term biological age is used to show that this is an estimate of age based upon the biological development of the individual, which may not relate directly to the calendrical aging of individuals as the exact date of birth remains unknown.

Bibliography

Aitchison, N.B. 1994. Kingship, society, and sacrality: rank, power, and ideology in early medieval Ireland. *Traditio* 49, 45–75.

Al Qahtani, S.J., Liversidge, H.M. and Hector, M.P. 2010. Atlas of tooth development and eruption. *American Journal of Physical Anthropology* 142(3), 481–490.

Allason-Jones, L. and Davis, M. 2002. Investigating 'jet' and jet-like artefacts from prehistoric Scotland. *Antiquity* 76, 812–825.

Allason-Jones, L. and Jones, J.M. 2001. Identification of 'jet' artifacts by reflected light microscopy. *European Journal of Archaeology* 4(2), 233–251.

Anderberg, A-L. 1994. *Atlas of Seeds Part 4: Resedaceae–Umbelliferae*. Stockholm, Swedish Museum of Natural History.

Anderson, A., Ashton, J.H., Boyce, A.J., Fallick, A.E. and Russell, M.J. 1998. Ore depositional process in the Navan Zn-Pb deposit, Ireland. *Economic Geology* 93, 535–563.

Andersson, E. 2003. *Tools for Textile Production from Birka and Hedeby. Excavations in the Black Earth 1990–1995*. Stockholm, Birka Studies 8.

Armstrong, E.C.R. 1933. *Catalogue of Irish Gold Ornaments in the Collection of the Royal Irish Academy*. Dublin, Stationery Office.

Ashton, J.H., Downing, D.T. and Finlay, S. 1986. The geology of the Navan Zn-Pb orebody. In C.J. Andrews, R. Crowe, S. Finlay, W.M. Pennell and J.F. Pyne (eds) *Geology and Genesis of Mineral Deposits in Ireland*, 243–280. Dublin, Irish Association for Economic Geology.

Ayoub, M., Symons, S., Edney, M. and Mather, D. 2002. QTLs affecting kernel size and shape in a two-rowed by six-rowed barley cross. *Theoretical and Applied Genetics* 105, 237–247.

Barton-Murray, R. 2012. Unidentified bone objects. In G. Eogan *Knowth. The Early Medieval Settlement, Excavations at Knowth 5: The Archaeology of Knowth in the First and Second Millennia AD*, 670–671. Dublin, Royal Irish Academy.

Barton-Murray, R. and Bayley, J. 2012. Metalworking equipment. In G. Eogan *Knowth. The Early Medieval Settlement, Excavations at Knowth 5: The Archaeology of Knowth in the First and Second Millennia AD*, 526–551. Dublin, Royal Irish Academy.

Bayliss, A and Grogan, E. 2013. Chronologies for Tara and comparable royal sites of the Irish Iron Age. In M. O'Sullivan, C. Scarre and M. Doyle (eds) *Tara from the Past to the Future*, 105–144. Bray, Wordwell.

Becker, K. 2010. *Rathgall, Co. Wicklow*. Archaeology Ireland Heritage Guide No. 51.

Becker, K. 2019. Iron Age settlement in mid-west Ireland. In D.C. Cowley, M. Fernández-Götz, T. Romankiewicz and H. Wendling (eds) *Rural Settlement. Relating Buildings, Landscape, and People in the European Iron Age*, 45–55. Leiden, Sidestone Press.

Behre, K.-E. 2008. Collected seeds and fruits from herbs as prehistoric food. *Vegetation History and Archaeobotany* 17(1), 65–73.

Berggren, G. 1981. *Atlas of Seeds Part 2: Cyperaceae*. Stockholm, Swedish Museum of Natural History.

Bermingham, N., Hull, G. and Taylor, K. 2012. *Beneath the Banner. Archaeology of the M18 Ennis Bypass and N85 Western Relief Road, Co. Clare*. Dublin, National Roads Authority.

Bhreathnach, E. 1995. *Tara A Select Bibliography*. Dublin, Royal Irish Academy.

Bhreathnach, E. 2011. Transforming kingship and cult: the provincial ceremonial capitals in early medieval Ireland. In R. Schot, C. Newman and E. Bhreathnach (eds) *Landscapes of Cult and Kingship,* 126–148. Dublin, Four Courts.

Bhreathnach, E. 2022a. Through a 'celtic' mist: the translation of sacred places into theatre spaces in medieval and early modern Ireland. In M. Henvey, A. Doviak and J. Hawkes (eds) *Transmissions and Translations in Medieval Literary and Material Culture*, 293–317. Leiden, Brill.

Bhreathnach, E. 2022b. *Caves, Woods and Crosses: Scandinavian Beliefs in Early Ireland*. Lecture given at Dublin History Festival, 6 October 2022. Available online at https://www.youtube.com/watch?v=G4ATSmRf1w8 [Accessed 30/9/2023].

Binchy, D.A. 1958. The fair of Tailtiu and the feast of Tara. *Ériu* 18, 113–138.

Blaauw, M. 2010. Methods and code for 'classical' age-modelling of radiocarbon sequences. *Quaternary Geochronology* 5, 512–518.

Black, S. and Scheuer, J.L. 1996. Age changes in the clavicle: From the early neonatal period to skeletal maturity. *International Journal of Osteoarchaeology* 6, 425–434.

Blackburn, M.A S. 2007. Presidential address 2007. Currency under the Vikings. Part 4: The Dublin Coinage c. 995–1050. *British Numismatic Journal* 78, 111–137.

Blackburn, M.A.S. 2007. Currency under the Vikings, Part 3. Ireland, Wales, Man and Scotland. *British Numismatic Journal* 77, 119–149.

Blackburn, M.A.S. 2008. Currency under the Vikings. Part 4. The Dublin coinage c. 995–1050. *British Numismatic Journal* 78, 111–137.

Blunt, C.E., Stewart, B.H.I.H. and Lyon, C.S.S. 1989. *Coinage in Tenth-century England.* Oxford, Oxford University Press.

Boardman, S. and Jones, G.E.M. 1990. Experiments on the effects of charring on cereal plant components. *Journal of Archaeological Science* 17(1), 1–12.

Bode, M.-J. 1998. *Schmalstede: Ein Urnengräberfeld der Kaiser- und Völkerwanderungszeit, Offa-Bücher* 78. Neumünster, Wachholtz Verlag.

Boessneck J. 1969. Osteological differences between sheep (*Ovis aries* Linné) and goat (*Capra hircus* Linné). In D. Brothwell and E. Higgs (eds) *Science in Archaeology: A Survey of Progress and Research*, 331–358. London, Thames and Hudson.

Bornholdt-Collins, K. 2003. *Viking-Age Coin Finds from the Isle of Man: A Study of Coin Circulation, Production and Concepts of Wealth.* Unpublished PhD Thesis, University of Cambridge.

Bornholdt-Collins, K. 2010. The Dunmore Cave [2] hoard and the role of coins in the tenth-century Hiberno-Scandinavian economy. In J. Sheehan and D. Ó Corráin (eds) *The Viking Age: Ireland and the West Proceedings of the Fifteenth Viking Congress, Cork, 2005,* 19–46. Dublin, Four Courts Press.

Boyle, J.W. 2004. Lest the Lowliest Be Forgotten: Locating the Impoverished in Early Medieval Ireland. *International Journal of Historical Archaeology* 8(2), 85–99.

Boyle, J.W. 2009. *The Production and Use of Bone and Antler Dress Pins in Early Medieval Ireland, c. AD 400–800.* Unpublished PhD dissertation, New York University.

Bradley, J. 1991. Excavations at Moynagh Lough, County Meath. *Journal of the Royal Society of Antiquaries of Ireland* 121, 5–26.

Brady, C., Barton, K. and Seaver, M. 2011. *The Hill of Slane Archaeological Project.* Unpublished report available online at https://eprints.dkit.ie/299/2/HoSInterim2011.pdf [Accessed 30/9/2023].

Brickley, M. 2004a. Guidance on recording age at death in juvenile skeletons. In M. Brickley and J.I. McKinley (eds) *Guidelines to the Standards for Recording Human Skeletal Remains. Institute for Field Archaeologists Paper* 7, 21–22.

Brickley, M. 2004b. Determination of sex from archaeological skeletal material and the assessment of parturition. In M. Brickley and J.I. McKinley (eds) *Guidelines to the Standards for Recording Human Skeletal Remains. Institute for Field Archaeologists Paper* 7, 23–25.

Britnell, W.J. 2000. Small pointed blades. In J.C. Barrett, P.W.M. Freeman and A. Woodward, *Cadbury Castle, Somerset: The Later Prehistoric and Early Historic Archaeology. English Heritage Archaeological Report 20,* 183–186. London, English Heritage.

Bronk Ramsey, C. 2009. Bayesian analysis of radiocarbon dates. *Radiocarbon* 51(1), 337–360.

Brothwell, D.R. 1981. *Digging Up Bones.* London, Natural History Museum.

Browning, B.L. and Browning, S.R. 2007. Rapid and accurate haplotype phasing and missing-data inference for whole-genome association studies by use of localized haplotype clustering. *American Journal of Human Genetics* 81(5), 1084–1097.

Browning, B.L. and Browning, S.R. 2013. Improving the accuracy and efficiency of identity-by-descent detection in population data. *Genetics* 194(2), 459–471.

Brück, J. 1999. Houses, lifecycles and deposition on middle Bronze Age settlements in southern England. *Proceedings of the Prehistoric Society* 65, 145–166.

Brück, J. 2019. *Personifying Prehistory. Relational Ontologies in Bronze Age Britain and Ireland.* Oxford, Oxford University Press.

Brunel, S., Bennett, E.A., Cardin, L., Garraud, D., Barrand Emam, H., Beylier, A., Boulestin, B., Chenal, F., Ciesielski, E., Convertini, F., Dedet, B., Desbrosse-Degobertiere, S., Desenne, S., Dubouloz, J., Duday, H., Escalon, G., Fabre, V., Gailledrat, E., Gandelin, M., Gleize, Y. and Pruvost, M. 2020. Ancient genomes from present-day France unveil 7,000 years of its demographic history. *Proceedings of the National Academy of Sciences of the United States of America* 117(23), 12791–12798.

Burgess, C. and Gerloff, S. 1981. *The Dirks and Rapiers of Great Britain and Ireland.* Munich, Beck/Prähistorische Bronzefund.

Byrne, F.J. 2004. *Irish Kings and High-Kings.* Dublin, Four Courts Press.

Byrne, R.P., Martiniano, R., Cassidy, L.M., Carrigan, M., Hellenthal, G., Hardiman, O., Bradley, D.G. and McLaughlin, R.L. 2018. Insular Celtic population structure and genomic footprints of migration. *PLoS Genetics* 14(1), e1007152.

Cagney, L. and O'Hara, R. 2009. An early medieval complex at Dowdstown 2. In M.B. Deevy and D. Murphy (eds) *Places Along the Way: First Findings on the M3,* 123–133. Dublin, National Roads Authority.

Cahill-Wilson, J. and Standish, C.D. 2016. Mobility and migration in late Iron Age and early medieval Ireland. *Journal of Archaeological Science Reports* 6, 230–241.

Cappers, R.T.J. and Bekker, R.M. 2013. *A Manual for the Identification of Plant Seeds and Fruits.* Groningen, Barkhuis and University of Groningen Library.

Carden, R.F. and Hayden, T.J. 2006. Epiphyseal fusion in the postcranial skeleton as an indicator of age at death of European fallow deer (*Dama dama dama*, Linnaeus, 1758). In D. Ruscillo (ed.) *Recent Advances in Ageing and Sexing Animal Bones*, 227–236. Oxford, Oxbow Books.

Carey, J. 2005. An old Irish poem about Mug Ruith. *Journal of the Cork Historical and Archaeological Society* 110, 113–134.

Carey, J. 2020. The end of the world at the ends of the earth: apocalyptic thought in medieval Ireland. In C. McAllister (ed.) *The Cambridge Companion to Apocalyptic Literature*, 156–171. Cambridge, Cambridge University Press.

Carlin, N. and Cooney, G. 2017. Transforming our understanding of Neolithic and Chalcolithic society (4000–2200 cal BC) in Ireland. In M. Stanley, R. Swan and A. O'Sullivan (eds) *Stories of Ireland's Past: Knowledge gained from NRA Roads Archaeology*, 23–56. Dublin, Transport Infrastructure Ireland.

Cassidy, L.M., Maoldúin, R.Ó., Kador, T., Lynch, A., Jones, C., Woodman, P.C., Murphy, E., Ramsey, G., Dowd, M., Noonan, A., Campbell, C., Jones, E.R., Mattiangeli, V. and Bradley, D.G. 2020. A dynastic elite in monumental Neolithic society. *Nature* 582(7812), 384–388.

Caulfield, S., O'Donnell, R.G. and Mitchell, P.I. 1997. 14C Dating of a Neolithic Field System at Céide Fields, County Mayo, Ireland. *Radiocarbon* 40, 629–640.

Chadbourne, K. 1994. Giant women and flying machines. *Proceedings of the Harvard Celtic Colloquium* 14, 106–114.

Chaitanya, L., Breslin, K., Zuñiga, S., Wirken, L., Pośpiech, E., Kukla-Bartoszek, M., Sijen, T., Knijff, P., Liu, F., Branicki, W., Kayser, M. and Walsh, S. 2018. The HIrisPlex-S system for eye, hair and skin colour prediction from DNA: Introduction and forensic developmental validation. Forensic science international. *Genetics* 35, 123–135.

Chambers, F.M., van Geel, B. and van der Linden, M. 2011. Considerations for the preparation of peat samples for palynology, and for the counting of pollen and non-pollen palynomorphs. *Mires and Peat* 7, 1–14.

Chique, C., Molloy, K. and Potito, A.P. 2017. Mid-Late Holocene vegetational history and land-use dynamics in County Monaghan, northeastern Ireland – the palynological record of Lough Muckno. *Journal of the North Atlantic* 32, 1–24.

Christadou, R. and Legrand-Pineau, A. 2005. Hide working and bone tools: experimentation design and applications. In H. Luik, A. Choyke, C. Batey and L. Lougas (eds) *From Hooves to Horns, from Mollusc to Mammoth. Manufacture and Use of Bone Artefacts from Prehistoric Times to the Present. Proceedings of the 4th Meeting of the ICAZ Worked Bone Research Group, Tallinn, 26–31 August 2003*, 385–396. Tallinn Book Printers Ltd.

Clapham, A.R., Tutin, T.G. and Warburg, E.F. 1962. *Flora of the British Isles: Second Addition*. Cambridge, Cambridge University Press.

Clark, L. and Long, P. 2010. *N7 Nenagh to Limerick High Quality Dual Carriageway, Archaeological Resolution Project. Gortybrigane Site 2, E2488 Co. Tipperary. Final Excavation Report*. Available online at https://repository.dri.ie/catalog/4q77v621k [Accessed 30/9/2023].

Cleary, K. 2005. Skeletons in the closet: the dead among the living on Irish Bronze Age Settlements. *Journal of Irish Archaeology* 14, 23–42.

Cleary, R.M. 2003. Enclosed Late Bronze Age habitation site and boundary wall at Lough Gur, Co. Limerick. *Proceedings of the Royal Irish Academy* 103C, 97–189.

Cohen, A. and Serjeantson, D. 1996. *A Manual for the Identification of Bird Bones from Archaeological Sites. Revised Edition*. London, Archetype Publications Ltd.

Colledge, S. and Conolly, J. 2014. Wild plant use in European Neolithic subsistence economies: a formal assessment of preservation bias in archaeobotanical assemblages and the implications for understanding changes in plant diet breadth. *Quaternary Science Reviews* 101, 193–206.

Colledge, S., Conolly, J., Crema, E. and Shennan, S. 2019. Neolithic population crash in northwest Europe associated with agricultural crisis. *Quaternary Research* 92(3), 686–707.

Collins, B. and Tierney, J. 2012. Macrofossil plant remains. In C. Cotter (ed.) *The Western Stone Forts Project: Excavations at Dún Aonghasa and Dún Eoghanachta. Volume 2*, 353–357. Dublin, Discovery Programme.

Comber, M. 2001. Trade and communication networks in early historic Ireland. *Journal of Irish Archaeology* 10, 73–92.

Comber, M. 2002. M.V. Duignan's Excavations at the Ringfort of Rathgureen, Co. Galway. *Proceedings of the Royal Irish Academy* 102C, 137–197.

Comber, M. 2004. *Native Evidence of Non-ferrous Metalworking in Early Historic Ireland. BAR International Series 1296*. Oxford, Hadrian Books.

Condit, T. 2013. Crimewave. *Archaeology Ireland* 27, 3.

Connolly, A. 2000. *The Palaeoecology of Clara Bog, Co. Offaly*. Unpublished PhD thesis, Trinity College Dublin.

Connolly, M. and Coyle, F. 2005. *Underworld: Death and Burial in Cloghermore Cave, Co. Kerry*. Bray, Wordwell.

Cooney, G. and Grogan, E. 1994. *Irish Prehistory – A Social Perspective*. Dublin, Wordwell.

Cooney, G. and Mandal, S. 1998. *The Irish Stone Axehead Project: Monograph I*. Bray, Wordwell.

Coulter, C. 2015. Consumers and artisans. Marketing amber and jet in the early medieval British Isles. In G. Hansen, S. Ashby and I. Baug (eds) *Everyday Products in the Middle Ages*, 110–121. Oxford, Oxbow Books.

Coulter, S., Pilcher, J., Plunkett, G., Baillie, M., Hall, V., Steffenson, J.P., Vinther, B., Clausen, B. and Johnsen, S. 2012. Holocene tephras highlight complexity of volcanic signals in Greenland ice cores. *Journal of Geophysical Research* 117, 1–11.

Coyle-McClung, L. 2013. The Late Iron Age Lull – not so late after all. *Emania* 22, 73–83.

Coyle-McClung, L. and Plunkett, G. 2020. Cultural change and the climate record in final prehistoric and early medieval Ireland. *Proceedings of the Royal Irish Academy* 120C, 129–158.

Crabtree, P.J. and Campana, D.V. 2007. Worked bone. In S.A. Johnston and B. Wailes, *Dún Ailinne: Excavations at an Irish Royal Site, 1968–1975. Museum of Archaeology and Anthropology Monograph 129*, 127–131. Philadelphia, University of Pennsylvania.

Crawford, P. 2014. The Coleraine Hoard and Romano-Irish relations in Late Antiquity. *Classics Ireland* 21, 41–118.

Cronin, R., Downey, L., Synott, C., McSweeney, P., Kelly, E.P., Cahill, M., Ross, R.P. and Stanton, C. 2007. Composition of ancient Irish bog butter. *International Dairy Journal* 17, 1011–1020.

Crummy, N. 1983. *The Roman Small Finds from Excavations in Colchester 1971–79*. Colchester, Colchester Archaeological Trust.

Crummy, N. 2016. Small finds. In L. O'Brien, *Bronze Age Barrow, Early to Middle Iron Age Settlement and Burials, and Early Anglo-Saxon Settlement at Harston Mill, Cambridgeshire, East Anglian Archaeology 157*, 59–64. Bury St Edmunds, Archaeological Solutions Ltd.

Cunningham, B. 2000. *The World of Geoffrey Keating. History, Myth and Religion in Seventeenth-century Ireland*. Dublin, Four Courts.

Curran, S. 2019a. *Hidden Depths and Empty Spaces? A Remote Sensing Approach to the Exploration of Settlement Patterns, Identity and Social Hierarchy in Early Medieval Ireland (AD 400–1100)*. Unpublished PhD thesis, University College Dublin.

Curran, S. 2019b. The archaeology of settlement and society in early medieval Monaghan. *Ulster Journal of Archaeology*, 75, 52–69.

D'Arcy, S.A. 1900. An account of the excavation of two Lake-Dwellings in the neighbourhood of Clones. *Journal of the Royal Society of Antiquaries of Ireland* 10, 204–236.

Davies, O. and Quinn, D.B. 1941. The Irish Pipe Roll of 14 John, 1211–1212. *Ulster Journal of Archaeology* 4, 1–76.

Davis, S.R. 2011. The unseen Hill of Ward: new insights from LiDAR data. *Archaeology Ireland* 25(4), 36–40.

Davis, S.R. 2013. *The Hill of Ward: A Samhain Site in County Meath. 2013.* Archaeology Ireland Heritage Guide 63.

Davis, S.R., Carey, C. and Richley, E. 2017. A history of gathering at the Hill of Ward. In F. Beglane (ed.) *Gatherings: Past and Present. Proceedings from the 2013 Archaeology of Gatherings International Conference at IT Sligo, Ireland. BAR International Series S2832*, 86–101. Oxford, Archaeopress.

Davis, T. 2001. Mount Vernon Memorial Highway: changing conceptions of an American commemorative landscape. In J. Wolschke-Buhlman (ed.) *Places of Commemoration: Search for Identity and Landscape Design*, 131–185. Washington DC, Harvard University Press.

Delaney, S. and Murphy, E.M. 2022. *The Forgotten Cemetery: Excavations at Ranelagh, Co. Roscommon.* Dublin, Transport Infrastructure Ireland.

Delaney, S. and Roycroft, N. 2003. Early medieval enclosure at Balriggan, Co. Louth. *Archaeology Ireland* 17(2), 16–19.

Dennell, R.W. 1972. The interpretation of plant remains: Bulgaria. In E.S. Higgs (ed.) *Papers in Economic Prehistory*, 149–159. Cambridge, Cambridge University Press.

Derwin, J., Gabbett, M., Keane, S., Long, M. and Martin, J. 2002. Raised Bog National Heritage Areas Project 2002. Report prepared for Dúchas, the Heritage Service. Available online at https://www.npws.ie/sites/default/files/publications/pdf/Derwin_et_al_2002_Raised_Bog_NHA.pdf [Last Accessed 4/12/2023].

Dillon, M. 1951. The Taboos of the Kings of Ireland. *Proceedings of the Royal Irish Academy* 54C, 1–36.

Dineen, P.S. 1927. *Irish-English Dictionary/Foclóir Gaedhilge agus Béarla.* Dublin, Irish Texts Society.

Dobbs, M. 1930. The Ban-shenchus [part 1]. *Revue Celtique* 47, 283–339.

Doherty, C. 1980. Exchange and trade in early medieval Ireland. *Journal of the Royal Society of Antiquaries of Ireland* 110, 67–89.

Dolan, B. and Cooney, G. 2010. Lambay lithics: the analysis of two surface collections from Lambay, Co. Dublin. *Proceedings of the Royal Irish Academy* 110C, 1–33.

Doorenbosch, M. 2013. *Ancient Heaths: Reconstructing the Barrow Landscapes of Central and Southern Netherlands.* Leiden, Sidestone Press.

Dowling, G. 2006. The liminal boundary: an analysis of the sacral potency of the ditch at Ráith na Ríg, Tara. Co. Meath. *Journal of Irish Archaeology* 15, 15–37.

Dowling, G. 2011. The architecture of power: an exploration of the origins of closely spaced multivallate monuments in Ireland. In R. Schot, C. Newman and E. Bhreathnach (eds) *Landscapes of Cult and Kingship*, 213–231. Dublin, Four Courts Press.

Dowling, G. 2015. Exploring the hidden depths of Tara's hinterland: Geophysical survey and landscape investigations in the Meath–North Dublin Region, Eastern Ireland. *Proceedings of the Prehistoric Society* 81, 61–85.

Dowling, G. and Cahill-Wilson, J. 2014. Tracing the footprints of our ancestors. *Archaeology Ireland* 28(1), 20–22.

Dowling, G. and Schot, R. 2023. Gathering ground: unearthing 3000 years of prehistory at Faughan Hill, Eastern Ireland. *Proceedings of the Prehistoric Society* 90 (FirstView), 1–44 [doi:10.1017/ppr.2023.6].

Downey, C. 2013. Cúan ua Lothcháin and the transmission of the Dindšenchas. In G. Ó Riain and A. Ó Corráin (eds) *Celebrating Sixty Years of Celtic Studies at Uppsala University. Proceedings of the Eleventh Symposium of Societas Celtologica Nordica,* 45–61. Uppsala, Acta Universitatis Upsaliensis.

Doyle, M. 2014. Dress and ornament in early medieval Ireland - exploring the evidence. In B. Kelly, N. Roycroft and M. Stanley (eds) *Fragments of Lives Past: Archaeological Objects from Irish road Schemes. Archaeology and the National Roads Authority Monograph No. 11,* 67–80. Dublin, National Roads Authority.

Duffy, C. 2007. *2007:1417 – WARDSTOWN, Meath. Report on excavation license number 07E0388.* Available online at https://excavations.ie/report/2007/Meath/0018394/ [Accessed 30/9/2023].

Dulias, K., Foody, M.G.B., Justeau, P., Silva, M., Martiniano, R., Oteo-García, G., Fichera, A., Rodrigues, S., Gandini, F., Meynert, A., Donnelly, K., Aitman, T.J., Scottish Genomes Partnership, Chamberlain, A., Lelong, O., Kozikowski, G., Powlesland, D., Waddington, C., Mattiangeli, V., Bradley, D.G. and Richards, M.B. 2022. Ancient DNA at the edge of the world: Continental immigration and the persistence of Neolithic male lineages in Bronze Age Orkney. *Proceedings of the National Academy of Sciences of the United States of America* 119(8), e2108001119.

Dumville, D.D. 1997. *Councils and Synods of the Gaelic Early and Central Middle Ages.* E.C. Quiggin Memorial Lectures 3. Available online at https://www.asnc.cam.ac.uk/publications/Quiggin/ECQ%20Vol%203%201997%20Dumville.pdf [Accessed 30/9/2023].

Eastman, D.L. 2016. Simon the Anti-Christ? The Magos as Christos in Early Christian Literature. *Journal of Early Christian History* 6, 116–136.

Eastman, D.L. 2022. Simon the composite sorcerer. *New Testament Studies* 68, 407–417.

Edwards, K. 1988. Hunter-gatherer/agricultural transition and the pollen record in the British Isles. In H.J.B. Birks, *The Cultural Landscape: Past, Present and Future*, 255–267. Cambridge, Cambridge University Press.

Edwards, N. 1990. *The Archaeology of Early Medieval Ireland.* London, Routledge.

Eogan, G. 1957. A Hoard of Gold Objects from Drissoge, Co. Meath. *Journal of the Royal Society of Antiquaries of Ireland* 87(2), 125–134.

Eogan, G. 1965. *Catalogue of Irish Bronze Age Swords.* Dublin, Stationery Office.

Eogan, G. 1968. 'Lock-Rings' of the Late Bronze Age. *Proceedings of the Royal Irish Academy* 67C, 93–148.

Eogan, G. 1997. 'Hair-rings' and European Late Bronze Age society. *Antiquity* 71(272), 308–320.

Eogan, G. 2000. *The Socketed Bronze Axes in Ireland.* Marberg, Franz Steiner Verlag Wiesbaden GmbH.

Eogan, G. and Shee-Twohig, E. 2022. *Excavations at Knowth Volume 7: The Megalithic Art of the Passage Tombs at Knowth, Co. Meath.* Dublin, Royal Irish Academy.

Erdtman, G. 1943. *An Introduction to Pollen Analysis*. New York, Ronald Press.

Ettlinger, E. 1952. The association of burials with popular assemblies, fairs and races in ancient Ireland. *Etudes Celtiques* 6, 42–43.

Faegri, K. and Iversen, J. 1989. *Textbook of Pollen Analysis 4th Edition*. New Jersey, Blackburn Press.

Fanning, T. 1994. *Viking Age Ringed Pins from Dublin. Medieval Dublin Excavations 1962–1981. Series B, vol. 4*. Dublin, Royal Irish Academy.

Fenwick, J. 2021. *Rathra: A Royal Stronghold of Early Medieval Connacht*. Abbeytown, Roscommon County Library.

Finlay, N. 2000. Outside of life: traditions of infant burial in Ireland from Cillin to Cist. *World Archaeology* 31(3), 407–422.

Fischer, C.-E., Pemonge, M.-H., Ducoussau, I., Arzelier, A., Rivollat, M., Santos, F., Barrand Emam, H., Bertaud, A., Beylier, A., Ciesielski, E., Dedet, B., Desenne, S., Duday, H., Chenal, F., Gailledrat, E., Goepfert, S., Gorgé, O., Gorgues, A., Kuhnle, G., Lambach, F., Lefort, A., Mauduit, A., Maziere, F., Oudry, S., Paresys, C., Pinard, E., Plouin, S., Richard, I., Roth-Zehner, M., Roure, R., Thevenet, C., Thomas, Y., Rottier, S., Deguilloux, M.-F. and Pruvost, M. 2022. Origin and mobility of Iron Age Gaulish groups in present-day France revealed through archaeogenomics. *iScience* 25(4), 104094.

FitzGerald, M. 2007. Catch of the Day at Clowanstown, Co. Meath. *Archaeology Ireland* 21(4), 12–15.

FitzGerald, M. 2008. Bone artefacts from Chancellorsland Site A. In M. Doody, *The Ballyhoura Hills Project, Discovery Programme Monograph 7*, 315–320. Bray, Wordwell.

FitzGerald, M. 2012. Textile production. In G. Eogan *Excavations at Knowth 5: The Archaeology of Knowth in the First and Second Millennia AD*, 552–563. Dublin, Royal Irish Academy.

Fitzpatrick, E. 2009. Native Enclosed Settlement and the Problem of the Irish 'Ring-fort'. *Medieval Archaeology* 53, 271–307.

Flanagan, M.T. 2010. *The Transformation of the Irish Church in the Twelfth Century*. Oxford, Boydell and Brewer.

Forbes, D. 1868. Researches in British mineralogy. *London, Edinburgh and Dublin Philosophical Magazine and Journal of Science* 35, 171–184.

Ford, R.I. 1988. Quantification and qualification in paleoethnobotany. In C.A. Hastorf and V.S. Popper (eds) *Current Paleoethnobotany: Analytical Methods and Cultural Interpretations of Archaeological Plant Remains*. 215–222. Chicago, University of Chicago Press.

Forester, T. 2001. *Giraldus Cambrensis: The Conquest of Ireland*. Available online at https://www.yorku.ca/inpar/conquest_ireland.pdf [Accessed 30/9/2023].

Fredengren, C. 2007. Lisnacrogher in a landscape context. *Journal of the Royal Society of Antiquaries of Ireland* 137, 29–40.

Fuller, D.Q., Stevens, C. and McClatchie, M. 2014. Routine activities, tertiary refuse and labor organization: social inferences from everyday archaeobotany. In M. Madella, M. Lancelotti and M. Savard (eds) *Ancient plants and people: contemporary trends in archaeobotany*, 174–217. Tuscon, University of Arizona Press.

Gaffney, C.F. and Gater, J. 2003. *Revealing the Buried Past: Geophysics for Archaeologists*. Stroud, Tempus Publishing

Gale, R. 2003. Wood based industrial fuels and their environmental impact in lowland Britain. In P. Murphy and P.E.J.

Wiltshire (eds) *The Environmental Archaeology of Industry*, 30–47. Oxford, Oxbow Books.

Gale, R. and Cutler, D. 2000. *Plants in Archaeology*. Otley, Westbury and Royal Botanic Gardens, Kew.

Gardiner, M., Megarry, W.P and Plunkett, G. 2019. A Late Bronze Age field system and settlement on the Antrim Plateau: preliminary results. *Journal of Irish Archaeology* 28, 49–58.

Gaskell-Brown, C. and Harper, A.E.T. 1984. Excavations on Cathedral Hill, Armagh, 1968. *Ulster Journal of Archaeology* 47, 109–162.

Gavin, F. 2013. Insular military style silver pins in late Iron Age Ireland. In F. Hunter and K. Painter (eds) *Late Roman Silver Within and Beyond the Frontier: the Traprain Treasure in Context,* 415–426. Edinburgh, Society of Antiquaries of Scotland.

Gerriets, M. 1985. Money among the Irish: Coin hoards in Viking Age Ireland. *Journal of the Royal Society of Antiquaries of Ireland* 115, 121–139.

Giacometti, A. 2011. Reconstructing the human landscape before, during and after the lifespan of a ringfort at Lusk, Co. Dublin. In C. Corlett and M. Potterton (eds) *Settlement in Early Medieval Ireland in the Light of Recent Archaeological Excavations*, 157–168. Dublin, Wordwell.

Gifford-Gonzalez, D. 2018. *An Introduction to Zooarchaeology*. Cham, Springer.

Gilchrist, R. and Mytum, H.C. 1986. Experimental archaeology and burnt animal bone from archaeological sites. *Circaea* 4, 29–38.

Ginn, V. and Plunkett, G. 2020. Filling the gaps: a chronology of Bronze Age settlement in Ireland. *Journal of Irish Archaeology* 29, 41–62.

Gleeson, P. 2015. Kingdoms, communities, and Óenaig: Irish assembly practices in their northwest European context. *Journal of the North Atlantic* 8, 33–51.

Goodall, I.H. 1990. Knives. In M. Biddle (ed.) *Object and Economy in Medieval Winchester*, 835–861. Oxford, Clarenden.

Graham, B.J. 1975. Anglo-Norman settlement in County Meath. *Proceedings of the Royal Irish Academy* 75C, 223–249.

Gretzinger, J., Sayer, D., Justeau, P., Altena, E., Pala, M., Dulias, K., Edwards, C.J., Jodoin, S., Lacher, L., Sabin, S., Vågene, Å.J., Haak, W., Ebenesersdóttir, S.S., Moore, K.H.S., Radzeviciute, R., Schmidt, K., Brace, S., Bager, M.A., Patterson, N., Papac, L., Broomandkhoshbacht, N., Callan, K., Harney, É., Iliev, L., Lawson, A.M., Michel, M., Stewardson, K., Zalzala, F., Rohland, N., Kappelhoff-Beckmann, S., Both, F., Winger, D., Neumann, D., Saalow, L., Krabath, S., Beckett, S., Van Twest, M., Faulkner, N., Read, C., Barton, T., Caruth, J., Hines, J., Krause-Kyora, B., Warnke, U., Schuenemann, V.J., Barnes, I., Dahlström, H., Clausen, J.J., Richardson, A., Popescu, E., Dodwell, N., Ladd, S., Phillips, T., Mortimer, R., Sayer, F., Swales, D., Stewart, A., Powlesland, D., Kenyon, R., Ladle, L., Peek, C., Grefen-Peters, S., Ponce, P., Daniels, R., Spall, C., Woolcock, J., Jones, A.M., Roberts, A.V., Symmons, R., Rawden, A.C., Cooper, A., Bos, K.I., Booth, T., Schroeder, H., Thomas, M.G., Helgason, A., Richards, M.B., Reich, D., Krause, J. and Schiffels, S. 2022. The Anglo-Saxon migration and the formation of the early English gene pool. *Nature* 610(7930), 112–119.

Griffiths, R. 2012. Record ID: YORYM-CEE620 - EARLY MEDIEVAL hoard. The Portable Antiquities Scheme/ British

Museum. Available at: https://finds.org.uk/database/artefacts/record/id/504460 [Accessed: 2/3/2023].

Grimm, E.C. 1992. *TILIA and TILIA-GRAPH: Pollen Spreadsheet and Graphics Programs*. Volume of abstracts 8th International Palynological Congress, Aix-en-Provence.

Grogan, E. 2005. *The North Munster Project. Volume 2: The Prehistoric Landscape of North Munster*. Dublin, Discovery Programme.

Grogan, E. 2008. *The Rath of the Synods, Tara, Co. Meath: Excavations by Seán P. Ó Ríordáin*. Dublin, Wordwell.

Grogan, E., Eogan, G., Rees, R., Butler, V.G. and Henderson, J. 1987. Lough Gur excavations by Seán P. Ó Ríordáin: further Neolithic and Beaker Habitations on Knockadoon. *Proceedings of the Royal Irish Academy* 87C, 299–506.

Grogan, E., Condit, T., O'Carroll, E., O'Sullivan, A. and Daly, A. 1996. Tracking the late prehistoric landscape in North Munster. *Discovery Programme Reports* 4, 26–46.

Gwynn, E. 1906. *The Metrical Dindshenchas vol. 4*. Dublin, Dublin Institute for Advanced Studies.

Gwynn, E. 1926–28. The dindshenchas in the Book of Uí Maine. *Ériu* 10, 68–91.

Hald, M.M. 2008. The use of archaeobotanical assemblages in palaeoeconomic reconstructions. In N. Marchetti and I. Thuesen (eds) *ARCHAIA: Case Studies on Research Planning, Characterisation, Conservation, and Management of Archaeological Sites*, 223–229. *BAR International Series 1877*. Oxford, Archaeopress.

Hall, R.A. 1974. A check-list of Viking-Age coin finds from Ireland. *Ulster Journal of Archaeology*, 36–37, 71–86.

Hall, V.A. 2011. *The making of Ireland's landscape since the Ice Age*. Cork, Collins Press.

Hall, R.A., Allen, S.J., Evans, D.T., Hunter-Mann, K. and Mainman, A.J. 2014. *Anglo-Scandinavian Occupation at 16–22 Coppergate: Defining a Townscape*. York, York Archaeological Trust.

Hall, V.A. 2003. Vegetation history of mid- to western Ireland in the 2nd Millennium AD: fresh evidence from tephradated palynological investigations. *Vegetation History and Archaeobotany* 12(1), 7–17.

Hall, V.A. and Pilcher, J. 2002. Late-Quaternary Icelandic tephras in Ireland and Great Britain: detection, characterization and usefulness. *Holocene* 12, 223–230.

Halpin, A. and Newman, C. 2006. *Ireland An Oxford Archaeological Guide to Sites from Earliest Times to AD 1600*. Oxford, Oxford University Press.

Hamilton, D., Haselgrove, C. and Gosden, C. 2015. The impact of Bayesian chronologies on the British Iron Age. *World Archaeology* 47, 642–660.

Hannah, E. 2023. A chronology for unenclosed settlements in early medieval Ireland: settlement patterns in the late first millennium AD. *Proceedings of the Royal Irish Academy* https://muse.jhu.edu/pub/423/article/892669/pdf [Accessed 30/9/2023].

Harvey, E.L. and Fuller, D.Q. 2005. Investigating crop processing using phytolith analysis: the example of rice and millets. *Journal of Archaeological Science* 32(5), 739–752.

Hather, J.G. 2000. *The Identification of the Northern European Woods. A Guide for Archaeologists and Conservators*. London, Archetype Publications Ltd.

Hawkes, A. 2021. The excavation of two prehistoric ring-ditches and associated burials at Kilbrew, Co. Meath. *Journal of Irish Archaeology* 30, 25–48.

Hayden, B. 2014. *The Power of Feasts*. New York, Cambridge University Press.

Heald, A. 2005. *Non-ferrous metalworking in Iron Age Scotland, c. 700 BC–AD 800*. Unpublished PhD thesis for University of Edinburgh.

Heidel, B. and Handley, J. 2006. *Selaginella selaginoides*. Available at: https://www.fs.usda.gov/Internet/FSE_DOCUMENTS/stelprdb5206971.pdf. [Accessed 28/9/2023].

Hencken, H. 1942. Ballinderry Crannóg No. 2. *Proceedings of the Royal Irish Academy* 47C, 1–76.

Hencken, H. 1950. Lagore Crannog: An Irish royal residence of the 7th to 10th Centuries AD. *Proceedings of the Royal Irish Academy* 53C, 1–247.

Henry, P. 1999. Development and change in late Saxon textile production: an analysis of the evidence. *Durham Archaeological Journal* 14–15, 69–76.

Herity, M. 1974. *Irish Passage Graves: Neolithic Tomb-builders in Ireland and Britain 2500 B.C*. Dublin, Irish University Press.

Herity, M. 1993. Motes and mounds at royal sites in Ireland. *Journal of the Royal Society of Antiquaries of Ireland* 123, 127–151.

Heuschele, H. and Selander, J. 2014. The chemical ecology of Copepods. *Journal of Plankton Research* 36(4), 895–913.

Hicks, R. and Ward Elder, L. 2003. Festivals, deaths, and the sacred landscape of Ancient Ireland. *Journal of Indo-European Studies* 31, 307–336.

Hillman, G. 1973. Crop husbandry and food production: modern models for the interpretation of plant remains. *Anatolian Studies* 23, 241–244.

Hillman, G. 1981. Reconstructing crop husbandry practices from charred remains of crops. In R. Mercer (ed.) *Farming Practice in British Prehistory*, 123–162. Edinburgh, Edinburgh University Press.

Hillman, G. 1984. Interpretation of archaeological plant remains: ethnographic models from Turkey. In W. van Zeist and W.A. Casparie (eds) *Plants and Ancient Man, Studies in Palaeoethnobotany*, 1–41. Rotterdam, A.A. Balkema.

Hillman, G., Mason, S. De Moulins, D. and Nesbitt, M. 1996. Identification of archaeological remains of wheat: the 1992 London workshop. *Circaea* 12, 195–209.

Hillson, S. 1992. *Mammal Bones and Teeth: An Introductory Guide to Methods and Identification*. Dorset, Dorset Press.

Hogan, J. 1932. The Irish Law of Kingship, with special reference to Aileach and Cénel Eogain, *Proceedings of the Royal Irish Academy* 40C, 186–254.

Hubbard, R.N.L.B. and Clapham, A. 1992. Quantifying macroscopic plant remains. *Review of Palaeobotany and Palynology* 73, 117–132.

Hunt, C. 2013. Fire, rush-lights and pine at Navan? *Emania* 13, 41–47.

Hunter, F. 2008. Jet and related materials in Viking Scotland. *Medieval Archaeology* 52, 103–117.

Hunter, F. 2016. 'Coal money' from Portpatrick (south-west Scotland): reconstructing an early medieval craft centre from antiquarian finds. In F. Hunter and A. Sheridan (eds) *Ancient Lives. Objects, People and Place in Early Scotland. Essays for David V. Clarke on his 70th Birthday*, 281–302. Leiden, Sidestone Press.

Hunter, F. and Sheridan, A. 2014. Lignite, oil shale and cannel coal artefacts. In I. Russell and M.F. Hurley (eds)

Woodstown – A Viking Age Settlement in Co Waterford, 320–323. Dublin, National Roads Authority.

Hunter, F.J., McDonnell, J.G., Pollard, A.M., Morris, C.R. and Rowlands, C. 1993. The scientific identification of archaeological jet-like artefacts. *Archaeometry* 35, 69–89.

Hurley, M.F. 1997a. Artefacts of skeletal material. In M.F. Hurley, O.M.B. Scully and S.W.J. McCutcheon (eds) *Late Viking Age and Medieval Waterford: Excavations 1986–1992*, 650–699. Waterford, Waterford Corporation.

Hurley, M.F. 1997b. Artefacts of Skeletal Material. In R.M. Cleary, M.F. Hurley and E. Shee Twohig (eds) *Skiddy's Castle and Christ Church Cork*, 239–273. *Excavations 1974–77 by D.C. Twohig*. Cork, Cork Corporation.

Hurley, M.F. 2003. Artefacts of skeletal material. In R.M. Cleary and M.F. Hurley *Excavations in Cork City 1984–2000*, 329–348. Cork, Cork City Council.

Ingrouille, M.J and Eddie, B. 2006. *Plants: Diversity and Evolution*. Cambridge, Cambridge University Press

Inizan, M.L., Reduron-Ballinger, M., Roche, H. and Tixier, J. 1999. Technology and Terminology of Knapped Stone. Nanterre, CREP. Available at https://eclass.uoa.gr/modules/document/file.php/ARCH178/TerminologyKnappedStone.pdf [Accessed 30/9/2023].

Irish National Statute Book. 2005. Available at: http://www.irishstatutebook.ie/2005/en/si/0587.html [Accessed 9/12/2022].

Jacomet, S. 2006. *Identification of Cereal Remains from Archaeological Sites* (2nd edition, trans. by J. Greig). Basel, Archaeobotany Laboratory, IPAS, Basel University.

Jacomet, S. 2007. Plant macrofossil methods and studies: use in environmental archaeology. *Encyclopaedia of Quaternary Science* 4, 2384–2412.

Jensen, B., Pyne-O'Donnell. S., Plunkett, G., Froesel, D., Hughes, P., Sigl, M., McConnell, J., Amesbury, M., Blackwell, P., van den Bogaard, C., Buck, C., Charman, C., Clague, J.J., Hall, V.A.., Koch, J., Mackay, H., Mallon, G., McColl, L. and Pilcher, J. 2014. Transatlantic distribution of the Alaskan White River Ash. *Geology* 42(10), 875–878.

Johnston, P. and O'Donnell, L. 2008. Appendix V. Analysis of the charred plant remains and charcoal. In G. Stout and M. Stout (eds) *Excavation of an Early Medieval Secular Cemetery at Knowth Site M, County Meath*, 128–148. Dublin, Wordwell.

Jones, C., Carey, O. and Hennigar, C. 2011. Domestic production and the political economy in prehistory: evidence from the Burren, Co. Clare. *Proceedings of the Royal Irish Academy* 111C, 33–58.

Jones, C., McVeigh, T. and Ó Maoldúin, R. 2015. Monuments, landscape and identity in Chalcolithic Ireland. In K. Springs, *Landscape and Identity: Archaeology and Human Geography. BAR International Series 2709*, 3–26. Oxford, Archaeopress.

Jones, G. 1984. Interpretation of archaeological plant remains: ethnographic models from Greece. In W. van Ziest and W.A. Casparie (eds) *Plants and Ancient Man – Studies in Paleoethnobotany*, 42–61. A.A. Rotterdam, Balkema.

Jones, G. 1987. A statistical approach to the archaeological identification of crop processing. *Journal of Archaeological Science* 14, 311–323.

Jones, G. and Halstead, P. 1995. Maslins, mixtures and monocrops: on the interpretation of archaeobotanical crop samples of heterogeneous composition. *Journal of Archaeological Science* 22, 103–114.

Jones, H. and Young, R.M. 1897. A diary of the proceedings of the Leinster Army, under Gov. Jones. *Ulster Journal of Archaeology* 3(3), 153–161.

Jones, M.K. 1985. Archaeobotany beyond subsistence reconstruction. In G.W. Barker and C. Gamble (eds) *Beyond Domestication in Prehistoric Europe*, 107–128. New York, Academic Press.

Kearns, T., Martinón-Torres, M. and Rehren, T. 2010. Metal to mould: alloy identification in experimental casting moulds using XRF. *Historical Metallurgy* 44(1), 48–58.

Keating, G. (ed.) 1726. *General History of Ireland*. Dublin, Cluer and Campbell.

Keddy, P.A. 2010. *Wetland Ecology: Principles and Conservation*. Cambridge, Cambridge University Press.

Kelly, E.P. 2006. *Kingship and Sacrifice: Irish Bog Bodies and Boundaries. Archaeology Ireland, Heritage Guide 35*. Bray, Wordwell.

Kelly, F. 1999. Trees in Early Ireland. *Irish Forestry* 56(1), 40–56.

Kelly, F. 2000. *Early Irish farming: A Study Based Mainly on the Law-texts of the 7th and 8th Centuries AD (Vol. 4)*. Dublin, Institute for Advanced Studies.

Kenny, M. 1987. The geographical distribution of Irish Viking Age coin hoards. *Proceedings of the Royal Irish Academy* 87C, 507–525.

Kenny, N. 2010. Charcoal production in Medieval Ireland. In M. Stanley, E. Danaher and J. Eogan (eds) *Creative Minds. Archaeology and the National Roads Authority Monograph Series No. 7*, 99–116. Dublin, National Roads Authority,

Kerr, R.E. 1990. *Wall of Fire – The Rifle and Civil War Infantry Tactics*. Unpublished thesis, Fort Leavenworth, Kansas. Available at https://apps.dtic.mil/sti/pdfs/ADA227467.pdf [Accessed 30/9/2023].

Kerr, T.R. 2007. *Early Christian Settlement in North-West Ulster. BAR British Series 450*. Oxford, BAR Publishing.

Kerr, T.R., McCormick, F. and O'Sullivan, A. 2013. *The Economy of Early Medieval Ireland. Early Medieval Archaeology Project (EMAP) Report 7 (1)*. Available at https://researchrepository.ucd.ie/entities/publication/1fe28690-3f33-4497-b0fc-75ce-51fa7e0a/details [Accessed 30/9/2023].

Kerr, T.R., Swindles, G.T. and Plunkett, G. 2009. Making hay while the sun shines? Socio-economic change, cereal production and climatic deterioration in Early Medieval Ireland. *Journal of Archaeological Science* 36(12), 2868–2874.

Kinsella, J. 2010. A new Irish early medieval site type? Exploring the 'recent' archaeological evidence for non-circular enclosed settlement and burial sites. *Proceedings of the Royal Irish Academy* 110C, 89–132.

Knight, J.A. 1985. *Differential Preservation of Calcined Bone at the Hirundo Site, Alton, Maine*. Unpublished Masters Thesis, University of Maine.

Knörzer, K.H. 1971. Urgeschichtliche unkrauter im rheinland.ein beitrag zur entstehungsgeschichte der segetalgesellschaften. *Vegetation* 23, 89–111.

Körber-Grohne, U. 1981. Crop husbandry and environmental change in the Feddersen Wierde, near Bremerhaven, northwest Germany. In M.K. Jones and G.W. Dimbleby (eds) *The Environment of Man: The Iron Age to the Anglo Saxon*

Period, 287–307. *BAR British Series 87*. Oxford, BAR Publishing.

Krogsrud, L.M. 2012. Checklist of Viking-Age silver hoards from Ireland. *Journal of the Royal Society of Antiquaries of Ireland* 142/143, 59–73.

Küçükdemirci, M. and Sarris, A. 2020. Deep learning based automated analysis of archaeo-geophysical images. *Archaeological Prospection* 27, 107–118.

Lanigan, H.M. 1964. *Jet Bracelets in Ireland: Rings of Fossil Wood.* Unpublished Master of Arts Thesis, University College Dublin.

Lawson, D.J., Hellenthal, G., Myers, S. and Falush, D. 2012. Inference of population structure using dense haplotype data. *PLoS Genetics* 8(1), e1002453.

Leask, H.G. 1933. Rathmore Church, Co. Meath. *Journal of the Royal Society of Antiquaries of Ireland* 3(2), 153–166.

Lenihan, O. and Dennehy, E. 2010. N9/N10 Kilcullen to Waterford Scheme: Phase 3, Kilcullen to Carlow. Archaeological Services Contract No. 5 – Resolution, Kilcullen to Moone and Athy Link Road. Final Report on archaeological investigations at Site E2982, in the townland of Moone, Co. Kildare. Available online at https://repository.dri.ie/catalog/th840d851 [Accessed 30/9/2023].

Leslie, S., Winney, B., Hellenthal, G., Davison, D., Boumertit, A., Day, T., Hutnik, K., Royrvik, E.C., Cunliffe, B., Lawson, D.J., Falush, D., Freeman, C., Pirinen, M., Myers, S., Robinson, M., Donnelly, P. and Bodmer, W. 2015. The fine-scale genetic structure of the British population. *Nature* 519(7543), 309–314.

Lipscombe, M. and Stokes, J. 2008. *Trees and How to Grow Them.* London, Think Books.

Liversidge, H.M., Herdeg, B. and Rosing, F.W. 1998. Dental age estimation of non-adults. A review of methods and principles. In K.W. Alt, F.W. Rosing and M. Teschla-Nicola (eds) *Dental Anthropology, Fundamentals, Limits and Prospects*, 419–442. Vienna, Springer.

Lovejoy, C.O. 1985. Dental wear in the Libben population: Its functional pattern and role in the determination of adult skeletal age at death. *American Journal of Biological Anthropology* 68, 47–56.

Lucas, A.T. 1953. The horizontal mill in Ireland. *Journal of the Royal Society of Antiquaries of Ireland* 83, 1–36.

Lucas, A.T. 1973. National Museum of Ireland Archaeological Acquisitions in the Year 1970. *Journal of the Royal Society of Antiquaries of Ireland* 103, 177–213.

Lundström-Baudais, K.A., Rachoud–Schneider, M., Baudais, D. and Poissonnier, B. 2002. Le broyage dans la chaîne de transformation du millet (*Panicum miliaceum*): outils, gestes et écofacts. In H. Procopiou and R. Treuil (eds) *Moudre et Broyer: I. Méthodes*, 155–180. Paris, Comité des Travaux Historiques et Scientifiques.

Lyman, R.L. 1994. *Vertebrate Taphonomy.* Cambridge, Cambridge University Press.

Lyne, E. 2021. Lissaniska – location, location, location! *Archaeology Ireland* 35(1), 24–29.

Lyne, E. 2022. Archaeological excavation report, 17E0328 Lissaniska, County Kerry. https://repository.dri.ie/catalog/2n506t61m [Accessed 30/9/2023].

Lynn, C.J. 2007. Inauguration rites of rulers in Ireland and Carinthia: a note. *Ulster Journal of Archaeology* 66, 132–138.

Macalister, R.A.S. 1919. Temair Breg: A study of the remains and traditions of Tara. *Proceedings of the Royal Irish Academy* 34C, 231–399.

Macalister, R.A.S. 1949. *The Archaeology of Ireland.* London, Methuen.

MacLeod, S.P. 2003. Oenach Aimsire na mBan: Early Irish seasonal celebrations, gender roles and mythological cycles. *Proceedings of the Harvard Celtic Colloquium* 23, 257–283.

Madgwick, R., Grimes, V., Lamb, A.L., Naderbragt, A.J., Evens, J.A. and McCormick, F. 2019. Feasting and Mobility in Iron Age Ireland: Multi-isotope analysis reveals the vast catchment of Navan Fort, Ulster. *Nature Scientific Reports* 9, 19792.

Maguire, R. 2021. *Irish Late Iron Age Equestrian Equipment in its Insular and Continental Context.* Oxford, Archaeopress.

Mahon, W. 1988. Glasraige, Tóecraige, and Araid: evidence from ogam. *Proceedings of the Harvard Celtic Colloquium* 8, 11–30.

Mallory, J.P. and Woodman, P.C. 1984. Oughtymore: An early Christian shell midden. *Ulster Journal of Archaeology* 47, 51–62.

Mandal, S. 1996. Irish Stone Axes: Rock and Role of the Petrologist. *Archaeology Ireland* 10(4), 32–35.

Mandal, S. 1997. Striking the balance: The roles of petrography and geochemistry in stone axe studies in Ireland. *Archaeometry* 39(2), 289–308.

Mandal, S. and Cooney, G. 1996. The Irish Stone Axe Project: A Second Petrological Report. *The Journal of Irish Archaeology* 7, 41–64.

Mandal, S., Cooney, G., Grogan, E., O'Carroll, F. and Guinan, B. 1992. A review of the petrological techniques being utilised to identify, group, and source Irish stone axes. *Journal of Irish Archaeology* 6, 1–11.

Margaryan, A., Lawson, D.J., Sikora, Martin, Racimo, F., Rasmussen, S., Moltke, I., Cassidy, L.M., Jørsboe, E., Ingason, A., Pedersen, M.W., Korneliussen, T., Wilhelmson, H., Buś, M.M., de Barros Damgaard, P., Martiniano, R., Renaud, G., Bhérer, C., Moreno-Mayar, J.V., Fotakis, A.K., Allen, M., Allmäe, R., Molak, M., Cappellini, E., Scorrano, G., McColl, H., Buzhilova, A., Fox, A., Albrechtsen, A., Schütz, B., Skar, B., Arcini, C., Falys, C., Jonson, C.H., Błaszczyk, D., Pezhemsky, D., Turner-Walker, G., Gestsdóttir, H., Lundstrøm, I., Gustin, I., Mainland, I., Potekhina, I., Muntoni, I.M., Cheng, J., Stenderup, J., Ma, J., Gibson, J., Peets, J., Gustafsson, J., Iversen, K.H., Simpson, L., Strand, L., Loe, L., Sikora, Maeve, Florek, M., Vretemark, M., Redknap, M., Bajka, M., Pushkina, T., Søvsø, M., Grigoreva, N., Christensen, T., Kastholm, O., Uldum, O., Favia, P., Holck, P., Sten, S., Arge, S.V., Ellingvåg, S., Moiseyev, V., Bogdanowicz, W., Magnusson, Y., Orlando, L., Pentz, P., Jessen, M.D., Pedersen, A., Collard, M., Bradley, D.G., Jørkov, M.L., Arneborg, J., Lynnerup, N., Price, N., Gilbert, M.T.P., Allentoft, M.E., Bill, J., Sindbæk, S.M., Hedeager, L., Kristiansen, K., Nielsen, R., Werge, T. and Willerslev, E. 2020. Population genomics of the Viking world. *Nature* 585(7825), 390–396.

Marguerie, D. and Hunot, J.Y. 2007. Charcoal analysis and dendrology: data from archaeological sites in north-western France. *Journal of Archaeological Science* 34, 1417–1433.

Marsh, R. 2013. *Meath Folk Tales.* Dublin, The History Press.

Martin, A. and Barkley, W.D. 1973. *Seed Identification Manual.* Berkeley, University of California Press.

■

Martiniano, R., Caffell, A., Holst, M., Hunter-Mann, K., Montgomery, J., Müldner, G., McLaughlin, R.L., Teasdale, M.D., van Rheenen, W., Veldink, J.H., van den Berg, L.H., Hardiman, O., Carroll, M., Roskams, S., Oxley, J., Morgan, C., Thomas, M.G., Barnes, I., McDonnell, C., Collins, M.J. and Bradley, D.G. 2016. Genomic signals of migration and continuity in Britain before the Anglo-Saxons. *Nature Communications* [Online] 7(1). Available at https://www.nature.com/articles/ncomms10326 [Accessed 30/9/2023].

Matthews, S. 2011. Chelsea and Ballintober swords: Typology, chronology and use. In M. Uckelmann and M. Mödlinger (eds) *Bronze Age Warfare: Manufacture and Use of Weaponry. BAR International Series 2255*, 85–106. Oxford, BAR Publications.

McCaughey, T.P. 1960. Tract on the chief places of Meath. *Celtica* 5, 172–176.

McClatchie, M. 2014. Food production in the Bronze Age: analysis of plant macro-remains from Haughey's Fort, Co. Armagh. *Emania* 14, 33–48.

McClatchie, M. 2018. Barley, rye, and oats. In S.L. Lopez Varela (ed.) *Encyclopedia of Archaeological Sciences.* Available online at https://onlinelibrary.wiley.com/doi/10.1002/9781119188230.saseas0057 [Accessed 30/9/2023].

McClatchie, M., Whitehouse, N., Schulting, R., Bogaard, A. and Barratt, P. 2009. Cultivating societies: new insights into agriculture in Neolithic Ireland. *Dining and dwelling – archaeology and the National Roads Authority Monograph Series 6, 1–8.* Dublin, Wordwell

McClatchie, M., Bogaard, A., Colledge, S., Whitehouse, N., Schulting, R., Barratt, P. and McLaughlin, T. 2016. Farming and foraging in Neolithic Ireland: An archaeobotanical perspective. *Antiquity* 90, 302–318.

McClatchie, M., McCormick, F., Kerr, T.R. and O'Sullivan, A. 2015. Early medieval farming and food production: a review of the archaeobotanical evidence from archaeological excavations in Ireland. *Vegetation History and Archaeobotany* 24(1), 179–186.

McCormick, F. 1985. Faunal remains from prehistoric Irish burials. *Journal of Irish Archaeology* 3, 37–48.

McCormick, F. 2008. The decline of the cow: Agricultural and settlement change in early medieval Ireland. *Peritia* 20, 209–224.

McCormick, F. 2009. Ritual feasting in Iron Age Ireland. In G. Cooney, K. Becker, J. Coles, M. Ryan, and S. Sievers (eds) *Relics of Old Decency: Archaeological Studies in Later Prehistory*, 405–412. Dublin, Wordwell.

McCormick, F. 2013. Agriculture, settlement and society in early medieval Ireland. *Quaternary International* 346, 119–130.

McCormick, F. and Murphy, E. 2012. Food remains: mammal, bird, fish and shellfish. In C. Cotter (ed.) *The Western Stone Forts Project: Excavations at Dún Aonghasa and Dún Eoghanachta. Vol. 2,* 153–165. Dublin, Wordwell.

McCormick, F. and Murray, E.V. 2006. The mammal bones from Mooghaun, Co. Clare: Preliminary report. In E. Grogan (ed.) *The North Munster Project: Volume 1. The Later Prehistoric Landscape in Southeast Clare*, 303–306. Bray, Wordwell.

McCormick, F. and Murray, E. 2007. *Excavations at Knowth Vol 3: Knowth and the Zooarchaeology of Early Christian Ireland.* Dublin, Royal Irish Academy.

McCormick, F., Kerr, T.R., McClatchie, M. and O'Sullivan, A. 2014. *Early Medieval Agriculture, Livestock and Cereal Production in Ireland, AD 400–1100. BAR International Series 2647.* Archaeopress, Oxford.

McKinley, J.I. 2004. Compiling a skeletal inventory: disarticulated and co-mingled remains. In M. Brickley and J.I. McKinley (eds) *Guidelines to the Standards for Recording Human Skeletal Remains. Institute for Field Archaeologists Paper 7,* 14–17.

McLaughlin, T.R., Hannah, E. and Coyle-McClung, L. 2018. Frequency analyses of historical and archaeological datasets reveal the same pattern of declining sociocultural activity in ninth to tenth century CE Ireland. *Cliodynamics* 9(1), 1–24.

Mead, G.R.S. 1892. *Simon Magus: An Essay on the Founder of Simonianism Based on the Ancient Sources with a Re-Evaluation of his Philosophy and Teachings.* London, The Theosophical Society.

Meehan, R. and Warren, W.P. 1999. *The Boyne Valley in the Ice Age.* Dublin, Geological Survey of Ireland.

Miksicek, C.H. 1987. Formation processes of the archaeobotanical record. *Advances in Archaeological Method and Theory* 10, 211–247.

Mitchell, G.F. 1986. *Reading the Irish Landscape.* Dublin, Country House Publishing.

Mitchell, G.F. and Ryan, M. 1997. *Reading the Irish Landscape.* Dublin, Town House.

Molloy, K and O'Connell, M. 2004. Holocene vegetation and land use dynamics in the karstic environment of Inis Oirr, Aran Islands, Western Ireland. *Quaternary International* 113, 41–61.

Monk, M.A. 1986. Evidence from macroscopic plant remains for crop husbandry in prehistoric and early historic Ireland: a review. *Journal of Irish Archaeology* 3, 31–36.

Monk, M. and Power, O. 2012. More than a grain of truth emerges from a rash of corn-drying kilns? *Archaeology Ireland* 26(2), 38–41.

Moore, D. 2022. Athboy Town Centre Project, Athboy, Co. Meath. Cultural Heritage Impact Assessment. Available online at https://consult.meath.ie/ga/system/files/materials/7595/App%20F%20-%20Cultural%20Heritage%20Impact%20Assessment.pdf [Last Accessed: 1/12/2023].

Moorrees, C.F.A., Fanning, E.A. and Hunt, E.E. 1963. Formation and resorption of three deciduous teeth in children. *American Journal of Physical Anthropology* 21, 205–213.

Morahan, M. 2014. 2014:034 – Curleyland/Mill Land, Meath. Available at https://excavations.ie/report/2014/Meath/0023783/ [Accessed 30/9/2023].

Morris, H. 1926. The Battle of Ocha and the Burial Place of Niall of the Nine Hostages. *Journal of the Royal Society of Antiquaries of Ireland* 16(1), 29–42.

Müller-Lisowski, K. 1923. Texte zur 'Mog Ruith sage'. *Zeitschrift für keltische Philologie* 14, 145–163.

Müller-Lisowski, K. 1938. La légende de saint Jean dans la tradition irlandaise et le druide Mog Ruith. *Études celtiques* 3/5, 46–70.

Mullins, C. 2012. Bone Points. In C. Cotter (ed.) *The Western Stone Forts Project: Excavations at Dún Aonghasa and Dún Eoghanachta. Volume 2,* 104–118. Dublin, Wordwell.

Murphy, D. 1893. *Cromwell in Ireland A History of Cromwell's Irish Campaign.* Dublin, Gill and Son.

Murphy, E. and McCormick, F. 1996. The faunal remains from the inner ditch of Haughey's Fort, third report: 1991 excavation. *Emania* 14, 47–50.

Murphy, M. and Potterton, M. 2010. *The Dublin Region in the Middle Ages: Settlement, Land-use and Economy*. Dublin, Four Court Press.

Naismith, R. 2017. *Medieval European Coinage 8: Britain and Ireland c. 400–1066*. Cambridge, Cambridge University Press.

Neef, R., Cappers, R. and Bekker, R. 2012. *Digital Atlas of Economic Plants in Archaeology*. Groningen, Barkhuis and Groningen University Library.

Nevin, F. 2021. Application of the Eidt phosphate spot test to geophysical features at Raystown early medieval settlement complex, Co. Meath. *Journal of Irish Archaeology* 30, 127–140.

Newman, C. 1997. *Tara: An Archaeological Survey*. Dublin, Discovery Programme.

Newman, C. 2005. Recomposing the archaeological landscape of Tara. In E. Bhreathneach (ed.) *The Kingship and Landscape of Tara,* 361–409. Dublin, Four Courts.

Newman, C., O'Connell, M., Dillon, M. and Molloy, K. 2007. Interpretation of charcoal and pollen data relating to a late Iron Age ritual site in eastern Ireland: a holistic approach. *Vegetation History and Archaeobotany* 16(5), 349–365.

Ní Ghabhláin, S. 1996. The origin of medieval parishes in Gaelic Ireland: The evidence from Kilfenora. *Journal of the Royal Society of Antiquaries of Ireland* 126, 37–61.

O'Brien, E. 2021. *Mapping Death: Burial in Late Iron Age and Early Medieval Ireland*. Dublin, Four Courts Press.

O'Brien, M.A. 1962. *Corpus genealogiarum Hiberniae I*. Dublin, Institute for Advanced Studies.

O'Brien, R. 2012. *2012:561 – Rathnadrinna, Lalor's-Lot, Tipperary*. https://excavations.ie/report/2012/Tipperary/0023550/ [Accessed 30/9/2023].

O'Brien, R. and Fitzgerald, M. 2012. Bone spindle whorls. In C. Cotter (ed.) *The Western Stone Forts Project: Excavations at Dún Aonghasa and Dún Eoghanachta. Volume 2*, 135–137. Dublin, Wordwell.

O'Brien, W. 2017. The development of the hillfort in prehistoric Ireland. *Proceedings of the Royal Irish Academy* 117C, 3–61.

O'Brien, W. and Hogan, N. 2021. *Garranes: An Early Medieval Royal Site in South-West Ireland*. Archaeopress, Oxford.

O'Brien, W. and O'Driscoll, J. 2017. *Hillforts, Warfare and Society in Bronze Age Ireland*. Oxford, Archaeopress.

OCarroll, E. and Mitchell, F.J.G. 2016. Quantifying woodland resource usage and selection from Neolithic to post Mediaeval times in the Irish Midlands. *Environmental Archaeology* 11(2), 1–14.

O'Carroll, F., Shine, D., McConnon, M. and Corway, L. 2016. The Blackfriary Button. *Ríocht na Midhe* 28, 30–35.

O'Connell, A. 2009. Archaeological excavation report, E3074 Lismullin 1 Vol 3 Images, County Meath. Available online at https://repository.dri.ie/catalog/5h743983m. [Accessed 30/9/2023].

O'Connell, A. 2013. *Harvesting the Stars. A pagan temple at Lismullin, Co. Meath. NRA Scheme Monographs 11*. Dublin, National Roads Authority.

O'Connor, T.P. 1998. On the difficulty of detecting seasonal slaughtering of sheep. *Environmental Archaeology* 3, 5–11.

O'Connor, T. 2008. *The Archaeology of Animal Bones*. Stroud, Sutton Publishing.

O'Curry, E. 1878. *Lectures on the Manuscript Materials of Ancient Irish history: Delivered at the Catholic University of Ireland, During the Sessions of 1855 and 1856*. Dublin, W.A. Hinch.

Oddy, A. 1993. Gilding of metals in the old world. In S. La Niece and P. Craddock (eds) *Metal Plating and Patination*, 171–181. London, Butterworth-Heinemann.

O'Donnell, L. 2007. The wood and charcoal. In E. Grogan, L. O'Donnell and P. Johnston (eds) *The Bronze Age Landscapes of the Pipeline to the West: An Integrated Archaeological and Environmental Assessment*, 27–69. Bray, Wordwell.

O'Donnell, L. 2009. Charcoal analysis. In C. Baker (ed.) *The Archaeology of Killeen Castle, Co. Meath*, 113–124. Dublin, Wordwell.

O'Donnell, L. 2018. Into the woods: Revealing Ireland's Iron Age woodlands through archaeological charcoal analysis. *Environmental Archaeology* 23, 240–253.

O'Donnell, L. 2021. *Charcoal analysis from Clonee, Clonee Data Centre, Co. Meath. Licence numbers: 16E0092, 15E0577, 16E0038, 16E0117, 16E0118, 16E0150, 16E0151, 16E0417, 16E0175, 16E0195, 16E0194, 16E0196, 16E0227, 16E0259, 16E0270, 16E0337, 16E0284, 16E0368, 16E0494, 16E0634, 17E0063, 18E0143, 18E0144*. Unpublished report for Irish Archaeological Consultancy Ltd.

O'Donnell, L., Gearey, B., Hill, C.B., Hopla, E.J. and McKeon, J. 2021. Landscape and environment. In F. Walsh (ed.) *The Road to Kells: Prehistoric Archaeology of the M3 Navan to Kells and N52 Kells Bypass Road Project*, 25–42. Dublin, Transport Infrastructure Ireland.

O'Donovan, J. 1836. *Ordnance Survey of Ireland: Letters, Meath*. Available online at https://www.askaboutireland.ie/aai-files/assets/ebooks/OSI-Letters/MEATH_14%20E%202.pdf [Accessed 30/9/2023].

O'Driscoll, J. 2017. A multi-layered model for filling the gaps: a chronology of Bronze Age settlement in Ireland. Bronze Age hillforts in Ireland and Europe. *Journal of Irish Archaeology* 26, 77–100.

O'Driscoll, J. 2023. Head for the hills: Nucleated hilltop settlement in the Irish Bronze Age. *Journal of World Prehistory* 36, 1–47.

Ó Duinn, S. 1992. The siege of Knocklong: Forbhais Droma Damhghaire. Available online in translation at https://celt.ucc.ie/published/T301044/index.html [Accessed 30/9/2023].

Ó Floinn, R. 2000. Freestone Hill, Co. Kilkenny: a reassessment. In A.P. Smyth (ed.) *Seanchas. Studies in Early and Medieval Irish Archaeology, History and Literature in Honour of Francis J. Byrne*, 12–29. Dublin, Four Courts Press.

O'Hara, R. 2009. Collierstown 1: a Late Iron Age–early medieval enclosed cemetery. In M.B. Deevy and D. Murphy (eds) *Places Along the Way: First Findings on the M3*, 83–100. Dublin, National Roads Authority.

O'Keeffe, T. 2021. *Ireland Encastellated AD 950–1550. Insular Castle-building in its European Context*. Dublin. Four Courts.

O'Leary, A.M. 2017. Constructing the magical biography of the Irish druid Mog Ruith. In A. Classen (ed.) *Magic and Magicians in the Middle Ages and Early Modern Time. The Occult in Pre-modern Sciences, Medicine, Literature, Religion, and Astrology*, 219–230. Berlin, De Gruyter.

Olsen, S.L. 2003. The bone and antler artefacts: their manufacture and use. In N. Field and M. Parker Pearson (eds) *Fiskerton. An Iron Age Timber Causeway with Iron Age and Roman Votive Offerings: the 1981 Excavations*, 92–110. Oxford, Oxbow Books.

Ó Murchadha, D. 2002. Carman, site of Óenach Carmain: a proposed location. *Éigse* 33, 57–70.

O'Riain, P. 1972. Boundary associations in early Irish society. *Studia Celtica* 7, 12–29.

Ó Ríordáin, S.P. 1941. The excavation of a large earthen ring-fort at Garranes, Co. Cork. *Proceedings of the Royal Irish Academy* 47C, 77–150.

Ó Ríordáin, S.P. 1945. Roman material in Ireland. *Proceedings of the Royal Irish Academy* 51C, 35–82.

Ó Ríordáin, S.P. 1949. Lough Gur excavations: Carraig Aille and the 'Spectacles'. *Proceedings of the Royal Irish Academy* 52C, 39–111.

Ó Ríordáin, S.P. 1954. Lough Gur excavations: Neolithic and Bronze Age houses on Knockadoon. *Proceedings of the Royal Irish Academy* 56C, 297–459.

Ó Ríordáin, S.P. and Hartnett, P.J. 1943. The excavation of Ballycatteen Fort, Co. Cork. *Proceedings of the Royal Irish Academy* 49C, 1–43.

Orpen, H.G. 1911–20. *Ireland Under the Normans*. Oxford, Clarendon Press.

O'Sullivan, A. 2017. Magic in early medieval Ireland: some observations from archaeological evidence. *Ulster Journal of Archaeology* 74, 107–117.

O'Sullivan, A. and Kenny, N. 2008. A matter of life and death. *Archaeology Ireland* 22, 8–11.

O'Sullivan, A. and Kinsella, J. 2013. Living by a sacred landscape: interpreting the early medieval archaeology of the Hill of Tara and its environs, AD 400–1100. In M. O'Sullivan, C. Scarre and M. Doyle (eds) *Tara – From the Past to the Future*, 363–386. Dublin, Wordwell.

O'Sullivan, A. and Nicholl, T. 2011. Early medieval settlement enclosures in Ireland: dwellings, daily life and social identity. *Proceedings of the Royal Irish Academy* 111C, 59–90.

O'Sullivan, A., McCormick, F., Kerr, T. and Harney, L. 2014. *Early Medieval Ireland, AD 400–1100*. Dublin, Royal Irish Academy.

O'Sullivan, A., McCormick, F., Kerr, T. R. and Harney, L. 2021a. *Early Medieval Dwellings and Settlements. In Early Medieval Ireland, AD 400–1100: The evidence from archaeological excavations*, 47–138. Dublin, Royal Irish Academy.

O'Sullivan, A., McCormick, F., Kerr, T. R. and Harney, L. 2021b. *Farming in Early Medieval Ireland. In Early Medieval Ireland, AD 400–1100: The evidence from archaeological excavations*, 179–214. Dublin, Royal Irish Academy.

O'Sullivan, M. 1987. The art of the passage tomb at Knockroe, County Kilkenny. *Journal of the Royal Society of Antiquaries of Ireland* 117, 84–95.

O'Sullivan, M. and Downey, L. 2006. Moated Sites. *Archaeology Ireland* 20(4), 34–36.

Pagan, H. 2008. The pre-reform coinage of Edgar. In D. Scragg (ed.) *Edgar, King of the English*, 192–209. Woodbridge, Boydell and Brewer.

Pales, L. and Lambert C. 1971. *Atlas ostéologique pour servir à l'identification des mammifères du quaternaire*. Paris, Éditions du Centre national de la recherché scientifique.

Patterson, N., Isakov, M., Booth, T., Büster, L., Fischer, C.-E., Olalde, I., Ringbauer, H., Akbari, A., Cheronet, O., Bleasdale, M., Adamski, N., Altena, E., Bernardos, R., Brace, S., Broomandkhoshbacht, N., Callan, K., Candilio, F., Culleton, B., Curtis, E., Demetz, L., Carlson, K.S.D., Edwards, C.J., Fernandes, D.M., Foody, M.G.B., Freilich, S., Goodchild, H., Kearns, A., Lawson, A.M., Lazaridis, I., Mah, M., Mallick, S., Mandl, K., Micco, A., Michel, M., Morante, G.B., Oppenheimer, J., Özdoğan, K.T., Qiu, L., Schattke, C., Stewardson, K., Workman, J.N., Zalzala, F., Zhang, Z., Agustí, B., Allen, T., Almássy, K., Amkreutz, L., Ash, A., Baillif-Ducros, C., Barclay, A., Bartosiewicz, L., Baxter, K., Bernert, Z., Blažek, J., Bodružić, M., Boissinot, P., Bonsall, C., Bradley, P., Brittain, M., Brookes, A., Brown, F., Brown, L., Brunning, R., Budd, C., Burmaz, J., Canet, S., Carnicero-Cáceres, S., Čaušević-Bully, M., Chamberlain, A., Chauvin, S., Clough, S., Čondić, N., Coppa, A., Craig, O., Črešnar, M., Cummings, V., Czifra, S., Danielisová, A., Daniels, R., Davies, A., de Jersey, P., Deacon, J., Deminger, C., Ditchfield, P.W., Dizdar, M., Dobeš, M., Dobisíková, M., Domboróczki, L., Drinkall, G., Đukić, A., Ernée, M., Evans, C., Evans, J., Fernández-Götz, M., Filipović, S., Fitzpatrick, A., Fokkens, H., Fowler, C., Fox, A., Gallina, Z., Gamble, M., González Morales, M.R., González-Rabanal, B., Green, A., Gyenesei, K., Habermehl, D., Hajdu, T., Hamilton, D., Harris, J., Hayden, C., Hendriks, J., Hernu, B., Hey, G., Horňák, M., Ilon, G., Istvánovits, E., Jones, A.M., Kavur, M.B., Kazek, K., Kenyon, R.A., Khreisheh, A., Kiss, V., Kleijne, J., Knight, M., Kootker, L.M., Kovács, P.F., Kozubová, A., Kulcsár, G., Kulcsár, V., Le Pennec, C., Legge, M., Leivers, M., Loe, L., López-Costas, O., Lord, T., Los, D., Lyall, J., Marín-Arroyo, A.B., Mason, P., Matošević, D., Maxted, A., McIntyre, L., McKinley, J., McSweeney, K., Meijlink, B., Mende, B.G., Menđušić, M., Metlička, M., Meyer, S., Mihovilić, K., Milasinovic, L., Minnitt, S., Moore, J., Morley, G., Mullan, G., Musilová, M., Neil, B., Nicholls, R., Novak, M., Pala, M., Papworth, M., Paresys, C., Patten, R., Perkić, D., Pesti, K., Petit, A., Petriščáková, K., Pichon, C., Pickard, C., Pilling, Z., Price, T.D., Radović, S., Redfern, R., Resutík, B., Rhodes, D.T., Richards, M.B., Roberts, A., Roefstra, J., Sankot, P., Šefčáková, A., Sheridan, A., Skae, S., Šmolíková, M., Somogyi, K., Somogyvári, Á., Stephens, M., Szabó, G., Szécsényi-Nagy, A., Szeniczey, T., Tabor, J., Tankó, K., Maria, C.T., Terry, R., Teržan, B., Teschler-Nicola, M., Torres-Martínez, J.F., Trapp, J., Turle, R., Ujvári, F., van der Heiden, M., Veleminsky, P., Veselka, B., Vytlačil, Z., Waddington, C., Ware, P., Wilkinson, P., Wilson, L., Wiseman, R., Young, E., Zaninović, J., Žitňan, A., Lalueza-Fox, C., de Knijff, P., Barnes, I., Halkon, P., Thomas, M.G., Kennett, D.J., Cunliffe, B., Lillie, M., Rohland, N., Pinhasi, R., Armit, I. and Reich, D. 2022. Large-scale migration into Britain during the Middle to Late Bronze Age. *Nature* 601(7894), 588–594.

Payne, S. 1973. Kill-off patterns in sheep and goats: the mandibles from Aşvan Kale. *Anatolian Studies* 23, 281–303.

Penton, S. 2008. *Cumwhitton, Cumbria. Analytical Investigation of Jet-like Objects from a Viking Cemetery*. Portsmouth, English Heritage.

Peters, C.N. 2015. He is not entitled to butter: the diet of peasants and commoners in early medieval Ireland. *Proceedings of the Royal Irish Academy* 115C, 79–109.

Photos-Jones, E. 2005. Analysis of crucible lid and crucible contents. In A. Crone and E. Campbell (eds) *A Crannog of the First Millenium A.D.: Excavations by Jack Scott at Lough Glashan, Argyle 1960*, 138. Edinburgh, Society of Antiquaries Scotland.

Pilcher, J.R. and Hall, V.A. 2001. *Flora Hibernica*. Cork, Collins Press.

Pilcher, J.R., Hall, V.A. and McCormick, F. 1996. An outline tephrochronology for the Holocene in the north of Ireland. *Journal of Quaternary Science* 11(6), 483–494.

Pilcher, J.R., Hall, V.A. and McCormick, F. 1995. Dates of Holocene Icelandic volcanic eruptions from tephra layers in Irish peats. *Holocene* 5, 103–110.

Pirie, E.J.E. 1986. *Post-Roman Coins from York Excavations, 1971–81*. London, Council for British Archaeology.

Plahter, U. 2011. Analyses of jet-like objects. In D. Skre (ed.) *Things from the Town: Artefacts and Inhabitants in Viking-age Kaugang, Kaupang Excavations Project Publication Series, Vol. 3. Norske Oldfunn 24*, 133–141. Aarhus, Aarhuis University Press.

Plunkett, G. 2009. Land-use patterns and cultural change in the Middle to Late Bronze Age in Ireland: inferences from pollen records. *Vegetation History and Archaeobotany* 18(4), 273–295.

Plunkett, G., McDermott, C., Swindles, G.T. and Brown, D.M. 2013. Environmental indifference? A critique of environmentally deterministic theories of peatland archaeological site construction in Ireland. *Quaternary Science Reviews* 61, 16–31.

Power, P. 1947. The bounds and extent of Irish parishes. In S. Pender (ed.) *Feilscribhinn Torna*, 218–224. Cork, Cork University Press.

Powell, T.E. 1995. The idea of the three orders of society and social stratification in early medieval Ireland. *Irish Historical Studies* 29(116), 475–489.

Pregesbauer, M., Trinks, I. and Neubauer, W. 2014. An object oriented approach to automatic classification of archaeological features in magnetic prospection data. *Near Surface Geophysics* 12, 651–656.

Pungas, P. and Vosu, E. 2012. Dynamics of liminality in Estonian mires. In H. Andrews and T. Roberts (eds) *Liminal Landscapes: Travel Experiences in Spaces In-Between*, 87–103. London, Routledge.

Purcell, E. and Sheehan, J. 2013. Viking Dublin: enmities, alliances and the cold gleam of silver. In D.M. Hadley and L. Ten Harkel (eds) *Everyday Life in Viking Age Towns: Social Approaches to Towns in England and Ireland, c. 800–1100*, 35–60. Oxford, Oxbow Books.

Rackham, H. 1989. *Pliny (the Elder) Natural History*. Harvard, Loeb Classical Library.

Raftery, B. 1969. Freestone Hill, Co. Kilkenny: An Iron Age Hillfort and Bronze Age Cairn. Excavations by Gerhard Bersu, 1948–1949. *Proceedings of the Royal Irish Academy* 68, 1–108.

Raftery, B. 1972. Irish hill-forts. In C. Thomas (ed.) *The Iron Age in the Irish Sea Province. Council for British Archaeology Research Report 9*, 37–58. London, Council for British Archaeology.

Reddy, S.N. 1991. Complementary approaches to Late Harappan subsistence: an example from Oriyo Timbo. In R.H. Meadow (ed.) *Harappa Excavations 1986–1990: A Multidisciplinary Approach to Third Millennium Urbanism*, 127–135. Madison, Prehistory Press.

Reddy, S.N. 1997. If the threshing floor could talk: integration of agriculture and pastoralism during the Late Harappan in Gujarat, India. *Journal of Anthropological Archaeology* 16, 162–187.

Reddy, S.N. 2003. *Discerning Palates of the Past: An Ethnoarchaeological Study of Crop Cultivation and Plant Usage in India*. Ann Arbor, Prehistory Press.

Reimer, P., Austin, W., Bard, E., Bayliss, A., Blackwell, P., Bronk Ramsey, C., Butzin, M., Cheng, H., Edwards, R., Friedrich, M., Grootes, P., Guilderson, T., Hajdas, I., Heaton, T., Hogg, A., Hughen, K., Kromer, B., Manning, S., Muscheler, R., Palmer, J., Pearson, C., van der Plicht, J., Reimer, R., Richards, D., Scott, E., Southon, J., Turney, C., Wacker, L., Adolphi, F., Büntgen, U., Capano, M., Fahrni, S., Fogtmann-Schulz, A., Friedrich, R., Köhler, P., Kudsk, S., Miyake, F., Olsen, J., Reinig, F., Sakamoto, M., Sookdeo, A. and Talamo, S. 2020. The IntCal20 Northern Hemisphere radiocarbon age calibration curve (0–55 cal kBP). *Radiocarbon* 62, 725–757.

Reuille, M. 1995. *Pollen et Spores d'Europe et Afrique du Nord*. Marseilles, Laboratoire de Botanique, Historique et Palynologie.

Rheinisch, S. 2013. Uncovering an Anglo-Norman manor and deserted medieval village. *Archaeology Ireland* 27(3), 32–35.

Riddler, I. and Trzaska-Nartowski, N. 2009. *Lismullin 1 (A008/021) Worked Antler and Bone Objects*. Unpublished report for the National Roads Authority, Dublin.

Riddler, I.D. and Trzaska-Nartowski, N.I.A. Forthcoming. Objects and waste of antler and bone. In A. Lynch, C. Manning and K. Wiggins *Excavations at Dublin Castle, 1985–6. Volume II: the Viking Period*. Dublin, Department of Housing, Culture, Tourism and the Gaeltacht.

Riddler, I.D. and Trzaska-Nartowski, N.I.A. 2013. Objects of antler, bone and ivory. In C. M. Hills and S. Lucy *The Anglo-Saxon Cemetery at Spong Hill, North Elmham. Part IX: Chronology and Synthesis*, 92–155. Cambridge, MacDonald Institute Monographs.

Riddler, I.D. and Walton Rogers, P. 2006. Early medieval small finds. In K. Parfitt, B. Corke and J. Cotter *Excavations at Townwall Street, Dover, 1995–6, The Archaeology of Canterbury, New Series III*, 255–318. Canterbury, Canterbury Archaeological Trust.

Riddler, I.D., Trzaska-Nartowski, N.I.A. and Hatton, S. Forthcoming. *An Early Medieval Craft. Antler and Bone Working from Ipswich Excavations 1974–1994*. East Anglian Archaeology, Ipswich, Suffolk Archaeology.

Riehl, S. 2019. Barley in archaeology and early history. In R.W. Hazlett (ed.) *Oxford Research Encyclopedia of Environmental Science*. 26 pp. Available online at https://www.oxfordreference.com/display/10.1093/acref/9780190496616.001.0001/acref-9780190496616-e-219 [Last accessed 4/1/2024].

Rissech, C. and Black, S. 2007. Scapular development from the neonatal period to skeletal maturity: A preliminary study. *International Journal of Osteoarchaeology* 17(5), 451–464.

Roche, H. 2002. Excavations at Ráith na Ríg, Tara, Co. Meath, 1997. *Discovery Programme Reports* 6, 19–83.

Rowley-Conway, P. 2018. Zooarchaeology and the elusive feast: from performance to aftermath. *World Archaeology* 50(2), 221–241.

Rubinacci, S., Ribeiro, D.M., Hofmeister, R.J. and Delaneau, O. 2021. Efficient phasing and imputation of low-coverage sequencing data using large reference panels. *Nature Genetics* 53(1), 120–126.

Russell, N. 2011. *Social Zooarchaeology: Humans and Animals in Prehistory*. Cambridge, Cambridge University Press.

Rydin, H and Jeglum, J. 2006. *The Biology of Peatlands*. Oxford, Oxford University Press.

Rynne, E. and Prendergast, E. 1962. Two souterrains in county Meath, *Riocht na Midhe* 2, 37–43.

Scheuer, J.L. and MacLaughlin-Black, S. 1994. Age estimation from the pars basilaris of the fetal and juvenile occipital bone. *International Journal of Osteoarchaeology* 4, 377–380.

Scheuer, J.L., Musgrave, J.K. and Evans, S.P. 1980. The estimation of late fetal and perinatal age from limb bone length by linear and logarithmic regression. *Annals of Human Biology* 7(3), 257–265.

Scheuer, L. and Black, S. 2000. *Developmental Juvenile Osteology*. London, Academic Press.

Schiffels, S., Haak, W., Paajanen, P., Llamas, B., Popescu, E., Loe, L., Clarke, R., Lyons, A., Mortimer, R., Sayer, D., Tyler-Smith, C., Cooper, A. and Durbin, R. 2016. Iron Age and Anglo-Saxon genomes from East England reveal British migration history. *Nature Communications* 7(1). Available from: http://dx.doi.org/10.1038/ncomms10408 [Accessed 23/9/2023].

Schmid, E. 1972. *Atlas of Animal Bones*. Amsterdam, Elsevier.

Schot, R. 2006. Uisneach Midi a medón Érenn: A prehistoric 'cult' centre and 'royal site' in Co. Westmeath. *Journal of Irish Archaeology* 15, 39–71.

Schutkowski, H. 1993. Sex determination of infant and juvenile skeletons: I. morphological features. *American Journal of Physical Anthropology* 90, 199–205.

Schweingruber, F.H. 1978. *Microscopic Wood Anatomy*. Birmensdorf, Swiss Federal Institute for Forest, Snow and Landscape Research.

Scott, B.G. 1981. Goldworking terms in early Irish writings. *Zeitschrift fur Celtische Philologie* 38, 242–254.

Scott, B.G. 1991. *Early Irish Ironworking*. Ulster Museum, Belfast.

Seaver, M. 2016. *Meitheal, The Archaeology of Lives, Labours and Beliefs at Raystown, Co. Meath*. Dublin, Transport Infrastructure Ireland.

Seaver, M. and Brady, C. 2011. *Heritage Guide No. 55: Hill of Slane*. Dublin, Wordwell.

Seetah, K. 2005. Butchery as a tool for understanding the changing views of animals. In A. Pluskowski (ed.) *Just Skin and Bones? New Perspectives on Human-Animal Relations in the Historic Past. BAR International Series S1410*. Oxford, Archaeopress.

Sellwood, L. 1984. Objects of bone and antler. In B.W. Cunliffe *Danebury. An Iron Age Hillfort in Hampshire. Volume 2. The Excavations, 1969–78: the Finds, CBA Research Report 52*, 371–395. London, Council for British Archaeology.

Shaffrey, R. 2022. Medieval and post-medieval writing slates and pencils. *Finds Research Group Datasheet 56*. Unpublished factsheet for the Small Finds Research Group.

Sheehan, J. 2007. The form and structure of Viking Age hoards: the evidence from Ireland. In J. Graham-Campbell and G. Williams (eds) *Silver Economy in the Viking Age*, 149–161. Walnut Creek, Left Coast Press.

Sheehan, J. 2018. Reflections on Kingship, the Church, and Viking Age Silver in Ireland. In J. Kershaw, G. Williams, S. Sindbæk and J. Graham-Campbell (eds) *Silver, Butter, Cloth: Monetary and Social Economies in the Viking Age*, 104. Oxford, Oxford University Press.

Shee-Twohig, E. 1981. *The Megalithic Art of Western Europe*. Oxford, Oxford University Press.

Sheridan, J.A., Cooney, G. and Grogan, E. 1992. Stone axehead studies in Ireland. *Proceedings of the Prehistoric Society* 58, 389–416.

Shine, D. 2008a. 2008:981 – Drissoge, Rathcarran/Rathcairn and Wardstown, Rathcairn, Meath. https://excavations.ie/report/2008/Meath/0019994/ [Accessed 30/9/2023].

Shine, D. 2008b. 2008:982 – Rathcairn, Meath. https://excavations.ie/report/2008/Meath/0019995/ [Accessed 30/9/2023].

Shine, D. and Travers, C. 2011. Excavations in Athboy, Co. Meath. *Archaeology Ireland* 25(2), 19–22.

Shingurova, T. 2018. The story of Mog Ruith: perceptions of the local myth in seventeenth-century Ireland. *Proceedings of the Harvard Celtic Colloquium* 38, 231–258.

Silver, I.A. 1963. The ageing of domestic animals. In D. Brothwell and E. Higgs (eds) *Science in Archaeology: A Survey of Progress and Research*, 250–268. London, Thames and Hudson.

Silver, I.A. 1969. The ageing of domestic animals. In D. Brothwell and E. Higgs (eds) *Science in Archaeology*, 283–302. London, Thames and Hudson.

Skoglund, P., Stovå, J., Götherström, A. and Jakobsson, M. 2013. Accurate sex identification of ancient human remains using DNA shotgun sequencing. *Journal of Archaeological Science* 40, 4477–4482.

Smith, A.N. 2007. Worked bone. In J. Hunter *Investigations at Sanday, Orkney. Vol 1: Excavations at Pool, Sanday. A multi-period Settlement from Neolithic to Late Norse Times*, 459–514. Kirkwall, Historic Scotland.

Speed, L 2020. *Bronze Age Metalworking*. Available online at https://finds.org.uk/counties/blog/tag/metal-working/ [Accessed 20/3/2023].

Stace, C. 2010. *New Flora of the British Isles: Third Edition*. Cambridge, Cambridge University Press.

Stevens, P. 2017a. Early medieval jet-like jewellery in Ireland: production, distribution and consumption. *Medieval Archaeology* 61, 239–276.

Stevens, P. 2017b. *Preliminary Scientific Analysis of Jet-like Jewellery from Early Medieval Ireland: An Exploratory Study*. Unpublished report for the Royal Irish Academy.

Stockmarr, J. 1971. Tablets with spores used in absolute pollen analyses. *Pollen et Spores* 13, 615–621.

Stout, M. 1997. *The Irish Ringfort*. Dublin, Four Courts.

Stout, G. and Stout, M. 2010. Early landscapes: from prehistory to plantation. In F.H.A. Aalen, K. Whelan and M. Stout (eds) *Atlas of the Irish Rural Landscape*, 31–65. 2nd ed. Cork, Cork University Press.

Stuiver, M., and Reimer, P.J. 1993. Extended ^{14}C database and revised CALIB radiocarbon calibration program. *Radiocarbon* 35, 215–230.

Summerfield, R.J. 1974. *Narthecium ossifragum* (L.) Huds. *Journal of Ecology* 62, 325–339.

Sutherland Graeme, A. 1913–1914. An account of the excavation of the Broch of Ayre, St Mary's Holm, Orkney. *Proceedings of the Society of Antiquaries of Scotland* 38, 31–51.

Swift, C. 2000. The local context of Oenach Tailten. *Riocht na Midhe* 11, 25–47.

Swindles, G. 2003. *Testate Amoeba, Peat Bogs and Past Climates*. http://www.microscopy-uk.org.uk/mag/indexmag.

html?http://www.microscopy-uk.org.uk/mag/artjun03/gsamoebae.html [Accessed 30/9/2023].

Theuerkauf, M-L. 2022. Dindshenchas Érenn. *Cork Studies in Celtic Literatures* 7. University College Cork.

Thomas, J. 1996. *Time, Culture and Identity: An Interpretive Archaeology*. London, Routledge.

Thompson, G.B. 1996. Ethnographic models for interpreting rice remains. In C. Higham and R. Thosarat (eds) *The Excavation of Khok Phanom Di a Prehistoric Site in Central Thailand. Volume IV: Subsistence and Environment: The Botanical Evidence (The Biological Remains, Part II)*, 119–150. London, The Society of Antiquaries of London.

Tolonen, K. 1991. Advances in peatland palaeoecology on environmental changes. In M. Botch, O.L. Kuznetsov and I.P. Khizova (eds) *Studies of Mire Systems of* Fennoscandia, 25–34. Petrozavodsk, Institute of Biology of Petrozavodsk.

Tourunen, A. 2008. Fauna and fulachta fiadh: animal bones from burnt mounds on the N9/N10 Carlow Bypass. *Roads, Rediscovery and Research Archaeology and the National Roads Authority Monograph Series* 5, 37–44.

Troels-Smith, J. 1955. Karakterisering af løse jordater. *Danmarks Geologiske Undersøgelse Rapport IV* 3, 1–73.

Turney, C.S.M., Wheeler, D.J. and Chivas, A.R. 2005. Carbon isotope fractionation in wood during carbonization. *Geochimica et Cosmochimica Acta* 70, 960–964.

Tylecote, R.F. 1986. *The Prehistory of Metallurgy in the British Isles*. London, Institute of Metals.

Ubelaker, D.H. 1999. *Human Skeletal Remains: Excavation, Analysis and Interpretation*. Washington, DC, Smithsonian Institute Press.

van der Veen, M. 1992. *Crop Husbandry Regimes: An Archaeobotanical Study of Farming in Northern England 1000 BC–AD 500*. Sheffield, J.R. Collis Publications.

van der Veen, M. 2007. Formation processes of desiccated and carbonized plant remains, the identification of routine practice. *Journal of Archaeological Science* 34, 968–990.

van der Veen, M. and Jones, G. 2006. A re-analysis of agricultural production and consumption: implications for understanding the British Iron Age. *Vegetation History and Archaeobotany* 15(3), 217–228.

Verrill, L. and Tipping, R. 2010. Use and abandonment of a Neolithic field system at Belderrig, Co. Mayo, Ireland: Evidence for economic marginality. *Holocene* 20(7), 1011–1021.

von Post, L. 1924. *Das genetische System der organogenen Bildungen Schwedens*. Quatrième commission, commission pour la nomenclature et la classification des sols, 287–304. Rome. Comité International de Pédologie.

Vincent, P. 1990. *The Biogeography of the British Isles: An Introduction*. London, Routledge.

Vogel, J.S., Southon, J.R. and Nelson, D.E. 1987. Catalyst and binder effects in the use of filamentous graphite for AMS. In H.E. Gove, A.E. Litherland and D. Elmore (eds) *Proceedings of the 4th International Symposium on Accelerator Mass Spectrometry. Nuclear Instruments and Methods* B29, 50–56.

Wagner, G. 1988. Comparability among recovery techniques. In C.A. Hastorf and V.S. Popper (eds) *Current Paleoethnobotany: Analytical Methods and Cultural Interpretations of Archaeological Plant Remains*, 17–35. Chicago, University of Chicago Press.

Walsh, F. 2020a. A multivallate ringfort at Knockhouse Lower, Co. Waterford. *Journal of Irish Archaeology* 29, 119–138.

Walsh, F. 2020b. Who lives in a ringfort like this? *Archaeology Ireland* 34(3), 36–39.

Walsh, F. 2021. *The Road to Kells: Prehistoric Archaeology of the M3 Navan to Kells and N52 Kells Bypass Road Project*. Dublin, Transport Infrastructure Ireland.

Walsh, P. 1916. Irish Ocha, Ochann. *Ériu* 8, 75–77.

Walton Rogers, P. 2001. The re-appearance of an old Roman loom in medieval England. In P. Walton Rogers, L. Bender Jørgensen and A. Rast-Eicher, *The Roman Textile Industry and its Influence: a Birthday Tribute to John Peter Wild*, 158–171. Oxford, Oxbow Books.

Walton Rogers, P. 2007. *Cloth and Clothing in Early Anglo-Saxon England AD 450–700, Council for British Archaeology Research Report 145*. York, Council for British Archaeology.

Warner, R.B. 1976. Some observations on the context and importation of exotic material in Ireland, from the first century B.C. to the second century A.D. *Proceedings of the Royal Irish Academy* 76C, 267–292.

Wastegård, A., Hall, V.A., Hannon, G., van den Bogaard, C., Pilcher, J.A., Sigurgeirson, S. and Auoadottir, M. 2003. Rhyolitic tephra horizons in northwestern Europe and Iceland from the AD 700s and 800s. *The Holocene* 13, 277–283.

Wastegård, S. and Davies, S. 2009. An overview of distal tephrochronology in northern Europe during the last 1000 years. *Journal of Quaternary Science* 24(5), 500–512.

Waterman, D.M. 1951. Excavations at Dundrum Castle, 1950. *Ulster Journal of Archaeology* 14, 15–29.

Watts, S. and Pollard, A.M. 1998. *Identifying Archaeological Jet and Jet-like Artifacts using FTIR. Postprints: Infrared and Raman Users Group Conference at the V & A*. Sept. 1995, 37–52. Available online at http://irug.org/uploads/event/irug-2-postprints.pdf [Accessed 30/9/2023].

Weissensteiner, H., Pacher, D., Kloss-Brandstätter, A., Forer, L., Specht, G., Bandelt, H-J., Kronenberg, F., Salas, A. and Schönherr, S. 2016. HaploGrep 2: Mitochondrial Haplogroup Classification in the Era of High-Throughput Sequencing. *Nucleic Acids Research* 44(W1), W58–63.

Welton, J.E. 2003. *SEM Petrology Atlas, Chevron Oil Field Research Company, Methods in Exploration Series No. 4*. Tulsa, Oklahoma, American Association of Petrology Geologists.

Wheeler, E.A., Bass, P. and Gasson, P.E. 1989. IAWA list of microscopic features for hardwood identification. *IAWA Bulletin* 10(3), 219–332. Rijksherbarium, Leiden.

Whitfield, N. 2008. 'More like the work of fairies than of human beings': the filigree on the 'Tara' brooch, a masterpiece of late Celtic metalwork. *ArcheoSciences* 33, 235–241.

Whitefield, A. 2017. Neolithic 'Celtic' fields? A reinterpretation of the chronological evidence from Céide Fields in north-western Ireland. *European Journal of Archaeology* 20(2), 257–279.

Whitehouse, N.J., Schulting, R.J., McClatchie, M., Barratt, P., McLaughlin, T.R., Bogaard, A., Colledge, S., Marchant, R., Gaffrey, J. and Bunting, M.J. 2014. Neolithic agriculture on the European western frontier: the boom and bust of early farming in Ireland. *Journal of Archaeological Science* 51, 181–205.

Woodman, P.C. 1978. *The Mesolithic in Ireland: Hunter-Gatherers in an Insular Environment. British Archaeological Reports British Series* 58. Oxford, BAR Publishing.

Woodman, P.C. 1987. The impact of resource availability on lithic industrial traditions in prehistoric Ireland. In P. Rowley-Conwy, M. Zvelebil and H.P. Blankholm (eds) *Mesolithic Northwest Europe: Recent Trends 1987*, 138–146. Sheffield, Department of Archaeology and Prehistory, University of Sheffield.

Woodman, P.C., Finlay, N. and Anderson, E. 2006. *The Archaeology of a Collection: The Keiller-Knowles collection of the National Museum of Ireland*. Wicklow, Wordwell Ltd.

Wood-Martin, W.G. 1886. *The Lake Dwellings of Ireland: Ancient Lacustrine Habitations of Erin commonly called Crannogs*. London, Longmans, Green and Co.

Woods, A.R. 2013. The coinage and economy of Hiberno-Scandinavian Dublin. In S. Duffy (ed.) *Medieval Dublin XIII*, 43–69. Dublin, Four Courts Press.

Woods, A.R. 2014. Monetary activity in Viking-Age Ireland: The evidence of the single-finds. In R. Naismith, M.R. Allen, and E. Screen (eds) *Early Medieval Monetary History: Studies in Memory of Mark Blackburn*, 295–330. Farnham, Ashgate.

Woods, A.R. 2015. Prelude to Hiberno-Scandinavian coinage: the Castle Street and Werburgh Street hoards. In H.B. Clarke and R. Johnson (eds) *The Vikings in Ireland and beyond: Before and After the Battle of Clontarf*, 355–372. Dublin, Four Courts Press.

Wright, P. 2005. Flotation samples and some paleoethnobotanical implications. *Journal of Archaeobotanical Science* 32, 19–26.

Wyse-Jackson, P. 2018. *Irish Trees and Shrubs*. Belfast, Appletree Press Ltd.

Yeloff, D., Charman, D., van Geel, B. and Mauquoy, D. 2007. Reconstruction of hydrology, vegetation and past climate change in bogs using fungal microfossils. *Review of Palaeobotany and Palynology* 146, 102–145.

Zak, J. and Widman, H.G. 2004. Fungi in stressful environments. In G. Bills and M. Foster (eds) *Biodiversity of Fungi*, 303–317. Burlington, Elsevier Academic Press.

Zeder, M.A. and Lapham, H.A. 2010. Assessing the reliability of criteria used to identify postcranial bones in sheep, *Ovis*, and goats, *Capra*. *Journal of Archaeological Science* 37, 2887–2905.

Zohary, D., Hopf, M. and Weiss, E. 2013. *Domestication of Plants in the Old World*. Fourth Edition. Oxford, Oxford University Press.